Retired,

Rehabbed,

Reborn

The Sacred Landmarks Series

Laura Wertheimer, Editor   Michael J. Tevesz, Founding Editor

Revelations: Photographs of Cleveland's African American Churches
  Michael Stephen Levy

Resplendent Faith: Liturgical Treasuries of the Middle Ages
  Stephen N. Fliegel

Seeking the Sacred in Contemporary Religious Architecture
  Douglas R. Hoffman

Eric Mendelsohn's Park Synagogue: Architecture and Community
  Walter C. Leedy Jr.   Edited by Sara Jane Pearman

A Higher Contemplation: Sacred Meaning in the Christian Art of the Middle Ages
  Stephen N. Fliegel

Dedication: The Work of William P. Ginther, Ecclesiastical Architect
  Anthony J. Valleriano

A Guide to Greater Cleveland's Sacred Landmarks
  Lloyd H. Ellis Jr.

Retired, Rehabbed, Reborn: The Adaptive Reuse of America's Derelict Religious Buildings and Schools
  Robert A. Simons, Gary DeWine, and Larry Ledebur, with Laura A. Wertheimer

The Sacred Landmarks series includes both works of scholarship and general-interest titles that preserve the history and increase understanding of religious sites, structures, and organizations in northeast Ohio, the United States, and around the world.

RETIRED, REHABBED, REBORN

The Adaptive Reuse of America's Derelict Religious Buildings and Schools

Robert A. Simons,

Gary DeWine, and

Larry Ledebur

with Laura A. Wertheimer

The Kent State University Press

Kent, Ohio

Cleveland State University
College of Liberal Arts
and Social Sciences

Published in cooperation with Cleveland State University's
College of Liberal Arts and Social Sciences

Published in cooperation with Cleveland State University's College of Liberal Arts and Social Sciences

 This publication is made possible in part by the generous support of Furthermore: a program of the J. M. Kaplan Fund.

Library of Congress Catalog Number 2016008084

ISBN 978-1-60635-256-4

Manufactured in Korea

LIBRARY OF CONGRESS CATALOGING-IN-PUBLICATION DATA

Names: Simons, Robert A.

Title: Retired, rehabbed, reborn : the adaptive reuse of America's derelict religious buildings and schools / Robert A. Simons, Gary DeWine, and Larry Ledebur ; With Laura A. Wertheimer.

Description: Kent, Ohio : The Kent State University Press, 2016. | Series: The sacred landmarks series | Includes bibliographical references and index.

Identifiers: LCCN 2016008084 (print) | LCCN 2016008543 (ebook) | ISBN 9781606352564 (pbk. : alk. paper) ∞ | ISBN 9781631012549 (ePub) | ISBN 9781631012556 (ePDF)

Subjects: LCSH: Church facilities--Remodeling for other use--United States. | Church buildings--Remodeling for other use--United States.

Classification: LCC NA5205 .R48 2016 (print) | LCC NA5205 (ebook) | DDC 726.5/1--dc23

LC record available at http://lccn.loc.gov/2016008084

21 20 19 18 17   5 4 3 2 1

CONTENTS

Case Studies

Dead or dying buildings are a serious and endemic issue in many communities, especially mature ones facing change and population shifts away from the urban core. Both negative and positive factors shape the disposition of these buildings. On the negative side the properties may be an eyesore, often creating anxiety among neighboring stakeholders. Also, the owners/sellers are frequently in the midst of economic hardship. They may be faced with the choice of either keeping open a facility that has lost its viability (often doing so on a shoestring budget that leads to deferred maintenance) or closing and disposing of a beloved facility. Sometimes the selling entity faces mass closings of its buildings in a short time period. On the positive side, these buildings represent an opportunity to recycle a beloved structure, to capture and retain all that is best about people's memories, and to do so in a way that is both profitable and sustainable. Positive externalities (important benefits to society beyond the simple dollars and cents of developer investment and return) accompany these projects, which is a good thing because these deals often require substantial public subsidies to attain and sustain economic viability.

The idea for this book was born on a golf course (on the fairway, second shot, the 4th hole, a par 5, at Airport Greens in Cleveland, Ohio), on a breezy morning in early November 2006. Roby Simons and Gary De-Wine were talking about what Gary wanted to do now that he was about to retire after thirty years in community development

at the city of Euclid, Ohio. Gary wanted to write a book on empty shopping centers, and Roby countered with "dead" churches. We hooked up with Larry Ledebur, Roby's colleague and a professor in the Maxine Goodman Levin College of Urban Affairs at Cleveland State University, who had an active interest in church rehab projects. This developed into a book proposal to a publisher in 2007. We added several authors from the Cleveland area in completing our work, many of them graduate students in CSU's Levin College. Gary DeWine was in charge of selecting the case studies. After the other publisher withdrew support for the project due to a steep decline in the real estate market in 2010, we searched for another publisher. Kent State agreed to move forward in June 2011, but primarily for the religious buildings portion of the project. The rest is written in these pages.

The lead author and project coordinator is Robert A. (Roby) Simons. Gary DeWine and Larry Ledebur are also intellectual leaders of the project. This trio was assisted by four graduate students at Cleveland State University: Youngme Seo, Eugene Choi, Satya Subha Vyakaranam, and Adam Saurwein, who contributed as lead and junior authors on one or more chapters or case studies. Rose Zitiello and Scott Dimit are senior practitioners in city planning and architecture, respectively, and played a key role in two of these chapters. The exhibits and graphic illustrations in the book were prepared by Francis Demaske. Francis is an associate professor of Graphic and Interactive

Design at Edinboro University in Edinboro, Pennsylvania. He has been teaching at Edinboro since 1991. He received his MFA in Graphic Design and Illustration from Kent State University in 1992, and his BFA in Graphic Design and Illustration from Kent State University in 1989. Francis Demaske has been involved in the visual communication field since 1983. For the case studies, we also relied upon the participation of a myriad of project developers and other stakeholders in helping us to understand the projects and accurately represent their stories. Where appropriate, some proprietary information was protected and the anonymity of some individual players was maintained. Subha Vyakaranam and Eugene Choi provided the demographic data and maps for the case studies. Adam Saurwein, plying his sharp editorial eye in the task of master internal editor and quality control officer for the project, made a project written by nine authors read as if written in one voice. Kelly Kinahan and Shannon Walker provided supplementary research and worked on the glossary of terms in the final stages of production, and series editor Laura Wertheimer ruthlessly polished the prose.

ACKNOWLEDGMENTS

The authors would like to thank our chapter coauthors, including Dr. Eugene Choi; Scott Dimit; Adam Saurwein, Esq.; Dr. Youngme Seo; Subha Vyakaranam; and Rose Zitiello, Esq., who worked with us as a team at Cleveland State University over the three-year period when this book was written, just before the great recession.

Special thanks to Laura Wertheimer, our diligent and energetic series editor, who cleaned and scrubbed this project until it read like it was written by a single author.

We were glad to work with Diane Wilkoff, our final copy editor and compliance policewoman, who saw that we fully complied with The Kent State University Press's scrupulous requirements, and essentially polished off the last 1 percent.

The authors wish to thank and acknowledge all the fifty or more people who talked to us in putting together this book, mostly during the case studies.

We owe a debt of gratitude to the folks at The KSU Press, who worked with us for over two years to bring this book to its final stages, and helped us resurrect this book from the ashes of the Great Recession.

Thanks to Cleveland State University's College of Liberal Arts and Social Sciences, and to the Levin College of Urban Affairs at Cleveland State University, for their financial support of this project.

Thanks to five peer-reviewers who provided feedback, including Howard Goldberg, David C. Feltman, Michael J. Crosbie, Elizabeth C. Murphy, and Douglas Hoffman, who provided lots of constructive suggestions and helped us strengthen this book.

Thanks also are due to Francis Demaske, our graphics expert, who skillfully assembled our pictures, maps, and charts into images almost as beautiful as the buildings they represent.

And most of all, we thank our wives Donna Simons, Carol DeWine, and Susan Whitelaw, who served as our ballast, keeping things in our lives moving along with their support, thus giving us the freedom to compile this creative work, which took way too long to finish, but will hopefully be worthwhile for our readers to benefit from.

1

INTRODUCTION

Robert A. Simons

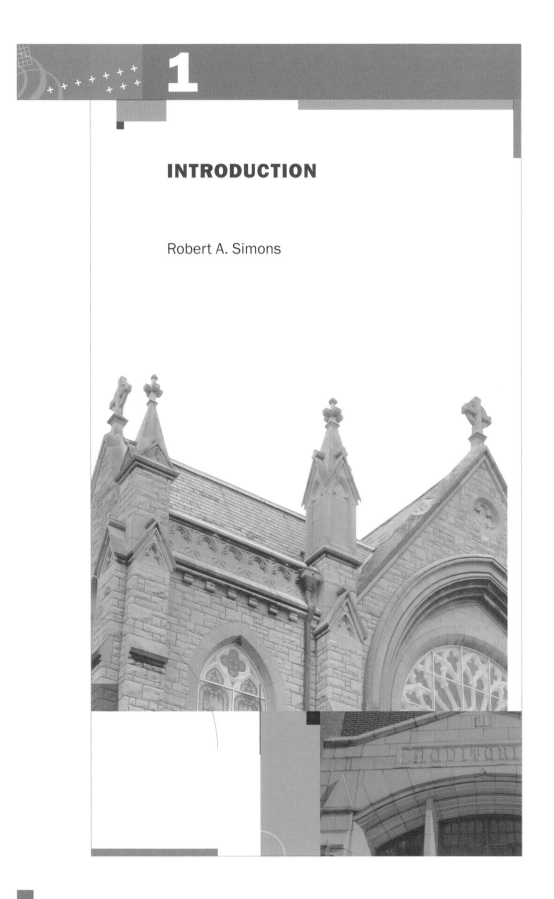

Purpose and Scope

This book is addressed to developers, planners, architects, public officials, and not-for-profit community organizations, school district real estate administrators, and owners and managers of religious buildings. The subject at hand is finding sustainable new uses for religious buildings in the United States. While the focus is on these religious buildings, the lessons found in this book may also be applied to other vacant or underutilized public and institutional structures and school buildings that face many of the same problems and challenges.

There is a considerable backlog of underutilized, abandoned, or otherwise empty churches and other religious buildings in the United States. Every year over one thousand religious buildings become vacant in the United States. At the end of 2008, more than thirteen hundred churches and religious buildings in the United States were for sale (CoStar 2008). The market absorbs some of them, but others may languish for years. The formerly religious structures are often well located, prominent, attractive, eligible for tax credits, and available for redevelopment. The reuse of these important structures also offers an opportunity to capture their embodied energy, and their intrinsic and historical features boost the goal of sustainability. In general and especially in hard economic times (at press time, 2009–13), rehabbing these desirable structures may present a profitable opportunity for developers and permit sellers to recoup some value from these assets. Neighbors and other stakeholders may also be better off as historic structures are retained and the urban fabric of our communities is preserved. Redevelopment of churches is also sustainable and "green" because existing resources are better utilized, and their typical location (central city or suburbs) is consistent with infill development, and hence discourages urban sprawl.

This book is a tool for developers and others interested in reusing these important buildings. Often the structures are prominent, and have substantial nostalgic and historical value to former users and other community stakeholders. These characteristics present unique opportunities and potentially higher marketing success, but may also impose some additional constraints, such as neighbors' "Not in My Backyard" concerns, known to developers as "NIMBYs." Each rehab deal appears to be unique and tricky, but, as we show, there are identifiable patterns of successful and unsuccessful approaches. These patterns are addressed in turn throughout the redevelopment process. Ten separate case studies of adaptive reuse outcomes for religious buildings and public schools that have achieved varying degrees of success are also featured. In addition, several vignette mini-cases appear within various chapters to illustrate specific points.

The goal of this book is to increase the ease with which private and not-for-profit developers can identify, conceptualize, acquire, redevelop, and profitably market religious buildings for adaptive reuse. However, there is a public or social aspect to sustainability and to the preservation of these special structures, and for many people saving these structures goes well beyond dollars and cents. Chapter 9 is devoted to this theme, but this theme is also woven throughout this book.

The book is divided into four parts. The first section, comprising the first two chapters, provides historical background and context. It addresses underlying trends and typical redevelopment processes for religious buildings (primarily churches), and presents statistical results of several hundred redevelopment project outcomes. The second section, with five chapters, addresses the steps needed to establish that a project is feasible in practice. These steps include: assessing the design needs and market potential for the project, conducting a financial analysis and obtaining financial backing, and securing planning approval as needed. The third section has three chapters that, in turn, question whether the real estate market is the only viable approach to redeveloping religious structures, examine a trend of converting secular structures to sacred ones (e.g., conversion of commercial space to churches), and systematically review the case studies examined in this book to provide policy considerations and lessons learned. The fourth section gives detailed financial and redevelopment case studies for ten projects or development situations, several of which have multiple components or phases. While we focus largely on formerly religious buildings, we also include three cases of rehabilitated schools, primarily to illustrate the utilization of historic preservation tax credits, and to examine more closely the potential for negative financial outcomes.

Background Trends Section

The background information presented in this section helps lay the foundation for understanding the complex real estate development opportunity offered by adaptive reuse of sacred buildings. As will become apparent, one key to making these projects economically viable is to acquire them at the lowest possible cost. Thus, developers need to know the context of the opportunity for property acquisition, and this means understanding trends in religious observance. Developers must also understand the economic and political perspectives of the sellers of these specialized buildings in order to time their acquisition effectively. The successful project, we have found, begins before the building is available. These chapters therefore suggest ways that a developer can anticipate opportunities to purchase a building for reuse.

Furthermore, developing a new line of real estate project expertise, in this case merchant rehabbing, has a steep learning curve. There is a huge amount to be learned, and developers must assess their fixed cost (both financial capital and human capital) in learning the ropes for this tricky niche market. Doing one of these deals may not make sense: doing five deals might.

Chapter 2 provides background on religious activity in the United States as it relates to the supply and demand for religious buildings. More than 80 percent of the U.S. population is affiliated with a religious faith, but the religious landscape is not static. As this chapter explains, changes both in the total membership of different religious denominations and in the size and composition of congregations within them affect the number of sacred buildings available for reuse, while interdenominational variations in the relationship between individual congregations and their denomination's leadership bodies affect when and how the owners of a sacred structure will dispose of it if it can no longer serve its original purpose. However, successful reuse of a building also depends upon adaptation to the demographic and underlying economic factors in the community in which it is located. Filtering of religious building stock and the economics of the process by which religious buildings change use are also addressed. This includes different denominations' increasing expenses, local demographic changes in congregations, and consolidation of congregations.

Chapter 3 provides statistical analysis of a data set of more than two hundred rehabilitated religious building and school projects in the United States to determine what locational factors and building attributes are associated with different types of development projects. It features a type of regression analysis (multinomial logit) in which the dependent variable is development outcomes (condo, apartment, retail, office, and cultural use), and independent variables include religious denomination, area demographics, building characteristics, and locational factors. The chapter identifies several factors that are good predictors of successful outcomes. Some information about the spot market for religious buildings (from CoStar) is also analyzed.

Practical Feasibility Section

Chapter 4 addresses the architectural factors to consider in rehabbing religious buildings. It examines issues such as religious design, energy use, parking and construction, and the implications of these issues for associated excess costs. The chapter features an experienced rehab architect's walk-through checklist for a potential project, as well as several relative cost analyses that compare rehab projects to new construction for both residential and nonresidential projects. Finally, it briefly addresses the operating cost differentials between new and rehab projects.

Chapter 5 discusses two techniques for conducting market analysis on religious building rehab projects: "highest and best use" analysis and "market niche" analysis. The chapter provides a tutorial of each technique followed by examples of its application to four possible rehab outcomes: conversion to condominiums, conversion to residential apartments, reuse for commercial purposes, and cultural reuse. These analyses integrate market demographics, location and traffic factors, and building and lot characteristics to determine best outcomes for several different types of property.

Chapter 6 is the financial toolbox chapter. It covers the basics of a project's financial structure that may be applied to the rehabilitation of religious buildings, including debt, equity, construction loans, and permanent financing. Because many of these deals involve public/private partnerships, the chapter also addresses the following topics: joint ventures, public loans and grants, HOME funds, community development block grants (CDBG), U.S Department of Housing and Urban Development (HUD) direct loan program, nonprofit foundations, historic preservation tax credits (HPTC), low-income housing tax credits (LIHTC), historic easements, bank loans, New Market Tax Credits, property tax abatement, brownfield funds, loan guarantees, tax increment financing (TIF), revenue bonds, general obligation (GO) bonds, and Economic Development Administration (EDA) funds.

Chapter 7 is also a financial analysis chapter, but it looks beyond individual financial tools and provides integrated examples of redevelopment. It includes spreadsheets featuring pro forma cash flow and related models. Sample financial models and discounted cash flow analysis for different types of religious building projects are also provided. Examples include a church-to-condo build out and sell-off project and the conversion of a former school to apartments with historic preservation and low-income housing tax credits. This latter example is provided because many religious building campuses also include school buildings.

Chapter 8 sets forth an overview of the planning-approval process and then focuses on potential off-site impacts and winning community approval. Other topics covered include zoning and rezoning, code compliance, and dealing with property sellers, planners, NIMBYs, neighbors, and historic preservation advocates. The chapter uses several vignette mini-cases to illustrate both positive and negative implications of the rezoning process.

Policy Section

Chapter 9 addresses adaptive reuse issues affecting the community, including factors related to landmarks and historical status, the integrity of the urban fabric, and public subsidy decisions. While this book generally seeks to further the ease with which the private market can identify, conceptualize, acquire, develop, and profitably market the adaptive reuse of religious buildings, this chapter recognizes that these special structures often carry a public or social value that goes beyond dollars and cents. It features a case involving religious to secular adaptive uses.

Chapter 10 addresses the other side of religious to secular transformations, i.e., the process of changing secular uses to religious ones. This chapter looks at the phenomenon of megachurches, including the reuse of shopping centers, patterns of development and potential reuse, demand, size, zoning, and land use issues.

The final analytical chapter (Chapter 11) summarizes the findings and lessons learned from the case studies conducted for this book. It methodically examines ten former religious buildings and schools that were redeveloped into residential uses or commercial/cultural projects. While the cases generally focus on the projects themselves, this case study chapter focuses on particular issues related to the adaptive reuse of schools and churches. For example, particular cases look at the hierarchical disposal process for certain religious buildings, developer and nonprofit teaming, and a large master planned project. Separate tables analyze common elements in the financial, physical, and locational aspects of the cases. The final part of this chapter was developed with input from all the authors. It addresses lessons learned and policy recommendations that flow from this book for developers, community religious leaders, school administrators, and urban planners. These distilled lessons should enable interested parties to approach rehabilitation of these deals with realistic expectations, assist in avoiding common pitfalls, and increase the chances for project success.

Case Study Section

The book concludes with ten case studies of projects that have attained partial or full success. The case studies were composed by their authors using fieldwork, photos, financial outcomes (usually accompanied by a summary table), and interviews with developers. We considered several factors when selecting which projects to highlight for case studies. First, the case studies all include data drawn from individuals with direct knowledge of the project. Each case has been reviewed by either the developer or other key individuals involved in each project, and several cases have been reviewed by multiple stakeholders. Second, although Ohio is the focal area of these case studies (represented by three projects within the state and one from nearby Buffalo, New York), the data set used in the statistical analyses within this book is national. We therefore include a range of geographically diverse case studies, including urban cases from New York City, Boston, and St. Louis, one from New Mexico, and two from Arkansas: one from the small town of St. Joseph, Arkansas, and one from Little Rock and Hot Springs. Third, the case studies, which include both Catholic and Protestant churches and three repurposed public schools, cover a variety of property types that become available for reuse.

Finally, they illustrate both the range of financing mechanisms available for repurposing religious structures and the spectrum of possible financial outcomes.

Most of the edifices discussed were classified as historic landmarks within their communities. Each case study, in general, has both common characteristics and unique features that made the adaptive reuse plan either successful or unsuccessful. Some plans were well developed and benefited from favorable market conditions and quick absorption, while others still struggle with financial difficulties and are unfinished, or were unable to attain the vision of the property that the developers hoped for.

Chapter 12: Red Door Church, Cleveland Heights, Ohio

This former Lutheran church in Cleveland Heights, Ohio, was advantageously located in an area with immediate access to museums and hospitals. The church was built in 1932 on a 1.5-acre lot and a school wing was added later. The vacant but attractive, well-maintained gray stone church building with a red door was put on the market for sale and sold to a private developer. The adaptive reuse plan converted this church building into five rehabbed condominiums, with an additional fifteen new residential condominiums on the oversized lot. The total development cost was about $8 million. The project hit the market window and the rate of return to the developer was positive.

Chapter 13: Jamaica Performing Arts Center, Jamaica, Queens, New York

The empty First Dutch Reformed Church in Queens, New York, built in 1859, was adaptively reused and redeveloped as the 18,000-sq.-ft. Jamaica Performing Arts Center (JPAC). The redevelopment plan pro-vided high-quality cultural services to the community under the sponsorship of the city of New York Department of Cultural Affairs. Unlike other case studies in this book, this project was not profit-driven, and raised $20 million in capital and operating subsidies mostly from city sources. The city leases this stunning gem to the non-profit operator for just $1 per year.

Chapter 14: Urban Krag, Dayton, Ohio

The Deutsche Evangelical Reform Church sat empty for almost twenty years before it was converted to the Urban Krag Rock Climbing Gym during the 1990s. Local residents recognized the importance of having a small business occupy an otherwise vacant building in their community. This low-budget restoration project is meaningful since the historic building was saved from demolition and preserved, and the business contributes to the city's tax base.

Chapter 15: Saints Peter and Paul Catholic Church, South Boston, Massachusetts

Consisting of a church, rectory, and small garage with 35,700 sq. ft. on 0.82 acres, the Saints Peter and Paul Church (built in 1844) was located near the "T" on a main commercial street near downtown Boston. The property was redeveloped into thirty-six condominium units on six floors, designed for young singles or couples. An additional eight units were built in the rectory. Accomplished without public subsidies, the $16 million adaptive reuse plan was successful, and the developer made a positive return and retained two premium units as rental properties. The Boston condo market supported good market absorption.

Chapter 16: Babeville, Buffalo, New York

The Babeville project, corporate headquarters of Righteous Babe Records in downtown Buffalo, involved the conversion of a Methodist church to a music-retail-tenanted commercial project. The structure was in poor condition when a private developer spent $10 million on the church rehab and tenanted the project with several related music uses, including a studio, corporate offices, and art gallery, while preserving the main sanctuary as a twelve-hundred-seat concert hall. Substantial federal New Market Tax Credits, historic tax credits, and other local government subsidies were used. The deal struggles to sustain positive cash flow.

Chapter 17: St. Louis Catholic Archdiocese, and St. Aloysius Church, St. Louis, Missouri

In 2005 the Roman Catholic Archdiocese of St. Louis disposed of twenty church properties following an orderly process that is examined in the first part of this case study. The second half of this case study focuses on one of those properties, the St. Aloysius Gonzaga Church, which was sold to a private developer through a request-for-proposal (RFP) process and demolished for single-family housing development. The case demonstrates that an analysis of possible adaptive reuses for an existing building sometimes reveals that demolition is the most viable option.

Chapter 18: St. Joseph Church, Fayetteville, Arkansas

This project involved redevelopment of a former church, school, and an old sanctuary on a 2.2-acre site located in a historic district in Fayetteville, Arkansas. The area is gentrifying, and the three church buildings were converted to for-sale condominiums and rental apartments. The total project cost was approximately $4.5 million, and the project's rate of return is expected to be handsome. Proactive public discourse by both the developer and the church succeeded in generating public support for the project.

Chapter 19: West Tech High School, Cleveland, Ohio

The conversion of the vacant West Tech High School, four miles southwest of downtown Cleveland, Ohio, involved converting 368,000 sq. ft. of the school building to 189 low- and moderate-income housing units on 5 acres of a 20-acre site. The remaining 15 acres were partially developed into for-sale housing. In spite of substantial public subsidies (historic preservation and low-income housing tax credits) and alumni efforts, the original two developers failed to stabilize the project, attaining occupancy of only 55 percent. Also, only nine units were sold of the twenty-one dwelling units offered for sale. Ultimately, the project went through a mortgage foreclosure and three owners until it was turned around. When it was eventually leased up, completed, and sold to an operating firm, it was worth less than one quarter of what it cost to acquire and renovate. Although this project is now profitable, it is worth only about 20 percent of the redevelopment costs.

Chapter 20: Clinton Cultural Campus, Hot Springs, Arkansas

Two linked buildings (each about 40,000 sq. ft.) on a 5-acre historic school campus site in downtown Hot Springs, Arkansas, were converted into a total of seventy units of subsidized and market-rate multifamily apartments between 2000 and 2005. The project had both historic preservation and low-income housing tax credits. The redevelopment plan was undertaken by the partnership of a for-profit developer and a nonprofit organization. The $8 million project was a bricks-and-mortar success and garnered considerable market acceptance. While the building restoration and occupancy may be considered successful, this deal suffers financial difficulties and has had trouble sustaining positive cash flow. This case also discusses the broader experience of a developer and nonprofit entity that partnered on several successful school rehab deals in central Arkansas.

Chapter 21: The Lofts at Albuquerque High, Albuquerque, New Mexico

The Albuquerque High School Master Plan project was a multifaceted redevelopment of a well-located downtown high school over a decade or more. The project included redevelopment of 175,000 sq. ft. for residential, retail, and office space in four buildings that had been vacant for over twenty years. Financial strategies for the $41 million project included use of historic tax credits and city bonds. The successful project highlights benefits of master planning.

The authors hope that you find as much joy and satisfaction in reading this book as we have found in writing it. And now, dear reader, go forth and learn how to redevelop these important buildings. Leave no building behind, and go turn "prophets" into profits.

Reference

CoStar Data Services. 2008. http://www.costar.com/.

BACKGROUND TRENDS

2

THE CHANGING LANDSCAPE OF SACRED BUILDINGS

Larry Ledebur and

Eugene Choi

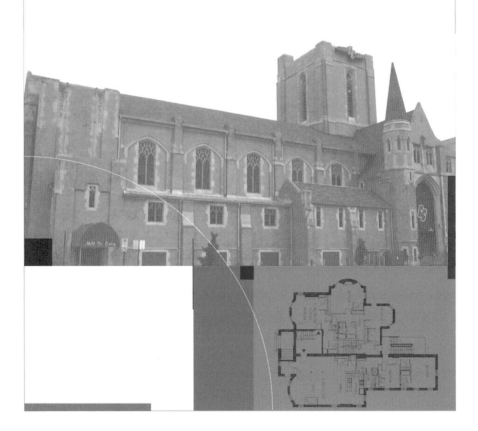

ar from being fixtures in the urban landscape, the population of congregations is a constantly shifting array—some coming, some going, others moving and still others reinventing themselves (Ammerman 2001).

The study of adaptive reuse of structures built for religious purposes raises two initial questions. First, why do these buildings lose their congregations and need to close? In the last decades of the twentieth century, the United States experienced a paradoxical increase in the number of religiously affiliated individuals accompanied by a decrease in the number of religious structures as church buildings throughout the country were shuttered. Second, where are redundant religious structures most likely to be found in the mosaic of cities and suburbs, exurban and rural areas? This question is a critical one because location is perhaps the most important determinant of a successful adaptive reuse of a building, particularly market uses.

These questions are best answered by approaching religious buildings not as brick and mortar, but rather as structural artifacts. The built environment of structures, infrastructure, and public spaces can be seen collectively as the fabric of place astride the geography of the urban region. Central cities and their neighborhoods, suburbs, and exurbs, as well as rural villages beyond the cities' peripheries, are both defined and divided by an overlying lattice of governmental jurisdictions. While these political and administrative boundaries remain largely fixed, the populations within them continually ebb and flow. One component of this ebb and flow is successive waves of immigrants, often of shared ethnic or racial heritage, who are first concentrated in cities. Over time these urban populations then out-migrate to suburbs and exurbs, sometimes eventually re-urbanizing. The geography of an urban space and its environs then becomes a dynamic mosaic that is culturally enriched and demographically diversified by a continually shifting urban population. Sacred buildings become both markers mapping out patterns of socioeconomic and ethnic changes within the metropolitan and rural areas of the United States and signifiers of the natural evolution of religious communities.

Why Do We Have Redundant Religious Buildings?

Church closures are a common fact of modern life. Economic trends undoubtedly contribute to the creation of redundant houses of worship. The economic decline of core cities causes a loss of urban population, followed by the relocation of once-urban congregations. The buildings they leave behind remain as abandoned hulks, surrounded by urban decay, as new churches are built to accommodate people living in more recently constructed suburban buildings. Demographic changes therefore produce redundant and threatened religious structures,

"Great for worship then! Great for retail now!"

Edward Koren/*The New Yorker* Collection/The Cartoon Bank

some to be destroyed, some to be reborn in another religious use, and others to be saved by adaptations to other uses.

The number of religious congregations within the United States has generally increased since 1970, although the rates of congregational change differ significantly across states (see Chapter 2 Appendix for details). An increase in congregations may mean that most religious structures remain in use for their original purpose, but some surplus buildings could still enter the market in older (typically central city) locations. Regions that experience a decline in congregations would certainly see redundant religious structures becoming available for adaptation and reuse.

As is shown below, the religious bodies in the United States that have had the largest net loss in congregations are the United Methodist Church, the Presbyterian Church (PCUSA), and the Roman Catholic Church. They are therefore the religious bodies most likely to put religious buildings on the market for reuse. It should be noted that the number of facilities that become available at any given time may be even greater than the number of congregations lost during that period due to demographically driven "turnover" or "churn"—that is, when a congregation close to the urban core matures and relocates, typically to a suburban or exurban location, their old facility may become available to other denominations or eventually to the private market for redevelopment.

Exhibits 2-1 and 2-2 contain data on the net change in the number of congregations by religious body in the United States in the two-decade period between 1980 and 2000. Faiths with the highest gains are shown in Exhibit 2-1. The Southern Baptist Convention had the highest net gain, with an increase of approximately 6,000 congrega-

tions during this period. The Church of Jesus Christ of Latter-Day Saints had a net gain of approximately 4,900 congregations, and the Assemblies of God had a net gain of approximately 2,500 congregations. These congregations are followed by National Association of Free Will Baptists, Judaism (all denominations),[1] and the Church of God of Prophecy. In general, these growing faiths are less likely to have large numbers of buildings available for adaptive reuse.

Faiths with the largest decrease in net congregations are shown in Exhibit 2-2. Among the top twenty religious bodies in this group, a net 6,400 congregations were lost between 1980 and 2000, about 320 per year. The United Methodist Church had the highest net loss of 2,688 churches between 1980 and 2000, followed by the Presbyterian Church (PCUSA) with a net loss of 1,509 churches. Catholics had almost 500 fewer churches. One main reason for the net reduction in congregations in the United States is the loss of adherents, but this did not hold true for all denominations. For example, the number of adherents in the Catholic Church and Baptist Missionary Association of America increased, but both denominations experienced a net loss of congregations.[2]

More recent data suggest a possible turnaround in the Catholic Church. According to the Catholic Information Project conducted by United States Conference of Catholic Bishops (2006), the number of congregations (i.e., parishes) increased 1 percent from 2000 to 2004. Though this number indicates a reversal of the trend of loss, the number of Catholic parishes remains relatively flat compared to the rate of increase within the number of Catholic adherents. It would seem that the leaders of Catholic dioceses are addressing the urban population loss by merging or consolidating two

Exhibit 2-1 Net Gain in the Number of Congregations (Top 20): 1980–2000

Religious Bodies	Theology	Congregations (Net Change)	Adherents (Net Change)	Change (%) (Adherent)
Southern Baptist Convention	Evangelical Protestant	6,061	3,668,418	23
Church of Jesus Christ of Latter-Day Saints	Other Theology	4,882	1,557,003	58
Assemblies of God	Evangelical Protestant	2,498	955,497	60
National Association of Free Will Baptists	Evangelical Protestant	2,466	254,170	NA
Jewish (all denominations)	Jewish Faith	2,246	220,425	4
Church of God of Prophecy	Evangelical Protestant	1,858	91,106	NA
Wesleyan Church	Evangelical Protestant	1,657	381,459	NA
Pentecostal Church of God	Evangelical Protestant	1,173	101,921	NA
Independent, Non-Charismatic Churches	Evangelical Protestant	1,084	1,116,769	NA
International Church of the Foursquare Gospel	Evangelical Protestant	1,045	188,668	119
Seventh-Day Adventist Church	Evangelical Protestant	935	268,830	41
Presbyterian Church in America	Evangelical Protestant	772	207,073	191
Old Order Amish Church	Evangelical Protestant	765	12,878	15
Church of God (Cleveland, Tennessee)	Evangelical Protestant	761	506,027	108
Evangelical Free Church of America, The	Evangelical Protestant	728	215,109	305
Christian and Missionary Alliance, The	Evangelical Protestant	665	163,145	97
Independent, Charismatic Churches	Evangelical Protestant	621	935,168	NA
Greek Orthodox Archdiocese of America	Orthodox Christian	518	427,659	NA
International Pentecostal Holiness Church	Evangelical Protestant	518	123,329	104
Lutheran Church-Missouri Synod	Evangelical Protestant	424	-96,798	-4

Source: ARDA.
Note: The numbers of Jewish adherents in 1980 originally obtained from ARDA are incorrect. Therefore, we referred to American Jewish Year Book of 1981 and applied their figure of 5.92 million Jewish adherents in 1980. No change could be made to the net change in number of congregations.

or more parishes and then disposing of the properties of the closed parishes according to the diocese's merger policies. A case study of the St. Louis Archdiocese experience is included later in this book (Chapter 17).

Dimensions of Adaptive Reuse

As is explained above, a congregation is not necessarily permanently connected to its original place of worship. Once a building loses its congregation and sacred func-

tion, a number of possible outcomes for the structure emerge:

1. *Mothballing:* The owners of the structure can choose to maintain but not use the building in anticipation of some future use by the congregation, or eventual sale or lease of the building.

2. *Dereliction:* If the structure is not maintained it will inevitably suffer the ravages of time, vandalism and decay, often becoming a derelict eyesore on the

landscape and the community in which it stands. These crumbling, deteriorating buildings are haunting reminders of former sacred uses and indicators of economic, demographic, and social changes in the communities in which they are located.

3. *Destruction:* Many structures that no longer serve their sacred function are de-molished. This is sometimes done to clear the land for other, usually secular, uses. Typically demolition occurs when a building stands in a location with commercial or residential possibilities. In these cases the land has greater market value without the structure. Demolition can also be a preferred alternative when congregations, denominations, or

Exhibit 2-2 Net Loss in the Number of Congregations (Top 20): 1980–2000

Religious Bodies	Theology	Congregations (Net Change)	Adherents (Net Change)	Change (%) (Adherent)
United Methodist Church	Mainline Protestant	-2,688	-1,172,612	-10
Presbyterian Church (U.S.A.)	Mainline Protestant	-1,509	-855,006	-21
Christian Church (Disciples of Christ)	Mainline Protestant	-906	-185,930	-15
Catholic Church	Catholic	-486	12,000,000	32
United Church of Christ	Mainline Protestant	-465	-384,164	-18
American Baptist Churches in the USA	Mainline Protestant	-187	-143,262	-8
Baptist Missionary Association of America	Evangelical Protestant	-72	24,713	9
Evangelical Lutheran Church in America	Evangelical Protestant	-52	-252,733	-5
Cumberland Presbyterian Church	Evangelical Protestant	-49	-10,388	-12
Free Methodist Church of North America	Evangelical Protestant	-3	-103,053	-52
Moravian Church in America– Northern Province	Mainline Protestant		-6,626	-20
Primitive Methodist Church in the USA	Evangelical Protestant		-7,144	-60
General Six Principle Baptists	Evangelical Protestant	1	25	-11
Brethren Church, The (Ashland, Ohio)	Evangelical Protestant	1	-2,024	NA
Albanian Orthodox Diocese of America	Christian Orthodox	2	395	NA
Fellowship of Evangelical Bible Churches	Evangelical Protestant	2	-899	-33
Two-Seed-in-the-Spirit Predestinarian Baptists	Evangelical Protestant	4	65	NA
Old Order River Brethren	Evangelical Protestant	5	540	NA
Christian Union	Evangelical Protestant	7	347	5

Source: ARDA

Note: The number of Catholic adherents between 1980 and 2000 obtained from ARDA seems overestimated compared to the number obtained from the Catholic Information Project (CIP) survey conducted by the United States Conference of Catholic Bishops in 2006. We used numbers from CIP rather than numbers from ARDA, so there was approximately a 12 million net gain in terms of adherents between 1980 and 2000.

faith hierarchies fear that any alternative uses of the structure will, in some way, tarnish or profane the sacred purpose it once served.

4. *Sacred adaptation:* In cities and metropolitan areas undergoing social, economic, and demographic transformations, some houses of worship that have lost their congregations and sacred purpose are acquired by other religious organizations. In older industrial regions it is not uncommon to find thriving congregations, often African American, in buildings that originally served other faiths and denominations. This denominational or faith filtration is an important process of transition that preserves the physical structures in sacred uses.

5. *Secular adaptation:* The lens that focuses this chapter is the adaptation of houses of worship to nonreligious or secular uses, as well as the potential to employ economic development strategies that incorporate the adaptive reuse of these structures.

The Changing Landscape of Sacred Places

The drivers of change in the landscape of sacred places are:

- births of new congregations
- deaths of existing congregations
- contractions and expansions of existing congregations
- out-migration and immigration of congregations

Births: New communities of worship are born, organize into congregations, and form new houses of worship. New congregations usually consist of faiths and denominations seeking to respond to or proselytize demographic groups or a growing population. They may occupy storefront churches or acquire existing available religious buildings, often in the suburbs or exurban fringes of metropolitan areas. They may also build new houses of worship.

Deaths: Communities of worship die when there no longer remains a critical mass of congregants to sustain either the mission of the congregation or its religious structure. The physical structure remains, but without its former function as a house of worship. Absent its former religious function, the structure is destined for adaptation to either sacred or secular reuse, mothballing, dereliction, or destruction. The congregation may fold or move away, following its members.

Contractions and expansions: Congregations experience a net increase in membership when the rate of new membership acquisition exceeds the rate of loss through exit and death. Absent excess physical capacity to accommodate growing membership, these congregations confront three basic options:

- Utilize the current facility more intensively through multiple services, etc.
- Expand the current facility on the existing or adjacent site, or remote sites.
- Leave the current facility and relocate to a larger structure with the required physical capacity.

The decision to relocate a congregation affects two structures: the new and the old. The relocation releases the vacated structure to the alternative uses. In turn, there are three sources of structures for the relocating congregation: (1) acquisition of an existing sacred building, (2) adaptation of an existing secular building, or (3) new construction.

Out-migration/immigration: Most contractions and congregational deaths occur in the urban core, and most but not all births and expansions are in suburban or exurban communities. Understanding the differential effects of change among communities within the landscape of space landmarks, therefore, also requires consideration of immigration and out-migration of communities of worship.

Many communities now contain formerly sacred buildings that have been vacated by deaths or out-migration of congregations. These vacated structures are either owned by nonprofit organizations, often the former congregation or denomination, or have been sold and are privately or publicly owned.

Placing the alternatives for use of vacated sacred buildings in the context of neighborhoods, communities, and jurisdictions requires investigation into how these decisions are made, by whom are they made, and why they are made. A thorough assessment of a building's potential reuse must also consider the public interest and allow for expression of stakeholder voices in these choices and outcomes.

Place Matters: Zones of Transition

The location of buildings that no longer serve the sacred purpose for which they were constructed is, in part, a function of patterns of development and decline in metropolitan and nonmetropolitan areas in the United States, as well as denominational change. These now redundant or surplus structures are found throughout metropolitan and rural areas. These areas include central cities and their historic downtowns, older inner-ring suburbs adjacent or in proximity to these core cities, bedroom communities and suburbs, rural areas and rural towns and villages.

What follows is a descriptive model of the transitions in the landscape of sacred landmarks of metropolitan regions. Although not all metropolitan areas are alike, this descriptive model should stimulate the reader's connections in patterns of change between their own communities and other metropolitan regions.

The four zones described below radiate outward from the urban core. With the exception of the central cities, each of these zones is composed of different communities and political jurisdictions that reflect the growth, the outward expansion, and in most cases the age (that is, the date of first settlement) of metropolitan areas.

1. Zone of Urban Landmarks

The urban landmark zone is generally the historic downtown area of the central cities of metropolitan regions that developed in the nineteenth century. Here are found many towering and often quite beautiful faith structures. In an era before twentieth-century skyscrapers, these imposing edifices with their vertical architecture and tall steeples tended to dominate and define the skylines of their cities. They orient residents to space and—through their bells—to time. Even today, in the second decade of the twenty-first century, these historic and architecturally significant structures remain historical and physical landmarks that give meaning and definition to urban space. They are, in effect, urban landmarks and urban monuments.

Many, if not most, of these downtown areas became zones of transition in the landscape of sacred landmarks in the latter decades of the twentieth century. The growing distress of central cities and suburbanization of religion and faith communities have exacted an inevitable and relentless toll on memberships of many downtown places of worship. Some, however, remain viable. Where this has occurred, typically in places with low home-to-church commuting costs, these churches often provide for the prestige and heritage needs of their increasingly suburbanized congregations. Mainstream

CASE STUDY
CHRISTIAN SCIENCE
Witness the Empty Churches and Ask Why

The Beginnings of Christian Science

Christian Science, like the Church of Latter-Day Saints and the Seventh-Day Adventists, is a religion that began in the United States. Its founder was Mary Baker Eddy, born in 1821 on a farm in New Hampshire. She suffered from poor health for many years, but in her forties discovered that she could heal herself through prayer, faith in God, and the "true sense of the spirit" (Simurda 2002). In 1875 she wrote *Science and Health,* which became the foundational scripture, along with the Bible, of the new religion. In 1894 she officially founded the Church of Christ, Scientist (CCS), based on the principle of self-healing through faith and prayer. Mary Baker Eddy died in 1910.

The Expansion Era

Mary Baker Eddy's message resonated with the spirit of the times. In an era before antibiotics, modern sanitation, and scientific diagnostic methods, mind cures of many kinds were popular. The notion that a sick person could be healed through the power of prayer was a popular one in an age when medicine could not help. The church grew from about nine thousand members in 1890 to nearly 270,000 worldwide in 1936 (Lindsay 2006, Simurda 2002). A building boom ensued, as the church built first the Mother Church in Boston and then branches in major cities across the country. New York, Chicago, and other major metropolitan areas were the sites for a number of church branches (Ivey 1999).

The new religion had a special appeal to women, who comprised about 75 percent of its recruits. During the Progressive Era, women took increasingly public roles, including efforts to reform the corrupt and slum-ridden cities. The CCS participated in the spirit of this movement. It built churches in urban areas, using classical architecture that reflected attitudes about harmony, regularity, and order in civic life. In contrast to many mainline Protes-tant churches, which expanded church-building in the suburbs, the CCS built churches mainly in the cities, in the upscale, white neighborhoods from which it drew most of its recruits. The church blended the secular (classical architecture) with the spiritual, which appealed to the urban upper- and upper-middle classes. The interior designs were influenced by women and often included small rooms with fireplaces for group meetings (Ivey 1999).

The Contraction Era

After World War II, the church began a period of decline, which accelerated in the 1960s and continues to this day. The church does not release membership numbers, so figures regarding changes are necessarily estimates. The *New York Times* reported that by 1989 the church had only about 170,000 members, many elderly, representing a loss of about 100,000 members since 1936 (Steinfels 1989). *USA Today* reported that the church had only about 106,000 members worldwide in 1992 (Lindsay 2006).

Quackwatch, an organization that monitors New Age healing projects, using data from the *Christian Science Journal*'s listings of practitioners (church-trained healers and spiritual leaders) and church organizations, reported that from 1971 to 2005 the number of practitioners in the United States declined from 4,965 to 1,161, and the number of churches declined from 1,829 to 1,010 (Barrett n.d.).

Another indication of the decline in church resources is the leasing and selling of church properties that have historical significance for the organization. To be sold are two historic homes of Mary Baker Eddy in Boston and in Washington, D.C.: the building that houses the *Christian Science Monitor*'s Washington office and a church located near the White House (Estes and Palmer 2005; Cook 2006). The church also plans to lease out office space on its historic 14-acre campus in Boston, which also houses the Mother Church and the Mary Baker Eddy Library since large staff cuts have left large vacancies in the administration buildings.

Derelict Church. Photograph: Larry Ledebur

The architecture of these massive churches is often either Neo-Gothic or Colonial, depending on the region of the country. Christian symbols, steeples, spires, and columns adorn the exterior of the building. Upon entering the church, one is greeted by a traditional foyer. . . . The sanctuary is often an exaggerated replica of the country church. A box shaped interior space contains long straight, uncomfortable wooden pews, hymnals, poor lighting, a crowded altar space, and many traditional symbols such as crosses, candles, descending doves, and stained glass windows. The image these congregations want to portray is "This is your parents' religion, but bigger and better. . . ."

The expansion of physical structures to accommodate growing congregations alters the landscape of faith-places of some central cities' downtowns, sometimes to the detriment of the building's present or future significance. Structural accretion changes the setting and spatial context of the original faith structure while also diminishing its visibility and architectural signature. The long-term viability of these megastructures is yet to be seen.

But many other churches in older downtowns have faced daunting challenges and often agonizing decisions about the future of their congregations and the structures in which they worship. Some challenged churches have struggled on, attempting to attract new membership and trying to establish or renew social missions that respond to the plight of their city and its changing demographics. Some churches that have suffered precipitous declines in membership have turned to endowments rather than contributions to keep them afloat as they attempt to redefine their roles and memberships in changing circumstances. Other churches have closed their

denominational churches in downtowns of central cities may thrive in unexpected ways. Some have grown and achieved megachurch proportions with two thousand or more worshipers attending their services per week.[3] In some cases the physical facilities housing these congregations have significantly expanded through a process of accretion adjacent to or around the original structure as new annexes, wings, sanctuaries, and "family life centers." These "expanded churches" often encompass whole city blocks and, at times, spill over to adjacent blocks. The structural growth of these "expanded churches" signals that they have prospered and grown, somehow countering the suburbanization of religion, even as the city struggled and declined around them. In his study of megachurches, Scott Thumma (1996) identifies the structures of worship described above as older "First Churches" of traditional Protestantism, but on a mega scale. He describes them as follows:

doors, either because their congregations could no longer sustain membership or operating revenues, or the congregation relocated to new facilities, sometimes within the central city, but more often to suburban locations. Their former houses of worship thus became available for alternative uses.

Some significant structures have been destroyed, either because alternative uses could not be found or to preclude a future use that might tarnish or profane the sacred purpose for which the building was originally created. Others have experienced less dignified deaths of dereliction and decay thorough ravages of time, vandalism, and arson.

Still others of these historic structures have survived through denominational or, in some cases, faith filtration. The downtown areas of many older cities house sacred structures that, having lost their former

congregations, have been acquired by congregations of other denominations or faiths, who then adapted the building to meet their own needs. African American congregations in particular have, through this process of denominational or faith filtration, come together to worship and fulfill their social missions in churches built by other congregations or even in former synagogues and temples. These buildings, adapted to new sacred uses, often continue to bear the embedded symbols and physical trappings placed there by their former owners.

Finally, some sacred structures vacated by their congregations have been adapted to secular uses. Zones of urban landmarks contain formerly sacred structures that have been reborn in a variety of secular uses, including public sector functions, nonprofit endeavors, and commercial enterprises. The profile of faith structures of downtown ar-

Landmark Church. Photograph: Larry Ledebur

eas in central cities and the transitions transforming this profile cannot be complete without recognizing the resurgence of storefront churches in distressed urban areas. These churches with their many parachurch functions represent a unique form of secular-to-sacred adaptation of retail and other commercial spaces. By and large, however, these buildings and spaces have no particular historical or architectural significance and hence do not constitute urban sacred landmarks to the wider community.

2. Zone of Cultural Heritage

The cultural heritage zone is also found within a central city. It lies adjacent to, and often surrounds, the downtown business district. The zone of cultural heritage encompasses the rich and diverse mosaic of ethnic neighborhoods that was created in the nineteenth century by waves of immigrants who sought the familiarity and security of communities that shared their ethnic cultures and customs. In these neighborhoods of common culture were built the many tall-steepled heritage churches that, along with the skyscrapers and landmark churches of downtowns, often dominate and define the skylines of central cities.

The latter half of the twentieth century was not kind to older neighborhoods of central cities. Socioeconomic trends and political policies eroded or destroyed the vitality of many of these ethnic neighborhoods and their communities of common culture. Freeways, planned and constructed without consideration for those affected, ruptured neighborhoods and ethnic communities. The relentless march to the suburbs drained neighborhoods and depleted communities of their residents, a process accelerated by the deterioration of central cities. Some neighborhoods fell prey to the wrecking ball of urban renewal. Many older urban neighborhoods lost their communities of ethnic culture. For some, even the remnant of that culture was lost as the neighborhood was claimed by other ethnic or racial groups filtering into the vacated housing.

The landscape of tall steeples, then, remains in a dramatically altered mosaic of neighborhoods in central cities. Some neighborhoods were able to sustain their ethnic identity despite the last century's winds of change in urban America. There, residents continue to value the ethnic heritage of the community and the sacred and heritage roles of their landmark churches. In many others, however, these heritage landmarks now stand isolated in deteriorating neighborhoods where residents no longer identify with the cultural heritage of community and its landmark houses of worship. Those who continue to value the faith structures' cultural heritage and functions often live in suburbs rather than the immediate neighborhood of the church. The congregations of churches in the cultural heritage zones are often declining, aging, and threatened.

This is the landscape of church consolidations and closings. Many churches in this landscape are Catholic, reflecting the faith of the immigrants who settled the neighborhood. In Boston, for example, the Catholic archdiocese is closing almost 25 percent of its churches. In Pittsburgh, Detroit, Cleveland, Boston, and St. Louis, as well as other dioceses, churches are either closed, in the process of closing, or targeted for closing.

Some structures in this zone are lost to dereliction and destruction with little fanfare, and the ethnic heritage and history that they once preserved may be irretrievably lost with them. In other cases, closing churches within this zone can be contentious, either because a church provides social services to the community beyond its own membership, or because the residents of the neighborhood value the structure as a community landmark even if they do not worship there or feel a connection to the building's cultural heritage. Sacred structures in distressed neighborhoods within the cultural heritage zone may sometimes successfully be adapted to houses of worship that better serve the denominations and faiths of the current residents.

Landmark structures in older distressed neighborhoods can also be adapted to secular or nonreligious uses. When a neighborhood perceives a sacred structure as a local landmark or symbol of community values, however, secular adaptation can be quite controversial. The neighborhood becomes an important stakeholder in the secular adaptation process, either because it is given a voice in the decision-making process or because it asserts a stake through community activism and confrontation. Neighborhood stakeholders almost invariably advocate for adaptive reuses consonant with community needs, vision, and goals, often preferring reuses that might contribute to economic redevelopment of the neighborhood. Some older neighborhoods in central cities' cultural heritage zone are being redeveloped through gentrification.[4] Gentrification results in a wider range of possibilities and opportunities for adaptation of former houses of worship to commercial uses consistent with rising real estate prices. Churches in areas being gentrified may be valued for high-end uses such as condominiums because people are willing to pay for the "sacred" atmosphere and the custom detailing in the architecture.

Within the cultural heritage zone, beyond the downtown and surrounding neighborhoods, is now found the megachurch, a phenomenon more typically associated with the zone of exurban expansion and its network of freeways and beltways. It is problematic to generalize about the architectural styles and structural forms of these houses of worship. Some appear to follow the more conventional architectural format of the expanded or "first" churches of downtowns. But Thumma (1996) also identifies a third, less common approach that blends the conventional form of downtown megachurches with a more nontraditional style: "This 'Composite' orientation attempts to retain some connection to traditional religion but also embraces modern architectural forms and a contemporary worship format. These megachurches of this type often superimpose a traditional building façade onto an unconventional, 'user-friendly' structure. The exterior, or at least the street exposure, of the church may appear 'church-like,' while the interior resembles a theater, with comfortable individual seating, state of the art sound and light system, and an adaptable performance stage. This building often has both conveniences of the nontraditional church building and the symbols and trappings of familiar Christianity."

In a few instances, central city megachurches have acquired mega secular facilities and adapted them to their sacred purposes. Two prominent examples—the Faithful Central Bible Church in Inglewood, California, and the Lakewood Church in Houston, Texas—are discussed in more detail in Chapter 10.

3. Suburban Zones

There is a tendency to refer to "suburbs" as relatively homogeneous. This is misleading. Suburbs vary significantly in their history, demography, and tax bases; in the age, experience, and income of their residents; and in social and economic vitality. In general, individuals and families choose suburban jurisdictions based on a variety of considerations such as kinship ties, the selection of amenities (such as schools, safety, infrastructure, neighborhoods, or proximity of shopping) offered by the location, and their ability and willingness to pay for their preferred mix of amenities through local taxes. One outcome of this "private choice" mechanism of residential/jurisdictional selection is the pronounced pattern of income segregation found in almost all urban regions.

The zone of first suburbs is composed of villages and towns that grew just beyond the confines of the core city. These jurisdictions are commonly referred to as "inner ring" or "first suburbs." Many inner-ring suburbs are the first and therefore the oldest jurisdictions that grew close to but beyond their central cities, usually in the latter part of the nineteenth century or early decades of the twentieth. The villages and towns that developed just beyond the core cities, indeed, were the first *edge cities*. They accommodated the population that grew rapidly in the United States as the nation urbanized. The first suburbs, while separate municipalities, were oriented to and under the economic sway of the core city. When central cities had the power to annex, many of the inner-ring villages and towns were incorporated into the municipal jurisdictions of their central cities, creating a blended zone where the zones of cultural heritage and first suburbs overlap.

The landscape of many early and older suburbs includes distinct and identifiable downtowns, reflecting their village and town origins. In many inner-ring suburbs are found faith structures that were constructed to serve congregations in a pre-automobile era that required longer travel time. Some of these suburbs have village landmark churches that orient these downtown areas in space and time. These pre-1920 houses of worship are in many ways similar to those found in zones of cultural heritage, although

often on a smaller architectural scale. They are often reflections of the immigrant waves that settled and grew the towns and villages on the periphery of larger cities.

The overlapping or blended zone also reflects the growth of denominations and faiths. The turn of the nineteenth century, for example, saw a rapid growth of Jewish and Christian Science congregations and their associated religious structures. Though the founding church of Christian Science is in the core of Boston, many of its structural artifacts in other metropolitan areas are in the blended zones of cultural heritage and inner-ring suburbs. Jewish communities, governed by congregations rather than a hierarchical leadership and less rooted in place, followed populations and constructed temples and synagogues in this blended zone (Gamm 2001). Faith structures in the zone of first suburbs also reflect the nineteenth-century growth of the seven sisters of Protestantism.

These first-ring nineteenth-century villages and towns on the periphery of central cities were reshaped by the successive tides of twentieth-century industrialization, the growing urbanization of the nation, and the spatial revolution wrought by the automobile. Industrialization tended to place these formerly tranquil peripheral villages and towns more firmly within the spheres of economic dominance of the central city, thereby making their fates and fortunes highly interdependent with those of their core cities. With growing urbanization and increasing incomes came an important process of housing filtration through which families sought to improve the size and quality of their residential structure by moving upward and outward.

The filtration process made lower-priced housing in core cities available to meet the needs of new immigrants and the influx of

African Americans to urban areas during and after World War II. This ongoing process altered, often significantly, the ethnic and racial composition of both the neighborhoods of the cultural heritage zone and the first-ring suburbs of core cities, and simultaneously increased income segregation in the nation's urban areas.

The white flight triggered in the 1960s, and the subsequent income flight as discrimination in housing was made illegal, added great impetus to the cycle of housing filtration, suburbanization, and income segregation in urban areas. Perhaps it was inevitable that the problems of the nation's core cities would begin to spill out beyond their jurisdictional confines. In many urban areas, suburbs adjacent or in proximity to central cities are now experiencing the symptoms of economic and social distress associated with core cities in the latter part of the twentieth century. When inner-ring suburbs encounter the same economic and demographic changes that neighborhoods in the zone of cultural heritage have confronted, the fates of houses of worship mirror those of sacred structures closer to the core cities: churches and synagogues that lose their congregations are either adopted by a different religious group, repurposed for secular uses, mothballed, or lost to demolition.

Certainly not all suburbs in proximity to central cities are suffering growing economic distress. Some remain enclaves of wealth and status with relatively stable residential populations and a supply of housing consistent with the needs and preferences of higher income residents. Proximity and ease of access to the central business district of the core city tends to make these locations desirable for those who can afford housing and the taxes needed to support often high-end public service expectations. Many of these wealthy enclaves, beyond but proxi-

mate to core cities of urban areas, have relatively stable faith communities, most often Protestant, that maintain and sustain existing faith structures and landmark churches.

4. Exurban Zone

"Exurban" and "exurbanism" refer to the spillover of urban sprawl and the forces of suburbanization into more rural areas beyond the boundaries of metropolitan areas. Exurban areas are zones of transition in which are found both the village landmark churches of the pioneers and first settlers of the area, and more recent (though still old) churches serving smaller cities and towns.[5]

Village landmark churches, some of which have been placed on the National Register of Historic Places, are typically significant because of their architecture, history, or most frequently, their setting. Village landmark churches are found as defining points on village greens and the skylines of villages and rural areas; by providing a focus for community identity, they become an important part of the "identity of place." Many of these structures continue to have active congregations that value and preserve the buildings, although diminished congregations and limited resources pose challenges. These structures also often have heritage significance apart from current congregations. Descendants of early church members may care deeply about these buildings with all their heritage and cultural associations. In villages and rural areas particularly, significance may include a graveyard where parents and ancestors are buried.

But the twentieth century has not been kind to the settings of many of these churches. Some have been lost to dereliction and demolition as congregations waned or built new churches. Others have been enveloped by the relentless urbanization and sprawl of the post–World War

II period. Many landmark buildings are marred and obscured by modern clutter: new and expanded streets and roads, telephone and power lines, road and business signage, traffic patterns, and visually intervening buildings. Still, some communities have been successful in protecting and even enhancing the settings of these landmark structures. Finally, some village landmark churches have been preserved in their original settings by adaptation to secular uses.

Conclusion

Metropolitan areas, counties, cities, and towns often provide listings and perhaps maps of locations of houses of worship. While serving a useful function, the lists and maps provided in Yellow Pages and directories are static images of the landscape of religion and their houses of worship. This frozen imagery of the present offers only veiled glimpses of the past, and only tantalizing hints of the changing landscape of sacred landmarks and the social, economic, and demographic forces it mirrors and reflects.

Notes

1. A further, more detailed analysis of this statistic may be misleading due to data aggregation bias. For example, the Jewish faith has at least four distinct, loosely affiliated branches: Orthodox, Conservative, Reform, and Reconstructionist. Further, according to a recent National Jewish demographic study, only about 60 percent of those self-identified Jews were affiliated with a congregation in the year 2000. Congregation sizes also vary substantially. Reform and Conservative Jewish congregations have a large average size (typically a few thousand members), whereas Orthodox Jews walk to synagogue, and their average congregational size is much smaller (typically a few hundred members). Because the Orthodox Jewish branch has a higher birthrate and a higher intergenerational denominational retention rate, this segment of the faith is growing faster than the rest

of the Jewish faith, and it is this trend that is likely driving the apparent increase in the number of Jewish congregations in the United States (Simons and Seo 2011). This analysis therefore indicates that caution should be used in deriving conclusions from the data in this chapter because other statistics presented may be similarly complex.

2. The reduction in Catholic churches may be partly explained by the fewer number of available priests.

3. Dr. Scott Thumma (1996) states: "At its most basic descriptive level, a megachurch is a congregation which has two thousand or more worship attendees in a week. However, size alone is an insufficient characterization of this distinctive religious reality. The megachurch is a new structural and spiritual organization unlike any other . . . they must be seen as a collective social phenomenon rather than as individual anomalous movements of spectacular growth or uniquely successful spiritual entrepreneurial ventures . . ." (n.p.).

4. This process is often controversial in itself. Gentrification occurs when higher income individuals and families purchase and restore older housing, which inevitably drive up housing prices, making this housing stock less accessible to lower income families.

5. The discussion of village landmark churches is abstracted from Ledebur and Whitelaw.

References and Works Consulted

American Jewish Committee Archives. 1981. *American Jewish Year Book*. http://www.ajcarchives.org.

Ammerman, N. 2001. "Still Gathering After All These Years: Congregations in U.S. Cities." In *Can Charitable Choice Work? Covering Religion's Impact on Urban Affairs and Social Services*, edited by Andrew Wash, 6–20. Hartford, Conn.: Leonard E. Greenberg Center for the Study of Religion in Public Life.

Association of Religious Data Archives, ARDA. http://www.thearda.com/.

Barrett, Stephen. n.d. Christian Science Statistics: Practitioners, Teachers, and Churches in the United States. Quackwatch. http://www.quackwatch.org/01QuackeryRelatedTopics/cs.html.

Christian Science. 2003. *Religion and Ethics News Weekly*. PBS, February 14. www.pbs.org/wnet/religionandethics/.

Cook, David T. 2006. "Christian Science Church—Stressing 'Mission Focus'—Cuts Real-Estate Costs." *The Christian Science Monitor,* April 14. www.csmonitor.com.

Diocese of Buffalo. http://www.buffalodiocese.org/.

Diocese of Cleveland. http://dioceseofcleveland.org/.

Estes, Andrea, and Palmer, Thomas C., Jr. 2005. "Christian Science Church May Sell, Lease Properties." *Boston Globe,* October 13. www.boston.com.

Fraser, Caroline. 1995. "Suffering Children and the Christian Science Church." *The Atlantic Online,* April. www.theatlantic.com.

Gamm, Gerald. 2001. "The Way Things Used to Be in American Cities: Jews, Protestants, and the Erosion of Catholic Exceptionalism, 1950–2000." In *Can Charitable Choice Work? Covering Religion's Impact on Urban Affairs and Social Services,* edited by Andrew Wash, 39–55. Hartford, Conn.: Leonard E. Greenberg Center for the Study of Religion in Public Life.

Ivey, Paul Eli. 1999. *Prayers in Stone: Christian Science Architecture in the United States: 1894–1930.* Urbana: University of Illinois Press.

Ledebur, Larry, and Susan Whitelaw. n.d. *Village Landmark Churches of Northeast Ohio.* Cleveland: Center for Sacred Landmarks, Maxine Goodman Levin College of Urban Affairs, Cleveland State University.

Lindsay, Jay. 2006. "Christian Science Church Aims for Growth Amid Struggles." *USA Today,* June 25. www.usatoday.com.

Pew Forum on Religion & Public Life. http://pewforum.org.

Simons, R. A., and Y. Seo. 2011. "The Effect of an Orthodox Jewish Campus on Nearby Residential Property Values: The Halo Effect." *International Real Estate Review* 14, no. 3: 330–53.

Simurda, Stephen J. 2002. "A Leap of Faith." *The Boston Magazine,* July. http://www.bostonmagazine.com/2006/05/a-leap-of-faith/.

Steinfels, Peter. 1989. "Plan to Expand Church Media Reveals Christian Science Rift." *New York Times,* January 4. http://query.nytimes.com.

Thumma, Scott. 1996. "Exploring the Megachurch Phenomena: Their Characteristics and Cultural Context." Hartford Institute for Religion Research. http://hirr.hartsem.edu/bookshelf/thumma_article2.html.

United States Conference of Catholic Bishops. 2006. *The Catholic Church in America: Meeting Real Needs in Your Neighborhood,* 1–19. Washington, D.C.: United States Conference of Catholic Bishops.

Wikipedia. "List of Former Christian Science Churches, Societies and Buildings." http://en.wikipedia.org/wiki/List_of_former_Christian_Science_churches%2C_societies_and_buildings.

Appendix: Religious Profile by State

As shown in Exhibit 2-A, the state that had the highest increase rate in the number of congregations between 1980 and 1990 was Nevada with a 49.3 percent increase, followed by Utah (44.3 percent increase), Hawaii (41.9 percent increase), and Alaska (40.8 percent increase). The states that had the lowest rate of change during this twenty-year period are North Dakota with a 8.5 percent rate of *decrease*, followed by Delaware (0 percent change) and West Virginia (0.9 percent rate of increase).

Regarding the net change in the actual number of congregations between 1980 and 2000, California, Florida, and Texas are the top three states with approximately 5,700, 3,900, and 2,800 net congregation gains, respectively, followed by New York (2,100) and Utah (1,900). North Dakota had the greatest net loss (128) followed by Delaware

(even) and West Virginia, which gained only thirty-six congregations.

The number of congregations per person shows little relationship to the outright numbers of congregations. For example, no states that have large number of religious entities are included in the top ten for congregations per person. The state with the highest ratio of churches per person is North Dakota with 0.00235 (one for every 435 people), followed by West Virginia (0.0023) and South Dakota with 0.0027. The tenth highest is Oklahoma with a ratio of 0.0017 (one church for every 588 people) and the twentieth highest is Alaska with a ratio of 0.00137.

Exhibit 2-B is a map that shows the number of congregations by state for the year 2000. Lighter shaded areas have fewer congregations, and darker areas have more congregations.

Exhibit 2-A U.S. Congregations by State, 1980–2000

States	1980	1990	2000	Congregations per person	People per congregations	Congregations increase rate (%)	Congregations net change
Alabama	7,744	8,447	8,343	0.002	533	7.2 (41)	599 (24)
Alaska	507	814	856	0.001	732	**40.8 (4)**	349 (35)
Arizona	2,046	2,766	3,307	0.001	1551	38.1 (6)	1,261 (11)
Arkansas	5,337	5,209	5,802	**0.002**	461	8 (38)	465 (29)
California	**11,215**	**14,427**	**16,920**	0.001	**2002**	33.7 (7)	**5705 (1)**
Colorado	2,298	2,813	3,228	0.001	1332	28.8 (9)	930 (17)
Connecticut	1,710	1,944	1,955	0.001	1742	12.5 (28)	245 (39)
D.C.	363	343	390	0.001	1467	6.9 (43)	27 (49)
Delaware	571	523	571	0.001	1372	0 (50)	0 (50)
Florida	6,150	8,577	10,078	0.001	1586	**39 (5)**	**3,928 (2)**
Georgia	7,134	8,300	8,962	0.001	913	20.4 (16)	1,828 (6)
Hawaii	546	758	939	0.001	1290	**41.9 (3)**	393 (33)
Idaho	1,344	1,600	1,855	0.001	698	27.5 (10)	511 (27)
Illinois	9,135	9,799	10,139	0.001	1225	9.9 (32)	1,004 (16)
Indiana	6,374	7,134	7,491	0.001	812	14.9 (22)	1,117 (13)
Iowa	4,386	4,560	4,584	0.002	638	4.3 (46)	198 (40)

Exhibit 2-A cont.

States	1980	1990	2000	Congregations per person	People per congregations	Congregations increase rate (%)	Congregations net change
Kansas	3,680	3,958	3,959	0.001	679	7 (42)	279 (38)
Kentucky	6,563	7,255	7,143	0.002	566	8.1 (37)	580 (25)
Louisiana	3,782	4,025	4,158	0.001	1075	9 (35)	376 (34)
Maine	1,270	1,336	1,301	0.001	980	2.4 (48)	31 (48)
Maryland	3,030	3,519	3,855	0.001	1374	21.4 (14)	825 (19)
Massachusetts	2,918	3,382	3,532	0.001	**1798**	17.4 (20)	614 (23)
Michigan	6,424	7,229	7,525	0.001	1321	14.6 (23)	1,101 (14)
Minnesota	4,705	4,981	5,114	0.001	962	8 (39)	409 (32)
Mississippi	5,090	5,433	5,505	**0.002**	517	7.5 (40)	415 (31)
Missouri	7,428	7,666	7,771	0.001	720	4.4 (44)	343 (36)
Montana	1,203	1,415	1,543	0.002	585	22 (13)	340 (37)
Nebraska	2,515	2,629	2,612	0.002	655	3.7 (47)	97 (43)
Nevada	475	664	937	0.000	**2133**	**49.3 (1)**	462 (30)
New Hampshire	760	896	872	0.001	1417	12.8 (26)	112 (42)
New Jersey	3,665	4,183	4,531	0.001	**1857**	19.1 (18)	866 (18)
New Mexico	1,543	1,824	2,026	0.001	898	23.8 (11)	483 (28)
New York	8,853	10,878	10,999	0.001	1725	19.5 (17)	**2,146 (4)**
North Carolina	**10,031**	**11,331**	**11,132**	0.001	723	9.9 (33)	1,101 (15)
North Dakota	1,635	1,622	1,507	0.002	426	-8.5 (51)	-128 (51)
Ohio	**9,732**	**11,086**	**11,166**	0.001	1017	12.8 (27)	1,434 (7)
Oklahoma	5,205	5,707	5,854	0.002	589	11.1 (30)	649 (22)
Oregon	2,501	2,908	3,155	0.001	1084	20.7 (15)	654 (21)
Pennsylvania	**11,872**	**13,284**	**13,104**	0.001	937	9.4 (34)	1,232 (12)
Rhode Island	491	554	572	0.001	**1833**	14.2 (24)	81 (44)
South Carolina	4,832	5,509	5,522	0.001	727	12.5 (29)	690 (20)
South Dakota	1,636	1,781	1,712	**0.002**	441	4.4 (45)	76 (45)
Tennessee	8,309	9,246	9,634	0.002	591	13.8 (25)	1,325 (10)
Texas	**15,628**	**16,961**	**18,466**	0.001	1129	15.4 (21)	**2,838 (3)**
Utah	2,419	3,319	4,343	0.002	514	**44.3 (2)**	**1,924 (5)**
Vermont	705	764	775	0.001	786	9.0 (36)	70 (46)
Virginia	6,310	7,490	7,736	0.001	915	18.4 (19)	1,426 (8)
Washington	3,305	4,092	4,649	0.001	1268	28.9 (8)	1,344 (9)
West Virginia	4,103	4,443	4,139	**0.002**	437	0.9 (49)	36 (47)
Wisconsin	4,623	5,023	5,181	0.001	1035	10.8 (31)	558 (26)
Wyoming	610	766	790	0.002	625	22.8 (12)	180 (41)

Source: ARDA; mapped by Eugene Choi
Note:
1. Top five states of each column are in bold.
2. Rankings of the increase rate and the net change are in parentheses.

Exhibit 2-B Number of Congregations

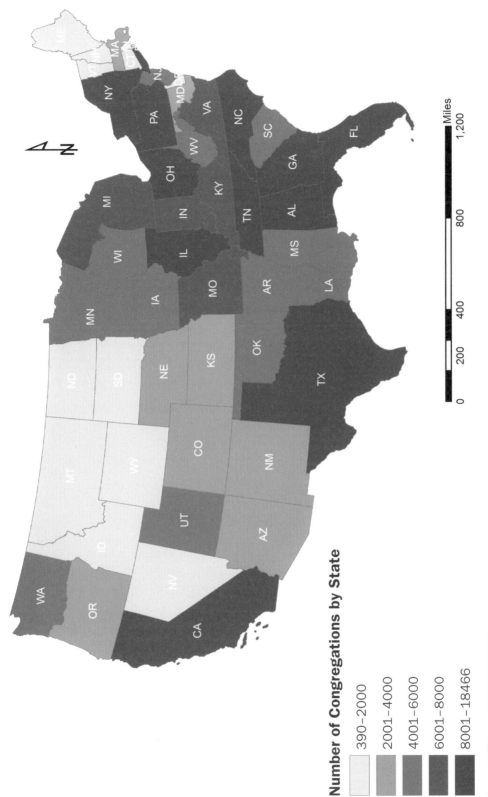

Number of Congregations by State

390–2000
2001–4000
4001–6000
6001–8000
8001–18466

Miles
0   200   400   800   1,200

Source: ARDA (map made by the authors)

3

A STATISTICAL ANALYSIS OF RELIGIOUS AND SCHOOL BUILDING REHABILITATION IN THE UNITED STATES

Robert A. Simons and
Eugene Choi

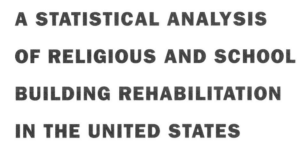

There has been very little statistical analysis of the factors associated with redevelopment outcomes of religious buildings and surplus school adaptive reuse projects in the United States. Knowing about these locational and physical property attributes is useful to developers and owners of potentially vacant properties because some factors may be positively associated with likely successful end uses, while others are negatively related to a particular end use. This knowledge can help the developer avoid making mistakes by choosing an incorrect use of a vacant property.

The purpose of this chapter is to determine which specific factors (site size, street access, location, etc.) are associated with end uses of adaptive reuse of religious buildings. This study uses a statistical analysis of the outcomes of over two hundred actual adaptive reuse projects to determine factors (variables) that affect project outcomes. The project end-use outcome (the dependent variable) is explained by a series of independent variables using a statistical technique known as a multinomial logit model. The independent variables, which include both supply-side and demand-side factors such as market demographics, building characteristics, and macro- and micro-locational characteristics, were derived from a review of previous studies on this subject. The logit models consider factors associated with five different development outcomes: apartments, condominiums, retail, office, and cultural uses. In order to properly address technical issues such as sample size and reference categories, we also include rehabbed school buildings in this analysis.[1]

In addition to the results of the statistical analyses, this chapter also provides an overview of the sales history of religious buildings that are currently on the market or that have been sold in the last four years.

Developing the factors that are featured in this chapter requires making reasonable compromises on quality of data for key factors, such as historic status, in order to get a complete data set for all properties used in the analysis. These trade-offs are acceptable for analysis of large data sets, and this work meets the standard of peer-reviewed research.[2] Further, some statistical analysis may not interest some readers. More complete data are found in the appendices for readers who wish to pursue the information in more depth.

Published Research on Factors Related to Adaptive Reuse

Three bodies of literature were reviewed: adaptive reuse literature, call option theory, and real estate reinvestment literature. Five major characteristics are significantly related to the end use of adaptive reuse projects: historic value, macroeconomic cycles, building structure characteristics, location characteristics, and demographic characteristics of the neighborhood. These characteristics may be classified as either internal or external factors. External factors include macroeconomic conditions, demographic changes, and location characteristics, while internal factors include building structure characteristics, historic value, and architectural value (Martin and Gamzon et al. 1978; Burchell and Listokin 1981; Bullen 2007).

Some of the research focuses on the details of the behavioral framework of the theory behind the timing of redevelopment, sometimes referred to as call option theory (Luehrman, 1998), divided investment timing into six stages: "invest now," "maybe now," "probably later," "maybe later," "probably never," and "invest never." The investment timing is determined by a property's value-to-cost and volatility characteristics. Higher value-to-cost with lower volatility drives "invest now," whereas, lower value-to-cost with higher volatility drives "invest never." If potential project initiators assume that a project's market is volatile, they will just wait and watch market conditions. On the other hand, if project initiators assume that a market is not volatile, they can more easily make the decision about whether to purchase the property or not, since they can make their decision primarily based on property value.

Moving to a more general perspective, adaptive reuse projects are a special kind of property reinvestment project. Under the assumption that a home reinvestment project and an adaptive reuse project would induce similar positive externalities,[3] this study considers the decision to convert an underused property into a new use to be similar to the decision to reinvest in a house.[4] Previous studies on property reinvestment have examined factors such as housing characteristics, community/neighborhood factors, and location characteristics (Laska, Seaman, and McSeveney 1982; Helms 2003). Garrod, Willis, Bjarnadottir, and Cockbain (1996) focused on the nonpriced benefits of renovating historic buildings. They point out that the nonpriced benefits[5] arise from a building's historical and architectural importance, its role in the community's development of a sense of identity, and its role in encouraging tourism and investment. In short, they considered historic value to be a key determinant that affects an owner's decision to renovate. With this literature in mind, we set forth below models to determine which independent factors are associated with particular development outcomes.

Building the Data Set and Descriptive Statistics of the Sample

The data set for this research was built backwards from religious building and school projects known to be redeveloped successfully through an extensive Internet search of newspapers, journals, and commercial real estate Web sites. Around 30 percent of the total cases were gathered from the database system of the Co-Star Group, which is the dominant commercial real estate information company.[6] This search discovered 369 properties, including 220 religious buildings and 149 schools, which had been adapted for reuse between 1990 and 2008. It was possible to identify project outcome types for 229 of these projects. A nonrandom subset of 209 of these cases forms the basis of the multinomial logit statistical analysis in this chapter. Exhibit 3-1 shows the location of the religious building and school rehab projects used in the statistical analysis.

Massachusetts, New York, California, and Texas are the four states in which adaptive reuse projects of religious buildings were most frequently initiated. School reuse projects were most frequently initiated in Massachusetts, New York, and Washington, D.C. No cases of adaptive reuse projects of religious buildings or schools were identified in ten states: Alaska, Idaho, Mississippi, Montana, North Dakota, Rhode Island, Vermont, West Virginia, Wyoming, and Hawaii (see Appendix 3-A for the rankings of all states).

Adaptive reuse project outcomes can be broadly divided into seven uses: residential rental housing, residential condominium, cultural use, office, retail use, school, and industrial use. Among 220 religious buildings, project outcomes for 144 properties could be determined. Of those 144 properties, housing was the most popular use: 10.4

Exhibit 3-1 Adaptively Reused Churches and Schools

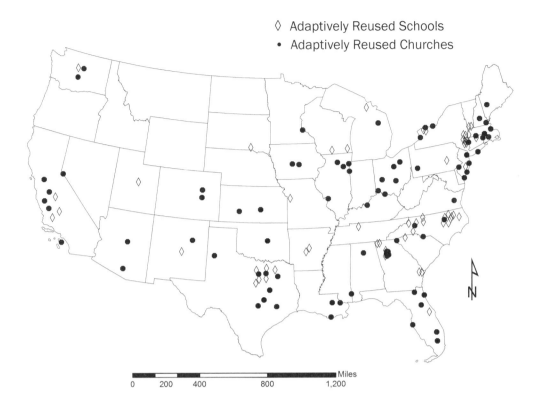

◊ Adaptively Reused Schools
• Adaptively Reused Churches

percent were reused as residential rental housing, and 23.6 percent were reused as residential condominiums. Cultural purposes (24.3 percent), retail (20.8 percent), offices (8.3 percent), and schools (11.8 percent) were also found. One religious building had an industrial reuse. Among 124 school properties, outcomes were identified for 85 buildings. By far the most popular end use was residential apartments (61.2 percent), and many of these were low-income housing. A total of 24.7 percent were reused as residential condominiums. The remaining 15 percent of identifiable school reuse outcomes included cultural purposes, offices, retail centers, and industrial sites.

Exhibit 3-2 shows detailed descriptive data for rehabbed religious buildings. Sellers' characteristics, location characteristics, building structure characteristics, census tract demographics, and the historic value of each religious building and school were all identified. The results are sorted by project outcomes.

The descriptive analysis shows that 29.9 percent of total reused religious buildings were sold by hierarchical organizations—the Catholic Church; the Church of Christ, Scientist; and similar religious denominations with a centralized financial structure. Their churches, when sold, are not financially autonomous; 42.5 percent had substantial historic value, 12.6 percent were located on local roads, 47.2 percent were located on collector roads, and 40.2 percent were located on major roads. A total of 26.8 percent of religious buildings were located on a street corner, and 48.0 percent of church reuse projects were initiated in the inner city or downtown.

Exhibit 3-2 Descriptive Statistics of Religious Buildings in the Sample

	OUTCOMES											
	Apartments		Condos		Cultural		Office		Retail		Total Known	
DESCRIPTION	N	%	N	%	N	%	N	%	N	%	N	%
OUTCOMES	15	10.4	34	23.6	35	24.3	12	8.3	30	20.8	126	87.40
HIERARCHICAL SELLER												
Yes	7	46.70	11	32.40	11	31.40	5	41.70	4	12.90	38	29.90
No	8	53.30	23	67.60	24	68.60	7	58.30	27	87.10	89	70.10
HAS HISTORICAL VALUE												
Yes	6	40.00	18	52.90	19	54.30	3	25.00	8	25.80	54	42.50
No	9	60.00	16	47.10	16	45.70	9	75.00	23	74.20	73	57.50
STREET TYPE												
Local	0		5	14.70	6	17.10	2	16.70	3	9.70	16	12.60
Collector	6	40.00	21	61.80	17	48.60	6	50.00	10	32.30	60	47.20
Main	9	60.00	8	23.50	12	34.30	4	33.30	18	58.10	51	40.20
CORNER LOCATION												
Yes	2	13.30	10	29.40	9	25.70	4	33.30	9	29.00	34	26.80
No	13	86.70	24	70.60	26	74.30	8	66.70	22	71.00	93	73.20
INNER CITY												
Yes	7	46.70	14	41.20	20	57.10	7	58.30	13	41.90	61	48.00
No	8	53.30	20	58.80	15	42.90	5	41.70	18	58.10	66	52.00
	Mean	SD	Mean	SD	Mean	SD	Mean	SD	Mean	SD	Sample Mean	Sample SD
Macro Economy												
Year Built	1929	31	1904	32	1893	52	1943	25	1932	36	1927	34
Interest Rate (%)	9.30	2.00	8.60	2.70	9.10	2.50	7.80	1.70	3.70	16.20	8.90	2.24

Exhibit 3-2 cont.

OUTCOMES

DESCRIPTION	Apartments		Condos		Cultural		Office		Retail		Total Known	
	N	%	N	%	N	%	N	%	N	%	N	%
Miles from Park	0.7	0.6	0.5	0.6	0.5	0.6	0.8	1.5	3.7	16.2	1.8	1.7
Miles from Lake	1.6	2.9	2.3	5.8	3.3	5.9	1.5	1.7	1.9	2.3	2.5	2.1
Miles from Highway	2.3	5	5	12.6	1.7	1.9	1.3	0.6	1.5	2.3	2.7	3.9
Miles from Airport	4.8	3.7	7.6	10.6	6.8	7.9	6	4.1	6.1	6.3	5.9	6.2
Building Structure												
Building Size (sq. ft.)	48,800	45,751	37,724	37,631	46,305	69,540	16,021	16,976	16,838	12,830	39,254	40,639
Story	2.3	0.8	2.6	1.3	2.3	0.9	1.8	1	1.5	0.8	2.4	0.9
Parking Space	31.9	33.6	25.6	16.3	37.8	55.4	23.9	26	45.8	30.7	33.9	39.5

Notes: SD means standard deviation, a measure of variance where smaller numbers are generally a good thing. Seventeen school reuses and one industrial reuse are not included in this table. Therefore 126 outcomes analyzed in this table represent 87.40% of total known outcomes, including school and industrial reuses.

To describe site and area characteristics of church reuse projects, location factors such as distance from the nearest park, lake, highway, and airport; building size; number of stories; and the number of available parking spaces were identified via use of the Internet. The average building size of reused religious structures was approximately 48,800 sq. ft. for apartment outcomes, 37,724 sq. ft. for condominium outcomes, 46,305 sq. ft. for cultural uses, 16,021 sq. ft. for offices, and 16,838 sq. ft. for retail uses (see Exhibit 3-2 for descriptive statistics).

Exhibit 3-3 shows the descriptive statistics for project outcomes of schools, which were most frequently repurposed for residential uses.

Findings indicate that 14.6 percent of reused schools had historic value; 17.1 percent were located on local roads, 48.8 percent were located on collector roads, and 34.1 percent were located on major roads. A total of 22.0 percent of the reused school buildings were located on a street corner, and 36.6 percent were initiated in the inner city or downtown. The average building size of schools that were reused for different purposes was 94,947 sq. ft. for apartment outcomes, 55,262 sq. ft. for condominium outcomes, 16,376 sq. ft. for cultural uses, and 26,247 sq. ft. for offices.

Statistical Model and Data

This study examines the outcomes of redeveloped religious buildings (primarily churches) and schools. It is expected that historic religious buildings and schools, unlike other old structures, retain their architectural identity and integrity. One hundred twenty-six religious buildings and eighty-three schools that are currently reused for another purpose are included in the sample for this study.

This study performs multinomial logit analysis on these religious buildings and schools. It uses five reuse categories (apartment, condominium, retail, office, and cultural use) as dependent variables. The outcomes are defined as:

- *Residential apartments:* This outcome includes market-rate rentals, senior housing, low-income housing, and combinations of these rental uses. Many of these projects use low-income tax credits and/or historic preservation tax credits.
- *Residential condominiums:* This outcome includes sale of residential market-rate condominiums, including loft-style condos.
- *Cultural:* The cultural use outcome includes museums, art centers, and concert halls used by both nonprofit and profit organizations. Rents are likely to be negligible.
- *Office:* This outcome includes buildings currently reused as office space, including both owner-occupied space and offices leased at or near market rates to other tenants.
- *Retail:* This outcome includes small strip centers, large-scale supercenters, restaurants, drugstores, single-tenant businesses, commercial parking lots, etc. Rents are expected to be market rate or substantial.

Explanatory (independent) variables were derived from the literature, and are described in Exhibits 3-2 and 3-3. They include: macroeconomic conditions; building characteristics; microlocation characteristics such as proximity to main roads, parks, and other amenities; and demographic characteristics, including income, education, and race. The analysis includes other relevant characteristics of the sellers. In particular, "hierarchical" and "nonhierarchical" sellers are identified. "Hierarchical" seller refers to an institution such as the Catholic Church, in which decisions to sell churches are made at an administrative level above the parish. These institutions may follow policies governing the merger or relocation of parishes that result in a net loss of churches that is larger, but also more controlled and economically efficient than, the sale of churches by what we categorize as "nonhier-

archical" sellers, in which church buildings are managed and sold by individual congregations, and are financially "stand-alone."

The multinomial logit regression model for this study and the technical aspects of the research methodology and detailed results are presented in Appendixes 3-B and 3-C.

Exhibit 3-3 Descriptive Statistics for Project Outcomes of Schools

DESCRIPTIONS	OUTCOMES									
	Apartments		Condos		Cultural		Office		Total Known	
	N	%	N	%	N	%	N	%	N	%
Outcomes	52	61.2%	21	24.7%	3	3.5%	6	7.1%	82	96.50%
Has Historical Value										
Yes	9	17.30%	3	14.30%	0		0		12	14.60%
No	43	82.70%	18	85.70%	3	100.00%	6	100.00%	70	85.40%
Street Type										
Local	11	21.20%	2	9.50%	0		1	16.70%	14	17.10%
Collector	21	40.40%	15	71.40%	2	66.70%	2	33.30%	40	48.80%
Main	20	38.50%	4	19.00%	1	33.30%	3	50.00%	28	34.10%
Corner Location										
Yes	9	17.30%	7	33.30%	1	33.30%	1	16.70%	18	22.00%
No	43	82.70%	14	66.70%	2	66.70%	5	83.30%	64	78.00%
Inner City										
Yes	14	26.90%	15	71.40%	1	33.30%	0		30	36.60%
No	38	73.10%	6	28.60%	2	66.70%	6	100.00%	52	63.40%
	Mean	SD	Mean	SD	Mean	SD	Mean	SD	Sample Mean	Sample SD
Macro Economy										
Year Built	1910	5	1913	39	1924	41	1977	15	1924	18
Interest Rate	9.60%	0.40%	8.70%	0.20%	7.20%	1.20%	7.70%	1.4	9.28%	0.90%
Location Characteristics										
Miles from Park	0.6	0.6	0.4	0.3	0.5	0.1	0.6	0.5	0.6	0.5
Miles from Lake	1.4	1.7	0.8	0.5	1	1	2.5	2.3	1.2	1.6
Miles from Highway	1.9	1.8	1.7	1.8	0.9	0.2	0.8	0.7	1.8	1.6
Miles from Airport	5.9	3.2	4.2	3.6	1.8	0.2	4	4	5.2	3.8
Building Structure										
Building Size (SF)	94,947	63,179	55,262	32,083	16,376	6,956	26,247	13,412	85,249	65,329
Story	3	0.7	2.7	1.1	2	0	1.7	0.8	2.7	0.9
Parking Space	56.6	34.5	40.9	36	25	0	71.3	26.1	59.6	38.4

Note: 1 retail reuse and 2 industrial reuses are not included in this table. Therefore 82 outcomes analyzed in this table represent 96.50% of total known outcomes that include retail and industrial reuses.

Empirical Results

Several multinomial logit models were run using the outcomes above as the dependent variable. Apartment use is the reference category[7] because it is the predominant reuse outcome. Exhibit 3-4 shows a summary of our results and compares each outcome to apartments. The factors associated with project outcomes can have either a positive or negative relationship. If there is no statistically significant result, that item is left blank. For further reference, and the actual parameter estimates, see Appendix 3-C.

Condominiums Compared to Apartments

- *Seller characteristics:* Compared to schools, religious buildings were more likely reused as condominiums than apartments. Properties sold by hierarchical organizations were less likely to be reused as condominiums. Accordingly, properties sold by nonhierarchical organizations were more likely to be reused as condominiums than apartments.
- *Macroeconomic factors:* Religious buildings and schools converted in years with a lower interest rate were more likely to be reused as condominiums. Projects located in the Farmbelt, Industrial Midwest, Mid-Atlantic Corridor, Mineral Extraction Region, and Northern California were more likely to be reused as condominiums than apartments.
- *Building characteristics:* More recently built religious buildings and schools were more likely to be reused as condominiums. Smaller religious buildings and schools were more likely to be reused as condominiums than apartments.
- *Location characteristics:* Religious buildings and schools closer to a park were more likely to be reused as condominiums. Properties farther from a high-

way or located on a street corner were more likely to be reused as condominiums than as apartments. However, religious buildings and schools located on main roads were more likely to be reused as apartments than condominiums.
- *Demographics:* Religious buildings and schools located in neighborhoods with a higher education level or a lower vacancy rate were more likely to be reused as condominiums.

Cultural Uses Compared to Apartments

- *Seller characteristics:* Religious buildings were more likely to be reused for cultural uses, while schools were more commonly reused as apartments. However, properties sold by hierarchical organizations were less likely to be reused for cultural purposes than properties sold by nonhierarchical organizations.
- *Macroeconomic factors:* Religious buildings and schools located in Northern California and the South were more likely to be reused for cultural purposes.
- *Building characteristics:* Newer religious buildings and schools were more likely to be reused for cultural purposes than as apartments.
- *Location characteristics:* When compared with apartments, religious buildings and schools located on a main road were more likely to be reused for cultural uses. Corner locations were also more significant for cultural uses than for apartment uses.
- *Demographics:* Religious buildings and schools located in neighborhoods with a higher educational level were more likely to be reused for cultural purposes. Religious buildings and schools located in neighborhoods with lower gross rent were also more likely to be reused for cultural purposes than for apartments.

Exhibit 3-4 Summary of the Logit Regression Results (Reference Category: Apartment)

Variable Groups	Condos	Cultural	Office	Retail
Seller Characteristics				
Church	More Likely****	More Likely****		More Likely****
Hierarchical	Less Likely**	Less Likely*		Less Likely****
Macro Economic Factors				
Interest rate	Lower***		Lower****	
Farmbelt	More Likely**		More Likely****	More Likely***
Industrial Midwest	More Likely**		More Likely****	More Likely****
Mid-Atlantic Corridor	More Likely***		More Likely****	
Mineral Extraction	More Likely*		More Likely**	More Likely****
Northern California	More Likely***	More Likely***	More Likely*	More Likely****
South		More Likely**	More Likely****	More Likely****
Southern California				
New England				
Building and Structure				
Age of structure	Newer****	Newer****		Newer***
Size	Smaller***		Smaller****	Smaller****
Stories				Fewer**
Parking spaces				
Location Characteristics				
Park	Closer**			
Lake				Closer**
Highway	Far**		Closer****	Closer**
Airport				
Corner location	More Likely****	More Likely**		More Likely**
Inner city			More Likely***	
Main road	Less Likely****	More Likely****		More Likely**
Local road	Less Likely*			
Collector road				
Demographics				
White			More***	More***
Young				More***
Education level	Higher*	Higher****		Higher**
Median income				
Owner-occupied				More*
Vacancy rate	Lower***		Lower**	Lower****
Gross rent		Lower***		Higher****
Historic Value				
Architectural style				More Likely**

Notes:
1: *, **, ***, **** denote statistical significance at 85%, 90%, 95%, and 99% level of confidence, respectively.
2. Blanks denote the statistical significance below an 85% level of confidence.

Offices Compared to Apartments

- *Macroeconomic factors:* Religious buildings and schools that were converted in years with lower interest rates were more likely to be reused as offices than as apartments. Projects located in the Farmbelt, the Industrial Midwest, the Mid-Atlantic Corridor, the Mineral Extraction Region, Northern California, and the South were also more likely to be reused as offices than apartments.
- *Building characteristics:* Smaller buildings and schools were more likely to be reused as offices than as apartments.
- *Location characteristics:* Religious buildings and schools located closer to a highway were more likely to be reused as offices compared to apartments. Properties located in the inner city or downtown were more likely to be reused as offices compared to apartments.
- *Demographics:* Religious buildings and schools located in neighborhoods with a higher percentage of white population were more likely to be reused as offices. Religious buildings and schools located in neighborhoods with lower vacancy rate were more likely to be reused as offices compared to apartments.

Retail Uses Compared to Apartments

- *Seller characteristics:* Religious buildings were more likely than schools to be reused as retail. However, religious buildings and schools sold by hierarchical organizations were more likely to be reused for apartment purposes than for retail.
- *Macroeconomic factors:* Religious buildings and schools located in the Farmbelt, the Industrial Midwest, the Mineral Extraction Region, Northern California, and the South were more likely to be reused for retail purposes.
- *Building characteristics:* Newer religious buildings and schools were more likely to be reused as retail than apartments. Smaller religious buildings and schools, and those with fewer stories, were more likely to be reused as retail.
- *Location characteristics:* Religious buildings and schools located closer to a lake were more likely to be reused as retail. Properties located closer to a highway, on a street corner, or on a main road were more likely to be reused as retail than as apartments.
- *Demographics:* Religious buildings and schools in neighborhoods with a higher percentage of white population, a younger population, or a population with a higher level of education were more likely to be reused as retail. Properties in neighborhoods with more owner-occupied housing, lower vacancy rates, and higher gross rents were more likely to be reused as retail.
- *Historic value:* Religious buildings and schools that were assumed to have more historic value were more likely to be reused as retail than as apartments.

Spot Market for Religious Buildings

This section summarizes the data regarding religious buildings and schools that were on the market at the end of 2008 (when this study was conducted) and those sold between 2005 and 2008.

CoStar Group, Inc. provided access to a database of properties for sale. In November 2008, CoStar listed 1,372 religious buildings that were on the market, and therefore were candidates for adaptive reuse.[8] The average building size for those properties was 12,673 sq. ft., and the asking sales price was $83 per square foot. Brief statistics of these buildings and their transaction particulars are presented in Appendix 3-D, Tables 3-D-1 (spot market) and 3-D-2 (sold property).

The CoStar Group's database system was searched for properties that were sold between 2005 and 2008, and 1,577 religious buildings were found. The average size of those buildings was 13,640 sq. ft. The asking sales price was $101 per square foot. Figures on the development outcomes (after transaction) of these buildings are presented in Appendix 3-D, Table 3-D-3. Approximately 5–7 percent of the religious buildings offered for sale had been redeveloped within the four-year window of the study.

Conclusion

The main goal of this chapter was to identify factors that affect decisions to adapt religious buildings (and, to some degree, schools) for particular uses. This chapter also provided information for religious buildings that are currently on the market and sold since 2005.

The database for this research included 209 known adaptive reuse project outcomes. Three separate literature perspectives were considered to derive the conceptual model for this study, and multinomial logit regressions were run to determine which variables were associated with five types of repurposing: apartments, condominiums, cultural purposes, offices, and retail uses.

Findings concerning the local market, location, and demographic factors associated with redevelopment outcomes are summarized below. Compared to apartments, which are typically located in older school buildings or hierarchical (primarily Catholic) churches, redevelopers of religious buildings should look for the following attributes[9]:

- *Condos:* newer structure, small church, not hierarchical, close to park, corner location, far from highway and from main road, higher education level, lower interest rate, lower rental vacancy rate in immediate area

- *Cultural:* newer structure, corner location, main road, lower rental rate
- *Office:* smaller building, lower interest rate, closer to highway, inner city location, higher percentage of whites in census tract, lower vacancy rate
- *Retail:* newer, small church, one story, not hierarchical, close to lake and highway, corner location, on highway or main road, younger demographic, whites in census tract, higher education level, more owner-occupied housing, lower interest rate, lower rental vacancy rate, higher rental rate, distinctive architecture

The findings in this study can have important implications for churches or other religious institutions that are suffering from a considerable decline in congregational size, developers who would like to initiate an adaptive reuse project, and public agencies who want to augment their tax bases through redevelopment. When the adaptive reuse of an old structure is needed, for example, results of this study can offer valuable basic information about which factors may play a significant role in the project and affect outcomes for the new use of a property. A developer may wish to compare a building's attributes and his or her preferred end use against the attributes and outcomes described above. If there is not a rough fit, or if there are too many negative signs, then the compatibility between the developer's idea and past market experience is poor, and that particular reuse idea may be less likely to succeed.

Notes

1. In order to properly conduct statistical analysis, a larger sample size of rehabbed projects allows more variables to be analyzed. Therefore, school buildings were included to boost the sample size and examine more projects with historic preservation and other types of public financial subsidy.

2. A related article by the authors using this data set was published in *International Real Estate Review* in 2009. None of the peer reviewers appeared to be concerned about the lack of incentive programs in the models, the lack of more detailed historical data about the buildings, or the use of visual inspection of Google images as a proxy for building status. Although certainly desirable, inclusion of these variables in the statistical model would have dramatically increased the number of hours required to build the data set.

3. An externality is defined as the action of an individual or company that is not included in its cost function and that results in external costs or benefits to another individual or company (DiPasquale and Wheaton 1996).

4. There are, however, several fundamental differences between an adaptive reuse project and a home reinvestment project. Adaptive reuse projects are initiated by various players, while home reinvestment projects are initiated by homeowners for their own purposes. Moreover, the initiator of a plan for adaptive reuse intends to change the property's original use, but under a home reinvestment plan the property's original purpose does not change.

5. Nonpriced benefits arise when people get enjoyment and satisfaction from a restored building and do not have to pay for access (Garrod, Willis, Bjarnadottir, and Cockbain 1996). Both nonpriced benefits, which are essentially private, and externalities, which may be public or private, justify public subsidy investments to encourage adaptive reuse.

6. http://www.costar.com/.

7. When outcome categories are multiple and unordered, multinomial logit regression is usually used. If there are five categories such as in our study, this analytical tool requires the calculation of four (five minus one) equations, one for each category to the reference category (apartments), to describe the relationship between dependent variables and independent variables.

8. Because this chapter considers only projects that adaptively reused existing structures, these figures do not include buildings that were demolished. The CoStar data represent a comprehensive but not exhaustive picture of the overall market; properties located in smaller markets where CoStar does not operate and properties sold outside the MLS system (e.g., for sale by owner, auction, sale by RFP) may not be found in their database.

9. While linking up these attributes with the intended use does not guarantee success, a statistically significant association has been found.

References and Works Consulted

Bogdon, A. S. 1996. "Homeowner Renovation and Repair: The Decision to Hire Someone Else to Do the Project." *Journal of Housing Economics* 5, no. 0017: 323–50.

Bullen, P. A. 2007. "Adaptive Reuse and Sustainability of Commercial Buildings." *Facilities* 25, no. 1/2: 20–31.

Burchell, R. W., and D. Listokin. 1981. *The Adaptive Reuse Handbook*. New Brunswick: The Center for Urban Policy Research, Rutgers, The State University of New Jersey.

DiPasquale, D., and W. C. Wheaton. 1996. *Urban Economics and Real Estate Markets*. Upper Saddle River, N.J.: Prentice-Hall, Inc.

Garrod, G. D., K. G. Willis, H. Bjarnadottir, and P. Cockbain. 1996. "The Non-priced Benefits of Renovating Historic Buildings: A Case Study of Newcastle's Grainger Town." *Cities* 13, no. 6: 423–30.

Gyourko, J., and A. Saiz. 2004. "Reinvestment in the Housing Stock: The Role of Construction Costs and Supply Side." *Journal of Urban Economics* 55, no. 2: 238–56.

Helms, A. C. 2003. "Understanding Gentrification: An Empirical Analysis of the Determinant of Urban Housing Renovation." *Journal of Urban Economics* 54, no. 3: 474–98.

Kulatilaka, A. 1999. *Real Options*. Boston: Harvard Business School Press.

Laska, B., J. M. Seaman, and D. R. McSeveney. 1982. "Inner-City Reinvestment: Neighborhood Characteristics and Spatial Patterns over Time." *Urban Studies* 19, no. 2: 155–65.

Luehrman, T. 1998. "Strategy as a Portfolio of Real Options." *Harvard Business Review* 7, no. 5: 13–37.

Malizia, E., and R. A. Simons. 1991. "Comparing Regional Classifications for Real Estate Portfolio Diversification." *Journal of Real Estate Research* 6, no. 1: 53–77.

Martin, T. J., M. A. Gamzon, N. G. Griffin, W. P. O' Mara, F. H. Spink Jr., D. Steller Jr., and M. A. Thomas. 1978. *Adaptive Reuse: Development*

Economics, Process and Profile. Washington, D.C.: Urban Land Institute.

Simons, R. A., and E. Choi. 2009. "Determinants of Redevelopment of Abandoned Churches and Schools." *International Real Estate Review* 13, no. 1: 79–108.

Simons, R. A., and J. Saginor. 2006. "Meta Analysis of the Effect of Environmental Contamination and Positive Amenities on Residential Property Values." *Journal of Real Estate Research* 28, no. 1: 71–104.

Smit, H. T. J., and L. Trigeorgis. 2004. *Strategic Investment: Real Options and Games.* Princeton, N.J.: Princeton University Press.

Tyler, N. 2000. *Historic Preservation: An Introduction to Its History, Principle, and Practice.* New York: W. W. Norton & Company, Inc.

Wilmott, P., J. Dewynne, and S. Howison. 1993. *Option Pricing: Mathematical Models and Computation.* Oxford: Oxford Financial Press.

Yacovissi, W., and C. R. Kern. 1995. "Location and History as Determinants of Urban Residential Density." *Journal of Urban Economics* 38, no. 2: 207–20.

Zielenbach, S. 2000. *The Art of Revitalization: Improving Conditions in Distressed Inner-City Neighborhoods.* New York: Garland.

Appendix 3-A Religious Buildings and Schools by States

STATES	Being Reused			On the Market			Sold Since 2005		
	Church	School	Total	Church	School	Total	Church	School	Total
AK	0	0	0	3	0	3	1	0	1
AL	2	0	2	25	1	26	11	0	11
AR	0	4	4	18	3	21	13	4	17
AZ	6	0	6	13	5	18	47	23	70
CA	**12**	4	16	66	11	77	**217**	**56**	**273**
CO	8	2	10	15	3	18	52	10	62
CT	2	3	5	6	0	6	17	2	19
DC	0	**13**	13	5	0	5	8	7	15
DE	0	0	0	3	0	3	1	0	1
FL	4	1	5	70	**20**	90	**144**	**71**	**215**
GA	6	6	12	55	5	60	75	10	85
IA	2	0	2	15	5	20	2	2	4
ID	0	0	0	4	0	4	2	0	2
IL	8	1	9	46	2	48	33	12	45
IN	1	0	1	49	4	53	19	2	21
KS	3	0	3	21	12	33	13	3	16
KY	3	0	3	15	3	18	8	1	9
LA	3	0	3	14	2	16	6	0	6
MA	**48**	**37**	**85**	12	6	18	65	29	94
MD	8	0	8	17	3	20	50	8	58
ME	5	0	5	6	2	8	3	1	4
MI	3	2	5	**90**	**17**	**107**	34	10	44
MN	2	0	2	27	5	32	27	9	36
MO	6	5	11	41	15	56	36	7	43
MS	0	0	0	10	0	10	0	0	0
MT	0	0	0	1	1	2	3	0	3

STATES	Being Reused			On the Market			Sold Since 2005		
	Church	School	Total	Church	School	Total	Church	School	Total
NC	4	12	16	51	4	55	46	12	58
ND	0	0	0	2	0	2	0	0	0
NE	1	1	2	4	1	5	3	1	4
NH	0	1	1	4	2	6	4	0	4
NJ	6	2	8	24	7	31	79	22	101
NM	1	1	2	8	4	12	3	0	3
NV	1	0	1	6	0	6	6	6	12
NY	**28**	**13**	**41**	82	**16**	98	121	**42**	**163**
OH	10	7	17	**111**	9	**120**	63	10	73
OK	1	0	1	32	5	37	10	0	10
OR	0	1	1	19	4	23	17	6	23
PA	11	12	**23**	56	12	68	57	24	81
RI	0	0	0	4	4	8	1	0	1
SC	3	1	4	33	6	39	12	2	14
SD	0	2	2	4	1	5	0	0	0
TN	0	1	1	33	4	37	17	0	17
TX	**12**	7	19	**148**	7	**155**	**143**	17	161
UT	0	1	1	1	3	4	0	3	3
VA	1	3	4	21	6	27	30	7	37
VT	0	0	0	1	0	1	0	0	0
WA	7	2	9	24	2	26	52	9	61
WI	2	4	6	28	8	36	24	6	30
WV	0	0	0	16	2	18	2	1	3
WY	0	0	0	1	0	1	0	0	0
Other	0	0	0	12	0	12	0	0	0
Total	220	149	369	1,372	232	1,604	1577	435	2,012

Note:
1. The top three states of each column are in bold.
2. Properties were not collected by random sampling.
3. There may be some overlap in the reuse and sold since 2004 figures.

Appendix 3-B Variable Descriptions for the Statistical Model

Explanatory Variables	Description
Seller Characteristics	
Church or school	School: 1; Church: 0
Hierarchical structure[1]	Yes: 1; No: 0
Macro Economic Condition	
Interest rate[2]	Average interest rate in rehab year
Geographic location[3] (Salomon Brothers' Definition)	Southern California Northern California Mineral Extraction Farmbelt South Industrial Midwest Mid-Atlantic Corridor New England: reference
Building Characteristics	
Age	Year built
Building size	In square feet
Story	Number of stories
Parking space	How many cars can be parked
Location Characteristics	
Park	Distance in miles
Lake	Distance in miles
Highway	Distance in miles
Airport	Distance in miles
Corner location	Yes: 1; No: 0
Inner city location	Yes: 1; No: 0
Street type[4]	Main Collector Local road : reference
Demographics (Census 2000)[5]	
White	% in tract
Young	Age 22~34; % in tract
Education	% of higher than bachelor's degree in tract
Income	Median household income in tract
Vacancy rate (Residential)	% in tract
Owner-occupied	% in tract
Rent	Median gross rent in tract
Historic Value	
Architectural Style[6]	Looking very good (from Internet images) (Yes: 1, No: 0). Research team met and clarified the standard

Notes:
1. It was assumed that all Catholic churches and Christian Scientist churches have a hierarchical decision-making structure.
2. Source for interest rate: Federal Reserve Historical Release.
3. Geographic location: See Malizia and Simons (1991).
4. Street Type: Collector roads collect traffic from local roads and distribute it to major roads, local roads have the lowest speed limit and carry low volumes of traffic, and main roads carry the largest volumes of traffic and are designed for high speeds.
5. Source for Demographics: 2000 U.S. Census.
6. Based on visual Internet inspection, it was assumed that if a church has a notable architectural style, the church has more historic value.

Appendix 3-C: Statistical Details and Model Results for the Study

The multinomial logit regression model for this study is expressed as:

$$y = f \text{ (SELLER, MACECO, BUILD, LOCAT, DEMOG, HSVLU)}$$

Where these factors are variables or vectors as follows:

y = A categorical variable indicating either "apartment," "condo," "cultural," "office," or "retail."

SELLER = Sellers' characteristics including church or school dummy and hierarchical structure dummy.

MACECO = Macroeconomic conditions, which are represented by interest rate in rehab year. This factor also includes U.S. economic geographic location designations based on Salomon Brothers definitions: Southern California, Northern California, Mineral Extraction, Farmbelt, South, Industrial Midwest, Mid-Atlantic Corridor, and New England (Simons and Saginor 2006).

BUILD = Building characteristics including age of property, building size in square feet, number of stories, and number of parking spaces.

LOCAT = Location characteristics, including distance from a highway, a park, an airport, and a lake; location in the inner city or not; location on a corner or not; and location on a main, a collector, or a local road.

DEMOG = Demographic characteristics of a property's tract, including percent white, percent young population, number of persons per household, percent more than bachelor's degree, median household income, vacancy rate, percent owner-occupied housing, and percent gross rent less than $450.

HSVLU = The historic value of properties was assumed based on visual Internet inspection that if a church has a notable architectural style, the church has more historic value.

The appendix continues with a description of regression diagnostics and model-fitting tests. Major results are as follows:

- The model is statistically significant for predicting outcomes of the adaptive reuse of religious buildings and schools at a 99 percent level of confidence, indicating that the model is statistically reliable.
- About 73 percent (out of a maximum of 100 percent) is being explained by the model based on Cox and Snell R-Square, and 77 percent is being explained based on Nagelkerke R-Square. These are satisfactory.

Additional statistical concerns in multivariate modeling are not a concern here:

- Homoscedasticity: Because the dependent variable for our model is categorical, the equal variance assumption underlying linear multiple regression is not appropriate. Therefore, this is not an issue in our study.
- Multicollinearity: No severe co-relations between independent variables were found.
- Spatial Autocorrelation: This is not an issue for this study because our cases—churches and schools—are spread all over the nation.

Finally, Tables 3-C-1 through 3-C-4 provide detailed results that underlie Exhibit 3-4.

Table 3-C-1 Condominium (Apartments as a Reference Category)

Variables	B	Std. Error	Wald[1]	Sig.
Seller Characteristics				
Seller = church (or schools)	2.746	0.587	21.892	0.000
Hierarchical Seller = Y	-1.069	0.631	2.874	0.090
Macroeconomic				
Interest Rate	-0.285	0.127	4.989	0.026
Farmbelt	1.615	0.902	3.204	0.073
Industrial Midwest	1.299	0.703	3.416	0.065
Mid-Atlantic Corridor	2.010	0.590	11.608	0.001
Mineral Extraction	1.327	0.851	2.430	0.119
Northern California	2.648	1.097	5.828	0.016
South	0.835	0.797	1.096	0.295
Southern California	-2.928	0.000		
New England (reference)	0.000			
Building Structure				
Age (Year Built)	-0.037	0.011	10.892	0.001
Building Size	-0.596	0.277	4.622	0.032
Story	0.136	0.251	0.293	0.589
Parking Space	0.005	0.005	0.715	0.398
Location Characteristics				
Distance from Park	-0.661	0.395	2.799	0.094
Distance from Lake	-0.073	0.082	0.791	0.374
Distance from Highway	0.116	0.070	2.769	0.096
Distance from Airport	0.002	0.045	0.002	0.961
Corner Location = Y	1.387	0.487	8.096	0.004
Inner City = Y	0.282	0.481	0.345	0.557
Street Type = local	-0.901	0.562	2.569	0.109
Street Main = main	-1.690	0.469	12.962	0.000
Street Main = collector (reference)	0.000			
Demographics				
White Population	-0.100	0.896	0.013	0.911
Young Population	0.594	3.184	0.035	0.852
Education	2.596	1.619	2.570	0.109
Median Income	-0.121	0.993	0.015	0.903
Owner Occupied	1.521	1.890	0.647	0.421
Vacancy Rate	-6.896	3.146	4.803	0.028
Gross Rent	-0.001	0.002	0.582	0.446
Historic Value				
Historic Value = Y	0.184	0.465	0.157	0.692

1. Test used in logistics regression for the significance of the logistic coefficient. Its interpretation is like the *F* or *t* values used for the significance testing of regression coefficients.

Table 3-C-2 Cultural Purposes (Apartments as a Reference Category)

Variables	B	Std. Error	Wald	Sig.
Seller Characteristics				
Seller = church (or schools)	5.230	0.754	48.076	0.000
Hierarchical Seller = Y	-0.969	0.650	2.226	0.136
Macroeconomic				
Interest Rate	-0.113	0.137	0.675	0.411
Farmbelt	1.185	1.151	1.060	0.303
Industrial Midwest	0.564	0.840	0.451	0.502
Mid-Atlantic Corridor	0.274	0.763	0.129	0.719
Mineral Extraction	1.330	1.013	1.724	0.189
Northern California	2.665	1.167	5.217	0.022
South	1.521	0.916	2.754	0.097
Southern California	-3.376	0.000		
New England (reference)	0.000			
Building Structure				
Age (Year Built)	-0.042	0.011	13.587	0.000
Building Size	-0.424	0.326	1.697	0.193
Story	-0.379	0.346	1.195	0.274
Parking Space	0.005	0.006	0.684	0.408
Location Characteristics				
Distance from Park	-0.134	0.330	0.165	0.684
Distance from Lake	0.009	0.081	0.013	0.908
Distance from Highway	-0.021	0.073	0.083	0.774
Distance from Airport	-0.016	0.048	0.116	0.734
Corner Location = Y	0.952	0.573	2.762	0.097
Inner City = Y	0.765	0.545	1.969	0.161
Street Type = local	0.072	0.662	0.012	0.914
Street Main = main	1.555	0.560	7.720	0.005
Street Main = collector (reference)	0.000			
Demographics				
White Population	0.453	1.115	0.165	0.685
Young Population	-2.258	3.666	0.379	0.538
Education	6.486	1.956	10.991	0.001
Median Income	-0.768	1.145	0.450	0.502
Owner Occupied	0.905	2.302	0.155	0.694
Vacancy Rate	0.185	3.553	0.003	0.959
Gross Rent	-0.004	0.002	4.597	0.032
Historic Value				
Historic Value = Y	0.284	0.549	0.003	0.296

Table 3-C-3 Offices (Apartments as a Reference Category)

Variables	B	Std. Error	Wald	Sig.
Seller Characteristics				
Seller = church (or schools)	1.370	0.959	2.042	0.153
Hierarchical Seller = Y	0.269	0.953	0.080	0.777
Macroeconomic				
Interest Rate	-0.647	0.235	7.589	0.006
Farmbelt	4.090	1.497	7.466	0.006
Industrial Midwest	3.993	1.203	11.015	0.001
Mid-Atlantic Corridor	3.517	1.185	8.817	0.003
Mineral Extraction	2.626	1.426	3.389	0.066
Northern California	2.363	1.544	2.343	0.126
South	4.739	1.356	12.208	0.000
Southern California	20.721	4804.816	0.000	0.997
New England (reference)	0.000			
Building Structure				
Age (Year Built)	0.003	0.015	0.037	0.847
Building Size	-1.256	0.401	9.835	0.002
Story	-0.330	0.475	0.483	0.487
Parking Space	-0.017	0.015	1.425	0.233
Location Characteristics				
Distance from Park	-0.004	0.085	0.003	0.958
Distance from Lake	-0.198	0.144	1.873	0.171
Distance from Highway	-1.051	0.346	9.225	0.002
Distance from Airport	-0.082	0.084	0.937	0.333
Corner Location = Y	1.062	0.769	1.905	0.168
Inner City = Y	1.667	0.756	4.862	0.027
Street Type = local	0.652	0.869	0.563	0.453
Street Main = main	0.589	0.664	0.786	0.375
Street Main = collector (reference)	0.000			
Demographics				
White Population	3.197	1.573	4.129	0.042
Young Population	0.295	6.014	0.002	0.961
Education	-1.479	2.981	0.246	0.620
Median Income	-1.130	1.704	0.440	0.507
Owner Occupied	2.971	3.229	0.846	0.358
Vacancy Rate	-8.376	4.658	3.233	0.072
Gross Rent	0.002	0.003	0.463	0.496
Historic Value				
Historic Value = Y	-0.271	0.840	0.104	0.750

Table 3-C-4 Retail Purposes (Apartments as a Reference Category)

Variables	B	Std. Error	Wald	Sig.
Seller Characteristics				
Seller = church (or schools)	6.679	1.061	39.612	0.000
Hierarchical Seller = Y	-3.249	0.823	15.598	0.000
Macroeconomic				
Interest Rate	-0.077	0.171	0.204	0.651
Farmbelt	3.250	1.320	6.059	0.014
Industrial Midwest	3.356	0.986	11.584	0.001
Mid-Atlantic Corridor	1.265	1.028	1.515	0.218
Mineral Extraction	4.402	1.222	12.970	0.000
Northern California	3.386	1.323	6.550	0.010
South	3.895	1.175	10.989	0.001
Southern California	-2.674	0.000	.	.
New England (reference)	0.000	.	.	.
Building Structure				
Age (Year Built)	-0.029	0.013	4.816	0.028
Building Size	-1.061	0.397	7.153	0.007
Story	-0.953	0.532	3.210	0.073
Parking Space	0.003	0.007	0.126	0.723
Location Characteristics				
Distance from Park	-0.002	0.072	0.001	0.981
Distance from Lake	-0.248	0.125	3.943	0.047
Distance from Highway	-0.204	0.137	2.219	0.136
Distance from Airport	-0.058	0.057	1.045	0.307
Corner Location = Y	0.769	0.690	1.243	0.065
Inner City = Y	0.942	0.688	1.877	0.171
Street Type = local	-0.327	0.875	0.140	0.709
Street Main = main	1.186	0.643	3.400	0.065
Street Main = collector (reference)	0.000	.	.	.
Demographics				
White Population	3.159	1.497	4.453	0.035
Young Population	12.593	4.946	6.482	0.011
Education	4.362	2.401	3.300	0.069
Median Income	0.784	1.505	0.271	0.603
Owner Occupied	4.405	3.028	2.116	0.146
Vacancy Rate	-14.605	5.295	7.608	0.006
Gross Rent	0.006	0.003	5.282	0.022
Historic Value				
Historic Value = Y	0.641	0.755	0.722	0.140

Appendix 3-D: Statistics for Religious Buildings on the Market (as of November 2008)

Table 3-D-1 Descriptive Statistics of Religious Buildings Currently on the Market

Data	N	Minimum	Maximum	Mean	Std. Deviation
Asking Price	1,360	$11,000	$30,000,000	$1,056,522	$1,595,075
Days on Market	1,360	3	1739	296	246
Lot Size (sq. ft.)	1,104	1,742	8,537,760	130,680	339,768
Building Size (sq. ft.)	1,360	800	319,196	12,673	15,176
Year Built	794	1823	2005	1951	33
Asking Price per sq. ft.				$83	
Floor Area Ratio (FAR)				0.1	
Total N	1,372				

Source: CoStar Group, Inc.

Table 3-D-2 Religious Buildings Sold from January 1, 2005, through November 30, 2008

Data	N	Minimum	Maximum	Mean	Std. Deviation
Sales Price	1,458	$14,500	$65,000,000	$1,421,516	$2,569,618
Building Size (sq. ft.)	1,577	1,070	218,816	13,640	17,553
Lot Size (sq. ft.)	1,424	1,307	348,480	36,286	9,234,720
Year Built	1,054	1800	2008	1954	30
Sales Price per sq. ft.				$104	
Floor Area Ratio (FAR)				0.4	
Total N	1,577				

Source: CoStar Group, Inc.

Table 3-D-3 Percentage of Religious Buildings Redeveloped from 2005 through November 2008

Religious Buildings Sold since 2005	2005	2006	2007	2008	Total
Total Sold	20	389	653	515	1,577
Redeveloped as Different Purposes	1	21	34	37	93
Reused by Churches	19	368	619	478	1,484
% Redeveloped	5.0	5.4	5.2	7.2	5.9

Source: CoStar Group, Inc.

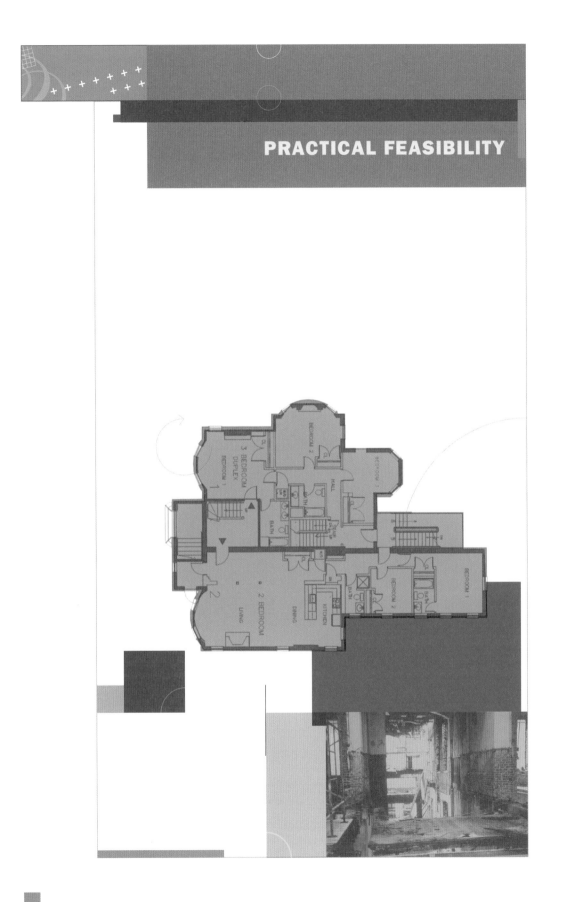

4

THE ARCHITECT'S PERSPECTIVE
on Relative Costs and Benefits of Building Rehabilitation Versus New Construction

Robert A. Simons, Scott Dimit, and Gary DeWine

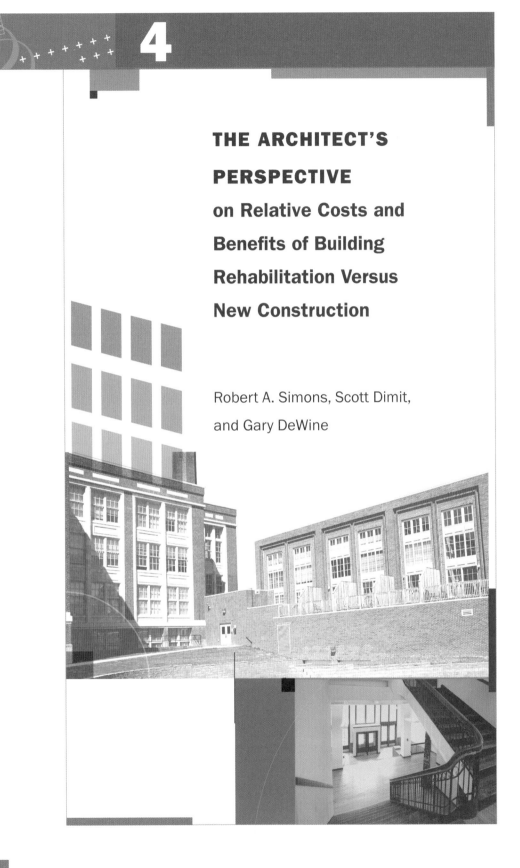

The developer of a former religious building for adaptive reuse could be a private development company seeking a return on investment, a nonprofit agency acting as developer for an altruistic reason (such as preservation of a historic structure), a public agency seeking either to expand its tax base or abate a nuisance, or a sole proprietor or speculator considering an investment. In some situations, several of these groups may collaborate to achieve their respective goals.

Control of the property can be obtained through several means: outright ownership, an option to purchase, a Request For Proposal (RFP) process, or possibly by taking advantage of a governmental action such as condemnation. It is best to conduct a due-diligence decision-making process at the predevelopment stage, prior to obtaining control. A team led by the developer and supported by an architect or construction expert should be assembled to assess both the financial and the physical feasibility of the project. Each project offers its own unique set of opportunities and constraints, with multiple disciplines collaborating and making an important contribution to the ultimate decision: *go* (i.e., proceed with the project) or *no-go* (i.e., walk away). Sometimes the decision to proceed can be made on the margin, i.e., the deal can be a *go* if the property can be acquired cheaply enough. This chapter offers a road map and some economic guidelines for making this decision from the design and architectural perspective.

In most situations an adaptive reuse rehabilitation (rehab) project can be brought to market at less expense than a comparable new construction, although this is not a guarantee. A rehab project may have more unexpected costs, but most require fewer additional investment dollars after site ac-quisition, making the deal attractive to some developers if the project is "bought right," especially in cost-sensitive down markets.

This chapter addresses the architect's approach and walk-through process, with an architect's development checklist provided. After this largely mechanical process, more creative items like key design elements and branding are addressed. Next, development cost comparisons are made for a typical rehab project compared with new construction at the same price point. This paired comparison is offered in substantial detail for a residential condominium. A summary comparison is provided for a church-to-office reuse, and the conversion of a school gym to condominiums.[1] After briefly addressing differences in operating costs between rehab and new projects, the chapter concludes with lessons and maxims for successful projects from the architect's perspective.

The Architect's Initial Assessment
Neighborhood Context

Any due diligence study for a building renovation project should begin with a thorough investigation of the neighborhood context surrounding the subject property. The process can provide important information on the type of product that should be provided along with pricing of the delivered final product. This becomes important later when the architect begins the design and project completion process. A developer should closely note the urban fabric and character of the neighborhood from a market-and-demand standpoint, and might ask the following questions:

- What is the predominant land use in the neighborhood? Is it zoned for residential, mixed use, or commercial business use, and is there market potential for the area to shift or reorient its traditional uses and potential value?

- What major anchors or institutions in the area can link to and support a renovation project and its successful use by providing patrons or residents, and how far from the subject property are these anchors located?
- Are there adjacent vacant properties in the neighborhood that could support future growth or provide additional use area? Are these same vacant properties a blighting influence at the present time?
- Are there recent previous building renovations in the area, and have they prospered?
- What is the current condition of the neighborhood, and where does it seem to be headed?

Most rehabilitation developers know their target work zones intimately, and for many the answers to these questions come almost by intuition. Many of the developers whose projects were the basis for the case studies in this book knew intuitively the market for their projects. Cleveland-based developer Michael Chesler from the Chesler Group, Inc. stresses that he "has to fall in love" with a building to make the initial commitment to renovate—likely a love that is a combination of seeing the future potential in a property as well as instinctively answering basic questions (e.g., "gut" project viability) in the affirmative (M. Chesler, personal communication, December 2008). A developer may allow his gut to direct decision-making, but prudence, equity partners, and lenders generally require that more formal market and economic planning augment a developer's intuition.

Because restoration projects for many historic buildings are eligible for the federal historic tax credit program administered through the National Parks Service, a due diligence study often includes basic historic research to determine the potential signifi-cance of a given building. For example, it is essential to know if the building is located in an officially registered historical district and if the building is currently listed—or if it has the potential to become listed—in the National Register of Historic Places. State historic registers and, in some communities, local historic registers also exist and may be a factor in establishing the project's eligibility for state or local historic tax credits. Historic significance of a project can include special physical characteristics of the structure, such as outstanding period features or exceptional expressions of a particular architectural style. The building might also have historic significance because of the original owner's personal story or because an event of historical importance took place within it.

In most states, the state historic preservation office administers these tax credit programs. While the historic listing process varies slightly from state to state, each historic preservation office can provide valuable help in assessing the historic potential of a given building during the project's investigation phase. Historic status may come into play when practical matters (like the placement of basic building infrastructure such as an external air conditioning unit) or market-driven remodeling (such as cutting a balcony into an historic roof to capitalize on a premium view) could conflict with tax credit program rules, which seek to preserve the original external appearance of the structure.

Basic zoning and planning restrictions should be explored and thoroughly understood at this early stage. A developer's architect is expected to quickly determine allowable use types, floor areas, density, building height restrictions, required number of parking spaces, required yard setbacks, and other important zoning restrictions. A visit to the municipal planning department or economic development office will also be valuable in determining the local community's planned future use for a given area, and establishing whether there are any community-sponsored incentives for renovation or redevelopment of a property.

Public incentives can include matching funds programs, storefront and facade renovation, property tax abatement, street and utility infrastructure improvements, streetscape programs, and a variety of other programs designed to assist redevelopment. Many neighborhoods, especially in urban areas, are supported by nonprofit community development corporations (CDCs) established to promote development, renovation, and general growth. A CDC can usually advise the developer on the basic social and economic history of a given area and can make introductions to key individuals who might support or oppose a given project. Neighborhood activist groups are usually on a first-name basis with CDC staff. Support from the local CDC is therefore essential if neighborhood design approval of a project is required or if any zoning variances are to be pursued, especially in a residential neighborhood.

Examination of the Existing Building Structure

The next step is to conduct a building pathology analysis on the structural and physical condition of the formerly religious building (or former school) to determine its sustainability. This process begins with the architect's first walk-through of the building being considered for reuse and is intended to identify, on an initial level, what is wrong and right with the building. In these preliminary investigations, the architect may also include an engineer who is an expert in assessing building condition and municipal building code compliance. While city hall's planning department and the

mayor may embrace the reuse of a former church or school, only the building department can issue a permit.

The building to be renovated should be thoroughly inspected to determine the various aspects of its existing state and also less apparent factors of suitability for its intended new use. It is preferable to know the new use before the inspection (see the "Highest and Best Use [HBU] Analysis" section in Chapter 5). In some cases, a quick walk-through with the building's broker or owner may reveal enough fatal flaws (e.g., severe physical deterioration, total functional obsolescence for the intended use, insufficient parking in a market where this is required, or an unsalvageable exterior shell) to dismiss the property outright as a rehabilitation prospect. If the project passes the initial inspection and walk-through assessment, a more thorough visit with a consulting team of engineers, architects, and contractors is usually in order. It is normally expected that the religious building will be remodeled to meet present-day building codes. Care must be taken that the upgrading satisfies safety and structural requirements. A professional who is familiar with the various codes can work to facilitate flexibility between the developer-owner and building department. Government building codes and historic preservation guidelines may allow for some interpretation along the margins, as we show in the Urban Krag case study (see Chapter 14). Further, many states have adopted sections of the International Building Code, which has intact sections dealing with historic preservation.

The walk-through of the subject property can often be further augmented by original as-built drawings of the building, if they exist. If these documents cannot be found, then the developer needs to consider the level of documentation that will be required to complete due diligence. The next level after the walk-through inspection is a nondestructive and perhaps destructive (e.g., sampling) evaluation of the building's physical condition. This evaluation is meant to determine the condition of building materials and to find building deficiencies, such as leaking roofs, air infiltration through windows and doors, and delaminating or failure of the building materials. Either way, a quick walk-through, or developer's "gut feel" should not replace a detailed, thorough analysis of a project's strengths and weaknesses.

The condition of the physical structure's components is one of the most obvious concerns for a developer. What type of structural system is used in the building, and is it in suitable condition for reuse? If not, what methods will be required to augment or repair the structure? If the building has a wood structure, is there any visible rotting, decay, sagging, or water damage to the beams or framing? If the building is framed in concrete, are there visible cracks, sagging, spalling, or rusted areas that might indicate deterioration or failure of hidden iron reinforcement? If bearing masonry is used, how tight are the masonry joints, and how square are the walls? What is the condition of the foundation system? A failed or deteriorated structure can be a deal killer for most planned renovations, so it is a good idea to consult a qualified and experienced structural engineer or architect early in the due diligence process.

Research of the condition of the building envelope is also of primary importance. The building's exterior protects and insulates the interior spaces from weather extremes and water infiltration, and most historic structures require updated windows, flashings, sealants, and insulation to yield modern building performance results. A masonry facade should be visually examined to assess the potential need for costly repairs such as replacing brick, repairing settlement cracks, pressure or chemical cleaning, tuck-pointing, and repairing stone lintels or other features. A majority of renovation projects require installation of new, high-performance insulated glass windows, so the number of window openings and the condition of the existing windows should be noted, as well as the conditions of the window heads, jambs, and sills. The state of the existing roof, insulation, sheathing, and framing should also be noted, and information about when the roof was last repaired or replaced should be obtained, if possible.

Environmental issues are becoming increasingly critical in determining an aged structure's suitability for renovation. The potential cost of remediation for environmental hazards, most notably asbestos and lead-based paint, is legendary. An environmental assessment determines the extent of hazards and estimates the cost of remediating them. While a full Phase I Environmental Site Assessment—and potentially Phase II, if warranted—is certainly an essential part of a planned property purchase, visual indicators are often present during the due diligence phase that can warn the developer that costly environmental remediation might be required.

Asbestos can likely be found in structures built or substantially renovated after 1870, especially for buildings constructed between about 1920 and 1950, when asbestos was used in pipe wrapping, floor tile, and exterior shingles. Postwar structures built before 1970 may contain asbestos-laden acoustic ceiling tile. Buildings should be thoroughly inspected visually for friable (potentially airborne) asbestos and other such materials, and if they are suspected, a professional environmental inspection should be commissioned. Vinyl floor tiles sized at 8" × 8" often contain asbestos fibers. These floor tiles might be costly to remove and dispose of legally. In some cases, asbestos and/or lead can be encapsulated or capped, which is typically cheaper, but this may present marketing issues if this information must be disclosed to a potential buyer or renter.

PCB (polychlorinated biphenyl) may be present in electrical systems, especially in transformers proximate to power lines. Hazardous materials in a building can include animal matter, such as pigeon and rodent droppings. In some areas of the United States high radon concentrations are a concern. It is rare but not unheard of for schools and churches to have oil or gasoline storage tanks, either in the basement or underground. If the building has been left open and exposed to the elements, water damage and toxic mold growth can often require complete removal of existing framing structures, floors, and walls. Toxic mold can also be a barrier to marketing residential units (Simons and Throupe 2005).

Other physical aspects of the existing building should be noted with an eye toward the intended future use of the renovated building. Window placement, size, and view potential should be considered based on intended use. Structural load-bearing wall and column placements should be considered, especially in residential projects. Existing circulation elements, such as elevators, escalators, open stairs, and fire egress stairs, should be noted for capacity and travel distance. Ceiling heights should be noted for future installation of mechanical systems, sprinklers, and lighting. Likewise, the condition of the existing floors should be checked for soundness, potential for the reuse of existing wood flooring, and suitability for new flooring finishes.

Site access and the potential for on-site parking are also important redevelop-ment factors that can be explored during the site visit. For example, is there capacity for garage parking either in the existing building or in an attached new structure? Is there adequate open land on the site for patron or visitor surface parking, and how can such parking be accessed? Would the parking meet zoning guidelines concerning setbacks, required capacity, and access drive sizes? How can truck loading and trash removal be facilitated for the renovated building? How can the fire department access the site with their trucks in the event of an emergency? A historic structure without land access or parking, especially for intended residential or office use, is usually extremely difficult to market and can prove unfeasible to renovate. This may be the case even if municipal parking code minimums (say, two spaces per 1,000 sq. ft. of building area) are attained because the market may require a higher standard (say, five parking spaces per 1,000 sq. ft. of building area).

Lastly, the special period features of the project should be noted with an eye to preserving and reusing them for added value. Perhaps a breathtaking entryway with stained-glass windows or a special wrought-iron railing might be restored. Period storefronts, often with cast-iron columns and trim, are present in many urban downtown locations and can be spectacular when restored. Likewise, interior columns, whether of wood or concrete, can be left exposed in offices and residential spaces, thereby adding an interesting historical reference and sense of place. The graceful arches and delicate yet far-off details in a church ceiling can become much more accessible when a penthouse unit is constructed, and the ceiling becomes touchably close.

A checklist reflecting the above information is found at the end of this chapter in Appendix 4-A.

Conclusions about the Initial Architectural Assessment

All the factors discussed above are incorporated into the schematic design phase, when the architect presents various design options for the space. These options take into consideration all the information previously assembled, such as market variables, physical layout of the property, opportunities for new infill construction, and zoning. This phase becomes particularly challenging when a vast interior void, such as the interior of a former church, school auditorium, or gym, needs to be adapted for another purpose, such as residential units or offices. The architect must take into consideration the market conditions in which the property is being developed along with construction costs. The goal is to advance a development plan that satisfies market realities while protecting the profit goals of the developer. From the input of the architect, the structural engineer, and general contractor, cost estimates are prepared that can be used to determine the financial feasibility of the particular adaptive reuse project, discussed in Chapter 7.

Design Elements to Mark and Brand the Product

Some of the best reasons for the renovation of any historic structure can be found in the building's inherent architectural features. Historic buildings represent a time capsule of sorts, illustrating the construction methods and the values of those who created them in a bygone era. In most cases, historic buildings were constructed with a "built-to-last" mentality, and as such they remain standing centuries after erection. The quality of construction alone is often a priceless asset, and it can become a branding feature for a renovation project. Thick load-bearing brick walls, 3 ft.-thick granite, and heavy timber frame construction were commonly used in churches and warehouse buildings built between 1850 and the early 1900s; today these exposed features offer a rich materiality and sense of place for popular modern loft offices or residences. Special masonry details, such as stone arches and lintels, keystones, and the like; detailed feature windows, transoms, and storefronts; and other restored exterior elements offer a unique, hard-to-duplicate identity to a renovated historic building, which in turn enhances the tapestry of the neighborhood context.

The Red Door Church project in suburban Cleveland, Ohio, for example, not only preserved most of the original exterior stonework and slate roof, but also retained the beautiful arched quarter-sawn oak trusses lining the sanctuary ceiling and showcased them in the interior of each condominium (see Chapter 12). Likewise, the church nave's original stained-glass window was preserved as a feature window in one lucky homeowner's living room. These and other special architectural features of the old stone church provided important design cues for the new cloister of townhouses that extend and emphasize the context of the renovation project. For example, each of the new townhouses has a distinctive red front door, just like the original church.

Unique building features can have a substantial marketing upside for developers because potential buyers or tenants will pay extra for them. Thus, retaining and featuring the distinctive aspects of the project are not only altruistic, but can also be profitable. Distinctive features also help brand the project and distinguish it from competitors in an otherwise "vanilla" or bland market.

Development Cost Comparisons

Having now examined the reasons for rehab and some of the pitfalls and upsides related to the redevelopment of religious buildings, we turn to discussion of how potential rehab developers may anticipate potential cost-related benefits and detractions of rehab compared with new construction. In addition to estimating potential project costs, it can assist in buying the property at the right price by showing the allowable project redevelopment costs, against which the offer price for the building must be framed.

This section contains three analyses. The first is a detailed examination of the relative overall development costs in dollars and percentages for a rehab conversion of a church to residential condominiums, compared to the *equivalent* (not reconstructed) new unit at the same price point.[2] The second analysis addresses the *hard cost only* development costs, comparing a new construction cost to the rehabilitation cost of converting a 10,000 sq. ft. church to office space. The same type of project cost data is compared in considering the construction of fifty-four condos within the interior volume of a former school gym.[3] The third analysis looks at the hypothetical operating costs between rehab and new construction for a residential project. This brief example largely addresses the difference in operational energy costs and its effect on property value.

Comparing Development Costs of Church Condo Rehab with New Construction

The financial analysis presented here is based on a compilation of several cases from this book. The Red Door Church (see Chapter 12), a residential development that entails a mix of 25 percent renovation and 75 percent new construction, along with the authors' twenty-plus years of experience teaching real estate cases and years of architectural experience with numerous rehab projects, make up the basis for the "new construction" scenario. The Saints Peter and Paul Church (see Chapter 15) and two components of the Fayetteville Church rehab project (see Chapter 18) form the basis for the "rehab" scenario. These cases took place at a similar time (mid-2000s) but in different markets. However, key elements of their cost structure (in percentages) are similar and allow generalization for instructional purposes. The examples presented here are for a hypothetical "typical" project, but since projects are unique, they should not be used as an absolute standard or guideline for cost analysis for any particular project. Nevertheless, the figures do illustrate the potential differences in costs between new construction and rehab construction.

Consider the following two hypothetical projects—one a new construction and the other an adaptive reuse project—with the same price points. Both projects consist of twenty-five residential condominium units with a construction cost of $165 per square foot and a sale price of $280,000 per unit. The 1,700-sq.-ft. units are constructed in a three-story building, for a total of 45,000 sq. ft. with fifty parking spaces on a 1-acre site. The total development cost (i.e., "all in") for the *new* project is $8 million. The total cost (also "all in") for the *rehab* project is $7.5 million. This model assumes that market demand for housing in this area is firm.

Exhibit 4-1 shows the relative costs for both the new and rehab projects. Sixteen cost line items, which can be grouped into three general categories, are provided. The first group (four items) deals with site acquisition and infrastructure costs. They include site acquisition (including standing structures), environmental remediation, site preparation (including parking and other site prep), and demolition. The following group (the next nine line items) incorporates structural hard costs (foundation, envelope, windows, HVAC, electrical, plumbing, rough carpentry, finish, and contingency line items). The last set (the final three items) includes soft costs, financing, and developer profit. The two columns on the left side of the table represent a new project, and the two columns on the right represent the rehab project. Both dollars and percentages are provided. Development costs are totaled to 100 percent, but, as mentioned above, the new project costs more (in this case about 6 percent more) than the rehab.

Acquisition and site infrastructure costs
The first cost group deals with site acquisition and preparation. All told, these four line items total 20 percent of total project cost for the proposed new construction, compared with 28 percent for the hypothetical rehab project. The first individual line item is site acquisition cost. Site acquisition cost for our generic $8.0 million new construction project is $960,000, or 12 percent of total new project cost. For the rehab project, the cost is $1.56 million, or 21 percent of total rehab cost. This is obviously a very large line item, and it is generally the largest single item for a rehabilitation project. Site acquisition for rehabs is usually substantially higher than for new projects, both in dollar terms and percentage, because it typically includes a standing structure that is structurally sound and may also be historically significant and attractive. The site may come with the possibility of historic tax credits and have a paved parking lot with some land attached. Some

Exhibit 4-1 Relative Development Costs of a Church Rehab into Condominiums, Compared with New Construction

Line Item	New Costs ($)	% of Total Costs	$ of Rehab Costs	% of Total
Land/Site Acquisition Including Buildings	960,000	12	1,575,000	21
Remediation/Asbestos	-	0	75,000	1
Site Preparation, Parking	640,000	8	300,000	4
Demolition	-	0	225,000	3
Building Foundation	400,000	5	150,000	2
Envelope	1,440,000	18	150,000	2
Windows	480,000	6	600,000	8
HVAC	400,000	5	525,000	7
Electricity	240,000	3	375,000	5
Plumbing	160,000	2	225,000	3
Rough Carpentry	1,040,000	13	1,050,000	14
Finish	400,000	5	450,000	6
Other / Contingency	320,000	4	450,000	6
Soft Costs	720,000	9	600,000	8
Financing	320,000	4	375,000	5
Developer Fee	480,000	6	375,000	5
Total	**8,000,000**	**100**	**7,500,000**	**100**

rehab sites in poorly performing markets, however, can be acquired for a very small amount (sometimes even for $1), especially if a public or nonprofit group is involved.

Environmental contamination remediation cost for our new construction project is assumed to be 0 percent of total project cost. In an actual situation, however, there may be environmental issues with the site, whether it is a contaminated brownfield site (it is not completely unusual to find buried tanks or contaminated soils) or a greenfield site (where wetlands may be an issue, for example). Many condominium and townhouse sites are located on greenfields and take advantage of nearby amenities, such as a waterfront, a scenic view, or a park. For the rehab project, the cost is $75,000, or 1 percent of total rehab cost. This is typically a very small line item. Still, the remediation cost for rehabs is generally substantially higher than for new projects because standing buildings may require asbestos mitigation or other environmental remediation. The buyer generally can expect to offset significant environmental costs (as well as other unusual extra costs of rehabilitation) against a lower property acquisition price.

With respect to parking and other site preparation costs, the expense for our new construction project is $640,000, or 8 percent of total new project cost. For the rehab project, the cost is $300,000, or 4 percent of total rehab cost. Site prep cost for rehabs is generally substantially smaller than for new projects, both in dollar terms and percentage. This is because new construction requires a lot of grading, utility work, and paving for parking lots, whereas rehab projects already have utilities and parking. Rehabilitation site prep normally consists of a less expensive reworking of what is already there: sprucing up, landscaping, and tweaking of access and visibility.

The last line item in this category is demolition. The demo cost for our hypothetical new construction project is zero, although for some urban sites there certainly may be some modest costs to remove older, smaller buildings. For the rehab project, the demolition cost is $225,000, or 3 percent of total rehab cost. Demolition costs for rehabs, although modest in scope, are generally higher than those encountered for new projects, both in dollar terms and percentage. This is generally due to removal of smaller outbuildings and gutting the unwanted parts of the interior of the church or school building before or during the rehab process.

Building hard costs

Building hard cost items begin with a construction-ready building site and work from the ground up. All told, these nine line items total 61 percent of total project cost for the proposed new construction, compared with 53 percent for the hypothetical rehab project.

The foundation cost line item for the generic $8.0 million new construction project is $400,000, or 5 percent of total new project cost. This item includes excavating and pouring a basement and supporting foundation for the lower exterior walls. For the $7.5 million rehab project, the cost is much lower, at $150,000, only 2 percent of total rehab cost. This is obviously a large line item for new construction, and foundation costs for rehabs are generally substantially lower than for new projects, both in dollar terms and percentage. Many rehabs have even lower foundation costs than this example, and indeed, the rehab of a sound existing building sometimes requires no foundation work at all.[4]

The building envelope cost (exterior walls, roof, trusses, and heavy framing) for our $8.0 million new construction project is

very large: $1.44 million, or 18 percent of to-
tal new project cost. The cost for the rehab
project is much smaller, at $150,000, only
2 percent of total rehab cost. In typical rehabs, this expense would involve stabilizing
the roof, or dealing with water leaks. Thus,
the building shell is the largest line item for
new construction, but is negligible for the
rehab project. The main reason for this difference is that the building shell expense in
rehabs has been largely accounted for in site
acquisition, which should include a viable
and attractive building exterior.

Window cost for the new construction project is $480,000, or 6 percent of to-
tal new project cost. For the rehabilitation
project, the cost is $600,000, or 8 percent of
total rehab cost. Window cost is therefore
modestly large for both new and rehab projects and is somewhat higher (and less pre-
dictable) in rehabs than for new projects,
both in dollar terms and percentage. Obviously this expense can vary widely with the
existing building type and the kind of windows that were used during the period of
construction. Rehabilitation projects of formerly religious buildings often have to work
with older, wooden windows that have gaps
or drafts, and therefore waste energy. The
glass may be only single pane, and retrofitting storms on these oddly shaped and
sized windows is more expensive. If the rehabs take advantage of historic preservation tax credits, this line item can grow
even bigger and may exhaust part of the
contingency budget because of the need to
provide expensive custom-made windows
to meet historic requirements.[5]

HVAC (heating, ventilation, and air conditioning) cost for our new construction
project is $400,000, or 5 percent of total new
project cost. For the rehab project, the cost
is $575,000, or 7 percent of total rehab cost.
HVAC cost is modest for both types of proj-

ects, but is generally somewhat larger for
rehabs than for new projects, both in dollar terms and percentage, because installing
modern, market-demanded forced-air integrated heating and cooling requires substantial ductwork. Also new buildings have more
efficient floor plates (the ratio of building
exterior to interior space) that allow more
efficient, cost-effective systems to be installed. Ductwork is readily incorporated
into walls in a new construction project, but
placing HVAC ducts in existing solid walls
is very messy and can be a hit-or-miss proposition in a rehab project. One alternative
for a rehab project is to use exposed (visible) ducts, but they can be unsightly unless
properly designed and installed. There may
be steam or radiant heating in some rehab
buildings, but the capacity and zone control
of these systems may be obsolete. Finally,
large fans and exhaust blowers may need
to be installed in attics or other places, and
sometimes this necessitates puncturing ceilings or rooflines for exhaust purposes. These
modifications can potentially run afoul of
historic preservation rules and regulations
that require preservation of the appearance
of the building's exterior.

The cost of installing the central electrical
box, meters, light fixtures, and electrical and
cable wiring for our new construction project
is $240,000, or 3 percent of total new project
cost. For the rehab project, the cost is
$375,000, or 5 percent of total rehabilitation
cost. Thus, in our hypothetical projects,
electrical is almost twice as expensive for
rehabs. However, electrical costs are a small
line item and roughly comparable for both
new and rehab projects, both in dollar terms
and percentage. Potential electrical problems
in a rehab project, which account for the
modest to substantial difference in cost that
favors new construction, include the uncer-
tain additional labor and reconstruction

costs associated with snaking and hiding electrical lines and hiding and installing individual meters. This example assumes no unusual problems, although some rehabs can incur even more expensive electrical costs. Excessive electrical costs can also consume contingency budgets.

Plumbing cost (which includes fire-prevention sprinklers) for our new construction project is $160,000, or 2 percent of total new project cost. For the rehab project, the cost is $225,000, or 3 percent of total rehab cost. Plumbing costs are a small line item, and are roughly comparable for both new and rehab projects, both in dollar terms and percentage. Potential problems related to retrofitting sewer (gravity flow) and water lines (pressurized) account for the modest difference in cost that favors new construction. Note, however, that the additional cost of tap-in fees for city sewer and water systems may negate the savings expected in new construction.

Rough carpentry, including all floors, interior walls, hallways, and drywall installation, is a large and relatively comparable cost for both rehab and new construction. Rough carpentry cost for our new construction project is $1.04 million, or 13 percent of total new project cost. For the rehab project, the cost is $1.05 million, comparable in dollar amount but a slightly larger 14 percent of total rehab cost. In some cases there could be larger costs associated with rough carpentry for rehabs versus new, unless the whole interior is to be gutted and entirely new floor structures, a more expensive element, have to be installed. Some projects can incur a larger carpentry cost, especially churches that are converted to housing, where the original building was a large open single-floor space in which multiple floors need to be added. School building adaptive reuse projects, where most of the construc-

tion is of sturdy concrete, concrete block, or brick, may self-select (in other words, avoiding inappropriately extensive interior wall reconfigurations) to work within the existing floor plate and room size configuration.

Finish includes painting, wall treatments, carpeting, and the relatively expensive kitchen and bathroom items, and is a moderate line item that is roughly comparable for both new and rehab projects, both in dollar and percentage terms. The finish cost for our new construction project is $400,000, or 5 percent of total new project cost. For the rehab project, the cost is $450,000, or 6 percent of total rehab cost. Potential budget issues for rehabs include retaining functionality while working around any available distinctive architectural features, such as ceiling detail, stone walls, and stained glass. Up-market units would likely have a larger tenant finish cost in the kitchen, with amenities such as granite countertops, but the units in this hypothetical case are not assumed to be luxury units, so their finish costs are moderate.

The contingency cost line is the big-risk item. While all real estate projects have some unknown cost overruns, the types of problems differ considerably among individual projects. For new projects, problems often lie in the ground with environmental issues, especially in urban infill projects. Other sources of cost overruns common to both new projects and rehabs include spikes in the cost of building materials and the inability to get subcontractors to do their job in the proper order, which may lead to cascading delays of other subcontractors or tradespeople. This in turn may lead to replacement of known subcontractors with those of unknown quality. Cost overruns may also be a construction management issue and can be partially overcome by making a construction manager arrangement with the builder (where there is typically a fixed fee, and the builder acts as general contractor and absorbs cost overruns), rather than using the fee builder approach (where the builder gets a single-digit percentage of costs while the owner is the general contractor and absorbs cost overruns). When there is a delay in sales, the contingency budget may get absorbed in financing charges.

Contingency costs are a modest line item and are generally larger for rehab projects, both in dollar terms and percentage. In our hypothetical projects, the contingency budget cost for our new construction project is $320,000, or 4 percent of total new project cost. For the rehab project, the cost is $450,000, or 6 percent of total rehab cost. While it is an industry standard in some circles to carry a contingency budget of 10 percent for any existing building renovation, many projects carry less or more contingency amounts depending on the "unknowns" perceived. For rehab projects, the contingency budget is typically allocated to basement, HVAC, plumbing, and infrastructure surprises, and dealing with the historic preservation authorities. At the end of the deal, any excessive contingency costs come right out of developer profit. On the other hand, incentives for efficiency can be encouraged by an arrangement that allows the contractor and developer to share the remaining contingency fund amount at a predetermined split rate upon the successful conclusion of the project.

Soft Costs, Financing, and Developer Profit

All told, these three line items total 19 percent of total project cost for the proposed new construction, compared with 18 percent for the hypothetical rehab project. Again, these costs would vary depending on the nature of the rehabilitation project, existing building conditions, and the services included. Soft costs for our new construction project are $720,000, or 9 percent of total new project cost. For the rehab project, the soft costs are $600,000, or 8 percent of total rehab cost. Soft costs include all out-of-pocket consulting costs, which predominantly consist of architectural and engineering fees but also include planning and market analysis, legal, and accounting fees. Soft costs are a modest to large line item and are roughly comparable for both new and rehab projects, both in dollar terms and percentage. Generally, new projects have more soft costs due to an emphasis on site layout, whereas rehabs working within an existing shell may not have these costs. In general, architecture and engineering (A & E) is usually more expensive for an existing building if major work is to be performed. Rehab projects may have higher fees related to managing the planning process (e.g., more not-in-my-backyard issues). For projects using historic tax credits or low-income housing tax credits, the legal and expert consultant fees for obtaining the funds and staying in compliance with program guidelines may be larger.[6]

Financing cost for our new construction project (in the form of a construction loan) is $320,000, or 4 percent of total new project cost. For the rehab project, the cost is $375,000, or 5 percent of total rehab cost. Financing is a modest line item and is roughly comparable for both new and rehab projects, both in dollar terms and percentage, but rehabs can expect a slightly higher cost. Some lenders are unfamiliar with rehabs because there are often few comparable projects, and so finding a lender may be more difficult. Potential problems in financing revolve around phasing and not getting too far out in front of the market, resulting in standing inventory that needs to be carried.

The lender may require a certain amount of units be presold before funding a project. The modest difference in financing cost favors new construction. In the 2014–16 time period of "iffy" times for homebuilders coming out of the Great Recession, smaller rehab projects may be considered lower risk, if properly managed.

The last line item is developer profit. The development fee for our new construction project is $480,000, or 6 percent of total new project cost. For the rehab project, the development fee is $375,000, or 5 percent of total rehab cost. The developer's fee is a modest line item (although the most important one for obvious reasons) and is roughly comparable for both new and rehab projects, both in dollar terms and percentage. However, new projects probably have a slight edge. The developer fee is tied closely to several factors, including keeping unplanned contingent costs down and buying the project at a low price in the first place.

In sum, this section has provided a teaching example of the differences in development costs for a church building to residential condominiums. Of course, actual costs will vary on a case-by-case basis, and these differences may be substantial. Further, some soft costs may include consultant fees that can prove invaluable to saving the project money, due to their particular expertise. If, for instance, the cost of the tax attorney is 1.5 percent of the project cost, but his or her work can yield an additional 15 percent for the project, the benefit far outweighs the expense.

Extension of Cost Analysis to School Buildings on Religious Campuses

This analysis was not conducted in the same detail for school buildings converted to apartments, but the following observations may be helpful.

With respect to site acquisition items, historic urban schools share many characteristics with vintage churches. However, their classroom-sized interior walls are almost always very solid and difficult to reconfigure. Sometimes classrooms can be combined, but retrofitting plumbing can be problematic and expensive. Whereas the religious building renovation approach is often concerned with construction of a whole new interior structure inside the existing religious shell, the primary concern for a school rehab might be retrofitting the existing floor plates into residential apartments or condos. However, schools, too, may have ancillary buildings, such as gymnasiums, in which a residential project may be built inside an existing shell. Also, schools often have large ball fields that can serve as the site for new construction projects, possibly incorporated into a larger rehabilitation project.

With respect to building hard costs for schools, foundation and rough carpentry expenses are likely to be lower than for the religious building because the walls are largely permanent and not able to be reconfigured. Window expense may be higher, since classrooms typically have many windows that are older and taller than those used in new construction. Retrofitting HVAC, electrical, and especially plumbing in solid concrete or cinderblock walls may also be more expensive than both new construction and rehab of a religious building. The finish expense may also be less because some school projects end up as low-income housing tax credit projects, which have lower rents and a lower level of tenant finish.

Soft costs and architectural fees should be roughly comparable in school rehabs as for religious buildings. Rehab of school buildings on religious campuses, however, presents two notable challenges. First, school floor plans may need to be heavily customized to accommodate the existing interior walls. Secondly, strategies may need to be found to minimize otherwise un-leasable space in large hallways. Meanwhile, the rehab of churches tends to involve the architectural and engineering challenges of adapting large volumes of space for reuse, while considering that the adaptation may be in direct contradiction of historic tax credit renovation guidelines.

Also, consultant fees (including legal and accounting) associated with historic preservation tax credits and low-income housing tax credits can be expensive. Financing of equity through tax credit programs can get complicated because it affects both the amount of bank debt (generally a much lower loan-to-value ratio) and the sources and timing of equity from investors. Also, from the experiences recorded in the cases in this book, profits appear smaller and harder to retain for school projects than for religious buildings, despite rehab costs, which are typically lower per square foot than for former religious buildings.

Construction Hard Cost Comparison

The second example set was created utilizing hard cost data obtained from Design Cost Data™/D4COST™, which supplies the construction industry with historical cost data from actual projects. The data can be updated to a new baseline date and location to provide a reliable cost estimate. The two paired comparisons (first, an office building, new and rehab; second, a residential project, new and rehab) are presented in Exhibit 4-2. These cost comparisons are hard costs only, so no acquisition costs, soft costs, financing, or profit are considered. Thus, the results will accentuate hard cost differences between new and rehab projects.

The first scenario compares the actual construction cost of a new 10,000-sq.-ft. office building (Castelli, 2008)[7] with the cost

for adaptive reuse of a church to be converted to office space. The second scenario compares the new construction cost for the fifty-three-unit double-height residential Markethouse Lofts, located in San Jose, California, with the Gym Lofts at Albuquerque High (see Chapter 21), which has fifty-four residential units constructed within the volume of the original gym building. Markethouse Lofts has 63,182 sq. ft. while the Gym Lofts comprises 68,018 sq. ft.

Because the projects have slightly different sizes, the most appropriate comparison is the percent differences. For example, the overall percentage difference (new/rehab) in cost for the first project, a 10,000-sq.-ft. office, is 26 percent ($2.2 million/$1.6 million), indicating rehab costs are a quarter less than comparable new construction. A summary of the differences follows.

Building elements where rehabs are less costly than new construction
- Concrete, since the foundation exists.
- Wood and plastic items, which are essentially the outside walls for the two new construction projects and the interiors for all.
- Thermal and moisture protection: Reusing the existing roof can be a significant savings for an adaptive reuse project, unless the roof has to be replaced.
- Mechanical and electrical: Surprisingly, these items were slightly less expensive for adaptive reuse projects examined.[8]

Building elements where rehabs are more costly than new construction
- Metals: Both reuse projects required structural steel and metal framing.
- Doors and windows: Meeting historic preservation requirements for replacement or restoration was more costly than for new construction.

Exhibit 4-2 Construction Hard Cost Comparison (Excluding acquisition and soft costs).

	10,000 sq. ft. Office New Construction versus Adaptive Reuse of Church circa 2008			54 Condo Units New Construction versus Adaptive Reuse of School Gym circa 2003			
	New Office Building ($)	Former Church ($)		New Lofts ($)	Former Gym ($)		Cost Comparison Reuse vs. New Construction
General Requirements	237,376	162,000	-32%	1,364,741	782,887	-43%	Less
Concrete	57,389		-100%	1,364,741	226,273	-83%	Less
Masonry	169,080	37,000	-78%	0	126,675		Varies
Metals	33,421	259,000	675%	358,244	504,722	41%	More
Wood and Plastics	285,434	25,000	-91%	1,688,876	425,340	-75%	Less
Thermal and Moisture Protection	101,727	12,500	-88%	281,478	201,047	-29%	Less
Doors and Windows	89,896	233,000	159%	477,659	704,594	48%	More
Finishes	508,715	198,000	-61%	1,194,148	1,189,634	0%	Varies
Specialties	14,900	8,500	-43%	63,972	33,370	-48%	Less
Equipment	7,976	3,000	-62%	78,473	131,854	68%	Varies
Furnishings					22,206		Varies as applicable
Conveying Systems	67,050	87,000	30%	48,619	69,839	44%	More
Mechanical	194,079	121,000	-38%	963,848	915,034	-5%	Less
Electrical	144,950	126,500	-13%	699,430	587,252	-16%	Less
Total Building Costs	**1,911,993**	**1,272,500**	**-33%**	**8,584,229**	**5,920,727**	**-31%**	**Less**
Existing Conditions							
Asbestos					72, 825		More
Demolition		39,000			178,735		More
Site Work	245,742	277,000	13%	1,023,556	58,075	-94%	Varies
Total Non-Building Costs	**245,742**	**316,000**	**29%**	**1,023,556**	**309,635**	**-70%**	**Varies**
Total Project Costs	**2,157,735**	**1,588,500**	**-26%**	**9,607,785**	**6,230,362**	**-35%**	**Less**

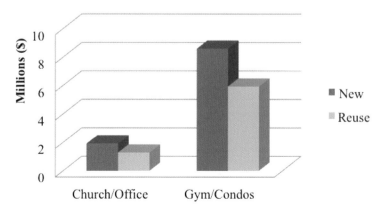

New Construction vs. Reuse

- Conveying systems: Installation of elevators was 30–40 percent more costly in reused buildings.

Variable costs from project to project
- Masonry: Brick and stone repair was an expense common to both adaptive reuse projects. The 10,000-sq.-ft. new office building was entirely brick.
- Finishes: Painting and decorating costs were identical for the condo projects but varied for the office projects.
- Site work: This item varied from site to site. In Albuquerque, the city built a parking garage, while the cost of parking and site development was the developer's expense for the new construction condos.

The value of an existing building shell and foundation in good condition is obvious if use can be made of the interior space. A greater amount of expense will be incurred with building elements such as windows, doors, and structural metals. Finally, site work is a variable depending on the requirements of the end user. Every project presents its own set of obstacles and opportunities.

Operating Expenses
The main operating cost difference between a rehabbed building and a new one is electric and gas utilities. This assumes cable, security, exterior maintenance, telephone, and water (and any other line items related to utilities) are the same. Thus, in Northern climates operating cost differences are accounted for by gas heat in the winter and some negligible air conditioning electrical expense in the summer. In Southern climates, heavy use of air conditioning in summer and some gas or electrical heat during the winter accounts for operating expense differences.

Consider for the sake of example two hypothetical scenarios: a new residential apartment unit and a rehab residential apartment unit. Both offer comparable space at similar price points. Assume that both units are 1,500 sq. ft., have three bedrooms, and are individually metered apartment units in a Northern climate. The units each rent for $1,400 per month.

To illustrate the point, assume that R-values (the traditional measure of resistance to heat flow, where higher R values are a better insulator and more energy efficient) in the windows, walls, and ceiling of the new construction are R-5, R-20, and R-30, respectively, which complies with the building code. In the run-of-the-mill, cost-minimizing rehab project, which does not feature a green building philosophy, the R-value of insulation (warm air rises) in windows, walls, and ceiling are R-2, R-10, and R-15, respectively (R-Values of Common Building Materials 2009). These values are generally below the levels recommended by today's building codes in temperate climates.

For the new unit, the heating cost in a winter month (e.g., February), would be $125, and the annualized total gas cost for heating purposes would be $950, or 68 cents per square foot per year. For the comparable rehab unit, the heating cost in a winter month would be $200, and the annualized total gas cost for heating purposes would be $1,500, or $1.07 per square foot.

Thus, holding constant other factors (e.g., summer air conditioning, gas for hot water) the additional difference in heating gas expense for each unit is $550 per year (39 cents per square foot), resulting in a substantially lower operating expense for the new unit in this analysis. Assuming efficient rental markets and capitalizing this one line item into value (at an income capitalization rate of 10 percent) indicates a "loss" in value of $5,500, or about 4 percent of its market value. This proportion would also hold for residential rental and commercial property, subject to similar use patterns. A similar result can be expected in warm climates where the primary cost is electricity used for air conditioning during summer months.

This analysis has been for net leasable space under tenancy. Any vacant, underutilized, and wasted space (e.g., hallways in large schools) can be really expensive to carry, and energy costs can quickly have a big negative effect on bottom-line operating costs, especially where the rents are gross instead of net or where the landlord absorbs operating costs. Further, higher initial expense (assuming better equipment) can produce lower operating costs, which can recoup the additional investment faster.

Chapter Summary

This chapter has addressed the architect's approach and walk-through process, looking at both neighborhood linkages and structural issues, with a building walk-through checklist provided in the appendix. After taking a brief look at key design elements and branding, a development cost comparison was made for a typical rehab project compared with new construction for the same price point. This paired comparison is offered in substantial detail for a residential condominium, and in summary fashion for an office project. Differences in operating costs between rehab and new projects were also addressed.

The prospective buyer-developer should conduct a thorough neighborhood analysis looking at linkages and potential for the project to be successful. The building walk-through should be systematic and should lead to a go/no-go decision based on the absence of deal-killer fatal flaws and on the ability to capitalize on the building's size, functionality with respect to market demand, and unique features. Branding and

features of the project should flow from the structure's distinctive and visible assets, if present.

With respect to cost differentials between new construction and rehab, site acquisition costs and related demolition costs for rehab projects are usually much higher than for new construction. However, site prep, foundation, and building shell expenses are expected to be substantially lower. Windows and doors, along with the installation of elevators, can be expected to be substantially higher. HVAC, plumbing, and electrical expenses can be expected to be variable: either modestly higher in rehabs or lower. The contingent cost line item is also more variable. Developer profits for construction can be dependent on managing contingent costs and buying the property cheaply.

Higher energy-related operating costs for rehab projects are a concern, and this is even more important where the prices are volatile, as in recent years. Energy prices alone can rob 3–5 percent of the value of a rehab project, compared with comparable new construction, holding all other factors constant.

Notes

1. The school gym example is included because it is not unusual for religious campuses to also have school buildings. These structures are fundamentally different than those intended for worship.
2. This detailed example is based largely on the costs incurred by developers of the projects described in the case studies in this book.
3. Both examples in this second set are based on construction hard costs obtained from Design Cost Data™/D4COST™.
4. Conversely, sometimes there are considerable foundation expenses for a rehab, such as when the basement requires reworking from a partially finished, 6 ft.-high dirt floor storage area into to a fully functional 8–10-ft.-high basement (see Babeville, Chapter 16, and Jamaica Queens Performing Arts

Center, Chapter 13, cases) or when a building must be shored up to accommodate more weight.

5. An alternative would be to consider Life Cycle Cost analysis, which could indicate in some situations that it is more cost effective *not* to replace the windows. Windows can be a major factor in heat loss and therefore energy consumption.

6. Note that historic preservation tax credits (HPTC) and low-income housing tax credits (LIHTC) are programs for residential rental properties, whereas our example examines for-sale residential properties. Thus, our hypothetical projects are generally incompatible for use with tax credits, although some mid- to upmarket residential rehab projects are maintained as rentals for the HPTC required five-year period, then converted to for-sale condos. See Chapters 6 and 7 for more detailed information on tax credits.

7. Published since 1958, *Design Cost Data* (*DCD*) provides the construction industry with actual, documented building costs for the purpose of conceptual cost estimating. Architects, general contractors, and other industry professionals submit their completed projects, along with the final cost to build, for publication in DCD. Published bimonthly, and distributed nationwide, *DCD* includes these projects along with square-foot cost guides, industry cost trends, and industry articles. In addition to *DCD* magazine this data is available in D4COST Software. D4COST Software was developed by *DCD* in the early 1990s and was the first industry software for conceptual cost estimating. D4COST includes 1,100 projects for use as models along with cost escalators and regional modifiers to target the projects to a new bid date and location. D4COST is an excellent tool for creating budgets before plans are drawn. Users can use D4COST to archive their own projects and data for estimating, creating a historical cost database, and marketing.

8. This result is contradictory to our earlier hypothetical example, in which rehab electrical was more expensive than new. The lesson here is that these costs may be variable based upon the specific situation, and a wide range may be expected. These costs may consume part of a contingency budget.

References and Works Consulted

Castelli, D. 2008. DC&D Technologies, Inc. *Design Cost Data Magazine/D4COST™* .

R-Values of Common Building Materials. http://www.stronggreen.com/docs/R-Values%20of%20Common%20Building%20Materials.pdf.

Simons, R. A., and R. Throupe. 2005. "An Exploratory Review of the Effect of Toxic Mold on Real Estate Values." *The Appraisal Journal* 73, no. 2 (Spring): 156–66.

APPENDIX 4-A: Existing Building Walk-Through Checklist

This is a thorough but not exhaustive list of factors that should be addressed during a building walk-through. Make notes about the condition of each item and those requiring further investigation.

Building Exterior and Site Issues

Access to site

Location of main highways and distances to ramps

Main feeder artery locations and distance to intersections

Access to bus and light rail public transportation

On-site access points

Building entries

Main access

Service entry

ADA

Access to site

Level path to entry

Parking Areas

Resident parking—capacity

Visitor parking—capacity

Street Parking—proximity

Enclosed parking potential—existing structures, basement, site available

Building Site Context

Neighborhood institutions and anchors—types and proximity to

Neighborhood use types

Adjacent property use types

Condition of neighboring properties

Availability of neighboring parcels—future expansion/immediate need

Presence of successful previous renovations—use types, if present

Historic landmark status of neighborhood

Building Itself

Existing building exterior conditions

Location of the structure on the site—setbacks—future additions possible

Condition and character of the building exterior

Condition of the exterior cladding—brick, wood, stone

Structural condition of the facades—cracks, damage, deterioration

Leaking condition of the existing doors and windows—damaged or missing

Presence of special historic features:

    Iron window lintel hoods, columns

    Special masonry features, arches, stone lintels, keystones, etc.

    Specialty glazing—divided lights, transoms, leaded glass, etc.

    Turrets, bay windows, storefronts, sunrooms

    Wrought-iron railings, balconies, etc.

Existing utility service to the building:

    Location of water main, sanitary, and storm sewer service to site

    Location of electrical service to the building site

    Location of gas service to site

Condition of existing landscaping

Condition of existing public sidewalks and streetscape features

Building Interior Conditions

Condition of primary structural system and building elements

Wood structure—sound, water-damaged, decayed or rotted, sagging

Concrete structure—damaged, sagging, reinforcement exposed, collapsed

Steel structure—damaged, rusted, decayed, collapsed

Foundations—sound, settled, cracked, decayed, damaged, pitched

Main floor structures—structure and thickness of members

Bearing walls—exposed brick, plastered, concrete, cracks, or settlement

Condition of existing roof, cladding membrane, shingles, etc.—leaks

Structural column bay spacing, depth of beams, ceiling heights

Circulation systems

Presence or condition of elevator/service elevator, ADA-compliant

Location and condition of fire egress stairs—code compliance

Open access stairs, historic entry lobby, mezzanine, etc.

Mechanical systems

Location, type, and condition of existing mechanical systems

Location and condition of HVAC distribution—ducted, radiator, etc.

Plumbing systems

Location and condition of main plumbing riser stacks

Location and condition of existing bathroom areas

Existence of and condition of sprinkler system, risers, distribution

Condition of roof drains, gutters, downspouts, etc.

Location of water main, meters, and hot water system if present

Electrical systems

Location of, size of, and capacity of existing main electrical service

Existing distribution and sub-panel locations—code compliance/adaptable

Interior and site environmental issues

Presence of visible signs of asbestos-containing materials:

-8" × 8" VAT floor tiles

-Presence of pipe sleeves or tank wrappings

-Pre-1960 duct sleeves

-Pre-1960 plaster wall or ceiling claddings

Presence of visible signs of lead paint

Presence of open-to-weather framing, flooring, attics with soaked wood

Visible presence of black mold

Presence of buried tanks or barrels of hazardous materials on site

Presence of any fuel service equipment on site

5

MARKET ANALYSIS TECHNIQUES FOR RELIGIOUS AND SCHOOL BUILDING REHAB PROJECTS

S. Subha Vyakaranam and
Robert A. Simons

market analysis is a thorough investigation of the demand and supply sides of the market. It is used to determine the attractiveness of a particular property to be used or reused in a certain way in its end-use market. A market analysis is intended to inform the financial analyst in matters related to unit absorption (net market acceptance of user units) and vacancy, price points, and amenities desired by the market. In the case of adaptive reuse, the market analysis consists of comparison of the compatibility of the existing structure (the supply side of the market) with the end-user market demand. Since an adaptive reuse project's physical location is constrained, the developer has no alternatives in terms of location or linkages and few options with respect to expansion of the physical structure. The developer does, however, have a wide range of potential alternatives to determine the best end use.

With respect to recycling existing buildings, the process begins with the assumption that the property has either been declared surplus or cannot be economically sustained by the current owner (the church or another entity). One common reason why reuse is a priority is that it presents an opportunity for the selling entity to both recover some financial value on the sale of the asset and preserve the historical importance of the building for its constituents or neighbors. Another reason for reuse is that the owner is seeking to avoid tax liability for a property that will lose its tax-exempt status when it ceases to operate as a tax-exempt property. Once the decision to sell has been made, other factors become important, such as potential developer profit, the increasingly high cost of new construction, and a commitment to sustainable design principles with the accompanying recovery of value embedded in the historic structure.

At the heart of any adaptive reuse project planning effort are five critical questions:

- What are the best economic new uses that do not detract from the cultural significance of the old structure?
- How well could the existing building accommodate and support the potential end use?
- What is that building's highest and best use for redevelopment?
- Is there enough market demand to absorb a project into the market?
- Does the financial analysis indicate reuse rather than demolition of the building(s)?

In order to address these points, this chapter presents two important techniques to help better analyze adaptive reuse market opportunities: highest and best use analysis (HBU), including both a basic and enhanced version, and market niche analysis. Highest and best use analysis takes the perspective of a site looking for a use. It is largely intuitive and is intended to narrow a long list of potentially desirable outcomes down to a short list of highly desirable ones, so that a more detailed market analysis can be performed. Once the HBU has been completed, the market analyst can perform a detailed market niche analysis to determine if sufficient net market demand is present for a specific, carefully defined project, and also set forth unit absorption rates and price points. A market study in turn feeds this demand-side data into a financial feasibility pro forma, which is beyond the scope of this chapter. A market study is also related to a marketing study, which seeks to market built space directly to potential users (often using data generated by the more general market analysis).

This chapter sets forth two forms of the HBU technique for narrowing multiple development outcomes down to a short list for further study. The chapter provides four examples of the basic HBU approach, and one example of an enhanced technique that allows weighting of decision factors. After this, the technique of market niche analysis is explained, and an example for a residential condo project is provided. Exhibit 5-1 provides an overview of the market analysis process.

Highest and Best Use (HBU) Analysis

Highest and best use analysis is an important concept that is widely used in real estate appraisal. It is based on the theory that the value of the property is directly related to the most profitable end use of that property.

An attempted analysis of highest and best use involves two considerations: [1] the most likely and profitable use of the site "as if va-

Exhibit 5-1 Overview of Market Analysis and Financial Feasibility Process

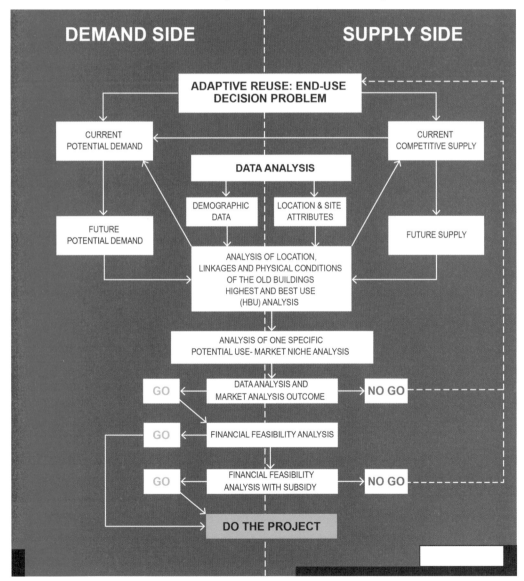

cant," [2] if a property is "already improved," it is the use that should be made of the property to maximize value for non-income producing properties or, maximize net operating income on a long range basis for investment properties. In cases where capital expenditure is necessary to renovate or improve an income producing property, these costs must provide a sufficient rate of return (to the owner) for the total amount invested in the site and building improvements.[1]

In order to be considered as the HBU, any potential use must be:

- *Legally allowable:* This restriction may exclude uses that cannot be expected to be allowed by zoning, uses forbidden by government regulations, and uses prohibited by deed restrictions or covenants.
- *Physically possible:* A potential use must be physically possible given the size, shape, topography, and other characteristics of the site.
- *Financially feasible:* This means that the proposed use of a property must generate adequate revenue to justify the costs of construction plus a profit for the developer. In the case of adaptive reuse, financial feasibility is maximized with the HBU of the site.
- *Greatly productive:* The use must generate the highest net return (profit) to the developer.

Thus, the best end use need not be the current use at the site, but the HBU analysis should yield results that indicate the best use, and the market-driven analysis should support this conclusion.

The HBU Matrix

Moving now from concept to practice, we present and operationalize two forms of HBU analysis: basic and enhanced. The ba-

sic approach provides the building blocks for narrowing many potential uses down to a short list, based on the site attributes of the property and on market conditions. The models we set forth are easily adapted by the market analyst to include more site attributes and potential end uses.

The basic HBU analysis is a scoring matrix for each potential type of end use. In this example, there are twenty-one site attributes (one per row), and eight columns, two columns for each potential end use. One column provides a description[2] of how each site attribute is scored, and the other provides the score[3] itself. The description provides information about the ideal condition of a site attribute for the potential end use listed at the top of the column. Therefore, the description and score may change for a particular attribute because the score indicated that appropriateness of the subject property (i.e., the vacant church or school) for the proposed end use listed at the top of each column. In our example, the scoring is done based on a scale from (−2) to (+2), where (−2) is not ideal, (0) is not applicable or neutral, and (+2) is ideal. Note that if a site factor scores equally for all potential end uses, it becomes a neutral factor in the HBU decision.

The potential use with the highest bottom-line score is the HBU for the subject property. Embedded in this analysis is the assumption that all site attributes are equally important. Note that due to the subjective nature of this process, absolute scores may differ considerably. Thus, the bottom-line highest score is the most important figure, and comparison of individual scores between analysts may not be valid. Exhibits 5-2 through 5-4 provide detailed results for three different redevelopment cases from this book.

Organization of the Site Attributes Used in HBU Analysis

There are several factors affecting adaptive reuse that play an important role in HBU analysis, including location and linkages, environmental and historical site characteristics, and market demand. Each factor may have several attributes, measured separately. These are addressed in turn as follows:

I. *Location and linkages:* As we all know, the three most important factors in determining the desirability of a property are "location, location, location." Location is the dominant part of real estate market analysis for real property because of its ability to determine the accessibility to other activities via linkages. A site with more linkages has more potential for development or investment. By "linkages" we mean access to private and public transportation, and distance from important amenity features that affect site desirability. Highest and best use is very dependent on the site having good linkages to appropriate transportation and activity generators.

   a. *Visibility/views:* This attribute accounts for view premiums from the property, including views of a city skyline or a shoreline. For commercial properties, this attribute focuses more on how prominently visible the site is, although prominent visibility can also be a positive attribute for residential uses.

   b. *Auto traffic:* The daily count of automobile traffic along the road or intersection near the property.

   c. *Pedestrian access:* Availability of pedestrian paths and access to the site.

   d. *Highway access:* The proximity to an interstate highway. Drive time of five minutes is considered ideal. Being too close can be a negative for some uses, such as single-family residential.

   e. *Subway/bus:* Proximity to public transportation, such as a subway or bus station. Too close is considered a disadvantage for some uses. Ideal distance from the property is about a two- to five-minute walk.

   f. *Airport access:* Proximity to the airport is an important factor. It is considered disadvantageous if the airport is less than a five-minute drive (because of noise) and ideal if it is between fifteen and thirty minutes away (for convenience of access).

   g. *Noise level:* The amount of traffic noise on the road nearby. Moderate to excessive noise is a negative in a residential neighborhood and has little effect in a commercial area.

   h. *Distance to nearest park:* Proximity to public places like parks is considered advantageous, especially in a residential neighborhood. Proximity of ¼ to 1 mile is ideal. This attribute should not affect commercial, industrial, and cultural properties, although retail may indirectly benefit because its market may be attracted to this feature.

   i. *Distance to bodies of water:* Proximity to bodies of water, like reservoirs, rivers, or lakes, is considered advantageous, especially in a residential neighborhood. Proximity of 1 mile is ideal. However, this attribute could negatively affect commercial, industrial, and cultural properties by serving as a barrier to access, or limiting the number of households within a primary market area.

II. *Environmental and historic site attributes:* This factor includes site zoning, size, and environmental legacy, as well as the building's design and its architectural character. When a building is historically important, the process of adaptive re-use must include discussions about reinforcing or changing its character. For example, can the existing building's style support interventions that represent a substantively different architectural language, or should renovations be consistent with the building's existing character? There is also the neighborhood and political influence exerted on buildings that become historic landmarks. These important structures may retain a long-standing and special positive memory in the minds of the local residents and stakeholders. Hence, end-use decisions are sometimes based solely on neighborhood support and political influence.

a. *Environmental condition of parcel:* This site attribute addresses any site deficiencies with respect to the presence of any environmental or brownfield issues. This attribute also captures the suitability of the site's physical topography and appearance for the proposed end use.

b. *Size of parcel:* This attribute captures how compatible the shape and size of the parcel are to the intended use.

c. *Distinctiveness and beauty of the structure:* This site attribute evaluates whether the existing building style has any distinctive or unusually attractive elements that would be positively viewed by its end-user market. Examples might include listing on historic registers, prominent facades or steeples, stained-glass windows, or a rare architectural style.

d. *Future expansion potential:* The expansion potential of the existing building is important. This attribute is an eval-

uation of the importance of "site tightness" with respect to extra land available for future expansion for each use.

e. *Adequate parking:* This attribute evaluates the adequacy of parking in relation to parcel size and type of use. Any development with adequate parking can be more easily leased or sold.

f. *Potential influence and neighborhood reaction:* This attribute measures the influence of any particular institution, especially the seller, in advocating a particular end use. It also considers the neighborhood reaction to the intended end use.

g. *Zoning:* This attribute tests the intended use's compatibility with the underlying zoning of the site and may also address compatibility with contiguous land uses.

III. *Market demand and financial feasibility:* This final factor analyzes whether the proposed end use is feasible from a market perspective, considering both supply and demand.

a. *Resident base:* The demographic data from the immediate area, including resident incomes, age, and race, typically measured in the particular census tract. This attribute also measures the importance of the resident base providing support for the intended end use.

b. *Daytime employment:* This attribute measures the importance of daytime employees for the particular end use. This is not important for residential or industrial end uses but does play a major role for commercial, cultural, and office end uses.

c. *Competition:* This attribute briefly analyzes the directly relevant competitors in the surrounding area.

d. *Market window:* This attribute captures whether conditions are appropriate for the intended use with respect to unmet demand and timing of competitors' entry into the marketplace.

e. *Financial window:* This attribute addresses changes to lending rules, interest rates, and other factors related to national economic cycles in the market for the proposed end use. This can affect perceived availability of capital and the discount rates used by a developer in investment analysis.

Basic HBU Matrix: Case Examples

Having laid out the building blocks of the highest and best use matrix, we now move to examples of the basic HBU technique. To demonstrate the HBU matrix, three cases were selected: Jamaica Performing Arts Center (church to performing arts center) in Queens, New York; Babeville (church to commercial) in Buffalo, New York; and Red Door Church (church to condominiums) in Cleveland Heights, Ohio.

The potential alternative use categories analyzed in these cases are cultural center, commercial use, and condominiums. These cases are representative of typical situations (see Chapter 3), and the selected end uses are based on data analysis outcomes. For churches, a quarter of the end uses were condominiums, one-tenth were apartments, and about a third were cultural projects. The balance of religious buildings became either office or retail end uses.

Jamaica Performing Arts Center

The Dutch Reformed Church in Queens, New York, was originally built in 1859. The church was designated as part of an urban renewal area by the city of New York because there was a need for the Social Security Administration (SSA) to locate an office complex in the area. The congregation using the church therefore moved into another building in the same neighborhood in the early 1970s. Eventually, the SSA plan changed, and the church remained vacant and deteriorating. To prevent the church from deteriorating completely, three local cultural groups—the Jamaica Center for Arts and Learning, the Cultural Collaborative of Jamaica, and the Black Spectrum Theater—formed a partnership to save the structure. Eventually it was converted to a performing arts center, called the Jamaica Performing Arts Center (JPAC). For more detail, refer to the JPAC case in the case study section of this book (Chapter 13).

The site of the Jamaica Performing Arts Center is a 1.5-acre lot located on a busy commercial street, about a half-hour subway ride from Manhattan. Highest and best use analysis was performed, and the highest scoring use was cultural center. Exhibit 5-2 provides the detailed scoring matrix for this case. Some explanation of the scoring is provided, as follows:

The church is prominently visible, scoring a +2 for all four potential uses due to its location on a busy road with a huge volume of auto traffic. The traffic activity is a disadvantage for a residential use, so it scored −2 for residential use. Conversely, it is an advantage for commercial uses, which scored +2. There is excellent pedestrian access to the site and hence scores +2. For end uses of commercial or cultural, the noise levels would be neutral (0) unlike residential uses, for which noise level score would be −2.

The site is ideally located less than a mile away from I-495, less than a thirty-minute drive to the airport, a five-minute walk from a subway (public transit), and it is readily walkable, but has no abutting parks or water bodies. All four potential uses scored a high +2 for all of these attributes.

The uses surrounding the church are generally mixed use, with mostly office and commercial and some residential rental housing. However, the compatibility of the structure would be an important obstacle to be taken into consideration, especially in a commercial- and office-dominated mixed-use neighborhood. Hence the resident base indicates that the site is better suited for a commercial use (+1), neutral (0) for a cultural use, and not suitable for residential uses (−2).

Zoning was appropriate for condos (+2), cultural uses (+2), and apartments (+2), but not commercial uses (−2) because the parcel would have to be rezoned to become a commercial use. There were no environmental concerns (+2) for all four potential uses for the site. Parking was less important, as the area contains substantial mixed-use development and nearly 70 percent of the people used public transportation since parking is limited. Thus, parking scores are negative (or −1) for all four end-use types.

Competition is an important factor in determining the market demand, but it scored a 0 for cultural and −2 for the rest. Here, the deciding factor was political influence and neighborhood reaction, which scored the highest for cultural (+2) and was not applicable (0) for the rest.

With respect to total scores, a cultural center is the best use for the property and has an end use total HBU score of 33. The other scores were 8 for condominiums, 19 for commercial, and 6 for apartments. The market window and the finances were not more encouraging for a cultural use than for any other use, but due to the political influence and potential neighborhood reaction, the project can be considered a socially driven but market-validated end use. Note that this high ranking score does not guarantee that there is market demand for the project, just that the site is more appropriately suited for a cultural end use compared to the other uses considered in the analysis.

Babeville

The former Asbury Delaware Methodist Church, now called Babeville, is located on Delaware Avenue at the corner of West Tupper Street in downtown Buffalo, New York. It has been a Buffalo landmark since its erection. The iconic church building is an imposing structure constructed of red medina sandstone with two monumental church spires. The church was closed in the early 1980s. A savior of the church materialized in 1995 when Scot Fisher, president of Righteous Babe Records (RBR), began an intense effort to save the church from certain demolition. The property now has been adapted to a mixed-use commercial project, with a mix of music-related tenants, including an art gallery. For more details, see the case study later in this book (Chapter 16).

The HBU scores for the Babeville project are set forth in Exhibit 5-3. Selected scores were awarded as follows: The site includes a prominently visible and attractive building (+2) due to its location and distinctive church structure. There is a good volume of auto traffic for downtown and the noise level was high, which makes it unsuitable for a residential use. However, if the end use were to be commercial or cultural, the volume of auto traffic would be an advantage (+2) and the noise level would have no effect (0). The site is just minutes from Kensington Expressway and a New York state highway. The airport is about a one-hour drive from the site, but a thirty-minute drive is ideal, so the site scored a −2 for all uses. There is no public transportation station that is less than a five-minute walk, so the site scored −2 for all the end uses. The church scored a +2 for its

Exhibit 5-2 Basic Highest and Best Use Matrix for Jamaica Performing Arts Center

Site Attributes	Church to Condominiums		Church to Cultural Use (Jamaica Performing Arts Center)		Church to Commercial		Church to Apartments	
	Description	Score	Description	Score	Description	Score	Description	Score
Visibility/Views	Views from the property; prominence of the site	2	Better if near an intersection or on a main road	2	Better if near an intersection or on a main road; proves advantageous for business	2	Views from the property; prominence of the site	2
Auto traffic	Lower the daily count, the better; less is better	-2	More is better	2	More is better	2	Lower daily count is better	-2
Pedestrian access	More pedestrian paths available to site is better	2	More pedestrian paths available to site is better	2	More pedestrian paths available to site is better	2	More pedestrian paths available to site is better	2
Highway access	5 min drive but not 1 mile	2	5 min drive but not 1 mile	2	5 min drive but not 1 mile	2	5 min drive but not 1 mile	2
Subway/Bus	Close is good, but too close is bad	2	Closer is better	2	Closer is better	2	Close is good, but too close is bad	2
Airport access	Half hr. drive is good; within 5 min drive or less is bad	2	Half hr. drive is good; within 5 min drive or less is bad	2	Half hr. drive is good; within 5 min drive or less is bad	2	Half hr. drive is good; within 5 min drive or less is bad	2
Noise level	Lower is better	-2	Does not affect the use to a great extent	2	Does not affect the use to a great extent	2	Lower is better	-2
Distance to nearest park	Nearer is better, preferably less than 1 mile	2	Nearer is better, preferably less than 1 mile	2	Nearer is better, preferably less than 1 mile	2	Nearer is better, preferably less than 1 mile	2
Distance to bodies of water	Nearer is better, preferably less than 1 mile	2	Nearer is better, preferably less than 1 mile	2	Nearer is better, preferably less than 1 mile	2	Nearer is better, preferably less than 1 mile	2
Day time employment	n/a = 0	2	n/a = 0	2	More is better	2	n/a = 0	2
Resident base	Whether the residential demographic base supports the intended use	-2	n/a = 0	1	n/a = 0	0	Whether the residential demographic base supports the intended use	-2
Adequate parking	Whether the site provides adequate parking in relation to parcel size and type of use; SITE SPECIFIC	-1	Whether the site provides adequate parking in relation to parcel size and type of use; SITE SPECIFIC	-1	Whether the site provides adequate parking in relation to parcel size and type of use; SITE SPECIFIC	-1	Whether the site provides adequate parking in relation to parcel size and type of use; SITE SPECIFIC	-1

Exhibit 5-2 cont.

Site Attributes	Church to Condominiums		Church to Cultural Use (Jamaica Performing Arts Center)		Church to Commercial		Church to Apartments	
	Description	Score	Description	Score	Description	Score	Description	Score
Zoning	Intended use compatibility; check for underlying zoning	2	Intended use compatibility; check for underlying zoning	2	Intended use compatibility; check for underlying zoning	-2	Intended use compatibility; check for underlying zoning	2
Condition of parcel (Environmental)	Existence of environmental concerns; parcel condition satisfactory/unsatisfactory	2	Existence of environmental concerns; parcel condition satisfactory/unsatisfactory	2	Existence of environmental concerns; parcel condition satisfactory/unsatisfactory	2	Existence of environmental concerns; parcel condition satisfactory/unsatisfactory	2
Size of parcel	Whether the size of the parcel is appropriate for the intended use	1	Whether the size of the parcel is appropriate for the intended use	2	Whether the size of the parcel is appropriate for the intended use	2	Whether the size of the parcel is appropriate for the intended use	-2
Distinctiveness and beauty of structure	Distinctiveness of structure; whether the form of the structure will match its intended function	2	Distinctiveness of structure; whether the form of the structure will match its intended function	1	Distinctiveness of structure; whether the form of the structure will match its intended function	2	Distinctiveness of structure; whether the form of the structure will match its intended function	1
Future expansion potential	Future expansion possibility	-2	Future expansion possibility	0	Future expansion possibility	-2	Future expansion possibility	-2
Competition	Market pressure/need	-2	Market pressure/need	0	Market pressure/need	-2	Market pressure/need	-2
Market window	Whether the market will allow or no	-2	Whether the market will allow or no	2	Whether the market will allow or no	-1	Whether the market will allow or no	-1
Financial window	National and local financial market window(s) for the intended use	-2	National and local financial market window(s) for the intended use	2	National and local financial market window(s) for the intended use	1	National and local financial market window(s) for the intended use	-1
Political influence and neighborhood reaction		0		2		0		0
Totals		8		33		19		6

Note: Default Values: 2 = ideal; 0 = not applicable or neutral; -2 = not ideal.

Exhibit 5-3 Basic Highest and Best Use Matrix for Babeville

Site Attributes	Church to Condominiums		Church to Cultural Use		Church to Commercial (Righteous Babe Records)		Church to Apartments	
	Description	Score	Description	Score	Description	Score	Description	Score
Visibility/Views	Views from the property; prominence of the site	2	Better if near an intersection or on a main road	2	Better if near an intersection or on a main road; proves advantageous for business	2	Views from the property; prominence of the site	2
Auto traffic	Lower daily count is better; less is better	-2	More is better	2	More is better	2	Lower daily count is better	-2
Pedestrian access	More pedestrian paths available to site is better	2	More pedestrian paths available to site is better	2	More pedestrian paths available to site is better	2	More pedestrian paths available to site is better	2
Highway access	5 min drive but not 1 mile	2	5 min drive but not 1 mile	2	5 min drive but not 1 mile	2	5 min drive but not 1 mile	2
Subway/Bus	Close is good, but too close is bad	-2	Closer is better	-2	Closer is better	-2	Close is good, but too close is bad	-2
Airport access	Half hr. drive is good; within 5 min drive or less is bad	-2	Half hr. drive is good; within 5 min drive or less is bad	-2	Half hr. drive is good; within 5 min drive or less is bad	-2	Half hr. drive is good; within 5 min drive or less is bad	-2
Noise level	Lower is better	-2	Does not affect the use to a great extent	0	Does not affect the use to a great extent	0	Lower is better	-2
Distance to nearest park	Nearer is better, preferably less than 1 mile	2	Nearer is better, preferably less than 1 mile	0	Nearer is better, preferably less than 1 mile	-2	Nearer is better, preferably less than 1 mile	2
Distance to bodies of water	Nearer is better, preferably less than 1 mile	2	Nearer is better, preferably less than 1 mile	0	Nearer is better, preferably less than 1 mile	-2	Nearer is better, preferably less than 1 mile	2
Day time employment	n/a = 0	0	n/a = 0	2	More is better	2	n/a = 0	2
Resident Base	Whether the residential demographic base supports the intended use	-2	n/a = 0	0	n/a = 0	0	Whether the residential demographic base supports the intended use	-2
Adequate parking	Whether the site provides adequate parking in relation to parcel size and type of use; SITE SPECIFIC	2	Whether the site provides adequate parking in relation to parcel size and type of use; SITE SPECIFIC	2	Whether the site provides adequate parking in relation to parcel size and type of use; SITE SPECIFIC	2	Whether the site provides adequate parking in relation to parcel size and type of use; SITE SPECIFIC	2
Zoning	Intended use compatibility; check for underlying zoning	2	Intended use compatibility; check for underlying zoning	2	Intended use compatibility; check for underlying zoning	-2	Intended use compatibility; check for underlying zoning	2

Exhibit 5-3 cont.

Site Attributes	Church to Condominiums		Church to Cultural Use		Church to Commercial (Righteous Babe Records)		Church to Apartments	
	Description	Score	Description	Score	Description	Score	Description	Score
Condition of parcel (Environmental)	Existence of environmental concerns; parcel condition satisfactory/unsatisfactory	2	Existence of environmental concerns; parcel condition satisfactory/unsatisfactory	2	Existence of environmental concerns; parcel condition satisfactory/unsatisfactory	2	Existence of environmental concerns; parcel condition satisfactory/unsatisfactory	2
Size of parcel	Whether the size of the parcel is appropriate for the intended use	2	Whether the size of the parcel is appropriate for the intended use	1	Whether the size of the parcel is appropriate for the intended use	2	Whether the size of the parcel is appropriate for the intended use	-2
Distinctiveness and beauty of structure	Distinctiveness of structure; whether the form of the structure will match its intended function	2	Distinctiveness of structure; whether the form of the structure will match its intended function	2	Distinctiveness of structure; whether the form of the structure will match its intended function	2	Distinctiveness of structure; whether the form of the structure will match its intended function	1
Future expansion potential	Future expansion possibility	-2	Future expansion possibility	-2	Future expansion possibility	-2	Future expansion possibility	-2
Competition	Market pressure/need	-2	Market pressure/need	-2	Market pressure/need	2	Market pressure/need	-2
Market window	Whether the market will allow or no	-2	Whether the market will allow or no	-2	Whether the market will allow or no	2	Whether the market will allow or no	-2
Financial window	National and local financial market window(s) for the intended use	-2	National and local financial market window(s) for the intended use	-2	National and local financial market window(s) for the intended use	2	National and local financial market window(s) for the intended use	-2
Political influence and neighborhood reaction		0		0		2		0
Totals		**2**		**7**		**14**		**-1**

Note: Default values: 2 = ideal; 0 = not applicable or neutral; -2 = not ideal.

proximity to parks and water bodies for residential uses, a 0 for cultural uses, and a −2 for commercial, since parks and water bodies do not have rooftops (households that could be potential shoppers or customers), and therefore these features detract from potential demand.

After evaluating data, it was observed that the local area would not support a residential use (−2). Zoning was appropriate for condos, cultural use, and apartments (+2), but not commercial, which scored −2 because the parcel had to be rezoned to become a commercial use. There were no environmental concerns, and adequate parking was an advantage (+2 for all uses).

Lack of competition was an important factor in determining the market demand, and it scored a +2 for commercial. The market and financial windows were not particularly encouraging, but there were interested investors and the neighborhood residents advocated for a commercial end use (scored +2 for commercial). The factor of political influence and neighborhood reaction also played an important role for the commercial use. Accordingly, a commercial use scored the highest overall with a score of 14, while condominiums scored 2, cultural uses scored 7, and apartments scored −1.

Red Door Church

The Red Door Church, which was redeveloped as the Brownstones at Derbyshire, was originally built in 1932 as a modest-sized First English Lutheran Church. Population declined and spread away from the urban core in the 1970s. In 1950, the church membership numbered three hundred families, but by 2002 fewer than fifty remained. The building was put on the market. When no religious groups emerged as buyers, developers acquired the property for conversion into residential condos (see Chapter 12).

At the time it was acquired by the developers, the site contained an 8,000-sq.-ft. church building and adjoining school wing on a 1.5-acre lot in Cleveland Heights, Ohio, a suburb of Cleveland. The site had an abundance of parking and undeveloped land.

Exhibit 5-4 shows the scores for this project. The site is prominently visible (scored +2 for all the end uses) due to its location and visibility from the street. The site is on a minor arterial street with a parkway median and has a moderately significant volume of auto traffic, which becomes a slight disadvantage for residential uses (−1), but represents a slightly favorable factor, scoring a 1, for the cultural and commercial uses. The traffic is also a disadvantage for residential uses because the traffic volume raises noise to a level that is not ideal, resulting in a score of −1 for both the residential uses. However, if the end use were to be commercial or cultural, the auto traffic would be a slight advantage (scoring a +1), and the noise level would have no effect (0). There are no interstate highways nearby, which is considered a disadvantage because most people would have to travel on local roads for at least fifteen minutes to reach the highway. Cleveland's main airport is about a half-hour drive from the site. Since a twenty-minute drive is ideal, the site scored a +1 for all the end uses. The closest public transportation station is less than a five-minute walk (scored +2 for all uses). Red Door Church scores a +1 for its proximity to parks and water bodies, as parks and water bodies are not quite reachable within a ten-minute walk from the site.

The upscale local demographics would support residential use and scored +2 for residential condominiums and a cultural center, unlike for commercial and apartments, which scored only a +1. The distinctiveness and beauty of the structure were

Exhibit 5-4 Basic Highest and Best Use Matrix for Red Door Church

Site Attributes	Church to Condominiums (Red Door) Description	Score	Church to Cultural Use Description	Score	Church to Commercial Description	Score	Church to Apartments Description	Score
Visibility/Views	Views from the property; prominence of the site	2	Better if near an intersection or on a main road	2	Better if near an intersection or on a main road; proves advantageous for business	2	Views from the property; prominence of the site	2
Auto traffic	Lower daily count is better; less is better	-1	More is better	1	More is better	1	Lower daily count is better	-1
Pedestrian access	More pedestrian paths available to site is better	1	More pedestrian paths available to site is better	1	More pedestrian paths available to site is better	1	More pedestrian paths available to site is better	1
Highway access	5 min drive but not 1 mile	-1	5 min drive but not 1 mile	-1	5 min drive but not 1 mile	-1	5 min drive but not 1 mile	-1
Subway/Bus	Close is good, but too close is bad	2	Closer is better	2	Closer is better	2	Close is good, but too close is bad	2
Airport access	Half hr. drive is good; within 5 min drive or less is bad	1	Half hr. drive is good; within 5 min drive or less is bad	1	Half hr. drive is good; within 5 min drive or less is bad	1	Half hr. drive is good; within 5 min drive or less is bad	1
Noise level	Lower is better	-1	Does not affect the use to a great extent	0	Does not affect the use to a great extent	0	Lower is better	-1
Distance to nearest park	Nearer is better, preferably less than 1 mile	1	Nearer is better, preferably less than 1 mile	0	Nearer is better, preferably less than 1 mile	1	Nearer is better, preferably less than 1 mile	1
Distance to bodies of water	Nearer is better, preferably less than 1 mile	1	Nearer is better, preferably less than 1 mile	0	Nearer is better, preferably less than 1 mile	1	Nearer is better, preferably less than 1 mile	1
Day time employment	n/a = 0	2	n/a = 0	2	More is better	2	n/a = 0	2
Resident base	Whether the residential demographic base supports the intended use	2	n/a = 0	2	n/a = 0	1	Whether the residential demographic base supports the intended use	1
Adequate parking	Whether the site provides adequate parking in relation to parcel size and type of use; SITE SPECIFIC	2	Whether the site provides adequate parking in relation to parcel size and type of use; SITE SPECIFIC	2	Whether the site provides adequate parking in relation to parcel size and type of use; SITE SPECIFIC	2	Whether the site provides adequate parking in relation to parcel size and type of use; SITE SPECIFIC	2
Zoning	Intended use compatibility; check for underlying zoning	2	Intended use compatibility; check for underlying zoning	2	Intended use compatibility; check for underlying zoning	-2	Intended use compatibility; check for underlying zoning	2

Category	Description				
Condition of parcel (Environmental)	Existence of environmental concerns; parcel condition satisfactory/unsatisfactory	2	2	2	2
Size of parcel	Whether the size of the parcel is appropriate for the intended use	2	0	-1	-2
Distinctiveness and beauty of structure	Distinctiveness of structure; whether the form of the structure will match its intended function	2	2	-1	0
Future expansion potential	Future expansion possibility	-2	-2	-2	-2
Competition	Market pressure/need	2	-2	-2	1
Market window	Whether the market will allow or no	2	0	-1	-1
Financial window	National and local financial market window(s) for the intended use	2	1	1	-1
Political influence and neighborhood reaction		2	-1	-2	0
Totals		**25**	**14**	**5**	**9**

Note: Default values: 2 = ideal; 0 = not applicable or neutral; -2 = not ideal.

complimentary for condos and cultural use, resulting in a +2 score, but did not seem very suitable for apartments (0) and commercial (−1).

Zoning was appropriate only for condos, cultural, and apartment uses, scoring +2, but not commercial, which scored −2 because the parcel would have to be rezoned to permit a commercial use. There were no environmental concerns, and adequate parking was an advantage, resulting in a score of +2 for all end uses.

Competition favored condominiums (+2). The lower score for cultural end use (−2) reflects the fact that Cleveland's powerful University Circle cultural agglomeration, including the main orchestra venue, several major museums, and related arts uses, is located less than 2 miles away, and that the subject property would be unable to effectively compete in this shadow. Commercial had a low score of −2 due to the fact that the neighborhood was primarily residential. The market window and finances were suitable for condominiums, scoring +2, unlike the other potential uses. Political influence and neighborhood reaction scored the highest for condos (+2).

Highest and best use analysis for the Red Door Church adaptive reuse project resulted in a high score of +25 for condominiums. Among the other uses, cultural scored +14, apartments scored +9, and commercial scored +5.

Enhanced HBU Matrix

The enhanced HBU analysis is very similar to the basic model except that there is an additional step: each site attribute is also weighted according to its perceived importance. There are three columns: weight, description, and score. The weighting is ranked on a I–III scale, with III as most important and I as least important. A detailed example is provided in Exhibit 5-5.

The previous three examples of the basic HBU matrix assumed that each site attribute was equally weighted. We now relax this assumption and explicitly weight the importance of each site attribute on a I–III scale, with the larger number indicating more importance. Now we will have both a raw score (as per the previous examples) and a new weighted score that is more sensitive to the analyst's reflections according to the relative importance levels assigned to each site attribute. For example, if a property has a raw, unweighted score of +2 for visibility and visibility is assigned an importance level of III, then it results in a weighted score of 6 (2 × 3). If visibility has a −1 raw score and a weighting factor of II, its weighted score is −2 (−1 × 2).

The Red Door Church case was used as an example for the enhanced HBU matrix, presented in Exhibit 5-5. This is similar to Exhibit 5-4, with twenty-one attributes and four end uses, but with extra columns that contain the weight of each site attribute and a weighted score. The matrix has five columns and twenty-one rows for each potential use. The columns are: Description,[4] Weight,[5] Weighting factor,[6] Score,[7] and Weighted score.[8] The rows are the site attributes discussed in the basic model. The use that has the highest *weighted score* is the most desirable one to further investigate.

The weights are arrived at by considering the four factors affecting the outcome of adaptive reuse.[9] The weighting scale is III for "very important," II for "somewhat important," and I for "not very important." For example, visibility has a level III importance for all the proposed uses in the Red Door case, but the importance of auto traffic differs by use. Where condos were assigned a weight of III, cultural uses reflected a relative importance level of only I. This is because a cultural use is a place visited only occasionally, so location with respect to auto traffic may not have that much importance as for the other uses. Some important attributes—like zoning, condition of parcel, size of parcel, distinctiveness and beauty of structure, competition, market window, financial window, and political influence and neighborhood reaction—may have the same level of importance, level III, for all the potential end uses.

The final results of the Red Door case using an enhanced HBU analysis yielded the following results: Condominiums are the most desirable end use with a weighted score of 66. A cultural use followed with a score of 31, then apartments with a score of 25, and finally commercial scored 8. Note that the results as determined by the relative order of scores, from highest to lowest, were essentially the same for the weighted and unweighted versions of this HBU analysis, but the analyst would have more confidence in the enhanced approach.

As a final note, the scores themselves are not as important as the order of the bottom-line total scores for the potential end uses. However, higher scoring end uses do deserve a closer look, while lower scoring ones are unlikely to be successful on the site. Finally, our example used twenty-one site attributes, but a valid HBU analysis can also be conducted with a smaller or larger number of well-selected site factors. We used four potential outcomes for simplicity, but this HBU analysis can also be prepared with as many potential outcomes as necessary. At least one of the alternative uses should be close to the "pre-analysis favorite" (if there is one). For example, if the project looks suitable for residential, consider market-rate apartments, low-income apartments, condos, and demolishing all structures to subdivide empty lots.

Market Niche Analysis

A market niche is a focused, quantifiable, and targetable portion or subset of a larger market. It is important to understand both the supply side and demand side of each market to identify a niche for a project. The residential form of this analysis is demonstrated using the Red Door Church case as an example to understand the supply and demand of housing stock in Cleveland Heights, Ohio, during 2006 (when the project was actively marketing units) and to analyze the market penetration rate and success the project achieved in filling the identified niche. This market niche analysis is predicated on housing sales price and tenure (rent vs. own), which is a simplification. Other extensions are also possible (e.g., buyer age, unit type), but these are not demonstrated here. A similar type of retail niche analysis is also possible for commercial/retail end uses. However, because commercial is a relatively unusual outcome for churches and rare for school rehabs, a detailed example is not provided here.[10]

To begin the analysis, housing supply and demand need to be established. The demand-supply analysis in Exhibit 5-6 shows both the total demand for housing (represented by number of households) present around the time of the sale of the Red Door Church condos and the total supply of new and existing homes by price range. This exhibit contains five major columns with between one and three subcolumns in each category. Starting at the left with household income for residents of Cleveland Heights, 2000 census data were extracted and inflated to 2006 dollars using the CPI-U[11] index.[12] The maximum house affordability range was calculated by multiplying the 2006 income range by a factor of 2.7 (Simons and Brennan 1996). The third major column reflects 2000 census data, based

Exhibit 5-5 Enhanced Highest and Best Use Matrix for Red Door Church

Site Attributes	Church to Condominiums (Red Door)					Church to Cultural U...			
	Description	Weight	Weighting factor	Score	Weighting score	Description	Weight	Weighting factor	Scor...
			a	b	a*b			a	b
Visibility/Views	Views from the property; prominence of the site	III	3	2	6	Better if near an intersection or on a main road	III	3	2
Auto traffic	Lower the daily count, the better; less is better	III	3	-1	-3	More is better	I	1	1
Pedestrian access	More pedestrian paths available to site is better	II	2	1	2	More pedestrian paths available to site is better	III	3	1
Highway access	5 min drive but not 1 mile	I	1	-1	-1	5 min drive but not 1 mile	III	3	-1
Subway/Bus	Close is good, but too close is bad	I	1	2	2	Closer is better	I	1	2
Airport access	Half hr. drive is good; within 5 min drive or less is bad	II	2	1	2	Half hr. drive is good; within 5 min drive or less is bad	II	2	1
Noise level	Lower is better	II	2	-1	-2	Does not affect the use to a great extent	II	2	0
Distance to nearest park	Nearer is better, preferably less than 1 mile	II	2	1	2	Nearer is better, preferably less than 1 mile	I	1	0
Distance to bodies of water	Nearer is better, preferably less than 1 mile	II	2	1	2	Nearer is better, preferably less than 1 mile	I	1	0
Day time employment	n/a = 0	II	2	2	4	n/a = 0	II	2	2
Resident base	Whether the residential demographic base supports the intended use	III	3	2	6	n/a = 0	II	2	2
Adequate parking	Whether the site provides adequate parking in relation to parcel size and type of use; SITE SPECIFIC	III	3	2	6	Whether the site provides adequate parking in relation to parcel size and type of use; SITE SPECIFIC	III	3	2
Zoning	Intended use compatibility; check for underlying zoning	III	3	2	6	Intended use compatibility; check for underlying zoning	III	3	2
Condition of parcel (Environmental)	Existence of environmental concerns; parcel condition satisfactory/ unsatisfactory	III	3	2	6	Existence of environmental concerns; parcel condition satisfactory/ unsatisfactory	III	3	2
Size of parcel	Whether the size of the parcel is appropriate for the intended use	II	2	2	4	Whether the size of the parcel is appropriate for the intended use	II	2	0
Distinctiveness and beauty of structure	Distinctiveness of structure; whether the form of the structure will match its intended function	III	3	2	6	Distinctiveness of structure; whether the form of the structure will match its intended function	III	3	2

Weighting score a*b	Church to Commercial Use					Church to Lofts				
	Description	Weight	Weighting factor a	Score b	Weighting score a*b	Description	Weight	Weighting factor a	Score b	Weighting score a*b
6	Better if near an intersection or on a main road; proves advantageous for business	III	3	2	6	Views from the property; prominence of the site	III	3	2	6
1	More is better	III	3	1	3	Lower daily count is better	II	2	-1	-2
3	More pedestrian paths available to site is better	II	2	1	2	More pedestrian paths available to site is better	III	3	1	3
-3	5 min drive but not 1 mile	III	3	-1	-3	5 min drive but not 1 mile	II	2	-1	-2
2	Closer is better	III	3	2	6	Close is good, but too close is bad	III	3	2	6
2	Half hr. drive is good; within 5 min drive or less is bad	II	2	1	2	Half hr. drive is good; within 5 min drive or less is bad	II	2	1	2
0	Does not affect the use to a great extent	II	2	0	0	Lower is better	II	2	-1	-2
0	Nearer is better, preferably less than 1 mile	I	1	1	1	Nearer is better, preferably less than 1 mile	II	2	1	2
0	Nearer is better, preferably less than 1 mile	II	2	1	2	Nearer is better, preferably less than 1 mile	II	2	1	2
4	More is better	II	2	2	4	n/a = 0	II	2	2	4
4	n/a = 0	II	2	1	2	Whether the residential demographic base supports the intended use	III	3	1	3
6	Whether the site provides adequate parking in relation to parcel size and type of use; SITE SPECIFIC	III	3	2	6	Whether the site provides adequate parking in relation to parcel size and type of use; SITE SPECIFIC	III	3	2	6
6	Intended use compatibility; check for underlying zoning	III	3	-2	-6	Intended use compatibility; check for underlying zoning	III	3	2	6
6	Existence of environmental concerns; parcel condition satisfactory/ unsatisfactory	III	3	2	6	Existence of environmental concerns; parcel condition satisfactory/ unsatisfactory	II	2	2	4
0	Whether the size of the parcel is appropriate for the intended use	II	2	-1	-2	Whether the size of the parcel is appropriate for the intended use	II	2	-2	-4
6	Distinctiveness of structure; whether the form of the structure will match its intended function	III	3	-1	-3	Distinctiveness of structure; whether the form of the structure will match its intended function	III	3	0	0

Exhibit 5-5 cont.

Site Attributes	Church to Condominiums (Red Door)						Church to Cultural U			
	Description	Weight	Weighting factor	Score	Weighting score	Description		Weight	Weighting factor	Sco
			a	b	a*b				a	b
Future expansion potential	Future expansion possibility	III	3	-2	-6	Future expansion possibility		III	3	-2
Competition	Market pressure/need	III	3	2	6	Market pressure/ need		III	3	-2
Market window	Whether the market will allow or no	III	3	2	6	Whether the market will allow or no		III	3	0
Financial window	National and local financial market window(s) for the intended use	III	3	2	6	National and local financial market window(s) for the intended use		III	3	1
Political influence and neighborhood reaction		III	3	2	6			III	3	-1
Totals				25	66					14

Note: Default values: 2 = ideal; 0 = not applicable or neutral; -2 = not ideal. I = not very important; II = to some level, important; III = very important.

on income strata, for the number of households in each price range for Cleveland Heights (left subcolumn in that sequence), as well as a small amount of demand from other nearby suburbs (1 percent outer-ring suburbs). This total represents the overall demand (number of households) at various price points along the affordability spectrum. For example, there are 4,976 households that could afford a housing unit valued between $163,000 and $245,000.

Column four contains the supply side of the equation. Using 2000 census data by price range and inflated to 2006 dollars, in addition to median contract rental data from the Census Bureau, the number of house and apartment units in each range was estimated.[13] To this number would be added any new units in the market area constructed since the last census, plus any residential competitive units actively being marketed, less any demolitions. Vacant units (from the U.S. Census) need to be distributed throughout the market as well, as U.S. Census data provide only detailed price information

about occupied units. So for this example, there are a total of 4,252 units in the same $163,000 to $245,000 price band.

Column five provides the results of the niche analysis, by price band. This is the net demand for housing (both for purchase and rental) by price range. Exhibit 5-6 shows that the net demand numbers for units valued below $65,000 are close to zero. At the other end of the market, the net demand figure for the $490,000 and up range is −611 (indicating a saturated, overserved market). In the price range of the proposed Red Door Church project, there was a gross demand for 9,719 (4,976 + 2,523 + 2,220) homes in the $163,000 to $490,000 price band. The gross supply for the same price band was 8,421 (4,252 + 2,193 + 1,976), leaving a net demand (demand less supply) of 1,298 units. Thus, the competitive balance in the price range where the Red Door project is competing is favorable because it is underserved. Since the project size is about twenty-five units, it would represent only about 2 percent of overall net demand. This is a modest market

hting ore *b	Description	Weight	Weighting factor	Score	Weighting score	Description	Weight	Weighting factor	Score	Weighting score
			Church to Commercial Use					**Church to Lofts**		
			a	b	a*b					
	Future expansion possibility	III	3	-2	-6	Future expansion possibility	III	3	-2	-6
	Market pressure/need	III	3	-2	-6	Market pressure/need	III	3	1	3
	Whether the market will allow or no	III	3	-1	-3	Whether the market will allow or no	III	3	-1	-3
	National and local financial market window(s) for the intended use	III	3	1	3	National and local financial market window(s) for the intended use	III	3	-1	-3
		III	3	-2	-6		III	3	0	0
				5	8				9	25

penetration rate, and indicates a *go* market outcome. This analysis validates that there were favorable market conditions for marketing the Red Door condominiums. This market analysis is corroborated by the actual project outcome: the project was a success and yielded profit to the developer. It was a successful, market-driven end use for the old historic church building.

Conclusion

This chapter has addressed adaptive reuse market analysis using two important tools: HBU analysis (basic and enhanced) and market niche analysis. The templates developed in the chapter are based on three major case studies: the Jamaica Performing Arts Center (church to performing arts center) in Queens, New York; Babeville (church to commercial) in Buffalo, New York; and the Red Door Church (church to condominiums) in Cleveland Heights, Ohio.

A basic highest and best use analysis for each project was demonstrated, and an enhanced version with weighted attributes

was developed for the Red Door Church project. A residential market niche analysis was also performed for the Red Door Church project, demonstrating the validity of unit price points and magnitude of the project compared with net market demand.

Highest and best use analysis and market niche analysis are important tools for developers to use in predevelopment workups of potential rehab projects. Especially in a soft market, understanding project strengths and weaknesses can not only help avoid making a bad mistake, but can also enhance understanding of site attributes and their relative attractiveness in light of various market price and unit characteristics. The next chapter examines the financial side of rehab project analysis and explains the use of debt and equity using financial tools available to move a project from the market analysis stage to the point of financial feasibility.

Exhibit 5-6 Residential Market Niche Analysis for the Red Door Church

	2006 Household Income Range[1]		2006 House Price Affordability Range Adjusted[2]		Number of Households in Range (Demand)[3]			Units in Range (Supply)[4]			Net Demand[5]
					Cleveland Heights	1% Outer Suburban	Total	Owner	Renter	Total	
1	Less than	$12,000	Less than	$32,000	2,095	136	2,231	489	1,653	2,142	89
2	$12,000	$18,000	$32,001	$49,002	847	127	974	235	663	898	76
3	$18,000	$24,000	$49,003	$65,337	1,247	133	1,380	523	774	1,297	83
4	$24,000	$30,000	$65,338	$81,672	1,074	146	1,220	516	537	1,053	167
5	$30,000	$42,000	$81,673	$114,342	2,343	310	2,653	1,139	1,281	2,420	233
6	$42,000	$60,000	$114,343	$163,347	3,517	430	3,947	2,121	1,349	3,470	477
7	$60,000	$90,000	$163,348	$245,022	4,416	560	4,976	3,158	1,094	4,252	724
8	$90,000	$120,000	$245,023	$326,697	2,191	332	2,523	1,847	346	2,193	330
9	$120,000	$180,000	$326,698	$490,047	1,960	260	2,220	1,803	173	1,976	244
10	$180,000	$240,000	$490,048	$653,397	565	70	635	1,156	90	1,246	(611)
TOTAL					**20,255**	**2,504**	**22,759**	**12,987**	**7,960**	**20,947**	

Data sources and calculations:

1. "2006 Income Range" = 1999 Income Range x Cleveland CPI-U change from 1999 to 2006 (17.2%)
2006 CPI-U of 195.3 minus 1999 CPI-U of 166.6 = change of 28.7, or 30.56%
2. "Affordability Range" = Income Range x 2.7 (conservative side of 2.5 to 3.0 rule of thumb ratio)
3. "Households" from 2000 U.S. Census Data: Household Income in 1999 for Cleveland
"Outer" = Most of outer-ring suburbs in Cuyahoga County @ 1% of households from 2000 U.S. Census Data
4. "Units in Range" in Cleveland
"Owner" units represent owner-occupied units from 2000 U.S. Census Data in Cleveland by Value. Range adjusted for CPI-U change.
"Renter" units represent capitalized value of median rents for renter-occupied units from 2000 U.S. Census in Cleveland by Gross Rent Range adjusted for CPI-U change.
5. Net demand = Total Households in Range less Total Units in Range.

Notes

1. Source: PROPEX.COM classroom (http://www.propex.com/C_g_hbuo.htm).
2. Description: This variable describes the site attribute in the context of the end use. The description helps in scoring that particular site attribute's suitability for that particular end use.
3. Score: The numerical score for the site attribute for the end use. The score indicates the importance of the attribute in decision-making for the end use.
4. Description: This variable describes the site attribute in the context of the end use. The description helps in scoring that particular site attribute's suitability for that particular end use.
5. Weight: The weight indicates the analyst's view of the level of importance of a particular site attribute.
6. Weighting factor: The factor that, when multiplied by the score, gives the weighted score.
7. Score: The numerical score of the site attribute for the end use. The score indicates the suitability of an attribute for the end use. This is the same as in the basic HBU matrix.
8. Weighted score: This is calculated by multiplying the score with the weighted factor for each site attribute.
9. The factor categories are: location, linkages, history and historic importance, and market demand and financial feasibility.
10. For example, see Simons and Brennan (1996).
11. CPI-U: Consumer Price Index for all urban users. Source: http://www.bls.gov/news/release/cpi.nr0.htm.
12. 2006 Income Range = 1999 Income Range × Cleveland CPI-U change from 1999 to 2006 (17.2 percent), where 17.2 percent was derived from: 2006 CPI-U of 195.3 − 1999 CPI-U of 166.6 = change of 28.7, or 17.2 percent.
13. Units in the range consist of "Owner occupied" and "Renter occupied" units. "Owner" represents owner-occupied units from 2000 U.S. Census Data from Cleveland Heights by value range adjusted for CPI-U change; "Renter" represents capitalized value of renter-occupied units from 2000 U.S. Census in Cleveland and Cleveland Heights by Gross Rent range adjusted for CPI-U change. For example, an $800 per month unit is multiplied by 12 to annualize revenues: $9,600. The net revenue after operating expenses is assumed to be 80 percent, yielding net operating income before taxes of $7,680. This is converted to value by dividing by the assumed cap rate of 9 percent, which results in a unit value of $85,300.

References and Works Consulted

Clapp, J. M. 1987. *Handbook for Real Estate Market Analysis.* Englewood Cliffs, N.J.: Prentice-Hall.

Conduct a Market Analysis. http://www.vainteractive.com/inbusiness/editorial/sales/ibt/market_analysis.html.

Fanning, S. 2005. *Market Analysis for Real Estate: Concepts and Applications in Valuation and Highest and Best Use.* Chicago: Appraisal Institute.

NetMBA. http://www.netmba.com/marketing/market/analysis/.

PropEx. http://www.propex.com/C_g_hbuo.htm.

Schmitz, A., and D. L. Brett. 2001. *Real Estate Market Analysis, a Case Study Approach.* Washington, D.C.: ULI—the Urban Land Institute.

Simons, R. A., and J. Brennan. 1996. "Development of Inner City Retail Niche Markets." In *Megatrends in Retail Real Estate,* edited by Jon Benjamin. Norwell, Mass.: Kluwer Academic Publishers.

6

FINANCING THE ADAPTIVE REUSE OF RELIGIOUS BUILDINGS AND SCHOOLS

Adam N. Saurwein and
Robert A. Simons

After determining that adequate market demand exists for an adaptive reuse project, the developer's next task is to determine whether the project is financially feasible. The developer must be able to secure adequate financing that covers development costs and meets lenders' equity requirements. Understanding financial tools is especially important in an adaptive reuse deal because creative financing tools and strategies often are required to make these deals successful. The purpose of this chapter is to illustrate the numerous sources of financing for the adaptive reuse of religious buildings and related structures such as educational facilities.

Redevelopment of religious and instructional buildings that originally had been constructed many years ago and for purposes different than their intended use after redevelopment can be a tricky proposition. While purchasing an existing building may save a developer some construction expenses, retrofitting churches for new uses can significantly increase other costs compared to new construction (see Chapter 4). The redevelopment of a property involves the balancing of these above-average costs and risks with a proportionate potential for return on total investment. Nevertheless, these increased costs can result in a gap between the total funds available for a project and the total cost of an adaptive reuse project. Gap financing tools can make feasible a project that suffers from increased development costs (relative to its end appraised value or cash flow and related ability to support debt) but is an otherwise viable project.

Even if a project involves financial complexities, these complexities usually can be managed using both conventional and creative real estate development practices. Despite their potential for increased costs and risks, historic churches and related build-ings are often ideal opportunities for using creative financing tools, such as historic preservation tax credits and nonprofit grants. The case studies in this book provide examples of projects with multiple layers of financing using many of the tools discussed in this chapter.

A deal's ownership structure can be altered to maximize financing opportunities. Some ownership vehicles (corporate structures) provide added opportunities to increase sources of capital, structure the decision-making authority for the project, and spread investment risk across several parties.

This chapter starts with a discussion of basic concepts of financing and common sources of equity and debt, including both private and public debt. It moves on to an explanation of the Developer's Toolbox, which catalogues the financial tools available for use in the adaptive reuse of churches and schools. The chapter concludes with a discussion of various forms of ownership of a real estate deal.

Equity

Any real estate deal is built on two basic concepts: equity and debt. The form of both equity and debt can range from rather simple, traditional sources of financing to complex and innovative financing tools.

Equity is essentially an amount of hard cash or cash equivalent that the developer contributes to a project, usually at the project's inception. Equity represents the extent to which a development team contributes financially toward project creation, with the rest of the project financed through debt instruments. If a project fails, the development team risks losing its equity contribution. Accordingly, these equity funds, including any pledged collateral, are the at-risk capital contribution to a project. Lenders require that a developer "have skin in the deal." This means that the lender may provide the loan only on the condition that the developer provides a percentage of the total project cost as an equity contribution.

Developers have several reasons for increasing the number of equity participants in a project. First of all, a developer may lack sufficient equity to meet the lender's requirements. Most developers are thinly capitalized. Developers often seek equity from nonbank sources to fill a gap in their equity contribution requirement. A developer may seek to fill the equity gap with capital contributions from another development partner or a community organization. Sometimes another party may hold a capital asset that is required for a project. If the developer cannot afford to acquire the property or if the property owner refuses to relinquish control of it, the developer can try to bring the owner into the deal as a partner. The property owner's capital asset can qualify as an equity contribution toward the project. There also may be tax advantages available to a private for-profit partner that contributes appreciated property to a partnership.

A second reason why developers seek equity contributions from other sources is to spread the risk associated with a project. Equity participants are personally invested in a project at least by the amount of equity that each contributes to the project. Equity is generally considered to be *at-risk* capital because if a project fails, the equity participants risk losing at least the amount of their equity investment. To reduce his or her individual risk exposure, a developer may seek additional equity partners to contribute a portion of the at-risk capital component of a project. This may consequently free up some of a developer's equity for use in other projects, enabling the diversification of a developer's portfolio.

Exhibit 6-1 All else being equal, lowering equity contributions increases rates of return.

Developer Equity	$10,000,000	$2,000,000
Cost of Project	$10,000,000	$10,000,000
Project before Tax Cash Flow	$750,000	$270,000
Annual Rate of Return on Equity	7.5%	13.5%

Third, reduced equity contributions potentially translate into higher rates of return on equity for a developer. This can be demonstrated by a simple example (see Exhibit 6-1). If a developer's initial equity investment is the entire $10 million project cost (that is, there is no debt service), and the project had a pretax annual cash flow of $750,000, then the project's rate of return on equity would be 7.5 percent (annual income of $750,000 divided by capital investment of $10 million). In contrast, a developer might reduce his or her capital contribution to $2 million and finance the remaining $8 million with debt. If the annual debt service is $480,000, the project's annual pretax cash flow is reduced from $750,000 to $270,000, but the project's rate of return on equity is increased to 13.5 percent ($270,000 annual income after debt service divided by $2 million equity contribution). This simplified example illustrates the dramatic impact that reducing equity contributions can have on increasing the rates of return.

Another important consideration regarding equity is the timing of the receipt of funds. Lenders usually require a developer to meet all cash equity requirements at the close of the deal. Some sources of equity, such as deferred tax credit equity, may not be available as a lump sum but rather are disbursed incrementally over a period of years. In such cases, the developer may need to sell the tax credits or seek a *bridge loan,* discussed later in this chapter, along with permanent financing to close a deal. Accordingly, developers need to pay close attention to when funds will be received and be prepared to use creative financing tools to fill any gaps in financing the deal.

Not all sources of equity would be ideal or even available for all real estate projects. Every project is different. Adaptive reuse projects are generally more complicated than new construction. However, the added complexity of these deals also provides an opportunity to use more creative sources of equity and debt.

Even though direct capital contributions are the simplest source of equity, adaptive reuse projects often require more creative forms of financing. Equity can come from numerous sources and take various forms. Fortunately, developers are not always limited to narrowly defined sources of equity.

Sometimes an adaptive reuse project has value to a community in addition to its potential cash flow. For example, the adaptive reuse of a historic structure may increase property values in a neighborhood or make the community a more attractive place to live. Cash may be available from a wider variety of sources, such as community development corporations and economic development agencies, when a project appears to be catalytic or have the potential to increase property values in a community.

The following discussion looks at both traditional and creative equity sources and types. Sometimes a source can define the type of equity, and sometimes a particular type of equity can come from several sources. However, the point of this chapter is to bring attention to the many sources and types of financing available. Accord-ingly, for the sake of simplicity, the term "source" is used here to indicate both a source of equity and a type of equity.

Developer and Partner Equity

Individual developers, general partners, limited partners, corporations, and real estate investment trusts (REITs) are examples of some of the most common sources of developer equity and equity participants. Whether the developer seeks general partners to share project risk and management or limited partners who only risk their capital without management responsibility is a decision that needs to be considered and negotiated, depending on the financial objectives of the parties involved.

Different equity partners have different investment objectives. Some equity participants may expect to receive a greater portion of the cash flows while others may prefer returns through the appreciated value of the property. Both the ownership structure and the capital structure have important tax implications that must be considered thoroughly with the help of a tax professional. These issues should be considered in conjunction with decisions regarding the project ownership structure, which is discussed in more detail below.

Capital Assets

The term "equity" has taken on an increasingly broad and expansive meaning. In addition to cash, other assets, such as control of an interest in land or other real property, can be contributed to the deal as cash equivalents. Therefore, a developer can limit his or her cash exposure and gain control of the property by making the landowner a general or limited partner in the deal. This strategy can decrease the amount of the developer's required up-front capital compared to the developer purchasing the property outright. In addition, making the landowner a partner may be necessary when the landowner is simply unwilling to relinquish control of his or her property. In either case, the developer may count the value of the property toward the lender's equity requirements.

Moreover, developers can often find creative ways to generate equity by creating value in a property. A common way to accomplish this value creation is through rezoning. Take, for example, a property originally located in a zoning district designated residential or institutional. Perhaps the neighborhood has changed through commercial development over the years. The land no longer may be suitable for residential or institutional development. Accordingly, the land will be less valuable for those uses than for commercial use. The developer could acquire the property at a discount and then rezone it to a more valuable use, such as commercial. If the new zoning designation reflects a higher and better use for the property than the old zoning designation, then the market value of the rezoned property should increase, thereby creating value. This property with its increased value may be contributed to the deal as equity.

Another related approach is to create value by improving real estate. For example, a developer could buy raw land and then construct improvements on that property. The new *value* of the land, plus improvements, should be worth more than the actual *cost* of the land and improvements. This newly created value may be counted as equity on the developer's books. This new value could be refinanced, used to collateralize loans, or realized through sale of the property. In the context of an adaptive reuse project, a developer can also create value in an existing property by making repairs, constructing capital improvements, or rehabbing an existing structure.

In-Kind Services

In-kind services also may create value and qualify as equity. For example, a developer usually charges a fee for providing development services to a project. A lender may allow—or even require—that the developer leave the development fee in the deal until the project is complete. In such a case, the development fee may qualify as an equity contribution.

Grants

Equity may also be available from other stakeholders in a project. A *grant* is a contribution of other people's money that does not have to be repaid. In addition to state and local governments, private or nonprofit organizations that have an interest in seeing a deal move forward are the usual sources for grant funding. Projects usually have to qualify for grant money by meeting certain criteria. Some grants are aimed at the redevelopment of specific types of properties, such as brownfield redevelopment, while others facilitate projects with specific uses, such as affordable housing.

In addition to privately funded community foundations, the federal government provides an annual allocation of community development block grants (CDBGs) to qualifying communities. The funds are often used to provide equity for development activities. Community development corporations (CDCs) often receive and administer allocations of CDBG funds. State, county, and municipal economic development agencies, in addition to CDCs, are usually excellent resources for identifying sources of grant funding.

Venture Capital (VC) Funds

Venture capital funds function in a role similar to the role of the limited partner, except venture capital funds usually demand an even higher return on their equity contribution. The returns may be in the form of a percentage of the cash flow from a project or an increase in the value of the real estate after sale. There are many different types of venture capital funds, including some that focus specifically on investment in real estate projects.

Easements

Developers can sell certain easements to generate equity for a project. Easements are legally enforceable agreements that grant the purchaser a particular interest in a property. Historic preservation easements grant the purchaser the right to protect an architectural or cultural resource. Conservation easements preserve green space and restrict development of parks and natural environments. Under some circumstances, the redevelopment of churches and schools can provide excellent opportunities to utilize these easements. These easements are usually purchased by organizations that seek to preserve historic buildings or to protect the natural environment. Often, such easements add value to a property by assuring that certain beneficial aspects of the property will be maintained in perpetuity. Be aware, however, that an easement becomes part of the chain of title. This means that the agreement can "run with the land" and remain in effect after the sale of the property—likely restricting future development plans, such as modification of a building or development of natural areas. Accordingly, this restriction has the potential to affect the value of the property either positively or negatively, so the decision to sell an easement should be considered thoroughly and made carefully.

Tax Credits and Their Conversion to Equity through Syndication

A tax credit is a dollar-for-dollar recognition of payment of taxes due. Tax credits function either as a reduction in the amount of taxes owed or, if they are *refundable tax credits,* as a dollar-for-dollar payment made by the government directly to the taxpayer through the tax system.

There are numerous state and federal tax credit programs geared toward facilitating challenging real estate development projects. Tax credit programs may be aimed at projects that involve the historic preservation of buildings, the construction or renovation of low-income housing, the creation of jobs, or the remediation of brownfields. A taxpayer qualifies for tax credits by meeting certain criteria and fulfilling the specific conditions of the relevant tax credit program. For example, a developer wishing to use federal historic preservation tax credits must perform historic preservation work on qualified buildings in accordance with standards set forth by the Secretary of the Interior. Tax credit programs also may require an ongoing compliance period. If a project falls out of compliance, a developer may be obligated to return the tax credits. Therefore, successfully meeting all program qualifications and maintaining compliance monitoring are important considerations in the successful utilization of tax credit programs.

Tax credit programs are not necessarily a source of equity by themselves. Developers certainly could choose to keep the tax credits and claim them on their income tax return. However, tax credits themselves are insufficient to provide equity to a project since tax credits involve a time element. Tax credits are not available until after work is complete and a taxpayer files a tax return. In addition, tax credit programs may cap the annual allowable tax credit at a certain limit but allow the credit to be taken over several years. These considerations make tax credits alone a poor source of equity at the inception of a project, the time when a developer needs equity the most. A developer often needs cash immediately to meet equity requirements for the construction phase of development. Fortunately, a developer can turn future tax credits into a present source of equity by syndicating the credits, hence converting a future stream of tax credits to a single present value figure.

A developer can sell the rights to future tax credits to generate an immediate equity contribution to a project. Tax credits can be assigned either to a direct investor or to a tax credit syndicator, who then finds investors willing to purchase the tax credits.[1] The price of tax credits varies with market conditions. The price of tax credits also depends on how soon the tax credits are received. For example, the benefits of historic preservation tax credits are received all at once upon a project's completion, so they are more valuable to investors than some of the other forms of tax credits, which are redeemable over a period of years and subject to strict compliance rules.

Investors purchase tax credits to lower their effective tax rates, increase their after-tax earnings, and even improve their corporate image. Financial institutions have traditionally played a significant role as direct investors in tax credits, which can offset their large tax liabilities. In 2009, there was an economic climate in which financial institutions faced lower tax liabilities due to decreased profits. Thus, the demand for tax credits fell, and this was reflected in lower (discounted) prices being paid for tax credits. In more up markets, the discount is typically reduced, and the stream of tax credits sells for closer to its full value.

Tax credit syndication typically involves an intermediary who markets tax credits to investors. Syndication of tax credits is subject to government regulation. Laws require syndicators to offer tax credit purchasers a prospectus disclosing the terms and risks of the investment. In addition, syndicators charge fees for their syndication services. Both regulatory compliance costs and syndication fees increase the cost and complexity of utilizing tax credits. Therefore, developers interested in tax credit syndication should take care to seek guidance from an organization familiar with managing tax credit syndication.

The Role of the Community Reinvestment Act in Tax Credit and Other Financing

The Community Reinvestment Act (CRA)[2] is a federal statute that requires commercial banks that receive Federal Deposit Insurance Corporation (FDIC) insurance to make credit available in neighborhoods where they take deposits. Accordingly, lending institutions seek eligible community development investment projects located in low- and moderate-income (LMI) census tracts[3] through *qualified community development investments*.[4] Qualified community development investments include direct investments and lending through community and economic development corporations. These investments bring commercial and housing development projects to fruition through special underwriting and significant capital, equity, and gap financing. Examples include fixed-interest capital investments to microenterprise organizations (including microfunds), intermediary lenders, credit unions, low-income housing tax credits (LIHTC) financing, new market tax credit financing, and financing to support new or substantially rehabbed units of housing. Other qualifying activities may include community-based child care and educational, health, or social services targeted to low- and moderate-income residents.

Private sources of equity or capital are often available from banks that purchase tax credits to fulfill their CRA requirements. It is worth noting that several years ago motivated institutions with CRA requirements, usually national and regional banks, paid more than $1 per dollar of tax credit in order to satisfy their CRA requirement. However, due to disruptions in the market, projects during and just after the Great Recession of 2008 were fetching considerably less. Nevertheless, the CRA is an instrumental government tool for making private financing available to projects. In addition to purchasing tax credits, institutions can fulfill their CRA requirement through offering community development investment loans and letters of credit as part of their CRA portfolio.

Historic Tax Credits

Adaptive reuse projects involving religious buildings and/or schools may qualify for historic tax credits, which are offered by the federal government and by many states. The official name of the federal program is Historic Tax Credit (HTC), while the state names may vary (Ohio's program, for example, is called the Historic Preservation Tax Credit program). The federal program is administered by the National Parks Service in conjunction with State Historic Preservation Offices (SHPO).[5] The federal program offers a 20 percent federal tax credit for qualified rehabilitation expenses. Like other tax credits, historic preservation tax credits may be sold to generate equity for the construction phase of an adaptive reuse project. State programs typically offer additional tax credits beyond the federal program.

Like many tax incentive programs, historic tax credits come with a number of rules and restrictions on use. To qualify for the historic tax credit, a structure needs to meet two basic criteria. First, the building must be certified as a historic structure by the National Park Service. The structure should either be located in a National Register Historic District and certified as contributing to the historic character of the district, or be registered individually on the National Register of Historic Places. The certification process is fairly straightforward.

Second, when the rehabilitation work is complete, the SHPO and National Park Service need to make a determination that the rehabilitation meets the Secretary of the Interior's *Standards for Rehabilitation*.[6] Alterations to the appearance of an historic building can disqualify the developer from taking the tax credits. Developers should consult an experienced historic preservation specialist when planning to use historic tax credits.

The amount of the historic tax credits the project would be eligible for is based on *qualified rehabilitation expenditures* (QRE). Eligible expenses for this program go beyond simply hard costs for "brick and mortar," and typically include some soft costs such as the developer fee and architect fees, but not land costs. The taxable basis for creating historic tax credits and low-income housing tax credits (see below) are not usually the same.

Historic tax credits are available for use only on income-producing properties, such as rental-residential, commercial, agricultural, or industrial. The property must be held by the tax credit applicant and used for an income-producing purpose during a five-year compliance period, or else the applicant risks having the tax credits revoked. However, after the five-year period, the property may be sold or converted for another use. Accordingly, residential rental properties may subsequently be converted to condominiums and sold off. The Willow Avenue Condominiums, part of the Lafayette Street Project case study in Fayetteville, Arkansas, shown later in this book, provides an excellent example of this strategy of holding residential rental units to satisfy the five-year compliance requirement for historic tax credits and then selling the units as condominiums.

Low-Income Housing Tax Credits

A developer should consider utilizing federal low-income housing tax credits (LIHTCs) when an adaptive reuse project involves the construction of affordable, residential rental property. These federal tax credits are allocated to states, which then administer the program through state housing agencies. The LIHTC program offers a tax credit that may be claimed over a ten-year period for qualified expenses, including property acquisition and rehabilitation expenses.

A developer considering participation in the LIHTC program should be aware that there are strict requirements for this program. The LIHTC program caps tenant rents at certain, published limits.[7] However, the rent limitations apply only to the portion of the rent paid by the tenant. Accordingly, other rental assistance programs, such as Section 8, may be used to raise the total rent above the level of LIHTC rent restrictions.

Program regulations establish a two-tiered system of occupancy and income thresholds: the 20–50 Rule and the 40–60 Rule. For the purpose of the 20–50 Rule, at least 20 percent of the units must be rent-restricted and occupied by households with incomes at or below 50 percent of the HUD-determined median income, adjusted for household size.[8] Likewise, the 40–60 Rule requires that at least 40 percent of the units must be rent-restricted and occupied by

households with incomes at or below 60 percent of the HUD-determined median income, adjusted for household size.[9] The entire property does not have to consist of low-income rental units, but the tax credit will be applied only to the qualified, low-income units.

The property usually must operate under these income limits for at least a thirty-year compliance period, as determined by written agreements with the agency issuing the tax credits. The minimum compliance period is fifteen years, with—except in certain circumstances—an additional fifteen-year "extended use period."

Adding to the complexity of the LIHTC program, two separate tax credit rates can apply to qualifying expenses, depending on several factors, including whether the project qualifies as a substantial rehab and whether the project is considered a federally subsidized project. The rates are nominally referred to as the 4 percent and the 9 percent credit rates, although the actual rates vary every month and are published monthly in a Revenue Ruling update by the IRS.[10] In December 2011, for example, the 4 percent rate was actually 3.20 percent, and the 9 percent rate was actually 7.47 percent. A state allocating agency competitively awards the 9 percent credit to projects for their qualifying construction costs (for new construction) or the substantial rehabilitation credit for projects financed with conventional debt. The 4 percent credit is available as-of-right for qualifying projects financed with tax-exempt municipal bonds. In addition, acquisition expenditures qualify only for the lower rate. A developer should consult an expert in the use of LIHTC to determine which expenses qualify for which rate.

In addition to the federal LIHTC program, many states offer state LIHTC programs.[11] Like other tax credits, these state and federal tax credits may be sold to generate acquisition and construction capital for the rehabilitation of a church or school into affordable residential rental property.

New Market Tax Credits

New Market Tax Credits (NMTCs) are a much less direct way for a developer to finance an adaptive reuse project, but they are worth mentioning. The NMTC program is similar to the LIHTC credit program in that both target low-income areas. However, while the LIHTC program is limited to financing rental housing, the NMTC program is much broader in scope and focuses on nonresidential, economic development activities.

The NMTC program is administered by the Department of the Treasury through the Community Development Financial Institutions Fund. The Department of the Treasury does not award NMTCs directly to a development project or developer, but rather allocates tax credits for distribution to community development entities (CDEs). A CDE is a corporation or partnership that has a mission of serving or providing investment capital for the benefit of low-income communities or people. CDEs include organizations such as community development corporations (CDCs), community development financial institutions (CDFIs), community development venture capital funds, and small business investment companies. Developers can consult their lender about NMTCs, since banks often have community development banking divisions that operate their own subsidiary CDE. CDEs receive tax credits in return for investments in eligible businesses, including real estate development. These investments may be in the form of low-interest loans, equity, or capital investments. Accordingly, depending on the particular programs available

through a CDE, the NMTC program may indirectly provide a developer with either equity or debt financing, or both.

According to the Community Development Financial Institutions (CDFI) Fund, through 2006 the NMTC program financed 550 projects nationally where the principal activity was the development or leasing of real estate. These projects represent almost half of the projects funded by NMTC and received almost 70 percent of the NMTC financing.[12] Accordingly, any developer working in a qualifying low-income area should research CDEs in the area. The CDFI Fund maintains both a searchable database of CDFIs awardees[13] and a list of certified CDFIs.[14] Developers should find these to be useful resources for identifying financing options through the NMTC program.

In addition, the NMTC can be combined with some other programs that may be useful to a developer of an adaptive reuse project. Often, schools and churches are located in older, lower-income neighborhoods. Adaptive reuse projects in these neighborhoods may be ideal recipients of equity through both the historic preservation tax credit program and the NMTC program. However, NMTCs generally cannot be combined with LIHTC, except in the case of certain mixed-use developments. Developers should consult the program regulations[15] or a consultant for more information. The Buffalo Babeville case study in this book uses New Market Tax Credits.

Debt

The remainder of a real estate development project that is not financed through equity is financed through debt. Debt may be characterized as loans, liabilities, or *other people's money.* Generally, debt must be repaid; however, some debt financing has characteristics of equity and may be considered a hybrid form of debt and equity. For example, some loans begin to amortize, but the balance of principal and interest is forgivable upon the fulfillment of certain conditions.

Debt is closely tied to *leverage,* which involves using financial instruments and borrowed capital to lower the amount of equity that a developer must contribute to a deal and to increase the developer's rate of return. To increase leverage, equity is replaced with debt. As debt-to-equity ratios increase, a project is said to become more highly leveraged. Lower equity requirements usually mean that the developer has less personal or corporate money at risk in the deal. A developer has a variety of options when using debt financing. Often, these various debt financing tools can be used in conjunction with one another.

However, increasing the use of debt sources may cause concern for the lender. Lenders have an expectation of being repaid. In order to ensure repayment, senior mortgage lenders have loan-to-value ratios of 80 percent or less and may also require that the developer offer collateral to secure the repayment of the loan. In the case of nonpayment of a debt, a lender can seize the collateral to satisfy the debt.

Whenever a developer seeks to use multilayered debt financing on a redevelopment project, the developer will have to negotiate the collateralization of each loan. Loans are either categorized as nonrecourse or recourse, depending on the source of collateral. *Nonrecourse* debt is secured by the financed property itself, rather than by personal guarantees of the developer or corporation. If the borrower defaults, the lender is *limited to seizing the financed property itself.* Conversely, the lender will typically require a developer or corporation to give a personal guarantee for a *recourse* loan. If the borrower defaults, then the lender may *seize the borrower's personal property,* such as stock or other assets, in addition to the financed property. Lenders will often require personal guarantees from less experienced developers or for riskier development deals.

When multiple lenders are involved in a deal, a developer also will have to address the *priority* that each lender has in the underlying collateral. Lenders usually want to be guaranteed a first-priority, or *senior,* position. If a borrower is forced into foreclosure, the first-position lender will have priority in being repaid (in full subject to available funds recovered) from the value of the collateral. However, sometimes lenders will agree to *subordinate* their debt when they believe that the subordinate financing will increase the value of the project, or at least not harm it. The increased property value then provides additional collateral to the lender, increasing the chances that the lender will be repaid in the event of default. Economic development agencies that provide debt financing to projects are often willing to take a second- or third-priority position in the project's capital structure, sometimes referred to as the *capital stack.* Other lenders also may be convinced to take a *junior* position, but they will charge a higher interest rate to compensate for their increased risk.

The use of debt helps spread the risk of loss. Developers seek to maximize the use of debt to minimize the exposure of their at-risk capital—their equity contribution. Instead of putting their own money at risk, they prefer to finance a project with *other people's money.* As noted earlier, by using other people's money to decrease their required equity contribution, developers can increase their rate of return on equity.

However, this can be a double-edged sword. Inexperienced developers may be required to give personal guarantees on loans.

During tough economic times, lenders may require that even experienced developers collateralize their loans with more than just the financed property. This places the developer's personal assets at a risk of loss. In addition, increasing the use of debt financing will increase the developer's debt service. The developer would then be required to use a greater portion of net operating income to service the debt. If the property suffers from excessive vacancy or operating expense increases, the developer would have a greater risk of default. This concern becomes even greater in the case of an economic recession or a downturn in the real estate market. Accordingly, developers need to carefully consider the proper capital structure of any project.

The next section describes several sources of debt that could be available to finance rehabilitation of formerly religious buildings and schools.

Construction Loans

There are two basic private loans involved in a real estate development deal: a construction loan and a permanent loan. A construction loan is typically an *interest-only,* short-term (a year or two) loan. The construction loan finances the construction phase of the redevelopment project, before there are any substantial cash flows. The developer usually makes several draws on the loan over the course of the construction phase. The construction loan is typically the senior mortgage. When construction is complete, the construction loan is replaced with a permanent loan.

Permanent Loans

A permanent loan is usually an amortizing, long-term loan. A permanent loan is sometimes referred to as a *take-out loan* because it takes the construction loan out of the capi-

tal stack and replaces it with permanent financing. Permanent loans may be fixed-rate or adjustable-rate. For properties that the developer intends to hold and lease after construction, the developer refinances the construction loan with a permanent first mortgage loan. A developer may secure in advance a commitment for take-out financing. The property needs to generate enough operating income to adequately cover the *debt service,* the amount owed to the bank each month to repay the debt. However, in the build-and-sell context, the developer will not have operating income or permanent financing. Instead, each purchaser (and there may be dozens as individual units are sold off) will obtain his or her own permanent financing, which will buy down/pay off part of the developer's construction loan at the time of purchase. However, if a developer must hold excess inventory for too long, the developer may have to seek a bridge loan or mezzanine loan.

Bridge Loans

Sometimes a developer needs a source of interim financing after construction is complete but before a property is sold or a permanent loan closes. Bridge loans—also known as *swing loans*—provide relatively quick, short-term financing to *bridge* this funding gap. Bridge loans carry a relatively high interest rate and are typically secured by the financed property.

Mezzanine Loans

A mezzanine loan is a specific type of bridge loan. While bridge loans are typically collateralized by the financed real estate, mezzanine loans are typically collateralized by the development company's stock and other assets, rather than the financed property. Occasionally, mezzanine financing takes the form of an equity investment with preferred returns, similar to limited partner equity. This form is not clearly debt or equity, but a hybrid. The term "mezzanine loan" may sometimes have a broader usage and refer to other types of subordinated debt outside bridge loans (e.g., without the time constraint between construction and permanent financing).

Wraparound Mortgage

A wraparound mortgage is a junior (subordinated) mortgage to finance the balance of an unpaid first mortgage, plus any remaining purchase money balance. A *wraparound* mortgage is often a form of seller financing, in which the seller acts as the lender for the new buyer. The seller/lender extends junior financing to a new buyer. Then the new buyer makes payments to the seller/lender, who is responsible for making payments on the first mortgage. The seller/lender can benefit in two ways. First, the seller typically adds a premium to the interest rate of the first mortgage in order to both cover the debt service on the first mortgage and provide the seller/lender with a profit. Second, the wraparound mortgage will typically be for a larger amount of principal than the balance of the first mortgage, providing the seller with the full amount of interest on the difference.

However, almost all wraparound mortgages are prohibited by a *due-on-sale clause* in the first mortgage agreement. A due-on-sale clause stipulates that the first mortgage may be called due upon the sale or transfer of ownership of the financed property. Since title is actually transferred in a wraparound mortgage arrangement, the due-on-sale clause is triggered, and the first lender is entitled to call the entire balance on the first mortgage due. If the seller cannot afford to pay the balance due on the first mortgage, the first lender would

have the right to foreclose on the property. Therefore, wraparound mortgage financing schemes generally should be avoided.

Forgivable Loans or "Soft Debt"

Forgivable loans, often referred to as "soft debt," are a hybrid of both debt and equity. Like a regular loan, forgivable loans usually require a repayment period. The loan is amortized over a long-term amortization schedule, but payments are required only for the first several years of the amortization period. Generally these programs condition loan forgiveness on the fulfillment of certain conditions aimed at encouraging development that benefits the community in some specific way. For example, some forgivable loans require that a certain number of jobs be created in order to qualify for forgiveness. Other loans are targeted to make high-quality housing affordable in certain neighborhoods. Upon fulfilling the conditions of the loan, the remainder of the loan is *forgiven,* either incrementally or all at once. Local economic development agencies are a common source of forgivable loans. These types of instruments may have tax consequences or advantages for the owner/ borrower with respect to mortgage interest deductibility and depreciation, so the reader is advised to check with an expert real estate accountant.

Bond Financing and Other Public Debt

Public entities can offer an additional source of debt financing. Municipalities have the ability to finance development through the issuance of bonds. The bonds can take several forms, including *general obligation bonds, revenue bonds,* and *tax increment financing.* From the point of view of the developer, bonds can be a source of equity to a project. However, these bonds function much more like debt instruments from the perspective of the issuing state or local government. Sometimes a state or municipality may be the developer of a project, so bond financing would function more like a source of debt.

It is important to note that the tax-exempt municipal bond market was disrupted by the recent downturn in the economy (the Great Recession), which tapered off in 2012. Many municipalities purchased insurance to boost their bond ratings. Unfortunately, many of the companies that insure municipal bonds are the same companies that guaranteed securities backed by subprime loans. The downgrading of the credit rating of these insurance companies has similarly impacted the rating of the municipal bonds that they have insured. Lower credit ratings on bonds have reduced the amount of capital available to municipalities for reinvestment, which has been detrimental to the feasibility of various publicly financed real estate development projects. Nevertheless, bond financing is likely to continue to play an essential role in the financing of redevelopment projects, so familiarity with the various types of bond financing is important.

General Obligation Bonds

General obligation (GO) bonds offer investors a return on their investment and are fully backed by the municipality's general taxing authority. In this sense, the bonds function as a debt for the issuing government entity and must be repaid through general tax revenues, special tax levies, or legislative allocations. However, when the bonds are purchased on the bond market, the sale generates revenues that function as equity that can be contributed to a project.

In the context of real estate development, GO bonds are most often used to offset the cost of infrastructure related to affordable housing development, although their use is not limited to such development. Since many jurisdictions require voter approval for the issuance of GO bonds, developers often must take care to build community support for a project before seeking bond financing. However, the use of GO bonds is quite rare in the context of the types of real estate projects (smaller rehabilitations) that are the focus of this book.

Revenue Bonds

Revenue bonds are similar to GO bonds in that they are issued by a municipality and sold to generate revenue for a project. However, unlike GO bonds, which are backed by the general taxing authority of a government entity, revenue bonds are backed only by the revenue generated from a particular project. Accordingly, revenue bonds are issued most often to finance a large, revenue-generating project, such as a stadium or a performing arts center. Revenue bonds are more common tools than GO bonds for financing real estate development but less popular than tax increment financing (TIF), discussed below. Because they are not backed by the full faith and credit of a local government, revenue bonds have a higher interest rate and are slightly riskier.

Tax Increment Financing

Tax increment financing is another form of bond financing. TIFs have become a popular method to finance a wide variety of development and redevelopment projects, and are popular, for example, for financing parking structures. The bonds are sold to generate revenue that is used to finance infrastructure and other public improvements necessary to facilitate a redevelopment project. Since investment in a neighborhood has a tendency to raise property values, property tax revenues increase. TIF bonds are repaid using these increased tax revenues—the *tax increment*—in a specific geographic area surrounding the development project. One significant advantage of using TIF, rather than other forms of bond financing, is that TIF usually does not require general voter approval, and is therefore easier and cheaper to obtain.[16] However, a TIF district must be formed and a specified percentage of those property owners must agree to this planned disposition of their future property taxes. In states where property tax abatement is common, use of a TIF generally prevents property tax abatement from being used.

The Developer's Toolbox

Exhibit 6-2 is a Developer's Toolbox of financial tools available for the adaptive reuse of religious buildings and schools. The table compiles the sources of equity and debt discussed above, together with some additional tools not discussed in detail in the text. The following sections describe the column headings and how to read the table.

- *Name:* This column collects the names of various financial tools. Sometimes the table contains a generic name for a source, such as *permanent loan,* and other times the source refers to a very specific program, such as the *Historic Tax Credit (HTC) Program.*
- *Type:* The type column generally categorizes each financial tool as *equity* or *debt.* However, some of the financial tools cannot be easily categorized as either, while other sources function as both debt and equity.
- *Source or Administering Agency:* This column gives a developer an idea of who to contact to secure a particular source of funding. Some of the programs are federally funded but administered locally, making a particular source or adminis-

tering agency difficulty to identify. Economic development agencies are usually helpful in identifying particular funding sources for development activities.
- *Description:* The program description provides a general overview of the program's function and purpose.
- *Eligibility:* Financial tools often have certain eligibility criteria that must be met. This column briefly describes general eligibility requirements. Many programs have very strict eligibility and compliance requirements, so check the individual program regulations or contact the administering agency for more information.
- *Limitations:* Certain programs are available only for specific purposes or are targeted at specific types of development projects. This column indicates potentially limiting factors in each program.
- *Compatibility:* Some programs are ideally paired with certain programs. Other programs are specifically prohibited from being used in conjunction with certain programs. The compatibility column offers developers suggestions for other sources of funding that can be used with a particular program and alerts developers about prohibited combinations of funding sources. Sources that can be combined with any other source are categorized as *universal.*
- *Web site:* Whenever possible, a web page with more information about each source of financing is included for convenient reference.

Ownership Structure and Its Impact on Financing

In addition to arranging the capital structure of a project, one of the most important considerations for a developer is the ownership structure of a project. Decisions regarding the ownership structure of

Exhibit 6-2 Developer's Toolbox for the Adaptive Reuse of Religious Buildings and Schools

Name	Type	Source or Administering Agency	Description
Developer Equity	Equity	Developer	The developer provides cash, property, or in-kind services to satisfy the lender's equity requirements.
General Partner Equity	Equity	General partner	Investors contribute equity in exchange for an ownership interest in a project, usually in proportion to the amount of equity contributed.
Limited Partner Equity	Equity	Limited partner	Investors contribute equity, usually in exchange for a negotiated, preferred return on the investment.
Nonprofit Foundations Grants	Equity	Nonprofit community foundations	Various foundations offer grants for projects that will have an economic, social, or cultural impact on a community.
Venture Capital	Equity	Venture capital fund	Investors or an investment fund contributes cash to projects with higher risk in exchange for a higher rate of return.
Brownfields Assessment and Cleanup Grants	Equity	U.S. EPA in conjunction with local government and economic development agencies	Assessment grants provide funds to inventory, characterize, assess, and conduct planning (including cleanup planning) for brownfield sites. Cleanup grants provide funds of up to $200,000 to carry out cleanup activities at a specific brownfield site owned by the applicant.
Community Development Block Grant (CDBG)	Equity	States, cities, and counties administer an allocation from HUD	The CDBG entitlement program allocates discretionary funds to larger cities and urban counties to develop viable communities by providing decent housing, a suitable living environment, and opportunities to expand economic opportunities. Grants can be used for a broad range of activities, including site acquisition, demolition, public works, and rehabilitation of public and private buildings.
Conservation Easement	Equity	Government agencies or land trusts	A legally enforceable land preservation agreement in which a landowner sells the right to develop real estate beyond a mutually agreed upon level to a government agency or a land trust for the purpose of land conservation.

Eligibility	Limitations	Compatibility	Website Link (as of March 2009)
N/A	There are no limitations; however, the more equity that is used by a developer, the more the developer is exposed to risk.	Universal	N/A
N/A	N/A	Universal	N/A
N/A	N/A	Universal	N/A
Eligibility varies. Check with individual foundations.	Limitations vary. Check with individual foundations.	Universal	http://foundationcenter.org/findfunders/
N/A	Venture capital investors expect a preferred return on their investment.	Universal	www.cdvca.org and http://www.occ.treas.gov/cdd/SBRG09032003.htm#VentureCapital
May not be available directly to a for-profit organization. However, applicants may be able to partner with local governments or redevelopment agencies to form eligible public-private partnerships.	Limitations on use are imposed by both federal and local rules.	Works well with other brownfield programs and CDBG	http://www.epa.gov/brownfields/applicat.htm
Cities and urban counties, which then allocate funds to individual projects. Priority of projects varies by jurisdiction.	Principally for low- and moderate-income persons in central cities, for the removal of slum or blight, or for urgent community development needs.	Compatible with most other programs	http://www.hud.gov/offices/cpd/community development/programs/entitlement/index.cfm and http://www.hud.gov/offices/cpd/community development/programs/stateadmin/index.cfm
Varies, since these are essentially privately negotiated agreements. Check with individual government agencies or land trusts.	Once recorded, an easement becomes part of the property's chain of title and usually "runs with the land" in perpetuity, which binds not only the owner who grants the easement but also all future owners. Future development of the property may be prohibited.	Compatible with most other programs	http://www.alcnet.org/protect/easements and http://www.nature.org/aboutus/howwework/conservationmethods/privatelands/conservation easements/

Exhibit 6-2 cont.

Name	Type	Source or Administering Agency	Description
Historic Preservation Easement	Equity	Information about these programs is compiled by the National Park Service in partnership with State Historic Preservation Offices, tax benefits are administered by the Internal Revenue Service, and easements are generally purchased by historic preservation organizations.	A preservation easement is a voluntary legal agreement that protects a significant historic, archaeological, or cultural resource. In addition, the owner may obtain substantial tax benefits. Under the terms of an easement, a property owner grants a portion of, or interest in, his or her property rights to an organization whose mission includes historic preservation.
HOME Investment Partnerships Program	Equity	States, cities, and counties administer an allocation from HUD.	The HOME program is a HUD-administered federal block grant to state and local governments. The grants can be used to implement housing strategies to increase housing opportunities for low-income households. Eligible uses of funds include demolition, housing rehabilitation, new construction of housing, and site acquisition for non-luxury housing. The program is targeted at creating affordable housing for low-income households.
Section 202 Supportive Housing for the Elderly	Equity	HUD	HUD provides a capital advance to finance the development of rental housing with supportive services for the elderly. As long as the housing remains available to very low-income elderly persons during the compliance period, the advance is interest-free and repayment of the advance is not required.
Federal Historic Tax Credit	Equity†	The program is administered by the National Park Service and the Internal Revenue Service in partnership with State Historic Preservation Offices.	Historic preservation tax credits offer a 10% or 20% tax credit for qualified rehabilitation expenses.

Eligibility	Limitations	Compatibility	Website Link (as of March 2009)
Only certified historic properties, listed in the National Register of Historic Places or located in a registered historic district and certified by the U.S. Department of the Interior as being historically significant to the district, are eligible.	Once recorded, an easement becomes part of the property's chain of title and usually "runs with the land" in perpetuity, which binds not only the owner who grants the easement but also all future owners. Future alterations to the property may be prohibited.	Can be used with historic tax credits and CDBG funds	http://www.nps.gov/hps/tps/tax/easement.htm
States, cities, and urban counties are eligible to receive HOME grants. In turn, those government entities award funding to for-profit, not-for-profit, and local housing authorities for eligible development projects.	HOME-assisted rental housing must comply with certain rent limitations, published each year by HUD. The program also establishes maximum per unit subsidy limits and maximum purchase-price limits. Participating jurisdictions are required to match funds from nonfederal sources. HOME-funded housing units are required to remain affordable for a specified compliance period.	Often used in conjunction with LIHTC and CDBG funds	http://portal.hud.gov/hudportal/HUD?src=/program_offices/comm_planning/affordablehousing/programs/home/
Private, nonprofit organizations and consumer cooperatives are eligible for funding.	Occupancy must remain open to very low-income households with at least one person 62 years of age or older.		http://www.hud.gov/offices/hsg/mfh/progdesc/eld202.cfm
Only certified historic properties, listed in the National Register of Historic Places or located in a registered historic district and certified by the U.S. Department of the Interior as being historically significant to the district, are eligible. This credit is available for properties rehabilitated for commercial, industrial, agricultural, or rental residential purposes.	Rehabilitation work has to meet the Secretary of the Interior's Standards for Rehabilitation as determined by the National Park Service. Only rehabilitation-related expenses are eligible for the tax credit.	CDBG, LIHTC, can be used with historic preservation easements	http://www.nps.gov/hps/tps/tax/index.htm and http://www.novoco.com/related_program/historic_tax_credit/index.php

Exhibit 6-2 cont.

Name	Type	Source or Administering Agency	Description
Low-Income Housing Tax Credit (LIHTC)	Equity†	HUD and state housing agencies	Provides a refundable tax credit for the acquisition and construction of new or existing affordable rental housing. Tax credits can be syndicated to generate equity for a project.
State Brownfield Tax Incentives	Equity or reduced property or income tax liability	State agencies generally administer these programs; the federal government previously has offered a tax credit, although the program has expired	These programs vary by state, but typically consist of tax credits, tax abatements, or tax deductions for qualifying brownfield cleanup and redevelopment projects.
New Market Tax Credit (NMTC)	Debt and/or equity, depending on the particular program	Community Development Financial Institutions (CDFI) Fund under the U.S. Department of the Treasury	The CDFI Fund was created to expand the availability of credit, investment capital, and financial services in economically distressed communities. Each year, tax credits are allocated for equity investments made to certain qualifying entities, known as Community Development Entities (CDEs), through the CDFI Fund. The CDEs make Qualified Low-Income Community Investments (QLICIs). QLICIs include, among other things, debt or equity investments in businesses and real estate projects in low-income communities.
Brownfields Revolving Loan Funds	Debt, although it may be forgivable	U.S. EPA in conjunction with local government and economic development agencies	Provides funds for local governments and community development organizations to provide low-interest loans and subgrants to carry out cleanup activities at brownfield sites.
Section 108 Loan Guarantee	Loan guarantee	HUD	HUD will guarantee up to five times a public entity's latest approved CDBG amount as security for loans for a broad range of capital intensive activities, including site acquisition, construction or rehabilitation of housing or public facilities, and installation of public infrastructure.

Eligibility	Limitations	Compatibility	Website Link (as of March 2009)
The development of residential rental properties meeting certain rent and occupancy criteria.	LIHTC programs have strict rent and occupancy limitations. Not all units in a development are required to follow these restrictions, but the tax credits are only available for the qualified units. Risk of recapture for noncompliance. Credits are claimed over a ten-year period.	Can be used with the HOME program, historic tax credits, and CDBG funds.	http://www.hud.gov/ offices/cpd/affordable housing/training/web/ lihtc/basics/ and http://www.novoco.com/ low_income_housing/ lihtc/irs_guidance.php
Eligibility varies. Check with individual states.	Limitations vary. Check with individual states.	Usually can be combined with other development tools.	http://www.epa.gov/ brownfields/partners/ finan_brownfields_epa_ print.pdf
The NMTC program requires that eligible projects be located in low-income communities or serve low-income persons.	Income limits and prohibited business uses. Generally not available for residential rental uses, unless part of a mixed use development, but may be used for for-sale residential. Risk of recapture for noncompliance.	Works well with Historic Tax Credits and brownfields programs. Not available for use with LIHTC.	http://www.cdfifund.gov/ what_we_do/programs_ id.asp?programID=5 and http://www.cdfifund.gov/ what_we_do/need_a_ loan.asp
May not be available directly to a for-profit organization. However, applicants may be able to partner with local governments or redevelopment agencies to form eligible public-private partnerships.	Limitations on use are imposed by both federal and local rules.	Works well with other brownfield programs and CDBG.	http://www.epa.gov/ brownfields/applicat.htm
Cities and urban counties, which then allocate funds to individual projects. Priority of projects varies by jurisdiction.	Principally for low- and moderate-income persons in central cities, for the removal of slum or blight, or for urgent community development needs.	Compatible with CDBG.	http://www.hud.gov/ offices/cpd/community development/programs/ 108/index.cfm

Exhibit 6-2 cont.

Name	Type	Source or Administering Agency	Description
Economic Development Initiative Grant	Loan guarantee or equity	States, cities, and counties administer an allocation from HUD	EDI grants enhance the security of guaranteed loans or the viability of projects financed with Section 108 loans by providing loan guarantees to local governments or providing equity directly to projects. These grants may be use for the same activities as Section 108 loan guarantees for the purpose of leveraging public and private dollars to create jobs for moderate- and low-income individuals.
Construction Loan	Debt	Banks	The proceeds of a construction loan finance the construction phase of redevelopment. Often a construction loan is an interest-only, short-term loan.
Permanent Loan	Debt	Banks	The proceeds of a permanent loan "take out" the construction loan. A permanent loan is generally an amortizing, long-term loan, although many have a balloon payment.
Bridge Loan	Debt	Banks, investment pools	Bridge loans typically provide relatively quick, short-term financing for real estate deals until a property is sold or refinanced. Bridge loans carry a higher interest rate than permanent financing and are typically secured by the financed property.
Mezzanine Loans	Debt, although sometimes functions like preferred equity, thus a hybrid	Private equity funds and investment pools	Mezzanine loans are a type of bridge loan. However, unlike bridge loans, mezzanine loans are typically collateralized by the stock of the development company itself, rather than the financed property. Occasionally, mezzanine financing takes the form of an equity investment with preferred returns, similar to limited partner equity.
Forgivable Loan Programs	Hybrid	Economic development agencies	Economic development agencies will offer low interest loans to qualifying projects in exchange for some benefit to the community, such as job creation or brownfield remediation. The loan will be on a long-term amortization schedule--for example, 20 years. After the borrower successfully meets the program requirements over a period of several years, the balance of the loan is forgiven.
General Obligation (GO) Bond	Hybrid	State or local government	GO bonds can be issued by a government entity to generate equity for a real estate development project. GO bonds are backed by the general credit and taxing power of the issuing jurisdiction.

Eligibility	Limitations	Compatibility	Website Link (as of March 2009)
Cities and urban counties, which then allocate funds to individual projects. Priority of projects varies by jurisdiction.	Used for industrial and commercial redevelopment of brownfield sites. Must be used in conjunction with a Section 108 loan guarantee.	Section 108 Loan Guarantees	http://www.hud.gov/offices/cpd/economic development/programs/edi/index.cfm
Lenders have minimum equity and debt service coverage requirements that must be met.	Limitations vary but generally depend on the borrower's creditworthiness and sometimes loan guarantees.	Universal	http://www.construction weblinks.com/Industry_Topics/Financing_for_Projects/Banks_Lenders/banks_lenders.html
Lenders have minimum equity and debt service coverage requirements that must be met.	Limitations vary but generally depend on the borrower's creditworthiness and sometimes loan guarantees.	Universal	http://www.construction weblinks.com/Industry_Topics/Financing_for_Projects/Banks_Lenders/banks_lenders.html
Eligibility varies. Check with individual lenders.		Universal	
Negotiated with lender or investor.	Requires personal guarantee of the developer and/or development company.	Universal	
Eligibility varies. Check with local economic development agencies.	Limitations vary. Check with local economic development agencies.		
Eligibility varies. Check with individual states and localities.	Usually requires voter approval.	Universal	N/A

Exhibit 6-2 cont.

Name	Type	Source or Administering Agency	Description
Revenue Bond	Hybrid	State or local government	Revenue bonds can be issued by a government entity to generate equity for a real estate development project. Revenue bonds are supported solely by the revenue generated from a specified source, such as a performing arts center or toll bridge.
Tax Increment Financing (TIF)	Hybrid	Usually municipalities or local taxing authorities	Tax increment financing is a form of bond financing. TIF uses the increased tax revenues in a district surrounding a redevelopment project to repay municipal bonds issued to finance infrastructure and other public improvements facilitating the redevelopment.

† Tax credit programs are not equity *per se*, but tax credits are often packaged and transmitted (via syndication) to generate equity for a pro

a real estate project can impact the financial structure of the deal, and vice versa. Various ownership forms provide opportunities for additional sources of financing and ways to spread risks and liabilities. The combination of the financial structure and the choice of ownership entity also can have significant tax implications. Some of the most common forms of real estate ownership are discussed below. There may be other, more creative, forms of real estate ownership available but not discussed here. Therefore, a developer should consult an attorney and accountant before making any decision regarding the optimal form of ownership for a development project.

Individual Ownership

The simplest form of real estate ownership is personal, individual ownership. This form of ownership gives a developer the greatest amount of control, but also exposes the developer to the greatest amount of risk and liability. This ownership form is rarely utilized for real estate development projects.

General Partnerships

Equity sources can be increased and liabilities spread through the use of a general partnership. In a partnership, multiple individuals or entities create a new entity (an LLC, discussed below) for the purpose of undertaking and managing a development project. The partners agree to share in the profits and losses of the partnership, usually based on the proportion of each partner's equity investment. Each partner has some management responsibility, and overall the general partnership has the controlling role in the project. This form of ownership also has the advantage of functioning as a pass-through entity for most tax purposes, avoiding the double taxation problem of Subchapter C corporations. Nevertheless, partners can be individually liable for the debts and actions of the partnership.

Limited Partnerships

General partnerships may supplement the raising of capital by including limited partners into a real estate deal. Limited part-

Eligibility	Limitations	Compatibility	Website Link (as of March 2009)
Eligibility varies. Check with individual states and localities.	Primarily used for public works projects. The projects must generate revenue.	Universal	N/A
Eligibility varies. Check with individual municipalities. TIF is often negotiated on a case-by-case basis.	Limitations vary. Check with individual municipalities. The terms of a TIF project are usually negotiated with individual municipalities on a case-by-case basis. Sometimes TIF financing is reserved for redevelopment projects in distressed neighborhoods.	Not compatible with property tax abatement.	http://www.realtor.org/smart_growth.nsf/Pages/tifreport?OpenDocument

ners usually contribute equity in exchange for a negotiated, preferred equity return. In addition, limited partners may not take an active role in controlling the partnership, but rather take the position of a "silent partner" and view the partnership as an investment opportunity. By including limited partners in a deal, a developer can increase the amount of equity available to a project. Profits, however, must typically be distributed first to limited partners before any remaining profits are distributed to general partners.

Even though an investor is nominally a "passive" investment partner, developers will no doubt be required to answer to those investors. Consequently, those perceived as the decision-makers in a project may not be wielding the real economic power. Developers need to keep this in mind when planning the capital structure of a project and be prepared to deal with demands and concerns of various investors, even those who are nominally limited partners or "passive" investors.

Corporations

Real estate projects can be owned by corporations. A corporation, sometimes referred to as a Subchapter C corporation for tax purposes, is a business entity in which shareholders invest in the corporation by purchasing shares, which are ownership interests in the corporation. The corporation is controlled by a board of directors, which hires management and oversees major decisions of the corporate entity. A corporation can provide opportunities for multiple investors to invest in the company. The corporate entity also generally shields the investors from any personal liability for the debts and actions of the corporation beyond their equity investment through the purchase of shares. However, corporations suffer from double taxation because the income of the corporate entity itself is taxed, then the distributions of the corporation are taxed as income to the corporation's shareholders. Accordingly, corporations are usually not formed specifically for the purpose of holding development-type real estate projects.

Limited Liability Companies

Most real estate projects in the United States are owned through a limited liability company. LLCs have characteristics of both a corporation and a partnership.[17] An LLC has the advantage of insulating developers from personal liability for the debts and actions of the LLC. In addition, an LLC is essentially a pass-through tax entity, with tax liability passing straight to the members of the LLC. The pass-though tax treatment of LLCs avoids the double taxation problem of corporations. Members of an LLC can be individuals, general partnerships, for-profit corporations, and nonprofit corporations.

Public, Not-for-Profit, and Community Organizations

When urban redevelopment or adaptive reuse of a property is being considered, not-for-profit and community organizations are commonly involved in the discussions. Community development corporations (CDCs) provide programs and services to support a neighborhood or community. CDCs often are focused on economic and neighborhood development. Various other community organizations also exist to support community development activities. CDCs and other community organizations have funds available for investment in projects that are expected to have a positive impact on a community. These groups tend to focus on projects that will benefit the greater community in some way. For example, a CDC may be interested in a project that adds housing to a neighborhood that has been losing population, or a community organization may support a project that preserves a historic or an iconic structure in a neighborhood. These groups can provide a developer with equity contributions, grants, or low-interest loans for an adaptive reuse project. In addition, CDCs can garner community support for a project and often can facilitate the approval and permit process with the municipality.

CDCs and community organizations can serve as developer, general partner, or limited partner in adaptive reuse projects in their community. Certain creative financing tools require a project to be developed in partnership with a not-for-profit community organization. Before embarking on an adaptive reuse project, a developer should identify any relevant community development corporations and other not-for-profit organizations that are potential partners or stakeholders. Engaging these organizations can provide financing to a project and facilitate the redevelopment process.

In addition, it has become increasingly important for public and nonprofit equity partners in a development to establish a long-term strategy to eliminate loan defaults in the event of cash flow or other failures by the developer that could place the project in jeopardy. This "work out" strategy should be prenegotiated so that it can be implemented without delay if necessary. Lenders may be more willing to fund a project when they are assured that a public entity is willing to assume responsibility for a project in case of the developer's default. For example, municipalities can guarantee loan repayments for a predetermined period of time to provide time to keep the project afloat while issues are resolved. Public development partners also should consider requiring personal guarantees from for-profit partners, securing other assets to collateralize a project, and negotiating in advance an intercreditor agreement with primary and potential secondary lenders.

Developers have a wide variety of sources for financing an adaptive reuse project. The capital structure of a project is composed of equity and debt, and influenced by the ownership structure of the deal. For convenient reference, sources of debt and equity are summarized in Exhibit 6-2. The sources of financing and ownership vehicles discussed in this chapter can be found throughout the case studies in this book and in the tables summarizing the case studies in Chapter 11.

Notes

1. For a further discussion of tax credit sale and syndication in the context of low-income housing tax credits, see http://www.hud.gov /offices/cpd/affordablehousing/training/web /lihtc/basics/syndication.cfm.
2. 12 U.S.C. § 2901 *et seq.*
3. To locate a census tract number by address, see http://factfinder.census.gov.
4. These categories are included per current guidelines provided by the Federal Financial Institution Examination Council (FFIEC) Q & As as guidance for lenders to comply with CRA. See http://www.ffiec.gov/cra/default .htm and http://edocket.access.gpo.gov/2009 /pdf/E8–31116.pdf.
5. General program regulations are published under title 36 C.F.R. § 67 of the Code of Federal Regulations, available at http://www .gpoaccess.gov/ecfr/index.html.
6. The Secretary of the Interior's *Standards for Rehabilitation* are published under 36 C.F.R. § 67.7, available at http://www.gpoaccess.gov /ecfr/index.html.
7. For a description of how maximum rents are determined, visit http://www.danter.com /taxcredit/rents.htm. A maximum rent and income calculator is available at http://www .danter.com/TAXCREDIT/getrents.HTML.
8. HUD income limits are available at http:// www.huduser.org/datasets/il.html.
9. HUD income limits are available at http:// www.huduser.org/datasets/il.html.

10. The actual rates are published monthly in a Revenue Ruling of the Internal Revenue Service. An index of applicable federal rates can be found at http://www.irs.gov/pub/irs-drop/rr-11–31.pdf. To find the rate, find this or a similar more updated document, click on the applicable month, and then look for Table 4 to find "Appropriate Percentages Under Section 42(b)(1)." However, these rates may be difficult for a layperson to find. The rates can also be found more easily on commercial Web sites.
11. See http://www.novoco.com/low_income_ housing/lihtc/state_lihtc.php for more information about individual state programs.
12. http://www.cdfifund.gov/what_we_do/nmtc /NMTCProgramProjectsFinancedThrough 2006.asp.
13. http://www.cdfifund.gov/awardees/db/index .asp.
14. http://www.cdfifund.gov/what_we_do/ programs_id.asp?programID=9#certified.
15. http://www.novoco.com/new_markets/ policy/index.php.
16. Another useful tool similar to TIF is a business improvement district (BID). A BID is a public-private partnership formed by business owners in a defined geographic area who elect to self-impose a special tax to provide services and invest in development projects in addition to what is already provided by the city government. However, the use of a BID to finance an individual redevelopment project is somewhat rare.
17. An S corporation is similar to an LLC in that both provide owners with limited liability protection from creditors and offer pass-through treatment for tax purposes. However, an S corporation generally has more formal requirements and offers less flexibility than an LLC.

## 7

DOLLARS AND CENTS
OF ADAPTIVE REUSE OF
RELIGIOUS BUILDINGS
AND SCHOOLS

Adam N. Saurwein and
Robert A. Simons

ot all religious building adaptive reuse projects are profitable without public subsidies. Sometimes communities find nonfinancial value in saving old buildings that are important to the community because they are highly visible landmarks or otherwise provide an amenity to the neighborhood. Often these projects are developed by nonprofit or public agencies and financed with heavy public subsidies and little expectation of financial returns, such as the Jamaica Performing Arts Center in New York, discussed in a case study in Chapter 13 of this book. However, most developers need to be sure that a project will return a profit. Developers also tend to rely heavily on debt financing. Accordingly, projects need to produce enough positive cash flow to cover expenses and debt service. Most importantly, a developer needs to be sure that he or she will receive some profit from the project, or else the project will not justify the amount of work required to make the project move forward. Therefore, it is important for developers to analyze the financial feasibility of a project to assess both the profitability of a project and its anticipated rate of return. Like all for-profit ventures, *if it doesn't make dollars, it doesn't make sense.*

This chapter covers real estate valuation and more complex cash flows over time than are presented in the case studies, which generally contain static sources and uses (at the time of project development) and stable year cash flows presented as a snapshot of the operating expenses and revenues for an unspecified time frame. Below, the topics of real estate valuation and calculating sources of project equity with tax credits are addressed. Sample cash flows for two projects—a church-to-condo development and sell-off deal with no subsidies, and a school-to-apartments deal with a mix

of low-income and market-rate tenants developed using historic preservation tax credits and low-income housing tax credits (LIHTCs)—are provided. The topic of captive tenants (owner-occupied commercial projects) is also briefly mentioned.

Financial Feasibility and Valuation

Financial feasibility analysis is a projection of expenses and revenues to assess the value of a project as accurately as possible. Sources of funds (debt and equity) are where the money to develop the deal comes from, which is covered in Chapter 6. However, the *value* of a project, generated in an appraisal, can be defined in several different ways. The three primary approaches to value are the *cost approach,* the *market approach,* and the *income approach.*

The Cost Approach to Value

The cost approach to value looks at the cost to acquire and construct a project. This approach focuses on the *uses of funds.* Chapter 4 of this book takes a closer look at various considerations related to the cost of completing adaptive reuse projects. In addition, there is a simplified pro forma included with each case study. Generally, the expense items capture the cost to construct a project. The total expenses, therefore, represent the value of a project in terms of cost. Subtracting the total cost, including finance charges and sales expense, from the total projected sales figures renders a *back of the envelope* analysis of the financial feasibility of a project. Many developers analyze the value of projects by measuring the return on total project cost. If projected revenues cannot exceed the cost of the project (including adequate return to capital invested), the project is a *no-go.* If revenues justify the project, a more detailed financial analysis, using the income approach to value, is justified. The cost approach to value is especially important to adaptive reuse projects to establish the qualified basis for various tax credit programs.

The Market Approach to Value

The market approach to value looks to the sales of similar properties to determine what price the market is willing to bear either for an entire project or for individual units in a project. The market approach is a form of appraisal that attempts to derive a value for a subject property by identifying its distinguishing characteristics and then identifying properties with similar characteristics that have recently sold in the subject property's market area. Some characteristics commonly used in real estate appraisal include the size of the property or unit, the year it was built, the number of bedrooms, and the number of bathrooms. Factors such as the style of the structure and the materials used to construct it are also considered. Comparable properties and sale figures can be found with the help of an appraiser or realtor, or by perusing public records.

The market approach is often difficult to apply to adaptive reuse projects because comparables, especially those sold recently enough to be instructive as to current market value, are relatively rare. Adaptive reuse projects almost always involve a unique property with distinguishing features, making comparable properties difficult to find. For example, old religious buildings and schools were often constructed with high-quality, traditional building materials, such as stone and brick, which may not be in common use today. In addition, the market may bear a higher price for a historic property or a property with an unusual architectural style than for ordinary properties.

An additional obstacle to finding comparable properties is the fact that the number of adaptive reuse projects is relatively small. Finding comparable projects even within an entire city's boundaries may be difficult. Moreover, since schools generally serve an entire neighborhood or municipality, they were not usually built in close proximity to one another. Since price is affected by the location of a property, comparing units in one neighborhood might provide an inaccurate assessment of the market potential for a property in a different neighborhood. Even within neighborhoods, some streets and locations are far more or less desirable than others.

Likewise, religious buildings were constructed to serve a particular neighborhood. Moreover, religious buildings have been constructed using a wide array of designs, materials, and architectural features. Residential units in a simple, small, rural, wood-frame Protestant chapel are not likely comparable to bilevel, loft-style units in a massive, Gothic stone church. Accordingly, the market approach to value may often be of little use for determining the value of a project. If the market approach is useful at all, it will most likely be used for evaluating projects in neighborhoods of large, old central cities that have undergone a renaissance of adaptive reuse. The market approach may also be useful for evaluating future phases of a phased project, based on the success of the sale of earlier phases.

The market approach is nearly useless for wholly unique projects and for projects that are essentially free, public facilities. Unique projects will have no comparable properties for comparison. Free, public facilities have no income and are generally not for sale, so valuation is more sophisticated, involving shadow rent or other nontangible returns.

Nevertheless, the preservation of an old structure as a public facility can add value to a neighborhood by increasing property values and, therefore, tax valuations around the property.

The Income Approach to Value

To be financially viable, a project must have sufficient cash flow to cover the cost of the project or to cover debt service and expenses. Ideally, a project's cash flow is at least 15–20 percent greater than its expenses and debt service. Since income from a project differs from the cost of a project, a project's value derived using the income approach may be very different from the value derived using the cost approach.

The income approach to value is based on a project's *net operating income* (NOI). This is easy to see in the example of residential apartments. The income calculation begins by calculating gross rental income from all units. However, some of the units will be vacant, so the revenues not collected from the projected vacant units must be excluded from gross rents. Even when tenants pay for their own utilities, owners of a property usually have at least some expenses related to the maintenance of common areas, cleaning, utilities, property taxes, maintenance reserves, marketing, and insurance of a property, all of which need to be subtracted from gross rental income. The remaining money is the NOI. This figure forms the basis of analysis using the income approach to value. Usually there is some sort of debt financing on the property, and NOI *less* debt service is before-tax cash flow. This is used for profit calculations, but not for value, which is calculated prior to debt.

Banks make lending decisions based on the potential *value* of a property, not on the property's *cost*. In addition, banks have certain limits about the portion of financing

that they are willing or able to provide to a project. Accordingly, they have certain equity requirements that a developer must meet in order to borrow money. The ratio of debt financing to equity financing in a project is known as the *loan-to-value* (LTV) ratio. A typical LTV ratio is 75–80 percent, although banks may require higher LTV ratios for riskier projects. Banks primarily use the income approach to determine the *value* of a property for the purposes of financing.

The value of a property under the income approach is affected by two main factors. The first is *net operating income*. Increasing the NOI generated by a property has a positive effect on a property's value. Increased expenses, however, can drag down NOI and reduce the value of a property. Owners must efficiently manage a property and monitor costs, not only to maintain the value of the property, but also to maintain sufficient income to service the debt on the property. NOI comes in a stream of cash flows over time, and is converted to present value through a discount rate, typically a figure of between 5 percent and 15 percent.

The other main factor affecting the value of a property is known as the *capitalization rate,* or *cap rate.* Defining the cap rate can be a difficult proposition. Different people define it differently, just as value can be defined in several different ways. Accordingly, the cap rate could refer to the ratio of NOI to capital cost, or it could mean the ratio of NOI to the property's value based on income.[1] When defining the cap rate based on the cost of a project, the cap rate serves as an estimate of how long it will take a project to pay for itself. For example, a project with a 5 percent cap rate will take approximately twenty years to pay itself off (i.e., 100 percent divided by 5 percent). For many common projects, cap rates are determined by a real estate appraiser acceptable to a specific lender, based on market conditions for similar projects.

There are more sophisticated calculations of the cap rate. One approach is essentially a weighted average of the cost of capital of both debt and equity, based on the proportions in which it is used. This approach renders a single cap rate that is aggregated by considering debt and equity separately. Generally, the debt and equity portions of financing are determined by the LTV ratio. Multiplying the cost of each type of capital by the proportion of the financing that it represents and then adding the results renders a cap rate.

For example, assume a project with an LTV ratio of 75 percent. If the bank will lend a maximum 75 percent of the *value* of the project and the borrower receives the maximum available financing, then the financing will essentially consist of 75 percent debt and 25 percent equity. If the interest rate on borrowed money is 6 percent, then 75 percent of the cap rate is 4.5 percent (i.e., 75 percent multiplied by 6 percent). The cost of capital can be defined as the rate of return that a developer expects to receive on his equity or cash contribution. If we assume that the developer expects a 10 percent return on equity, then the other 25 percent of the cap rate is 2.5 percent (i.e., 25 percent multiplied by 10 percent). Adding the debt and equity components of the cap rate renders a cap rate of 7 percent (i.e., 4.5 percent *plus* 2.5 percent).

Once the cap rate is determined, calculating the value of a project using the income approach to value is relatively simple. Under the income approach, *value* equals the NOI divided by the cap rate.[2] Therefore, a project with $100,000 of annual cash flow is worth $1 million at a 10 percent cap rate. Notice that if we instead use a 7 percent cap rate, the value of the project increases to $1,428,571.

Developers try to maximize the positive *spread* between the value of the project using the cost approach to value and the value of the project as determined by the income approach. This allows a developer to extract the maximum amount of value in a project, and fund the deal with less of his or her own money. This approach to value explains why developers constantly refinance properties: they are trying to extract the increased value of a property. Of course, refinancing works only when properties gain value, which is also consistent with the cap rate decreasing or NOI increasing. Projects that have a low NOI will have a low value. Projects with a negative NOI become a liability and have a negative value. Projects that have a lower value than cost have a *gap*, and these projects require subsidy for the deal to go forward.

Financial Models
The Church-to-Condos Deal

The rest of this chapter uses two financial models to demonstrate cash flows and financial returns. The first model is a build-and-sell conversion of a historic church to condominiums. The model assumes a church with a building footprint of about 35,700 sq. ft. After conversion, including the addition of floors within the church's main sanctuary space, the building is assumed to have a gross building area of 52,000 sq. ft. About 95 percent, or 49,000 sq. ft., of the gross built area is salable square feet, i.e., the area that will be portioned off into condos and sold. The other 5 percent accounts for common areas.

The redevelopment plan converts the church into forty-five condo units of various sizes, with an average size of almost 1,100 sq. ft. The average sales price is $265,000 per unit. For convenience, this project will be referred to as the *church-to-condos deal*.

Church to Condominiums. Photograph: Gary DeWine

Exhibit 7-1 is a sample pro forma for the church-to-condos deal. This example is important to understand because it closely resembles the pro forma included at the end of most case studies in this book. Much of the pro forma details project costs, as described in Chapter 4. The pro forma captures project expenses and shows how funds were used. The table also includes gross revenues from the sale of the condo units.

Though not included in this table, the sources of funds for this project are simple. The sources of funds come from developer equity and a construction loan. The developer of this project was not able to use historic preservation tax credits because the developer was not planning to hold the property as income-producing property for the required five years, but rather planned to sell the units immediately.

Also, note that soft costs are listed as a single line item in Exhibit 7-1 for the sake of simplicity, even though soft costs include fees paid to the numerous consultants needed to complete a successful redevelopment project. For example, a typical project may require the services of an appraiser, an architect, a mortgage banker, a marketing firm, and others.

Cash flows are the net amount of cash received and paid by a project to the owner over some defined period of time. Cash flows may be calculated on a monthly, quarterly, or annual basis. Cash flow for a for-sale redevelopment project will look considerably different than the operating cash flow of a rental property, which is held for a long period of time.

Exhibit 7-2 is a sample cash flow model for the church-to-condos deal. For-sale development projects are primarily financed using a construction loan, which generally requires only interest-only payments. The construction loan is disbursed incrementally over the course of construction. The developer *draws* on the loan to pay for construction costs, and the lender will require some assurance from the contractor or architect that the work is being satisfactorily completed and the project is on budget. Interest will accrue only on the outstanding balance as the developer draws on the loan.

Exhibit 7-1 Build-and-Sell Conversion of Church to Condos, Pro Forma

Site Acquisition	Project Total ($)	Project Cost (%)
Land/building acquisition (including option)	2,200,000	21.80
Site preparation		
Env. remediation: removal of asbestos	22,000	0.20
Other site preparation, incl. parking	100,000	1.00
Other exterior demolition	15,000	0.10
Construction costs		
Gutting and building prep	600,000	6.00
Building foundation	375,000	3.70
Structure and building envelope	1,625,000	16.10
Windows	425,000	4.20
HVAC	400,000	4.00
Electricity	278,000	2.80
Plumbing	220,000	2.20
Rough carpentry	1,240,000	12.30
Finish	800,000	7.90
Other / Contingency	422,000	4.20
Marketing & sales	196,000	1.90
Soft costs†	605,000	6.00
Financing fees @1%	75,773	0.80
Developer fee	480,000	4.80
Cumulative total expenses before interest	**10,078,773**	**100.00**
Construction loan disbursement	8,063,018	
Total interest	526,941	
Total Cost with Interest	**10,605,713**	
Revenues		
Units sold	45	
Gross Revenue	**11,925,000**	

† See Chapter 5 for a breakdown of various soft costs.

In for-sale redevelopment projects, the construction loan typically is retired, or *taken out,* as units are sold. Our example assumes that units are presold during the construction period as certificates of occupancy are issued. Although this has been the case for successful projects in recent years, this assumption may not be valid for all redevelopment deals under challenging market conditions. The tricky proposition with these projects, from the developer's perspective, is that they do not become truly profitable until the last few units are sold. Notice the line tracking "Equity" near the bottom of the table. The developer puts in equity at the front end but does not receive substantial profits until the last few units are sold at the end of the third year. Exhibit 7-3 shows the relationship between the construction loan balance and the developer's equity over

Exhibit 7-2 Cash flow, church condos

Assumptions and Project Description			
Building footprint sq. ft.	35,700	Avg. Sales Price per Unit	$265,000
Gross building sq. ft., after redevelopment	52,000	Acq. cost per completed building sq. ft.	$42.31
Net salable space (95%)	49,000	Acq. cost per original building sq. ft.	$82.76
Floor area coverage	146%	Mtg. interest rate	6.00%
# Units	45	LTV	80%
# Parking spaces	45	Gross sale revenues	$11,925,000
Avg. unit sq. ft.	1,089	Cost $/built sq. ft.	$203.96
		Sale $/built sq. ft.	$243.37

				Year 1			Year 2
Time period			Q1	Q2	Q3	Q4	Q1
Site acquisition	**Project Total**	**% Project Cost**					
Land/site acquisition (including option), includes existing structure	2,200,000	21.8%	$2,200,000				
Site preparation							
Env. remediation: removal of asbestos	22,000	0.2%		$22,000			
Other site preparation, incl. parking	100,000	1.0%		$50,000	$50,000		
Other exterior demolition	15,000	0.1%		$15,000			
Construction costs							
Gutting and building prep	600,000	6.0%		$100,000	$150,000	$150,000	$200,000
Building foundation	375,000	3.7%		$200,000	$100,000	$75,000	
Structure and building envelope	1,625,000	16.1%		$275,000	$375,000	$425,000	$375,000
Windows	425,000	4.2%		$50,000	$50,000	$125,000	$125,000
HVAC	400,000	4.0%			$25,000	$175,000	$125,000
Electricity	278,000	2.8%		$8,000	$20,000	$40,000	$60,000
Plumbing	220,000	2.2%		$20,000	$20,000	$30,000	$70,000
Rough carpentry	1,240,000	12.3%		$75,000	$225,000	$375,000	$375,000
Finish	800,000	7.9%					$100,000
Other/contingency	422,000	4.2%		$150,000	$50,000	$82,000	$120,000
Marketing & sales	196,000	1.9%					
Soft costs	605,000	6.0%	$65,000	$120,000	$140,000	$100,000	$105,000
Financing fees @ 1%	75,773	0.8%	$75,773	$-			
Developer fee	480,000	4.8%					
Quarterly total expenses			$2,340,773	$1,085,000	$1,205,000	$1,577,000	$1,655,000
Cumulative total expenses before interest	$10,078,773	100.0%	$2,340,773	$3,425,773	$4,630,773	$6,207,773	$7,862,773
Construction loan disbursement	$8,063,018	7,738,000		$1,085,000	$1,205,000	$1,577,000	$1,655,000
Outstanding principal balance	1.50%			$1,085,000	$2,306,275	$3,917,869	$5,631,637
Quarterly interest period	$526,936	5%		$16,275	$34,594	$58,768	$84,478
OPB with interest after debt repay				$1,101,275	$2,340,869	$3,976,637	$4,583,237
Total cost with interest	$10,605,709						
Revenues							

	Q2	Q3	Q4	Q1	Q2	Year 3 Q3	Q4	Year 4 Q1	
	$125,000	$50,000							
	$50,000	$25,000							
	$75,000								
	$80,000	$70,000							
	$70,000	$10,000							
	$120,000	$70,000							
	$200,000	$300,000	$200,000						
	$20,000								
	$36,000	$60,000	$50,000	$20,000	$20,000	$10,000		$-	
	$75,000								
			$480,000						
	$851,000	$585,000	$730,000	$20,000	$20,000	$10,000	$-	$-	
	$8,713,773	$9,298,773	$10,028,773	$10,048,773	$10,068,773	$10,078,773	$10,078,773	$10,078,773	
	$851,000	$585,000	$730,000	$20,000	$20,000	$10,000	$-	$-	
	$5,434,237	$4,967,875	$4,866,093	$3,826,210	$2,317,578	$776,317	$-	$-	
	$81,514	$74,518	$72,991	$57,393	$34,764	$11,645	$-	$-	$526,936
	$4,382,875	$4,136,093	$3,806,210	$2,297,578	$766,317	$-	$-	$-	

Exhibit 7-2 cont.

Time Period			Q1	Q2	Q3	Q4	Year 2 Q1
Site Acquisition	**Project Total**	**% Project Cost**					
Units sold	45						$
Gross revenue	11,925,000						$1,325,0C
Sales expense 5%							$66,25
Net proceeds before debt repayment							$1,258,75
Debt repayment @ 90% of proceeds			$-	$-	$-	$-	$1,132,87
Balance of sales to developer to equity							$125,87
Equity	$(2,340,773)		$(2,001,545)	$(2,001,545)	$(2,001,545)	$(2,001,545)	$(1,875,67
Net profit on deal	$723,194						
Project return on total cost	7%						
Return on equity	33%						

Does not account for "minor" cash calls of up to $100,000, nor reinvestment of investor funds.

School To Apartments. Photograph: Gary DeWine

time. Holding excess inventory at the end of the project leaves the risk on the developer. Accordingly, a quality market analysis identifying comparable projects, assessing how many units in the subject property the market can absorb, the competition's price points, and amenities required to be competitive in a market area is invaluable.

The School-to-Apartments Deal

Our other model is a school building (as part of a religious campus, or stand-alone) converted to apartments and will be referred to as the *school-to-apartments deal*. It is possible that the sanctuary and other religious buildings could be converted, but their highest and best use often is as condominiums. A rectory building could also be

| | | | | | Year 3 | | Year 4 | | |
Q2	Q3	Q4	Q1	Q2	Q3	Q4	Q1		
$5	$4	$5	$7	$7	$5	$4	$3		
$1,325,000	$1,060,000	$1,325,000	$1,855,000	$1,855,000	$1,325,000	$1,060,000	$795,000		
$66,250	$53,000	$66,250	$92,750	$92,750	$66,250	$53,000	$39,750		
$1,258,750	$1,007,000	$1,258,750	$1,762,250	$1,762,250	$1,258,750	$1,007,000	$755,250		
$1,132,875	$906,300	$1,132,875	$1,586,025	$1,586,025	$787,809	$-	$-		
$125,875	$100,700	$125,875	$176,225	$176,225	$470,941	$1,007,000	$755,250	$3,063,966	
$(1,749,795)	$(1,649,095)	$(1,523,220)	$(1,346,995)	$(1,170,770)	$(699,829)	$307,171	$1,062,421		
									$723,194

Exhibit 7-3 Debt versus equity, church condos deal

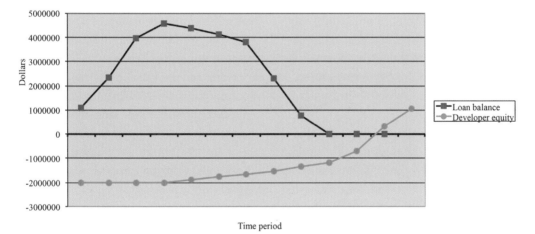

suitable for conversion to apartments, but rectory buildings are typically smaller, under ten units. The model assumes that a historic school on a church campus became available for redevelopment in a residential neighborhood that already had a substantial number of renters. The three-story building contains 121,000 sq. ft., of which about 100,000 sq. ft. are leasable. Only about 83 percent of the building area is as-

sumed to be leasable because school conversions often have wide hallways and large stairwells, rendering a higher *load factor,* or proportion of unusable or unrentable space.

The redevelopment plan for the school includes using sale to a private party and subsequent use of historic tax credits, and low-income housing tax credits (LIHTC).[3] The project is a mixed-income project with just over 20 percent of the apartments set

Exhibit 7-4 Sources of Funds, School-to-Apartments Deal

	Term	Amort.	Rate	Sources	% Total	LTV
Mortgage	30	30	6.00%	$9,410,510	62.20%	80.00%
Capital Contribution				$2,015,870	13.30%	
Phase I & 2 Enviro Grant				$41,500	0.30%	
Deferred Devel Fee				$944,572	6.20%	
HTC Equity to Project				$696,551	4.60%	
LIHTC Equity to Project				$2,024,593	13.40%	
Total Sources				**$15,133,596**	**100.00%**	

Note: LTV is calculated on the value of this project at $11.8 million, not on project costs of $15.1 million.

aside as qualifying low-income units subject to federal rent limitations in accordance with LIHTC regulations. Even though tax credits may be taken over time by developers, this analysis assumes they are syndicated and that the stream is capitalized in order to generate equity (a source of financing, one time, at the initiation only) for the project. Accordingly, there is more complexity in the sources of funds for this project. Exhibit 7-4 shows a table of the sources of financing for the project.

Notice that the sale of historic tax credits and LIHTC generates a total of almost 18 percent of the development funds for this project. Tax credit compliance and the sale or syndication of tax credits can be a tricky venture because of the need to follow complex regulations and to monitor the project to insure compliance. Accordingly, an expert in the use of tax credits should be consulted if tax credits are going to be used. This case is more complex because two separate programs are being utilized, and their compliance requirements are different.

This level of LIHTC is fairly "shallow," targeting a minimal amount of low-income tenants compared with most subsidy deals. Thus, this deal has a much higher loan-to-value ratio (.62) than most LIHTC deals, which typically have first mortgage LTVs in

the .3–.5 range. This is because this deal has been modeled with optimistic rental rates and relatively low expenses at 15 percent of gross revenues. With this in mind, Exhibits 7-5 and 7-6 are provided merely as simplified illustrations of how tax credits and their sale can provide equity to a project.

Exhibit 7-5 offers a simplified demonstration of how to calculate the value of historic tax credits and the value of their sale. Historic tax credits are available only for certain qualifying costs.[4] The federal historic preservation tax credit program provides a 20 percent credit for qualified rehabilitation expenses. Additional local or state tax incentives may also be available, and these are not modeled here. For simplicity, this example takes advantage of only federal tax credits. For this example, we have assumed that 30 percent of the construction hard costs (and no soft costs, a very conservative assumption), or about $4 million, qualified for the tax credits. This yields a tax credit of over $800,000, which the developer could take himself. However, the developer may not want to wait to file federal income taxes to receive the credit. Instead, the developer may sell the tax credits before beginning the project in order to generate equity.

Tax credits can be syndicated, but they often will fetch only a portion of their to-

Exhibit 7-5 HTC calculation, school apartments

Construction Costs		$13,343,880
Qualifying Rehabilitation Costs	30% of Constr. Cost	$4,003,164
Historic Tax Credit	20% of Qualifying Cost	**$800,633**
$ per dollar of credit		$0.87
Equity to Project		**$696,551**

Note these assumptions may not pertain to current market conditions.
The QRE shown above is conservative. Typically, QRE is higher than the construction cost because soft costs are included. Land and FF& E are not included.

Exhibit 7-6 LIHTC calculation, school apartments

	4% LIHTC 3.36%	9% LIHTC 7.84%
Acquisition Land and Bldg	$1,082	
Construction Costs		$224,552
Soft Costs		$8,421
Dev Fee		$15,895
Subtotal	**$1,082**	**$248,868**
Total Annual LIHTC Cr		**$249,950**
Over 10 yrs		$2,499,498
$ per dollar of credit		$0.81
Equity to Project		**$2,024,593**

tal value, especially under difficult market conditions, since there is some degree of risk involved for the tax credit investor if the project falls through. Thus, the investor must discount the returns from its face value to account for uncertainty and business risk, and to account for the time value of money since the investor will not receive the tax credits until sometime in the future. In our example, we assumed that the tax credits fetched 87 cents on the dollar, generating almost $700,000 of up-front equity for the project.

Similarly, Exhibit 7-6 provides a simplified example of tax credit calculation under the LIHTC program. As discussed in Chapter 6, there are two separate rates that can apply to a LIHTC project. In our example, most of our qualifying costs were eligible for the 9 percent rate because our project involved a substantial rehab. However, land and building acquisition costs are eligible only for the 4 percent rate. In addition, only construction expenses for the low-income housing units are eligible for the tax credit. Although up to 100 percent of a project is eligible for the LIHTC program, only

21.5 percent of the units in this project qualified as low-income units, and so only the costs associated with those units are eligible for the credit. Multiplying the qualifying eligible costs[5] from Exhibit 7-7 by the applicable federal rate generates the annual tax credit amounts listed in the table in Exhibit 7-6. The total annual tax credit is worth almost $250,000. Since the credit is available annually over ten years, the total ten-year tax credit is worth almost $2.5 million.

Like the historic tax credits, the developer typically chooses to sell the tax credits to generate capital for the project. Since LIHTC are recoverable over a longer period of time and have complex regulations requiring strict compliance monitoring, purchasers of tax credits are usually not willing to pay as much for LIHTC as for historic preservation tax credits. In our model, an investor was willing to pay 81 cents on the dollar for the tax credits, generating over $2 million of up-front capital for the project. This modeling assumes funds were received at once and that no bridge loan was required. Both discount percentage examples were representative of

Exhibit 7-7 Uses of Funds, School Apartments Deal

Uses of Funds	Per Unit	Total	% Total Cost with Financing	% Total Cost
Site Acquisition	$1,429	$150,000	1.00%	1.00%
Construction Costs	$127,085	$13,343,880	88.20%	88.60%
Soft Costs	$4,766	$500,396	3.30%	3.30%
Environmental	$238	$25,000	0.20%	0.20%
Development Fee	$8,996	$944,572	6.20%	6.30%
Contingency	$900	$94,457	0.60%	0.60%
Const. Loan Fin. Charges	$635	$66,719	0.40%	0.40%
Subtotal	**$143,412**	**$15,058,304**	**99.50%**	**100%**
Loan Origination Points 0.50%	$717	$75,292	0.50%	
Total	**$144,129**	**$15,133,596**	**100.00%**	

the market during the Great Recession, and tax credit equity discounts have improved (e.g., over 90 percent) as the U.S. economy has recovered.

Together, the historic preservation tax credit and the LIHTC generated over $2.7 million in capital for the formerly religious school building-to-apartments deal. This equity contribution can be seen on the sources of funds table in Exhibit 7-4.

Exhibit 7-7 shows a simplified table with the uses of funds. In this case, the city is assumed to be a player. The school district transferred the school to the city, which sold it to the developer for a modest $150,000. Note that this discounted acquisition price effectively functions as an indirect public subsidy for a project that will put a previously tax-exempt property back on the tax rolls and preserve a historic landmark for the community.

Exhibit 7-8 contains cash flows for the school-to-apartments deal. *Effective gross income* (EGI) is calculated by adding annual gross rent plus other income, and then subtracting vacancy. Since this is a LIHTC project, portions of the rents are rent-restricted according to the rules of the LIHTC pro-

gram. Expenses are subtracted from EGI to arrive at NOI. Both income and expenses are inflated using an inflation factor derived from the consumer price index (CPI).[6] As explained earlier, NOI can then be used to calculate the value of the project by dividing by the cap rate. For the purpose of illustration, we have calculated the value of the project in years three and five using the income approach to value and a cap rate of 8.5 percent. The results are listed in the line marked "Value."

This value, however, reflects only a snapshot of the project based on the cash flow of a single year. If the developer plans to hold the project for several years and then sell it, the project should return annual cash flow from operating income and then an appreciated reversion value at time of final sale. Because of the time value of money, the cash flows need to be discounted to present value. We have used the developer's own discount rate, which is essentially a *hurdle rate,* or minimum required rate of return, reflecting the developer's opportunity cost of making the investment.[7] This hurdle rate was converted to a discount factor, and then each NOI was multiplied by the discount factor to reflect the present value of the NOI for each year. These new cash flows are known as *discounted cash flows* (DCF). The sum of the present values for fifteen years of NOI was added to the present value of the net sales price of the project in year 15, discounted by 5 percent to reflect a sales commission. This total, which is $11.7 million, reflects the net present value (NPV) of the project. This is the project's value (the "V" in the LTV). At an 80 percent LTV, this generates a loan of $9.4 million.

Before-tax cash flow (BTCF) is calculated by subtracting the annual debt service from the NOI for each year.

The developer must take care—and a lender will surely require—that the project will have sufficient cash flow to repay the debt. The *debt service coverage ratio* (DSCR) is a measure of the adequacy of cash flow for the purpose of servicing debt. The DSCR is simply the NOI divided by the annual debt service. Since the first year of a project usually has unstable cash flows for a variety of reasons, including the fact that the project will likely have substantial vacancy before lease-up is complete, first-year cash flows are not often used as an accurate measure of stable cash flow. Accordingly, cash flows from a stable year, usually a year between years two and five, are used. Our DSCR in year 2 is 1.5, and in year 3 it is 1.6. Since most lenders require a DSCR of 1.15–1.20 or more, our project has sufficient debt coverage to make a lender comfortable with financing the project with a reasonable expectation of repayment.

The before-tax net present value, calculated in the same manner as NPV was calculated above, is also shown in Exhibit 7-8. At this point, we calculate the net present value of the investment before income taxes by taking the present value (PV) of the BTCF items for each of the fifteen years and adding the PV of sale, after repaying the outstanding principal balance on the loan. The total PV is $5.3 million, and from this is deducted the developer's stake in the deal, which includes cash up front, plus deferred development fee, totaling $3.0 million. The net present value (PV *less* investment) is positive, indicating this deal, as modeled, is a *go*. We have ended our model here without calculating the after-tax rate of return, which will vary depending on many factors and according to each individual's various other items of income or loss.

A Brief Word on Rates of Return

Developers employ various methods for evaluating rates of return on their investment. Rates of return are helpful for comparing alternative development projects and plans. Here, three basic methods of calculating rates of return are described. Certainly, more sophisticated methods of calculating rates of return exist, but these basic methods are offered as an introduction to calculating rates of return.

A basic measure many developers use is *return on total project cost,* which is stable year NOI divided by all development costs. This project has a return on project cost of 7 percent. This ignores both debt service and developer equity. An alternative method employs the same factors that are considered in determining the cap rate. The NOI divided by the cost of the investment renders the return on the asset. Typical cap rates range from 8 percent to 12 percent. Our project has a low 7 percent rate of return on the asset in the second year. However, this rate, along with the other rates of return, will generally increase as vacancy rates decrease and rents increase.

The *cash on cash return* measures how much cash a project generates in relation to the developer's equity investment. The cash

Exhibit 7-8 Cash flow, school-to-apartments

INCOME

Income Escalator	1.03		Year 1	Year 2	Year 3	Year 4	Year 5	Year 6
(Vacancy Rates)			20%	10%	7%	7%	7%	7%
Gross Full Rents			$1,087,560	$1,120,187	$1,153,792	$1,188,406	$1,224,058	$1,260,78
Gross LIHTC Rents			$218,851	$225,417	$232,179	$239,145	$246,319	$253,70
Other Income			$4,500	$4,635	$4,774	$4,917	$5,065	$5,21
Subtotal			$1,310,911	$1,350,239	$1,390,746	$1,432,468	$1,475,442	$1,519,70
Less Vacancy			$262,182	$135,024	$97,352	$100,273	$103,281	$106,37
Effective Gross Income			$1,048,729	$1,215,215	$1,293,394	$1,332,195	$1,372,161	$1,413,32
EXPENSES per Mo.								
Expense Escalator	1.03							
Real Estate Taxes			$21,187	$21,823	$22,477	$23,152	$23,846	$24,56
CAM, Utilities and Ins	$4.25		$93,500	$96,305	$99,194	$102,170	$105,235	$108,39
Mgmt Fee	5%		$52,436	$60,761	$64,670	$66,610	$68,608	$70,66
Reserves per Unit	$125.00		$13,125	$13,519	$13,924	$14,342	$14,772	$15,21
Total			$180,248	$192,407	$200,265	$206,273	$212,462	$218,83
NOI			**$868,481**	**$1,022,808**	**$1,093,128**	**$1,125,922**	**$1,159,700**	**$1,194,49**
Value					$12,860,332		$13,643,526	
PV Factor	1.000		0.901	0.812	0.731	0.659	0.593	0.535
PV Years			$782,415	$830,134	$799,286	$741,680	$688,225	$638,62
Sum of PV Years			$8,421,938					
PV Sale after Commission			$3,341,199					
Total PV			**$11,763,137**	7% return on project cost				
BTCF								
Mortgage $9,410,510	$0		0.072					
Annual Debt Service			$683,364	$683,364	$683,364	$683,364	$683,364	$683,36
BTCF			**$185,117**	**$339,444**	**$409,764**	**$442,558**	**$476,336**	**$511,12**
DSCR			1.27	1.50	1.60	1.65	1.70	1.75
Investor's BT Hurdle Rate	1.000		0.901	0.812	0.731	0.659	0.593	0.535
PV Years			$166,772	$275,500	$299,616	$291,527	$282,682	$273,26
Sum of PV Years			$3,507,957					
PV Sale			$1,770,154					
Total PV			$5,278,111					
Less Investment			$2,958,442	11% CoC ROR year 2				
Before Tax NPV			**$2,319,669**	**Invest**				

Year 7	Year 8	Year 9	Year 10	Year 11	Year 12	Year 13	Year 14	Year 15
7%	7%	7%	7%	7%	7%	7%	7%	7%
$1,298,604	$1,337,562	$1,377,688	$1,419,019	$1,461,590	$1,505,437	$1,550,601	$1,597,119	$1,645,032
$261,320	$269,160	$277,234	$285,551	$294,118	$302,941	$312,030	$321,391	$331,032
$5,373	$5,534	$5,700	$5,871	$6,048	$6,229	$6,416	$6,608	$6,807
$1,565,297	$1,612,256	$1,660,623	$1,710,442	$1,761,755	$1,814,608	$1,869,046	$1,925,118	$1,982,871
$109,571	$112,858	$116,244	$119,731	$123,323	$127,023	$130,833	$134,758	$138,801
$1,455,726	$1,499,398	$1,544,380	$1,590,711	$1,638,432	$1,687,585	$1,738,213	$1,790,359	$1,844,070
$25,298	$26,057	$26,839	$27,644	$28,474	$29,328	$151,038	$155,569	$160,236
$111,644	$114,993	$118,443	$121,996	$125,656	$129,426	$133,309	$137,308	$141,427
$72,786	$74,970	$77,219	$79,536	$81,922	$84,379	$86,911	$89,518	$92,204
$15,672	$16,142	$16,626	$17,125	$17,639	$18,168	$18,713	$19,275	$19,853
$225,401	$232,163	$239,127	$246,301	$253,690	$261,301	$389,971	$401,670	$413,720
$1,230,325	**$1,267,235**	**$1,305,252**	**$1,344,410**	**$1,384,742**	**$1,426,284**	**$1,348,242**	**$1,388,690**	**$1,430,350**
								$16,827,650
							After Commission:	$15,986,268
0.482	0.434	0.391	0.352	0.317	0.286	0.258	0.232	0.209
$592,597	$549,887	$510,255	$473,480	$439,356	$407,690	$347,192	$322,169	$298,949
								$3,341,199
$683,364	$683,364	$683,364	$683,364	$683,364	$683,364	$683,364	$683,364	$683,364
$546,961	**$583,871**	**$621,888**	**$661,046**	**$701,378**	**$742,920**	**$664,878**	**$705,326**	**$746,986**
								$15,986,268
1.80	1.85	1.91	1.97	2.03	2.09	1.97	2.03	2.09
								$8,469,459
0.482	0.434	0.391	0.352	0.317	0.286	0.258	0.232	0.209
$263,449	$253,357	$243,112	$232,810	$222,536	$212,357	$171,216	$163,632	$156,123
								$1,770,154

on cash return simply equals the BTCF divided by the developer's cash equity contribution. Our project has 11 percent second-year cash on cash rate of return. This approach focuses on the investor's equity when calculating return.

Another developer-equity focused method is the internal rate of return (IRR) on the before-tax cash flows, after debt service, over the entire holding period, including the sale. Typical before-tax IRR on equity ranges from 7 percent to 20 percent. Our project has a very positive NPV, indicating the return substantially exceeds the hurdle rate set by the developer.

Commercial Uses and Captive Tenants

When a developer rehabs a structure for an exclusive or dominant use by a firm or organization that the developer also controls, it is not unusual for the same individual to control more than one business entity related to the property (e.g., the main tenant and the separate corporation that owns only the real estate). As discussed in the section describing the various ownership structures for real estate deals in Chapter 6, each real estate project can be set up as its own LLC. So on one hand, an LLC legally owns the property and is responsible for maintenance, debt service, and taxes. On the other hand, another firm is the building's tenant and pays rent (not the mortgage) to the LLC that owns the real property. However, while expedient for other matters, this arrangement creates difficulty in cleanly evaluating the real estate deal and holding return (or loss) separate from the business that occupies the building.

Typically the real estate LLC collects rents from the operating company. Although there is a fixed rent schedule, if things get rough in the economy, the rental terms may become flexible because owner-

ship of the real estate shell corporation and operating company would likely be by the same individuals—beware not to kill the goose that lays the golden egg. Conversely, sometimes when the real estate corporation wants to refinance a loan, it may want higher rents to justify a higher value and, therefore, a larger loan. This can be accommodated if the firm's cash flow is sufficient.

All these moves make sense and are largely manageable if both the real estate entity and the operating entity are held by the same person or entity. However, when outside partners are involved (either in the original structure or by buying in over time), the situation can become even more complicated, and keeping the entities separate may be more important. Whoever covers any shortfalls in one or the other entity may incur liability on the mortgage notes or be responsible for cash calls, and the arrangement can become contentious. Interests may diverge, and the ownership structure of the entities becomes critical. It is best to keep the entities and their finances separate to begin with. The main focus in the cases in this book is on the real estate entity, rather than on the commingled finances of the operating and real estate entities. For example, the Babeville and Urban Krag case studies focus on the financial success of the real estate deals independent of the finances of the businesses that own and occupy the space. Then again, publicly subsidized projects may not need to be concerned about how much cash a project returns, such as the Jamaica Performing Arts Center, which generates a nominal $1 in rent per year through an arrangement with the public entity that owns it.

Nevertheless, commingling real estate ownership and business ownership is not advisable. Keep the entities separate.

Conclusion

Financing the adaptive reuse of a recycled building can range in complexity from relatively simple to a Gordian knot of complexity, especially when tax credits are involved. These subsidy programs can be tricky, and each deal is unique. Projects live and die by their ability to obtain financing and then amortize debt and pay expenses by maintaining positive cash flow. Assessing financial feasibility is as important a step as any for the success of a rehab project. Rehab projects should make sense. Although a few adaptive reuse projects are heavily subsidized by the public or a philanthropic organization in that they require little or no financial return (opting instead for some form of social return), most developers need to be involved in a project that makes sense. *And if it doesn't make dollars, it doesn't make sense.*

Notes

1. Recognizing that, in a discussion of the meaning of the income approach to value, defining the cap rate using the income approach to value renders circular logic. Nevertheless, making the point is useful. It not only highlights the difference between the effect of using the cost approach versus the income approach to value, but also defining cap rate in this way is useful when the value based on income is already known or has been calculated by a consultant, bank, or outside appraiser.

2. Be careful to use the same term, or time period, for NOI and for cap rate. In other words, the cap rate is usually calculated using *annual* interest rates; therefore, the *annual*—not monthly—NOI must be calculated and used to determine value. Annual NOI is simply a sum of the monthly NOI cash flows.

3. See Chapter 6 and its "Developer's Toolbox" for a more detailed discussion of tax credits and links to further information about them.

4. A link to more information is available in the "Developer's Toolbox" in Chapter 6. Additional guidance about applying the Secretary of the Interior's *Standards for Rehabilitation* for the historic tax credit program is available at http://www.nps.gov/hps/tps/tax/guidance.htm. However, experts experienced in historic preservation should also be consulted when determining qualifying costs for a project.

5. For simplicity, 21.5 percent of the qualifying costs from the "Uses of Funds," shown in Exhibit 7-7, was used.

6. In this case, an inflation factor of 3 percent was used for simplicity.

7. In this case, the assumption was that the developer's hurdle rate was 11 percent.

8

WINNING COMMUNITY APPROVAL
The Planning Process for Religious Building Adaptive Reuse Projects

Robert A. Simons, Rose A. Zitiello, and Gary DeWine

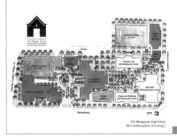

This chapter addresses various aspects of the predevelopment planning-approval process associated with acquisition and rehabilitation of religious buildings and potentially other community-oriented structures. Planning and redevelopment activities to consider include rezoning and zoning variances, preliminary and final planning and design approval, historic preservation, and gaining general community approval.

Rehabilitation of historically important structures is often politically complicated. The buildings may serve as neighborhood landmarks and hold fond memories and historic significance for neighbors and other stakeholders, many of whom may not reside proximate to the site location. Therefore, in addition to the development team and the property owner, important actors in the approval process may include: local and regional elected officials; nonprofit community development organizations; block clubs; government officials, such as planners and historic preservationists; and other stakeholders, including local residents and commercial neighbors.

This chapter provides insight and assists the developer in navigating some common pitfalls associated with project planning after the initial "back of the envelope" concept has been completed and adequate site control has been obtained.

The Developer's Checklist for Predevelopment and the Public Planning-Approval Process

Checklist:
1. Important contacts
2. Financial incentives
3. Historic building or area
4. Market feasibility
5. Financial analysis
6. Change-of-use zoning

7. Public outreach
8. Environmental issues

Project Planning

Remember: Time is money. Accountants, consultants, architects, lawyers, and other professionals all expect to be paid, usually by the hour, which means that maintaining priorities and tasks on time and on budget is important. There are many task and time-management tools, such as web-based Gantt Charts, available for development and construction management professionals. It is wise to develop a comprehensive checklist of tasks, responsible parties, priorities, and time lines at the very beginning of the project. See Exhibit 8-1 for a sample "Developer's Priority List."

1. Identify important contacts.

Identify important contacts with the local municipal or county planning departments who can provide process guidelines and who will have responsibility in the planning, permission, and approval process for the project.

2. Identify potential financial incentives for the project.

There may be a myriad of sources of financial assistance and incentives available to a developer. Each must be analyzed for eligibility and suitability for the project. For example, if the site is located in a low- or moderate-income census tract or if the project site area serves 51 percent or more of low- or moderate-income residents, the project may be eligible for public subsidies such as community development block grant funds or less restrictive philanthropic development loans and grants. Federal and state tax credit programs, such as new market or low-income housing tax credits, qualify for CRA (Community Reinvestment Act) credit to lenders. See Chapter 6 for details about various financing sources, including

Exhibit 8-1 Developer's Priority List

For: [Name]

Status	Priority	Due Date	Responsible Party	Project / Task	Notes	Date Closed or Completed

public financing and Community Reinvestment Act funding sources.

It is also important to note that when any federal grant or tax credit dollars are part of project financing, additional requirements may attach. Federally sourced funds for acquisition or rehabilitation assistance can trigger various local and federal requirements, such as the Davis-Bacon prevailing wage requirement and low- and moderate-income requirements for residential tenants or homeowners. If the rehab structure is occupied, additional Uniform Relocation Act notice requirements are triggered. Policies may require the developer to use best efforts or a specific percentage of the total project's budget for participation or set aside for disadvantaged business enterprises, such as small and minority- or female-owned businesses. Many of these factors may be on the table in the public-approval process.

3. Identify historically important buildings or designated historic neighborhoods.

Historic preservation concerns and historic landmark status frequently arise as issues in the redevelopment of religious buildings, either because the building itself is on a state historic list or the National Register of Historic Places, or because it is located in a locally designated historic district. If a building is notable for its historic architectural features or its social history, it may qualify for financial assistance through historic tax credits. The developer should seek out any local landmark or historic preservation boards or commissions as another resource to identify historic preservation considerations or requirements as part of the path toward planning approval.

A developer may find it appropriate to request historic designation for a building because of its age, architectural significance, or social significance.[1] The designation, however, may also carry state and local requirements for additional levels of design review to ensure adherence to historic preservation standards. The developer should seek the services of an architect with experience in historic preservation and historic tax credits so that requirements, costs associated with those standards, and available financial incentives are taken into consideration in the development pro forma. The developer should also keep in mind that neighbors, stakeholders, or local historic design or landmark commissions that object to the proposed alterations or end use of the building can use local and state historic designation as a tool to delay redevelopment, alteration, and even demolition of a building.

Take note that the use of federally sourced funds can trigger a Section 106 review. By law, citizens have a voice when federal actions will affect properties that qualify for the National Register of Historic Places. The Advisory Council on Historic Preservation publishes *Protecting Historic Properties: A Citizen's Guide to Section 106 Review,* which is designed to help citizens understand their rights.[2]

4. Complete a market-feasibility analysis.

With the recent contraction of credit in almost all financial sectors, and to a lesser degree during other times, lenders may request a market-feasibility analysis that eval-uates the current market conditions and market demand in the project area. If new units of housing will be put into service, the developer should prepare a market-feasibility study that includes an analysis of the area's median housing values, vacancy rates, and the presence of foreclosures and vacant or abandoned properties. The study should examine comparable price points, if there are any. The market study also should include demographics about potential buyers in the market, such as age, family size, and income. It is important for any analysis to describe the project's reasonable expectations for unit absorption. These topics are covered in Chapter 5 of this book.

5. Complete a financial analysis and pro forma.

A financial analysis should be developed to evaluate the project's sensitivity to alteration in project design, especially with respect to the number of units and the need for public subsidies. The financial analysis should be sufficiently detailed to compare and contrast what the developer wants from the project—including density, number of units, and related amenities desirable to generate maximum profit—and what the developer needs—such as the bottom-line minimum density to effectuate an acceptable return on investment and profit. A set of books should be kept for the project-level analysis, which can be made available to the general public or shown to public authorities for purpose of getting subsidies. A separate set of books should be retained in a proprietary manner for investors and partners to show return on equity, how income taxes will be paid, and how cash calls would be met. These topics have been covered in more detail in Chapters 6 and 7 of this book.

6. Zoning, change of use, and zoning variance considerations.

The developer's checklist includes careful research of the current zoning map, the zoning code, and the municipal comprehensive plan for both the project area and the adjacent properties. It is important to determine if the comprehensive or master plan is current, or if it has become outdated with the advent of nonconforming uses and developments. Development plans can be adopted for the purpose of either general planning guidance or strict enforcement of their provisions. Nevertheless, the zoning map is trump in this game. Performing a zoning analysis and carefully considering its applicability to the project can mitigate the risks associated with misunderstanding the intent of the zoning code or the relative importance that the local jurisdiction places on it.

A good rule of thumb is first to develop a concept or site plan that includes all exterior elevations and any site improvements, such as landscaping, fencing, sidewalks, and parking areas. This can be an effective tool in obtaining feedback about the project from stakeholders during design review or other public meetings. The developer's next step is to determine whether the project and its end use are consistent with the zoning code provisions and with adjacent land uses. If it is not, further zoning review is necessary. The developer should determine whether the project can be approved through a zoning variance, which is simpler than a rezoning because it allows exceptions to certain zoning provisions while maintaining the current use designation for the parcel.

The board of zoning appeals (BZA) typically has the administrative authority to grant a zoning variance. Preliminary and final rezoning and planning approvals and denials are conducted by the county or municipal planning board and may need legislative or administrative approval by the re-

spective city council or board members. An applicant who is denied a zoning variance is provided an opportunity to appeal the decision within a statutorily defined time limit, often thirty days, to a court with local or regional jurisdiction.

7. Public outreach.

Neighbors of the proposed project may be rightfully concerned about changes to the appearance, traffic, and potential nuisance related to a change of use in a historic religious structure or school. Managing this process for best possible outcomes is discussed in detail below, and focuses on managing meetings with neighbors and community groups, stakeholders of the historic structure's current owners and former patrons, rezoning, and successful management of integration of new space users into the existing urban fabric.

8. Environmental issues.

Due to heightened awareness of environmental hazards associated with historic buildings, lenders will typically require a Phase I environmental hazard assessment to be conducted before they issue a financing commitment. The developer should employ the services of a certified environmental engineer to conduct the Phase I assessment. This assessment includes a permit history of the building and its surroundings to identify any potential inherited problems, such as abandoned underground storage tanks. Testing the interior of the building for contaminants such as lead paint and asbestos, which require abatement, may be a contingency of financing. Additional review from the state Environmental Protection Agency office may be required if underwater storage tanks, toxic soil levels, or runoff from adjacent streams or drainage ditches are present. Sewer improvements may be necessary if the project involves construction of additional roof surface area, expanded paved or parking areas, or infrastructure improvements such as retention basins.

All these predevelopment activities should be identified as contingencies to be satisfied during the purchase option period. A motivated seller may want to participate and assist the developer in completing these actions.

Generic Planning-Approval Process

Once the developer is prepared to move forward, he or she should contact the local government staff in charge of planning approvals and concurrently make contacts with local elected representatives, such as the ward or district councilperson and the director of the local community development corporation. It is important to clearly define your project so that they can determine their level of support of or objections to the proposed use.

The next step is to begin the formal public planning-approval process. Because the building's new use (especially a residential or commercial end use) differs from its former use as a church (or perhaps a school), most rehabilitation projects of this type require submission of an application for rezoning, which is typically handled at the same time as preliminary or conceptual plan approval.

The concerns of neighbors and stakeholders should be considered in the initial project planning, so that any potential conflicts can be resolved by a mutually acceptable and minimally disruptive outcome. Neighbors will often express a number of concerns. Will the important or historic architectural features of the building be retained? Will construction noise or increased traffic disrupt the neighborhood? Is the project compatible with the current surrounding land use? What will be the effect on property values? Developers should an-

ticipate these questions and see them as issues to be addressed, not deterrents to the project. Failure to properly plan and manage this stage of the planning-approval process, however, can lead to delay or, in some cases, even fatal organized public opposition to a project.

It is very important to have an initial community meeting or open house well in advance of the rezoning hearing. The overarching goal of this meeting is to bring out and manage any community concerns. The developer may use it to fulfill statutory requirements, such as issuing notices to abutting landowners, or simply to offer information for the benefit of local residents, business owners, people with prior connections to the building, local historians, historic preservation activists, and other stakeholders. This meeting also gives the community stakeholders a way to voice their concerns and provides the developer with an opportunity to address issues that individuals raise one-on-one.

This meeting should take place in an informal and familiar setting, such as a community center, church basement, library, or other public place. Serving refreshments at the meeting is also a goodwill gesture, since most meetings are held in the evening and residents often bring their children.

After the developer has built public support, the project can move forward to the rezoning and preliminary plan-approval stage. This step can often be completed at one administrative hearing or meeting. Usually adjacent property owners, and sometimes also other property owners within a geographical area proximate to the proposed project, are sent notices of the hearing with an explanation of the action to be considered. Administrative approvals from the board of zoning appeals and, if applicable, the historic preservation committee should be scheduled within the same time period. Once preliminary approval is obtained, a project redesign period may be necessary so that the developer and architect can respond to community and public concerns raised at the hearing. In this case, the developer will make revisions to the project and reschedule the review for final approval.

Once final plan approval has been obtained, the final building drawings, including all mechanical systems, can be prepared and submitted for plan examination by the local building department. Once the drawings are approved and the building permit is issued, work can at last begin. When the site work is completed and building inspectors have verified that the work meets the local and state building codes, the developer will need to obtain a certificate of oc-

cupancy before tenant occupation of the structure is permitted.

A diagram setting forth an example of a generic planning-approval process for a retail development is provided below as Exhibit 8-2.[3]

Rezoning Is Not a Right

Rezoning a property is a serious issue, and a lot can go wrong even without neighbor opposition. Avoiding rezoning in the first place is a good strategy, so determine if the proposed use is allowed (e.g., is a use-by-right) under the current zoning laws. If rezoning is to be obtained, the proposed use must be compatible with the adjacent property uses and the local jurisdiction's zoning or comprehensive plans. Rezoning is not an absolute right, but a privilege that may

Exhibit 8-2 The Planning-Approval Process

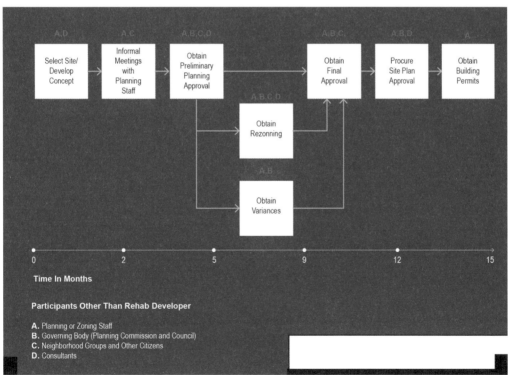

From "Planning Issues of Retail Development" by Robert A. Simons, page 280. In *Megatrends in Retail Real Estate,* ed. John D. Benjamin. Heidelberg: Springer, 1996. © 1996 Kluwer Academic Publishers. With permission of Springer.

How Not to Sell a Religious Building: Don't Take Rezoning for Granted[4]

In 2001, Young Israel (YI) was an Orthodox Jewish congregation of about 250 families that had ownership of a 30,000-sq.-ft. facility built around 1956. The site was situated on about 1.6 acres on the north side of a major arterial road in the city of South Euclid, a suburb of Cleveland, Ohio. The property was zoned single-family residential. Older religious buildings in the eastern suburbs of Cleveland were selling for about $25–$30 per above-ground building square foot (net of basement space). Thus, YI's building had an apparent value of about $450,000–$600,000 as a religious building. YI never intended to recycle the facility, just sell it to fund their new building off-site. The land uses adjacent to the YI facility were a fast food restaurant to the west, single-family residences abutting to the north and east, and multifamily residences to the south. However, located within 1/4 mile in a contiguous municipality was a substantial, existing commercial and retail structure of approximately 500,000 sq. ft.

In 2002, YI merged with a smaller congregation in a better location in the heart of the larger Orthodox neighborhood. YI acquired land in this nearby community and began to construct a new, larger facility. That year, they agreed to sell the old facility and set a purchase price of $1.3 million. They moved into their beautiful new facility in 2003, counting on funds from the sale of the old facility to help pay for the new one.

In 2003, YI had an offer of $1.2 million for a commercial use of its old facility, requiring demolition of the building subject to rezoning. After a year of failed negotiations regarding changing the land use with planning staff and other city officials, YI sought to rezone the site to commercial. Their application was denied at the local planning commission stage, but the commission's decision indicated that a multifamily use could be appropriate. Given a choice of seeking a buyer for a multifamily residential project or appealing the decision, YI chose to appeal the decision in the local court of common pleas. The court affirmed the decision of the planning commission.[5]

YI received inquiries of interest in 2005 and 2006 about constructing multifamily townhouses and a halfway house on the site, but due in part to the beginning of the Great Recession, none of the inquiries materialized into a sale. YI believed that the market value of the site was between $600,000 and $700,000. This assumed multifamily land with a density of sixteen to eighteen units, at $250,000 per unit, and that 15 percent of that was the land value. A private school reportedly offered $300,000–$400,000, but YI believed the offer was too low and declined.

YI's efforts to hold out for a higher price backfired. Over time the building became run-down, and legal fees, back taxes, and holding costs for repairs required by the city all added up. Meanwhile, the economy and housing prices peaked in late 2005 to early 2006. Then home prices started to soften, and unsold housing inventory began piling up. No buyers for the YI property emerged. The Great Recession of 2007–2009 froze the market for new projects, and the market window closed. In late 2007 the property was auctioned off for $300,000, and then demolished. The buyer, a member of the congregation (as of May 2014) now has a 1.5-acre site available with a cost basis of about $400,000.

Lessons learned: Do your homework. Set a realistic sales price based on existing market conditions (including zoning), not based on the equity needed to fund the move to a new facility. YI's need for funds led to clouded vision. If you get a decent offer, take it. Do not assume rezoning is a slam dunk. In YI's case nearly all the retail driving the potential commercial value of the property was in another community, and hence scarcely recognized by the city's zoning board. Community master plans did not necessarily line up with YI's plans.

be denied by the zoning board. Commercial and residential uses do not easily mix, especially in suburban markets. Rezoning that results in incompatible uses may be denied. Therefore, if the highest and best use ends up being not the most community-friendly use, delays in rezoning may result and the market window may close, leaving the rezoning applicant at a loss.

Winning Community Approval

The following items are a list of steps to win community approval for your project. Also, a checklist of planning and logistical suggestions and tips has been included in Appendix 8-A. Contained within this section are two vignettes on the pitfalls that can occur when a developer does not adequately address or plan for opposition to a project.

Know Your Audience

Religious and other community-oriented buildings may be vacant, but they are still important landmarks and hold an important place in people's memories. Do your homework. Research the local historical society, newspapers, and library. Then meet with neighbors, local business owners, and elected representatives to develop the building's social history into a concise narrative. Include this information as part of the project's historical file, to be used to relate to neighborhood and community groups. Next, flag any potential redevelopment issues, such as differences between the proposed site's use and neighboring land uses. Also, review census data for the city to identify potential issues, such as differences in the socioeconomic demographics of the proposed residents or a contrast between the value of the rehabbed housing and the expected income of new residents and the housing values and incomes of any stakeholders opposing the new project.

Identify Who Lives in the Zone of Influence

Rezoning and plan approvals almost always require formal notification of adjacent property owners, typically by direct mail and publication in a newspaper several weeks prior to the public hearing. These neighboring landowners are usually the key people within the first tier of potential residential stakeholders, those located within 500 ft. (about two blocks) of the project. People (primarily homeowners) living between 500 and 1,000 ft. of the proposed redevelopment project should be considered the second tier of stakeholders. One-on-one and small group meetings should be held with them to identify issues and concerns. Recently, many community groups have used social media such as Facebook, dedicated project web pages, or Twitter to reach and mobilize stakeholders.

Dot Your *i*'s and Cross Your *t*'s at the Front End

Zoning, fire, and safety codes may be triggered if a project requires a new building or adaptive reuse of an existing one. Meet with zoning administrators and the local planning department to answer several important questions:

- Are there any zoning or use restrictions?
- Is there a community master plan or neighborhood plan in place for the area?
- Does the building have any local, state, or national historical or landmark designations that may require an additional level of public involvement through the historical and social impact analysis mandated by HUD section 106? What parking requirements are related to the project's end use? Is this parking requirement adequate for market conditions? If not, what has to be done to amend or change the redevelopment plan to meet

A Costly Lesson in Not Knowing the Community

The former Jubilee Church, located at 700 Tuxedo Boulevard in the town of Webster Groves, Illinois, was built in 1900. The church was added to the National Register of Historic Places in November 2006. Its immediate surrounding neighborhood is exclusively residential.

A St. Louis–area developer began the process of acquiring the property from the church for conversion to condominiums in early 2005. The developer was experienced in the conversion of older buildings, including religious buildings, to new uses. State of Missouri Historic Tax credits could have played a role in financing the rehab portion of the project.

A meeting between the development team and the neighbors took place several months before the formal presentation at the planning commission meeting. The residents were given a two-day notice of the meeting, which was held just before Christmas. The public record indicates that the meeting was sparsely attended, and the development team learned there that residents did not want the project to become condos.

The developer's proposal, which was heard by the Webster Groves Planning Commission on July 10, 2006, was to convert the existing structure to a six-unit condominium. This would require a change of zoning from single-family residential to planned multiple-family residential.

The planning department staff explained the issues to be considered by the planning commission: the appropriateness of converting the church structures to six condominiums and how many dwelling units the site could support. The formal presentation to the commission ended, and the general public was then allowed to speak. More than twenty-five residents made public comments about the project—none supported it.[6]

The developer found himself in the middle of a hornet's nest of angry neighbors. Three hundred neighbors had signed a petition in opposition to the project, and the petition was placed into the city record. The developer, upon conclusion of the public portion of the hearing, formally withdrew the project.

The property was nonetheless transferred to the developer in September 2006, several months after the meeting. Using 20/20 hindsight, we can ask: Had the developer failed to list rezoning as a contingency of the purchase agreement? Wouldn't it have been better to have placed an option on the property? Shouldn't the developer have spent more attention to properly assess the expected public reaction to condos during the due diligence process?

As of 2009, the property was for sale and described as available for use as a meeting hall, school, day care, funeral home, church, or spectacular residence.[7]

The Jubilee Church case is an excellent example of the need for thorough preparation and research to determine the project's acceptability to neighbors. It can never be taken for granted or assumed that neighbors will accept a project. In this instance, the neighboring residents had valid concerns about the condo project. These concerns were voiced at the meeting before Christmas, but the development team ignored the message. The developer is now stuck with an asset that languishes on the market without an economically viable user.

the requirements corresponding with the proposed end use?

- Will the proposed new end use require alterations to the building in order to be in compliance with the city's building code, e.g., does a sprinkler system need to be added? What about Americans with Disabilities Act (ADA) compliance? Is there a sufficient number of fire exits?

Answering these questions at the front end will help to avoid unnecessary surprise and delay as the redevelopment plan progresses.

Identify the Off-Site Impact of the End Use

Proximate neighbors may fear that changes to the property's use pattern will negatively affect their quality of life. Ask yourself the following questions:

- Will the change in use cause more traffic?
- Will the rehab project impact limited parking that the neighbors depend on?
- If the intended use is commercial and the surrounding use is residential, what would be the hours of operation?
- Are there any noise, nuisance, or safety issues? If there are concerns, how can these factors be mitigated or buffered?

Project redevelopment can generate the classic NIMBY, i.e., not-in-my-backyard, issues. Fear of change may create CAVE people, i.e., citizens against virtually everything. These negative perceptions can usually be minimized through a well-thought-out plan that is consistent with local community standards.

Potential Opposition from Strict Historic Preservationists

When a building rehab is proposed, advocates of historic preservation and people with ties to the original buildings, such as former church members, may appear and en-

courage preserving the buildings just as they were in "the good old days." These people need to be heard and addressed. However, blind adherence to the principle of recreating prior conditions may doom a redevelopment project because of excessive costs that cannot be borne by the market or the development budget. As we discuss in the Urban Krag case study (Chapter 14), a developer can overcome opposition to change by showing how the end product will introduce a positive addition to the neighborhood. Neighbors rarely want to live in proximity to a deteriorated, underutilized, or vacant school building or church subject to vandalism and break-ins, which are public nuisances that negatively impact property values.

Types of Public Involvement Plans

If any federal, state, or local funding will be used in the predevelopment or construction of the site, there may be specific public involvement requirements, including public hearings or published notices in newspapers or libraries. Depending on the level of support for the proposed project, project developers should plan on including one or more of the following strategies to educate the public, resolve controversies, and obtain consensus: one-on-one meetings with key players, small focus groups, group workshops, open-house meetings, and newsletters/blogs.

Consensus Building

Consensus building requires answering the "What's in it for me?" question. Every project presents some obstacles to public consensus, but many of these obstacles can be overcome. What can a project planner offer that will win the hearts and minds of the neighbors? Be creative! Examples may include:

- Be prepared to reduce the size of the project somewhat to give the opposition a partial "win."

VIGNETTE CASE STUDY
Parking Can Be a Deal Killer

Tabernacle Fourth Baptist Church is located in the Wraggborough neighborhood of historic Charleston, South Carolina. By 2006, church membership had declined in numbers as many in the congregation moved away from the neighborhood. The church needed repairs that the remaining members could not afford. The church received an offer to purchase their building, so, assuming the conditions of the purchase agreement would be met (e.g., rezoning), they needed to find a place to relocate, starting at the time of the building's renovation.

The Patrick family was an experienced Charleston redeveloper of historic properties. Working with them, the church developed a proposal that would convert the church into a four-hundred-seat theater for the Charleston Stage Company. The mayor's office had been engaged in brokering the deal, but that support suddenly evaporated when community opposition to the plan materialized.

Parking was the most contentious issue. Charleston's code requires on-site parking of one space for every six seats. This ratio would be an impossible condition for the theater's developer to achieve. The issue could be resolved through a loophole if an agreement could be made to lease parking spaces within 400 ft. of the proposed theater. The city was planning to issue a request for proposals to build a parking deck that would satisfy the parking requirements.

Since the plan called for placing a theater, which is a commercial use, in a residential area, a zoning change was required. An appeal was made to the board of zoning appeals.

The Patrick family, their architect, and the head of the theater company met with the local homeowners association to garner support. They explained that the renovation would respect the interior of the historic church. Promises were made that the project would not adversely impact the neighborhood and that there would be no parking problems. Some neighbors were skeptical. Their concerns included the potential for an increase in traffic, cars, noise, people, and buses, which would threaten the tranquillity of their neighborhood. The implication was made that if the neighborhood did not agree to the project, someone could emerge at a later date with an offer to develop the property with more negative impacts to the neighborhood than a theater. The neighbors viewed this counterargument as a threat and became even more solidified against the theater proposal.

The community rallied to vigorously oppose and defeat the change of use. The Charleston Board of Zoning Appeals voted down the change of use in a split vote of 3–3 on May 2, 2006.

The lesson is that opposition can quickly mobilize and organize against an issue. Savvy public officials may quickly stop supporting a project with politically charged issues and save their political clout for another day.[8]

- Mitigate any visual changes to the property with berms or other buffers.
- Dedicate a public meeting space offered free to neighbors.
- Provide services to neighbors at a discount.
- Give financial support to local neighborhood block clubs, youth groups, or the elderly.
- Remediate neighborhood blight.
- Restore to productive use a socially or architecturally significant neighborhood landmark.
- Develop a permanent historical photo exhibit from the neighbors' collections, displayed prominently in the building.
- Conduct an artist competition for youth or adults and select winners' works for installation in the building.
- Sell bricks as part of a walkway or public space with donors' names on them as part of a capital-raising plan.

Maintain a Positive, Can-Do Attitude!

All community projects generate some change, and not all community members welcome change. The challenge is to minimize negative impacts throughout the development stage and maximize the benefits of the project to the neighbors and community. If your project needs rezoning or revisions to an existing comprehensive plan, planning approval usually requires a vote by a board or commission. Supporting unpopular projects means spending political capital, which is usually in short supply for any local entity.

The rehabilitation and restoration of an underutilized or vacant school or church usually takes place mostly within the existing shell of the building and so is less controversial than construction of a new building, since the exterior of the property appears to remain the same from the street. Nevertheless, assume that there are people who have an emotional investment in the property and that *any* change or improvement may not be welcomed.

There are essentially three groups of people with respect to this type of public process: those who favor the project, those who oppose it no matter what, and those who are on the fence and could be persuaded to support the project. Different strategies are suggested for each group. The folks who strongly oppose the project are most likely to get involved, followed by those strongly favoring the project. Neutral people are unlikely to get involved at all.

At one end of the spectrum are those individuals who oppose the project, but they may not be able to be convinced, no matter what. Often they may be more vocal than those who support the project. Make sure that those who do support it are heard.

It will be important to identify the people who favor the restoration project because they can provide support at public meetings when stakeholders are present and votes may be taken. Their support can often convince the naysayers to identify their basis for opposing the project, work through it, and give the project a second chance. Elected officials will want to hear substantial voter affirmation of a project before they support it, especially when the project arouses some controversy. Positive feelings can provide momentum for support by undecided citizens.

The opportunity for respectful exchange of views may encourage participants to rethink their positions because they can hear both sides. Above all, the developer should seek to minimize the dreaded "screamers at the mike" during public meetings. Community meetings that encourage discussion, such as workshops or open-house formats, can be more productive than using an open-mike format. Providing public comment or opinion cards can also be an effective tool for obtaining feedback on your project. In order to successfully accommodate this process, many developers find it useful to hire professional meeting planners who are experienced in convening a public forum.

In most cases, people are reasonable once their fears are relieved and they understand the project better. They want and deserve to be heard and feel respected. The developer should come prepared with some visible but financially benign concessions to accommodate people's concerns and provide political cover.

Conclusions

By following the steps set forth in this chapter, the developer will increase his or her chances of reaching a successful outcome through the planning process. These steps may be best handled by your team's planning professionals who are most familiar with handing group dynamics. This approach is a mix of art and science, but the most important part after getting some indication of public support is to get organized and develop a plan.

Notes

1. In some cases, the historic designation can also be initiated by other parties, such as a municipal authority, in an attempt to control development outcomes. Sometimes this may work against the developer's financial interests.
2. A helpful guide to understanding these rights can be found at http://www.achp.gov/citizens guide.pdf (last accessed Jan. 25, 2009).
3. For further reading on this and an additional source for examples on the steps followed in the general planning-approval process in the context of a retail center, see Robert A. Simons, "Planning Issues of Retail Development," in *Megatrends in Retail Property,* ed. John Benjamin (Boston: Kluwer, 1996).
4. Sources: Rabbi Naphtali Burnstein, personal interview, Feb. 6, 2008. *Young Israel of Beachwood v. City of South Euclid,* http://www .sconet.state.oh.us/rod/docs/pdf/8/2006 /2006-ohio-4379.pdf.
5. In this case the spiritual leader, a rabbi, was not involved in the nitty-gritty of the deal. The Young Israel leadership included real estate professionals and lawyers, and they even hired an outside law firm at one point during the zoning and appeal process.
6. Webster Groves Plan Commission, Meeting Minutes, July 10, 2006, http://www.webster groves.org/Archive.asp?ADID=61.
7. As of April 2009, the property was still listed at www.pattiahner.com/search/view_listing .html?mls=80019309. The site contains a detailed description of the property, photos, and an asking price. By December 2013, the Web site link was inoperative.
8. For a more detailed and contextual discussion of some of these issues, visit http:// charlestonwatch.com/baptist_church _wraggborough/.

Appendix 8-A: Checklist for Open Houses and Community Meetings

Objectives
- Facilitate good community relations
- Illustrate company policies, concept(s), and benefits
- Demonstrate and explain the phases of the project
- Dramatize public-private partnerships in action
- Convey the message of your concept
- Attract favorable publicity, and cultivate public goodwill and understanding
- Illustrate the "place-making" concept of planning* and effective utilization of public funds

Who is in charge?
- Consult with the project manager or administrator with oversight authority for the project
- Appoint a committee, if needed
- Name a coordinator, if needed
- Advise supervisors and obtain their support
- Choose staff, hosts, guides, and lecturer(s)
- Notify employees
- Designate a spokesperson

Guest list: Whom to invite
- Community stakeholders, employees, and end-users of the facility
- Customers and prospective customers (including taxpayers and county residents)
- Civic leaders and opinion molders
- Shareholders and financial community members (with prior approval)
- Educators
- Clergy

*"Place-making" is a term that began to be used in the 1970s by architects and planners to describe the process of creating squares, plazas, parks, streets, and waterfronts that will attract people because they are pleasurable or interesting. Landscape often plays an important role in the design process.

- Labor/jobbers
- Professional societies
- Community and economic development nonprofits (where applicable)
- Media (bloggers, newspapers, radio, and TV)
- Local, county, and state elected officials, e.g., mayor, city council members, commissioners, representatives
- Local, county, state department staffers
- Special guests suggested by administrators or elected officials

Setting the time and date
- Tie in with a special event
- Check with other local events to avoid conflicts
- Choose the least busy day of the week for stakeholders
- Set an alternate date in case of bad weather
- Set a plan for announcing any change, if necessary

Budget
- Estimate attendance
- Determine cost of refreshments, catering services, supplies, decorations, special safety precautions
- Determine cost of printing, displays, signs
- Determine cost of identification badges
- Determine cost of mailing expenses, postage, press kits
- Determine cost of transportation, if required

Facilities
- Select and mark adequate parking spaces
- Locate large, convenient reception area
- Establish simple registration procedure; assign staff
- Designate ample checkroom space, if required; assign attendant

- Prepare facilities to be seen:
  - All facilities must be clean and neat
  - Displays and machinery must be clean and in good working order
  - Tour route (if applicable) must be absolutely safe and free of obstacles
  - Information signs and arrows must be installed
- Arrange for adequate space to serve refreshments
- Install and test microphones and video equipment
- Put up suitable displays
- Make sure restrooms are convenient, clean, and clearly marked
- Brief your guides and conduct a practice run of the tour
- Instruct guides to be precise but not technical

Event format
- Arrange for a short welcome speech by an official or community leader
- Limit the size of tour groups for better manageability
- Route tours to save time and steps, to avoid unattractive areas, and to ensure safety and smooth, rapid movement of guests
- Schedule a question-and-answer period at the end of the tour
- Note problems for consideration in preparation for any subsequent tour or open house

Refreshments
- Select only quick-service items
- Obtain adequate paper containers and disposable utensils
- Arrange for necessary waste containers

Printed materials
- Invitations
- Programs, if required
- Company, developer, and industry literature
- Identification cards or badges
- Registration book
- Press kits

Displays
- Prepare displays with the scope of your company's activities and operations, photos of other successful projects, and the proposed project's importance to the community
- Prepare displays conveying company and industry messages

Publicity
- Invite press, television, and radio in advance and follow up on invitations the day of the event
- Distribute news releases in advance of the event
- Place advertising in advance of event, if needed
- Prepare material for reporters who attend
- Arrange for company executives and government officials to be available for interviews at the request of reporters
- Make sure that the company press officer maintains contact with all reporters throughout the event
- Distribute press kits to media while event is in progress
- Use the event as a springboard for future stories and interviews

Follow-up
- Encourage comments and suggestions from visitors
- Give recognition to employees who worked on the project
- Hold a critique to analyze and improve procedures
- Maintain a file of correspondence, press releases, reports, worksheets, and media coverage for future use
- Consider sending photographs and a follow-up letter to key people who attended

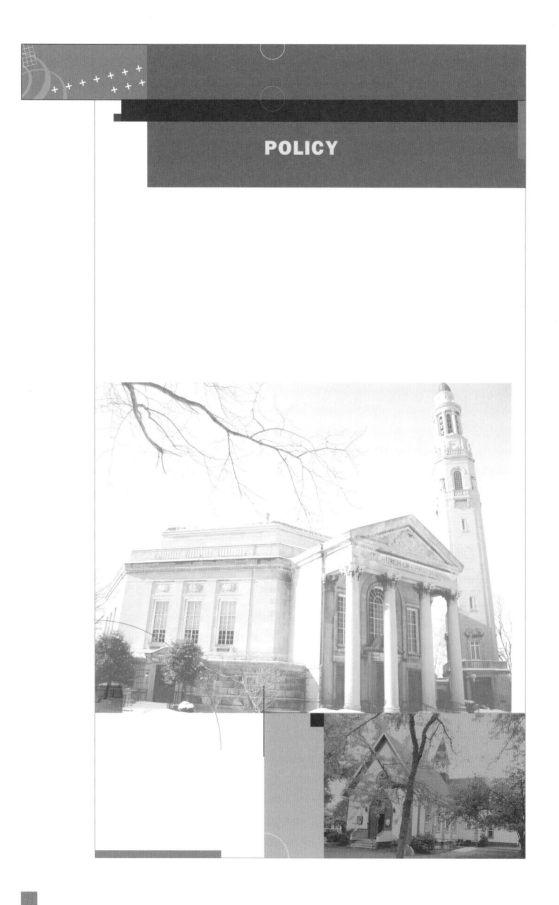

## 9

THE "HIGHEST AND BEST"
IN ADAPTIVE REUSES

Larry Ledebur

Adaptive reuses of former houses of worship are found in many shapes and forms. The range and variety of secular uses to which once-sacred places have been adapted will inevitably result in some types of adaptive reuses being more controversial. Thus, they likely require more difficult and contentious processes to win the support of local governments and communities.

This chapter addresses the critical issue of why *highest and best use* (HBU) as dictated by the marketplace and real estate values is not necessarily the highest and best use from the perspectives of local governments, historical societies, communities, former congregations, and religious administrative offices. Sharp disparities between public and market perspectives of highest and best use can sow the seeds of discord. Individuals or communities considering the adaptation of a former house of faith to a secular or nonsacred use, then, must understand the potential sources of controversy and conflict embedded in many of these projects, and should be aware of possible avenues of resolution.

Not all adaptive reuses are equal in the public eye. The aura of sacredness that adheres to the bricks and mortar of former houses of worship virtually ensures that many secular uses to which these buildings might be put will be viewed as inappropriate to some stakeholders. Adaptive reuse of former churches and synagogues, therefore, often becomes controversial in ways not necessarily encountered in reuse of other buildings. For this reason, market tests of HBU, such as rate of return, should not be the only or even the prevailing criteria for making decisions about "highest and best" or "appropriate" use of redundant houses of worship.

"Appropriate use," which is at the center of many controversies around secular uses of formerly sacred structures, does not have a commonly accepted meaning. The distilled essence of concern appears to focus on whether the proposed secular use is consistent with the embedded "sacredness" of the formerly sacred structure. The lack of a commonly accepted definition or meaning of "appropriate use" raises the question: Is the appropriateness of a particular secular use of a former house of worship simply in the eye of the beholder, or are there guidelines or decision criteria to assist communities in reaching at least some degree of consensus on appropriate uses of particular buildings and sites?

This chapter outlines a continuum along which the many secular adaptive reuses fall. The principle of this continuum is congruence of the proposed adaptive reuse with the original sacred purpose for which the building was constructed. Numerous vignettes and mini-case studies are presented to illustrate these issues. They also highlight the issues and controversies that surround many of these adaptations. At the epicenter of these controversies, almost always, is the focal issue: Does a house of worship, once the congregation has departed, become desanctified and, therefore, simply a building, or is "sacredness" embedded in the structure and minds and memories or people?

The Continuum of Uses of Former Houses of Worship

This section contains case studies that exemplify the range of adaptive reuses of former houses of worship. These reuses are organized along a continuum of the current use's level of congruence with the building's former religious functions. The starting point for understanding where various reuses fall on the continuum is a listing of commonly accepted functions of churches, synagogues, and other religious buildings.

SALE OF ORTHODOX JEWISH SYNAGOGUES

The Jewish faith has several branches, the largest of which are Reform, Conservative, and Orthodox. The following rules apply where Orthodox synagogues (often referred to as a "shul," a Yiddish word) can be sold.

There is a distinction between a private shul and a public one. A private shul is unincorporated, just an informal meeting place where prayer takes place, like in a private house's basement. These are easier to sell, with fewer rules, but they offer little in the way of redevelopment projects.

The more typical situation is a public shul, which is incorporated and has a community board. These buildings, once de-sanctified, can be sold for any end use except: a *mikvah* (ritual bath), tannery, bathhouse, or laundry (Talmud Megillah 27b). Additionally, no house of "ill repute" is permitted. Acceptable uses include: housing, school, bank, restaurant, and most bars.

When selling a building, some additional rules apply. However, if the building is demolished, there are no restrictions on how the land may be used.

So what makes a building holy to Jews? It's a place where people worship God. Also, the presence of holy objects such as the Torah makes it holy. Thus, most agree that the sanctuary is no longer holy after the Torah is removed. However, there is no formal de-sanctification ceremony.

A common buyer for religious buildings is a church. However, for Orthodox Jews, selling to a church (especially a Catholic one, or to a Buddhist community with statues of deities) may raise concerns about "idolatry." Jews (like Muslims) have a faceless and amorphous vision of the Supreme Being, and so use of concrete symbols is considered idol worship, which is prohibited. To overcome this issue, some Jewish sellers will use a middleman to create a legal fiction, and in this way the next user is acceptable.

Source: Rabbi Naphtali Burnstein, personal interview with Roby Simons, February 6, 2008.

Although different religions or denominations have different understandings of the uses of religious space, certain commonalties apply. Sacred functions can be categorized into two groups: "congregational functions" aimed at church members, and "social mission functions," which can overlap congregational functions but are intended for the wider community. The two typologies tend to both feature: maintenance of cemeteries, sacred art performances and exhibits, preservation and celebration of ethnic and cultural heritage, and developmental and family life programming for the community.

Examples of Congregational Functions
- Worship and other religious services
- Life-cycle ceremonies such as weddings, funerals, bar mitzvahs, and baptisms
- Congregational community meetings, recreational activities, meals, etc.
- Social services and charitable activities for the congregation
- Religious educational activities

Examples of Social Mission Functions
- Community meetings, recreational activities, meals, etc.
- Social services and charitable activities for the community

- Educational activities
- Activities that support community cohesiveness and promote community values and goals, including economic development and community advocacy

VIGIL CHURCHES

Sometimes, church closings can be painful regardless of the eventual reuse of the building. The term "vigiling" refers to a recent phenomenon in which parishioners of recently closed Roman Catholic churches organize to occupy the building around the clock so that the diocese administrators cannot lock the building and sell it. For vigilers, the bone of contention is not the proposed reuse, but the closing of the church itself. "I just don't want to give in to it," is the prevailing sentiment among vigilers (Vigiler quoted in Goodnough 2009).

This protest movement started four years ago in Boston and has spread to other parts of the country. Members of the closed parish organize shifts to occupy the building, preventing its sale while hoping that the administration changes its mind or pending appeals to the Vatican.

Vigilers conduct church services with lay members and, to the extent possible, maintain the regular functions of a parish church, even though some are without running water, heat, or electricity. "The Boston vigils were [according to one organizer] 'the longest-duration, broadest-based passive resistance movement' ever by American Catholics" (Goodnough 2009).

In addition to these functions that take place within the building, the building itself may have a special meaning to the congregation and to the community at large. It may be a community landmark, and it may be a symbol and a repository of the cultural and neighborhood history of the community.

The preceding listing of church functions gives a starting point for understanding the "Congruency Continuum" shown in Exhibit 9-1. At the "more congruent" end of the continuum are new uses that replicate some of the building's former functions, such as a former church that now houses a seniors' center and offers meals to low-income seniors, or a church transformed into a heritage center that celebrates and retains an ethnic group's customs and memories. A cemetery might also be connected to those who support the heritage center today. At the "less congruent" end of the continuum are functions far removed from or even antithetical to the building's former use as a sacred space, such as nightclubs, adult bookstores, and other adult entertainment. Between these two ends of the continuum is a large array of commercial and private uses.

Issues in Adaptation of Formerly Sacred Places

The adaptive reuse examples presented in this section show the range of reuses that are possible for former houses of worship. More importantly, they lend support to the theory that a continuum of acceptable reuses exists, depending on the extent to which the reuse replicates some of the functions of the house of worship when it was used for its original function. The continuum can be separated into two main sections, with nonprofit or public sector reuses tending toward the more "sacred" end and for-profit or private sector reuses tending toward the more secular end, some of which

Exhibit 9-1 Continuum of Secular Adaptive Reuses

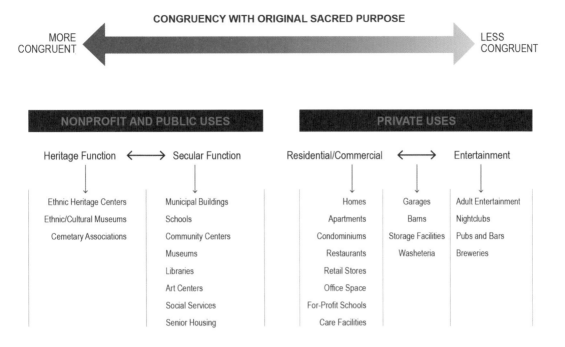

could be considered controversial, potentially sacrilegious, and even hedonistic. The examples presented here move from the least-congruent reuses to those that represent the highest and best use in the minds and eyes of nonmarket stakeholders.

Adult Entertainment

Some former houses of worship have become venues for entertainment, such as nightclubs, restaurants, brewhouses, and adult bookstores. Churches that undergo this fate may be located in declining inner cities that are trying to make an economic comeback as centers for evening and adult entertainment. The religious buildings tend to be large and structurally sound, making them attractive to developers who need large, open interior spaces. Renovations to the interior often retain some of the sacred architectural features, and the contrast between the former religious use and the current secular use may give added cachet to the new use. For some people, however, this deliberate juxtaposition of the sacred and the profane seems like a mocking of religion.

Electric Religion

Electric Religion is the name of a popular music band that has played at Clutch Cargo's, a large music and dance venue located in a former Congregational Church in Pontiac, Michigan. The title also captures the atmosphere of this club: loud, electronically amplified music performances, and dances in a former house of worship.

Pontiac is a small city about an hour from Detroit and is near large exurban developments. The First Congregational Church was built in 1925, when Pontiac was becoming a center for automobile production. Like many Midwest manufacturing centers, Pontiac began a long decline starting about 1950, and is now struggling with high unemployment and a downtown that

St. Boniface Church Conversion to the Ivory Theater, St. Louis, Missouri

St. Boniface Church is located in the historic Carondelet neighborhood of St. Louis. Bordering on the Mississippi River, the parish was established in 1860. The church, built in stages, was completed in 1890 in the Romanesque style with two 100-ft. towers on either side of its entrance. The property was added to the National Register of Historic Places in 2002. The site contains the church, a rectory constructed in 1921, and a school building dating from 1984.

A significant population decline had taken place in the 1990s, and the school was closed in 1995. The final decision to close the church was made partly because of a flood in 1993. The property became surplus as the Catholic population of the parish declined.

The property, with the church, rectory, and school, was sold by the archdiocese to Rothschild Allen, LLC, for $1.1 million in 2005, through a request-for-proposal (RFP) process. The archdiocese would not let a developer "cherry pick" portions of church property such as buying only the church. This strategy made sure the archdiocese would not be left with unsalable real estate. The archdiocese also required the purchaser to agree to deed restrictions, including limitations on alcohol sales and adult entertainment, in the former church.

Developer Pete Rothschild has a long history of redevelopment in St. Louis, beginning in 1969. His companies own and manage a thousand residential units and 600,000 sq. ft. of commercial space. He has a pioneer reputation: "After doing this sort of thing for 30 years, you get an intuitive sense of what's next," Rothschild said. "I think these (Carondelet) is what's next" (Hathaway 2007). The project, which was intended to jump-start redevelopment

in the Carondelet neighborhood, received $111,146 in remediation tax credits through the State of Missouri's Brownfield Redevelopment Program. Rothschild is in the process of converting the rectory next to the church into a restaurant and entertainment facility. The former school building houses a charter school, serving as a regular revenue stream from the property.

Rothschild's vision was to create a permanent home for several theater companies in the former church. He and his partner, Michael Allen, spent $800,000 to convert the church interior into an intimate performance space. The remodeling created stadium seating extending from the former altar area to the choir loft for 240 patrons. Other improvements included restrooms, dressing rooms, a box office, and state-of-the-art lighting and sound. The choir loft became a small cabaret and bar area serving "incidental" beer and wine. The incidental alcohol skirted the church prohibitions in the deed restrictions. Small theater space is at a premium in St. Louis, and although some visiting theater companies have said that the backstage space is inadequate, the Ivory fills a need.

The first show at Ivory Theater, named after a major street in the neighborhood because use of "St. Boniface" was prohibited, was a production of *Sex, Drugs, and Rock & Roll*. Initial advertising for the musical revue attracted the attention of the former owners and resulted in the Archdiocese of St. Louis winning a temporary restraining order to stop the performance. The suit contended the content might violate a condition of the building's sale that it not be used for shows aimed at "an adult audience rather than the general public."

But church officials agreed to dismiss the petition after reviewing a video of the show and talking with promoters. Both sides said

is attempting to attract restaurants, small theaters, and art galleries. The large church had formerly served Presbyterian and Congregational denominations. The last religious user was the Greater Life Christian Church, which put it on the market for about $600,000. Several churches were interested, but only the nightclub developers had the money to buy it (Sataline 1995).

About $500,000 was spent fixing broken

Ivory Theater, St. Louis, Missouri. Photograph: Gary DeWine

windows and replacing faulty wiring and plumbing. The atmosphere of the interior was changed from religious to "mystical." "The ceilings are now painted grape purple, gargoyles stand in place of religious statues and vinyl couches, instead of pews, line the former sanctuary" (Sataline 1995). Bars are located on each sidewall of the sanctuary.

The restaurant has a large, favorable location and is accessible to many suburban young people. It has a central auditorium and horseshoe-shaped balcony to house concerts, and secondary dance and performance areas in the basement and former bell tower. This conversion did not retain any architectural integrity in the exterior of the building. When windows break, plywood boards painted bright blue replace them. A large neon sign atop the building announces the club's name, Clutch Cargo's. Parking lots and decrepit buildings surround the building.

The club has become a popular destination for those who enjoy electronic music concerts. According to one reviewer: "Clutch Cargo's usually hosts three club nights per week for those who want to 'bump and grind,' featuring music ranging from techno, funk, Latin, alternative and everything in between. As an added bonus, Clutch Cargo's

a lack of communication led to the conflict. "We knew nothing about the plan," said Monsignor Vernor Gardin, vicar general of the archdiocese. "It could have been anything—nudity, simulated sex acts." Promotional materials suggested theatergoers leave children at home. Although some songs contain strong language, Rothschild said he didn't believe the performance violated the deed restriction(s). "The ad campaign from (the producer) New Line Theatre

was a little bit titillating, as well as the title of the play," said Rothschild. "We worked it out. There's no compromise. The show will go on as conceived" (Ratcliffe 2007).

The lesson learned is the deed restrictions cannot be taken lightly. Had the content been oriented to a mature audience, serious legal obstacles could have been encountered.

Vignette case study prepared by Gary DeWine

Clutch Cargo's, Pontiac, Michigan. Photograph: Larry Ledebur

was voted 'best bar to find a one-night stand' by the Metro Times in 2001" (Caruana 2003). A major feature of the club is that different concerts can be staged simultaneously in various parts of the building. Comments posted on the Web refer to the experience of moving from floor to floor for different concert experiences: "I love Clutch Cargo's. Where else can a group of people go and all be satisfied. If you don't like the music on one floor, just go to the next" (Planet99.com 2005).

The conversion from church to nightclub caused controversy in Pontiac, raising the question of appropriate use of former church buildings. The controversy was intensified by the original names proposed for the nightclub, "Sanctuary" and "Sanctum," which seemed sacrilegious to some. A city councilman told a reporter, "'But to think that somebody would be that brash to rub people's faces into the idea of a church being turned into a bar in such a sacrilegious way appalls me'" (Sataline 1995). A born-again Christian and city resident said, "I feel we are desecrating a sanctuary dedicated and consecrated to God." A director of

a city mission for the homeless had a somewhat different perspective. He was not offended by a church being converted to a nightclub, but regretted its location in an area where many hopeless, addicted people lived. He feared it would prove a temptation to those struggling to maintain sobriety. "If you have an empty heart, you're sad, you're depressed . . . you see a place where there seems to be joy, happiness. I think that's a tremendous temptation" (Sataline 1995).

On the other hand, one of the bar's owners, Nathan Vestal, emphasized the economic benefits of the conversion: "I came down to Pontiac eight years ago and there was a bar and all the rest of the storefronts were boarded up." He noted that for a city struggling to rebuild its downtown, the former church now houses a tax-paying enterprise. On the question of whether the building's former use as a church should be considered in its reuse, Vestal said that his father, a Presbyterian minister, told him, "'A church is people. A building is just mortar and stone'" (Salatine 1995).

This adaptive reuse vividly illustrates a conversion of a church to an entertainment venue that many consider antithetical to religion. Their anger was exacerbated by what felt like deliberate sacrilege or mockery of the building's former religious use and its architecture. The originally proposed names, "Sanctuary," and "Sanctum," had religious connotations. Another painful sacrilegious incongruity was maintaining a "mystical" interior as a setting for music and dancing that many associate with sexual license and widespread use of drugs and alcohol. Probably fueling the negative reception of this adaptive reuse in the community was the community's lost economic prosperity and current powerlessness, as it needed to accept almost any economic development activity that was willing to come there. The conversion of a large, landmark church representing a strong economic and community-oriented past to a nightclub for young people from other, more prosperous places seemed particularly defeating to the remaining residents of this struggling community.

"And on the Eighth Day, God Created Beer"

This logo is written on the mugs of The Church Brew Works, formerly St. John the Baptist's Roman Catholic Church. This adaptive reuse project is an example of an architecturally significant church, located in a declining city neighborhood of Pittsburgh, Pennsylvania, which has taken on new life as a brewery and restaurant.

The church was founded in 1878 to serve the Irish and Scottish Catholics who immigrated to work in the nearby steel mills. Skilled craftsmen created the decorative details of the building, including significant stained-glass windows and an unusual bell tower. Starting in the 1950s, the neighborhood began to lose population, and in 1993 the diocese closed the parish.

The church building lay dormant for three years. In 1996, after extensive renovation, "The Church Brew Works reopened the doors of St. John the Baptist" (Church Brew Works 2005). According to a Brew Works publication, the renovation tried to retain much of the original architectural and artistic detail of the building. "Painstaking attention to detail and the integrative reuse of existing fixtures all help to create a spectacular atmosphere to enhance your brewpub experience" (Church Brew Works 2005).

For example, the pews were cut to create the bar and the benches for tables. Bricks salvaged from a torn-down confessional were reused to make pillars for the outdoor sign. Another confessional now houses a gift shop. The "most breathtaking element" of the adaptive reuse project is the transformation of the altar to the area for brewing beer. According to the Brew Works, "Because the altar was built as a centerpiece of the church, the steel and copper tanks gleaming in the celestial blue backdrop is nothing less than captivating. This extraordinary view is only paralleled by the quality and taste of our beer" (Church Brew Works 2005).

This conversion from church to brewhouse evoked a range of responses in the community about appropriate use of former

Photograph: Dan Plunkett

Photograph: Church Brew Works/Nate Boguszewski

religious buildings. The History and Landmarks Foundation in Pittsburgh applauded the conversion because it preserved the historic nature of an architecturally significant building. The foundation gave the developer, Sean Casey, an award of merit for adaptive reuse. The diocese took the position that it could have been worse; a spokesman for the diocese, Rev. Ron Lengwin, told a reporter, "the church has no objections to the Brew Works, but would prohibit racier uses such as an exotic dance club." Public opinion is varied. The brewery's success suggests that religious trappings are not a barrier to many people's enjoyment of the beer, and may actually enhance their experience. However, waitresses told a reporter "some found the heavy church flavor a bit distasteful" (Lukasiak 2000).

In this adaptive reuse example, an important consideration was the retention of the exterior of the building as it had been when it was a church. This factor won the support of historic preservationists. For the people in the immediate neighborhood, the building still looked much the same as it had when it was a church, so it did not exacerbate the visibility of economic distress in the area. The use of religious trappings in conscious juxtaposition to the secular activities of the brewpub was kept inside, notably the use of the altar to house beer-brewing equipment. Another consideration is that the brewpub is essentially a restaurant and pub, a place for people to meet and dine together. It is not primarily a venue for raves or other events that seem to encourage licentious behavior. Perhaps for these reasons, the community reception of this church reuse was somewhat more positive than the conversion of the Pontiac, Michigan, church described above.

Office and Residential Uses

Former houses of worship may also be converted to private dwellings or to retail enterprises or offices. One such office project is discussed next.

Innovation in an Inspirational Setting

"Innovation in an inspirational setting" is the intent in the adaptive reuse of the First Church of Christ, Scientist, in Cleveland, Ohio, into the office for a consumer product-design firm. The new owners intend for the inspirational atmosphere of the interior to stimulate creativity and innovation. The church building, located on a hill overlooking an eastern suburb of Cleveland, has been a community landmark, "one of the most visible and beautiful landmarks in the city" (Litt 2003). The church, built in 1931, was designed by leading Cleveland architects Walker and Weeks. The facade resembles an old Roman temple, but the building is octagonal in shape and has a tall bell tower, which, when lit, is a beacon visible throughout the area.

The design firm maintained the exterior of the building almost intact and did very little remodeling to the interior, retaining the pipe organ, chandeliers, and Ionic columns. They changed the large, domed sanctuary into workstations for product designers. The balcony was converted to areas "for small, start-up companies to market new products created by the designers" (Litt 2003), and the basement, which used to house the Sunday school, is now used by engineers to create prototypes of new products. The owners said, "'We are really sensitive to the historic fabric of the building. It's a Walker and Weeks masterpiece, and we want to embrace that'" (Litt 2003).

The church's congregation, not large enough to keep the building intended for a thousand people, welcomed this adaptive

Nottingham Spirk, Cleveland, Ohio. Photograph: City Architecture/Bill Webb

Nottingham Spirk, Cleveland, Ohio. Photograph: City Architecture/Bill Webb, Nottingham Spirk, Cleveland, Ohio

reuse project. When the time came to sell the building, they were aware that the church's image in Cleveland could have been tarnished if the building was torn down. They turned down several offers before they received the current one.

This project is an example of an adaptive reuse to commercial purposes that has been met with approval from the congregation and the community. A key reason for public acceptance was the project's retention of the exterior of the building, which was seen as a community landmark. The building's location on a hill made it widely visible. The imposing architecture, the large size of the building, and the bell tower, lit at night, made the building visually pleasing and an inspiration to the surrounding neighborhood. Another positive feature of this project is that the commercial use capitalized on the religious heritage of the church. The church building was not treated simply as a large space in an affordable and appropriate location. Rather, its design, architecture, and history as a re-

ligious building were a large part of its appeal to the design firm. "'Everybody talks about innovation,' said John Nottingham, 53, the company's co-founder, as he stood in the sanctuary this summer. 'We're going to live it in an inspirational setting'" (Litt 2003).

Home Blessed Home
Conversion of houses of worship to condominiums or apartments is common (see Chapter 3). The conversion of Saints Peter and Paul Church to condominiums illustrates this adaptive reuse option, and some of the controversial issues that can arise in conversions of sacred buildings to private residences (see the case study in Chapter 15).

Saints Peter and Paul Church, in South Boston, Massachusetts, was built by Irish immigrants in 1848. The archdiocese closed the church in the late 1990s and sold it to developers in 2000 for $2.4 million. The conversion of this church into luxury condominiums has received much publicity because the conversion symbolizes at least two larger trends in the area: (1) the diminishing influence of the Catholic Church in the area due to the sex abuse scandal and population shifts, resulting in a constant drumbeat of church and parochial school closings; and (2) the gentrification of South Boston, which had for years been a declining, working-class enclave populated almost entirely by the descendants of Irish Catholic immigrants.

The church building is a large, granite structure in Victorian Gothic style. Its interior had the usual accoutrements of this style of church: stained-glass windows, statues, elaborately carved pews and other furniture, and sacred art. Following the usual procedure in the closing of Catholic churches, the archdiocese de-sanctified the church and removed its sacred objects, including crucifixes, chalices, and baptismal fonts (Vigue 2003). The archdiocese then sold the property to the McFarlands, local developers who converted the space into thirty-six luxury condominiums. The conversion left the exterior virtually intact and kept some religious emblems in place, including the interior's high plaster arches and the blue-painted ceiling with a painted gold cross. The developers removed the Stations of the Cross paintings, but have them available to sell to condominium buyers. The bell tower, a major architectural feature of the church, has been converted into the most expensive penthouse unit, and has "exposed beams, a wine cellar, and a balcony. . . . What about the bell itself, which tolled for so many high Masses and holy send-offs for the dead? 'If the buyer wants the bell, it will stay,' declared James McFarland. 'He can go up there and [clang] it. They can have themselves the biggest alarm clock in Boston.'"

Responses and reactions to this conversion of a beloved ethnic landmark into luxury housing have been very public and extremely varied. James McFarland, who was raised Catholic, said, "Being brought up Catholic, it was a bit strange to come into a church and tear it apart, but it's a de-sanctified church, so you have to keep telling yourself that when you're doing construction" (Lavoie 2004).

Some have expressed concern that potential buyers would be put off by the recent pedophilia scandals in the Catholic Church, even though this particular church was not involved. However, the condominiums, like others converted from churches in the Boston area, have proven to be very popular with buyers. A real estate broker, Lucas Garofalo, takes the view that the modern amenities, combined with unique, historic living spaces, make the condominiums so popular. "'People want a landmark, they don't want cookie-cutter,' he said. 'And because churches have such a strong connection to the history of a community, buyers love that. They also love granite countertops, hardwood floors, whirlpool tubs, stainless steel appliances, and high ceilings'" (Vigue 2003).

For some buyers, the attraction goes beyond the unique architectural detail and historic neighborhood associations of the building. A couple who bought a condominium converted from another church in the area was leery at first of living in a church since it seemed sacrilegious. But they changed their minds when they first went inside. The wife now says, "I am a very religious and spiritual person, and living here, for me, has always been like being cradled in God's hands. . . . Church is a place where all the noise in life dissipates and you have time to reflect. Places like this should always exist."

Neighborhood reactions have been less positive. One strong objection has been that a central landmark of an essentially working-class neighborhood was being turned into luxury condominiums, unaffordable by local residents. The conversion of Saints Peter and Paul's Church is part of a larger process of gentrification of South Boston, which has raised great concern about the availability of affordable housing for residents, especially seniors. South Boston's mayor, Ray Flynn, whose parents were married in the church, told a reporter that "People really feel hurt and a tremendous loss of community when they see their church close and then they see luxury condominiums being built on those locations, with Mercedes automobiles parked outside. . . . It takes a long time for people to not think of this as a sacred religious site" (Lavoie 2004).

The archdiocese is managing a process of closing and selling a large number of parish churches using established church policies.

A spokesman for the archdiocese has said, "It is not always accepting the highest offer. Church law very clearly spells out that when transferring or selling church property to someone else, the church's social mission must be taken into account. So it furthers the work of charity within society" (Lavoie 2004). He pointed out that an additional thirteen condominium units in the conversion of the rectory area around Saints Peter and Paul's were intended to be more affordable, and this expectation was spelled out in the sale agreement with the McFarlands.

As the archdiocese continues to divest itself of churches with declining populations, the Metropolitan Area Planning Council of Boston is engaged in helping neighborhoods understand and have a voice in the conversion of parish churches into housing. A spokesman for the council said, "Though towns will likely not have the final word on what happens to their local places of worship, they are trying to negotiate with the archdiocese for open space, housing or preservation of buildings. Now, suddenly and unexpectedly, the archdiocese has come across with the large infusion of church structures and communities are hoping [affordable] housing will be an option on that site" (Hillman 2004).

The conversion of Saints Peter and Paul's Church to luxury condominiums illustrates some of the issues that can arise in converting churches to homes. The adaptive reuse of this building was problematic in part because there were still many people in the neighborhood who had ties to the church. They felt a sense of loss when the church closed, and would have been unhappy about any adaptive reuse. No one seems to have objected to a housing reuse: the controversy focused on the conversion to luxury condominiums. The rapid gentrification of a long-established and closely knit working-class neighborhood being invaded by wealthy outsiders was exacerbated by the shortage of affordable housing in the area, and some low-income seniors felt squeezed out.

Nonprofit Secular Functions

Churches vacated by the religious groups that owned them may be taken over by nonprofit organizations. Nonprofits often have the goal of serving the public interest in some way, such as organizations focusing on social services, education, culture, and the arts. These reuses are closer to the original religious and sacred functions of the house of worship and are therefore higher on the "congruency" continuum. The following examples show some of the range of adaptive reuses in this category.

A Landmark in Their Lives

The conversion of St. Pius Church in Cincinnati, Ohio, to a neighborhood service center is an example of adaptive reuse that retains some of the community functions the building had when it was a Roman Catholic church.

According to a study conducted at the University of Cincinnati (Johnson 2004), St. Pius Church was built in 1911 to accommodate immigrating German Catholics. By the mid-twentieth century the population had changed to predominantly African American, and the number of practicing Catholics in the neighborhood declined. However, the huge church building had a large footprint as the major community landmark in a neighborhood consisting mainly of small family homes. The parish school remained active, even though 90 percent of the students were not Catholic. The school and church grounds remained important to community residents. "Local residents made use of social services offered by the church and neighborhood children used its grounds as a safe playground" (Johnson 2004). However, citing declining attendance, the archdiocese closed the school in 1990 and the church in 1998. The community felt the loss of this important symbol of community cohesion. The president of the neighborhood's community council and a parishioner of St. Pius (Pina) expressed the community's view: "A landmark in their lives was lost" (Pina 1998, as cited in Johnson 2004).

The neighborhood surrounding St. Pius, called South Cumminsville, has a high level of community cohesiveness, according to the University of Cincinnati study (Johnson 2004). It has the highest rate of minority home ownership in the city (Martinez 2004, as cited in Johnson 2004, 46). One reason for this cohesiveness is the nonprofit organization called Working in Neighborhoods (WIN). Started by two nuns in the 1980s, WIN serves several economically distressed Cincinnati neighborhoods, focusing on increasing home ownership and creating wealth. When the archdiocese put up the St. Pius Church building for sale, the only potential buyer was an asbestos-storage firm. At that point, WIN decided to purchase the property to house its administrative offices, and negotiated several low-interest loans to do so. The archdiocese agreed to sell to WIN, even though the commercial buyer offered a higher price, because WIN offered an adaptive reuse that more closely matched the church's social mission.

The sanctuary was refitted for administrative offices. The archdiocese removed many of the stained-glass windows before the sale, but a large rose window has been retained. The huge sanctuary space has been divided into two large areas: offices were built where the altar was, and the other half is split into community and computer education rooms. The building has retained its function as a center of neighborhood activity. The nuns who direct WIN have observed that residents are pleased that some of the spiritual feeling of the church has been retained and proud that they have "saved the parish" (Johnson 2004).

The adaptive reuse of St. Pius Church mitigated the closing of the church, always a painful and emotional issue for parishioners, former parishioners, and community residents. The neighborhood, consisting mainly of non-Catholic African Americans who were not connected to the religious ceremonies of the church, was deeply connected to the building and to its educational and social service missions. Transformation into the headquarters of an organization dedicated to the social mission of local economic development retained the original church's mission, and the adaptive reuse, in effect, "saved the parish."

"Nurturing . . . the Creative Life of Our Community"

This is the expressed mission and guiding focus of ArtCentric, a center for art in Corvallis, Oregon. Corvallis is a university town in the Willamette Valley, which, until the mid-twentieth century, was devoted primarily to agricultural and logging industries. In 1961 a group of public-spirited citizens formed the Corvallis Arts Council. Concurrently, a historic Episcopal church near downtown was available for use. The congregation had built a new church and sold the old building to the local Elks lodge, which could not use it, and offered to lend it indefinitely to the Arts Council. Crews of volunteers renovated the building: pews and altars were removed, and the entire building was renovated. The Arts Council operated in the building until 1970, when the Elks sold the lot on which the church stood. The Arts Council, faced with loss of their space, decided to move the historic church, and the city donated space in a nearby park, where the building was moved in 1972. In the process, the council secured the building's status on the National Register of Historic Places, which enabled the council to receive funds necessary to move the building.

The church building has historic and architectural value to Corvallis residents. The Episcopal church was built in 1889 in the Carpenter Gothic architectural style. The crossbeams and arches on the ceiling are patterned as the reverse of a railroad bridge, reflecting the architect's profession as a railroad engineer. In the renovation to an arts center, the main sanctuary has been divided, with the altar end now a gallery for large artworks, and the nave end a reception area and shop. The former vestry houses administrative offices. The base-

ment, formerly the Sunday school and parish hall, has been converted into a dance studio and classrooms for art lessons.

The local arts organizations offer concerts; lectures; classes in art, music, and dance; art exhibits; educational programming in the schools; and special programs for at-risk youth. The main sanctuary space is also available for rental for family and community events.

There is no record of any controversy surrounding this adaptive reuse. Many community groups worked actively and cooperatively over time to retain the building for a nonprofit use. The original Episcopal congregation, the Elks, the newspaper, the Arts Council, the city, and numerous volunteers worked together to maintain the historic building and create a successful transition from a place of worship to a community center for the arts.

Corvallis Arts Council, Corvallis, Oregon. Photograph: Scottlawphotography.com

The adaptive reuse of the church to an arts center is an example of an adaptive reuse in which some of the original functions of the building as a church were retained. The community welcomed the reuse because it was a way to retain a valued village landmark, and because the functions of the Arts Council seemed in keeping with some of the social mission of the original church. The perception of a church as a repository of art has been retained, as has the outreach to the community (Corvallis Art Center 2005).

"Hayti Hayti Handed Down"
The line "Hayti Hayti handed down" is from a poem by Darrell Stover, expressing the view that the St. Joseph Historic Foundation, located in Hayti, the traditionally African American district in Durham, North Carolina, is preserving an important heritage of the African American community. St. Joseph's African American Episcopal Church provides an example for the "most congruent" adaptive reuse of a church building, according to the Congruence Continuum shown in Exhibit 9-1. This empty church found new life as a heritage center.

The story of St. Joseph's begins with the arrival of Edian Markham, an African American Methodist Episcopal minister and former slave, to Durham in 1868. He established a church. In 1891 the African American community had grown more prosperous, and, with the additional support of wealthy white citizens, was able to build the substantial church that still stands. The brick structure is in the Gothic Revival style, with pronounced buttresses, towers, and bays, reminiscent of the Richardsonian Romanesque style of church architecture. The building contains a number of notable artistic and religious features, including an ornate pipe organ, an elaborate and historic tin ceiling, Art Nouveau light fixtures, and twenty-four stained-glass windows, some of which feature early black ministers of the church.

The building is prominently situated at the southeastern gateway to Durham, acting as a landmark and focal point of the historic Hayti district (Durham Convention & Visitors Bureau 2001; St. Joseph's Historic Foundation, Inc. 2005). The church was a prominent part of African American local history. Langston Hughes, W. E. B. Dubois, and Dr. Martin Luther King Jr. all made presentations at the church. W. E. B. Dubois is quoted as saying, "Never in all my travels have I seen a church as great as St. Joseph's" (St. Joseph's Historic Foundation 2005).

The Hayti community was dubbed the "Black Wall Street" during its heyday between 1900 and 1920 because of the thriving private enterprise of African American residents. Black-owned businesses included a barbershop, cosmetology school, grocery store, bank, hotel, hospital, construction firm, and many others. A resident of the town founded the North Carolina Mutual Life Insurance Company, the largest and one of the oldest black-owned businesses in the United States. His descendants still play an important civic role in the community (Whitfield and Champ 2005).

Urban renewal projects in the early 1970s decimated the Hayti neighborhood, when public housing buildings and freeways replaced much of the business district, nightclubs, and a Baptist church. The congregation of St. Joseph's built a new church south of town, "leaving empty and forlorn on its hill the handsome church building" (Ariail 2001). However, a coalition of historic preservation–minded community activists worked to preserve the building and turn it into a center celebrating black history and culture. They also wanted it to become a force for the economic revitalization of the Hayti district.

Both prominent black and white people led the effort to save the church (Ariail 2001). Through many decades of shared history and family relationships, people of both races felt a strong connection to the church and to the district's history. Folklorists and historians of blues and other African American musical forms also took a strong interest in creating a monument to preserve and celebrate black culture. In 2001 the church restoration was complete, and it became a four-hundred-seat hall with very good acoustics, which could showcase black theater and music.

The St. Joseph's Historic Foundation, Inc. and the Hayti Heritage Center conduct programming on African American history and culture, funded by a mix of private and public funding. Adding St. Joseph's Church as a center for performances has been a natural extension of their mission and has increased the visibility and support of the Heritage Center's work in the community. According to the executive director, Diane Pledger, "The entire community has embraced this, from school children giving $5, to every citizen who approved the bond issues. The community wanted us to save this building and turn it into something of use" (Ariail 2001).

The reuse of St. Joseph's African Methodist Episcopal Church into a heritage center celebrating African American culture exemplifies how a reuse can retain some of the original function of the church and also enhance and further that mission. St. Joseph's had traditionally served the functions of providing a focus for community cohesiveness and pride in the African American community, a function that has been expanded and enhanced. The church now books major artists, and hosts a widely attended major blues festival every year. The contributions and support of the entire community in this adaptive reuse effort indicate wholehearted acceptance and support for the reuse of the church building as a cultural heritage center.

The Community Vision and Goals Continuum

The preceding section gave examples showing that the "Congruency with Sacred Functions Continuum" was an important factor in perception of appropriateness of the adaptive reuse of a church. These functions included holding congregation-oriented religious services and offering material help in cases of emergency, and also functions fulfilling the social mission of the church, which involves charitable work in the community at large.

Another dimension addresses appropriateness: "Continuum of Congruency with Community Goals and Values." In this context, "community" refers to both the immediate neighborhood around the church and the larger community.

The community vision and goals vector places reuses along a continuum according to whether the reuse matches the hopes and plans the community has for itself. Exhibit 9-2 displays a matrix combining the two continuums, the "Congruency with Sacred Function" and the "Congruency with Community Goals" Continuum. The matrix has four quadrants:

(A) High Original Sacred Purpose, High Community Values/Vision
(B) High Original Sacred Purpose, Low Community Values/Vision
(C) High Community Values/Vision, Low Original Sacred Purpose
(D) Low Community Values/Vision, Low Original Sacred Purpose

Examples of quadrant A include the reuses of church buildings into nonprofit organizations to benefit the entire community, such as ArtCentric, the St. Joseph's Heri-

Exhibit 9-2 Diamond of Adaptive Reuse

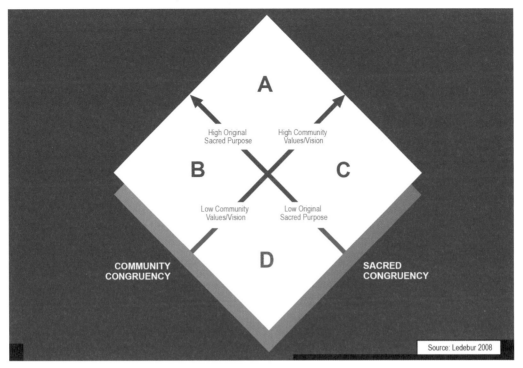

tage Center, and Working in Neighborhoods. These reuses retain some of the sacred functions and social mission of the original church, and are welcomed by the community.

For quadrant B possible examples might include the conversion of a church into a homeless shelter or home for troubled youth in a neighborhood that saw these new residents as problematic. Some of the original sacred functions of the church are retained in such a situation, mainly its social mission to help those in need, but the reuse is counter to the goals and vision of the community.

Quadrant C includes adaptive reuses that resonate with community values and vision but do not necessarily retain the church's original sacred purpose. The conversion of the Christian Science church in Cleveland, Ohio, is an example of a reuse in this quadrant. The reuse of the church into a for-profit design center did not retain the sa-

cred function of the church building, but it was congruent with community goals: to retain a landmark building that helped define the neighborhood and was a meaningful part of the personal geography of residents. It also helped the economic prosperity of the area by returning a building to the tax base. Another possible example is the reuse of a Catholic church in Pittsburgh to a brewhouse. Like the conversion of the Christian Science church, this renovation retained the exterior of a large, landmark church. At the same time, it met the goals of the larger community of contributing to the economic development of a declining downtown area.

Quadrant D includes adaptive reuses that are low in sacred function and are also incongruent with community values and vision. The conversion of the old landmark Methodist church in Pontiac, Michigan, to a youth-oriented nightclub is an example of reuses in this quadrant. The reuse was at the far end of the "Congruency with Original Sacred Function" of the building, and even seemed to mock the building's former sacred use. In addition, the reuse was not congruent with the vision and goals of the community. Though it did bring in needed tax revenue, it did nothing to retain and strengthen the values the community had and the way it wanted to develop an economic comeback. It appealed mainly to young people who were not resident in the community and whose contribution to the community was nil or even negative. Another example of a conversion in this quadrant is the reuse of a Catholic church as expensive condominiums. Housing for the relatively well-off is far down the continuum of Congruency with Original Sacred Function. The nearby community, South Boston, wanted housing but wanted affordable housing that would benefit local, working-class residents. The insertion of a luxury building (even though part was reserved for affordable housing) was not congruent with all the wishes of this neighborhood, though the economic redevelopment of South Boston may have been more congruent with the larger community, including metropolitan Boston governmental entities.

Conclusion: Appropriate Use and Highest and Best Use

With these two vectors in mind, it is possible to define appropriate use. Adaptive reuses can be labeled as appropriate to the extent that they are congruent with the original sacred function of the church, including its social mission, and with the values and vision of the community in which the church is located. Conversely, reuses that are not congruent with the original sacred purpose of the house of worship, or seem to mock it, and are not congruent with the values and vision of the surrounding community, can be called inappropriate uses.

For those interested in the conversion of former houses of worship to secular uses, the diamond of adaptive use provides a useful framework for:

(1) identifying nonmarket stakeholders such as local governments, community and neighborhood constituencies, historic preservation interests, and former owners and their congregations;

(2) assessing and understanding the stakes of these stakeholders and the nonmarket interests and public values that may catalyze community response and engagement in the fate and future of these buildings;

(3) anticipating public and community reactions to proposed adaptive reuses; and

(4) finding effective means of working with these nonmarket constituencies and stakeholders to address their issues and concerns, thus converting bad publicity and public opposition to support and approval or good publicity.

For example, an assessment might identify nonmarket public and community stakeholders deeply concerned about the fate and future of a redundant religious structure in terms of both the original sacred purpose of the building and its consistency with community values and vision (Quadrant A of the Diamond of Adaptive Reuse). Proposed adaptations that are highly congruent with the original sacred purpose and community vision and values are highly likely to receive community endorsement and support. However, it must be acknowledged that these uses may also require continuous public investment to remain economically viable, and that they pay no property taxes.

Proposed projects less congruent with these religious purposes and community values (Quadrant D), on the other hand, are more likely to be surrounded by controversy and opposition and entail high costs of winning public and community approval with the attendant risk of failure to garner this support. On the other hand, many of these uses are economically self-sustaining and contribute to the public coffers.

If the assessment of nonmarket stakeholders places the proposed project as highly congruent with original religious purpose but noncongruent with community values and vision (Quadrant B) the conflict and opposition will probably come from the surrounding community, neighborhood groups, and possibly local governments.

Finally, if the project is congruent with neighborhood values and vision but noncongruent with original sacred purpose, the probable sources of opposition are former congregants and their religious organization such as a Catholic diocese.

In concluding this chapter, it is useful to end where we began—with the issue of highest and best use. The underlying thesis of this chapter is that market values are not the only arbiter of the highest and best use of redundant houses of worship. Other nonmarket values come into play and may be considered in determining the best and most valuable use of structures for which there are public stakeholders such as local governments, communities, both neighborhood and communities of worship, and historic preservationists. Ultimately, in these cases, highest and best use will be determined through the interplay of the market for real estate and the market of public opinion.

References and Works Consulted

Ariail, K. 2001. "Preserving a Heritage." *The Independent Weekly*, June 27. http://www .indyweek.com/indyweek/st-josephs-historic -foundationhayti-heritage-center/Content ?oid=1183992.

Caruana, M. 2003. "Clutch Cargo's. Hear Here: The Best of Detroit and Even Some of the Rest." http://www.motorcityrocks.com/ carago.htm.

Church Brew Works. "History of St. John the Baptist's and Lawrenceville." www.church brew.com/church_history.html.

Corvallis Arts Center. 2005. www.artcentric.org.

Durham Convention & Visitors Bureau. 2001. "Historic St. Joseph's—Durham's Newest Performance/Meeting Venue." *Bull's Eye,* May/ June.

Goodnough, A. 2009. "In a Quiet Church Rebellion, Massachusetts Parishioners Keep the Faith." *New York Times,* January 6. http: //www.nytimes.com/2009/01/06/world/ americas/06iht-06vigil.19111393.html.

Hathaway, M. 2007. "Theater in Old Church Offers New Life: Neighborhood Gets Infusion of Townhouses, Stores, Offices and Excitement." *St. Louis Post-Dispatch,* September 27, B1.

Hillman, M. 2004. "Old School: Condos That Come from Unlikely Places." *Boston Business Journal,* October 8. www.bizjournals.com /boston/stories/2004/10/11/focus3.html.

Johnson, T. 2004. "Socio-economic and Political Issues in the Successful Adaptive Reuse of Churches." Master's thesis, University of Cincinnati, College of Design, Architecture, Art, and Planning, May 28.

Lavoie, D. 2004. "God's House Turned into Posh Condos." *Washington Times,* June 14. www .washtimes.com/business.

Litt, S. 2003. "Church's Transformation into Business Offers Answer to Many People's Prayers." *Cleveland Plain Dealer,* September 13.

Lukasiak, M. 2000. "Converting Churches, Mindful of Their Past." *Pittsburgh Tribune Review,* July 29, 2.

Martinez, Sister J. 2004. Interview by Tara A. Johnson and Beth Sullebarger, April 27. Cited in Johnson, 2004, 47.

Planet99.com. 2005. "Clutch Cargo's." http:// www.planet99.com/detroit/bars/9513x.html.

Ratcliffe, H. 2007. "Show Goes on, with Blessing: Church Officials Initially Objected to Performance of 'Sex, Drugs and Rock & Roll' at Old St. Boniface Church in Carondelet." *St. Louis Post-Dispatch,* September 29, A7.

Sataline, S. 1995. "An Old Pontiac Church Turned into a Bar Has Set Off . . . an Unholy War." *Detroit Free Press,* February 10, 1B.

St. Joseph's Historic Foundation, Inc. 2005. "St.

Joseph's Historic Foundation and the Legacy of the Hayti Community." www.hayti.org.

Talmud Bavli, Tractate Megillah. 2013. Edited by Hersh Goldwurm, 27b. Brooklyn, N.Y.: Mesorah Publications Ltd.

Vigue, D. 2003. "Converted." *Boston Globe,* March 23, J1. www.boston.com/.

Whitfield, K., and J. Champ. 2005. "Hayti Community." Meredith College School of Social Work. www.meredith.edu/socwork/Hayti%20two.htm.

FROM "TEMPLES OF CONSUMPTION" TO "TEMPLES OF FAITH"

Larry Ledebur and

S. Subha Vyakaranam

The primary focus of this book is the adaptation of redundant faith and learning structures to alternative commercial, nonprofit, or public enterprises. It is useful, however, to make a small detour into the adaptation of redundant secular buildings to houses of worship. This is the task of the current chapter. Many churches in the United States purchase secular structures to use as houses of worship. These religious enterprises can be found in storefronts, car dealerships, movie theaters, warehouses, malls, big-box stores, and many other buildings constructed for secular purposes. This chapter illustrates that the adaptive reuse of structures from sacred to secular is only one aspect of a larger phenomenon, the dynamic, multidirectional reuse of all types of structures from one use to another.

While there is growing recognition of religious organizations as a market for sale of commercial buildings, there are issues of which buyers and sellers should be aware. Clearly, although the number of nonmarket stakeholders is considerably smaller than in the adaptive reuse of former houses of worship to secular uses, there are some. Primary among these are the local taxing authorities, local governments that control permitting and zoning, and those who guide local zoning boards in considering zoning variances. At the core of this issue is the removal of commercial properties from the property tax base due to the nonprofit status of religious organizations. In many cases these adaptive reuses include and require substantial surface parking areas, which are also removed from the tax rolls.

In a few instances, megachurches have acquired mega secular facilities and adapted them to their sacred purposes. Two prominent examples are the Faithful Central Bible Church and the Lakewood Church in Houston (discussed below), both of which bought or leased former professional basketball coliseums to adapt to the functions of their megachurches. These secular-to-sacred adaptations are ironic in that some pundits have opined that sports coliseums may be the new and true cathedrals and sacred landmarks of secular urban America.

More recently, interest has focused on adaptive reuse of big-box retail stores for nonretail uses. A recent book, *Big Box Reuse,* has drawn national attention to this phenomenon (Christiansen 2008). Adaptations of big-box stores include indoor go-cart

Church built on the roof of a former commercial laundry. Korean Presbyterian Church, Queens, New York. Photograph: Brian Rose

raceways, gyms, senior resource centers, charter schools, Head Start programs, museums, libraries, health centers, and a peddler's mall, as well as one church, Calvary Chapel of Pinellas Park, Florida.

Big Boxes to God's McMansions

One reason for churches to adapt former big-box stores to meet their own needs is cost. These adaptations are often a less expensive alternative to new construction. Further, since big-box shopping space is located in areas zoned and operated as retail, churches avoid many, if not most, of the external stakeholder issues often encountered in building new churches in nonretail spaces. Since many of these big-box stores are located on the peripheries of metropolitan areas, they are highly accessible through transportation systems of beltways and turnpikes.

Part of the appeal is ready supply of these structures. Joel Garreau (2008) has argued:

> . . . we're going to have to figure out what to do with a whole lot of big boxes, and soon. There are thousands of them—vast prairies of Targets and Bed Bath & Beyonds and Costcos and Home Depots. Wal-Mart alone has 4,224 in the United States, more than half of them Supercenters into which, on average, you could comfortably fit four NFL football fields. . . .

> More typical, however, is the situation at Walmartrealty.com. At last count there were 189 Wal-Marts for sale, and not because business is bad. A typical available Wal-Mart might be a 40,000-square-foot store (about the size of a football field) that was replaced by a 80,000-square-foot store that was so successful it has been replaced with a 200,000-square-foot store just down the road. . . .

The following pages describe five adaptive reuses from megastructures to megachurches. The first is Lakewood Church in Houston, which adapted the former Compaq Center, an arena originally built for the Houston Rockets. The next three cases examine the secular-to-sacred adaptation of a former strip club in Atlanta; a mall in Lakeland, Florida; and an office building in Kirkland, Florida. The final case in this chapter serves as a reminder that the adaptive reuse of structures from sacred to secular, or vice versa, is only one aspect of a larger phenomenon, the dynamic, multidirectional reuse of all types of structures from one use to another. It is not an adaptive reuse of a secular building to a sacred use. It describes a megachurch, Without Walls International Church, located in Tampa Bay, Florida, which is now for sale, a victim of leadership problems, the mortgage crisis, and the spiraling downturn of the Florida real estate market.

"A Texas-Sized Sanctuary"

Pastor Joel Osteen used these terms to describe the new home of Lakewood Church in Houston, when in 2005 it moved into the former Compaq Center, an arena originally built for the Houston Rockets. Coincidentally, Osteen and his wife had their first date at the arena, nineteen years earlier (Associated Press 2005; Pristin 2004).

Large arenas designed for sporting events are not usually thought of as likely venues for religious services, although the idea that the main requirement for housing an evangelical worship service is a large, empty space hearkens back to the "tent revivals" of an earlier time. Lakewood Church is the largest American megachurch, with thirty thousand members, and the Compaq arena space, with its seating capacity for sixteen thousand, was just the right size

(Associated Press 2005). The church, which had its beginnings in an abandoned feed store in 1959, has grown fivefold since then. The new location is a visible indicator of the church's growth.

The arena, renovated at a cost of $75 million, has several advantages as a home for the church, according to Osteen. It is located near a major highway, making access easy for the large congregation. The interior provides space for the theatrical effects the church wants, such as good acoustics, a circular staircase (flanked by waterfalls) for the 250-member choir, a moving orchestra pit, and large video screens. There is room for all the technical equipment needed to broadcast the services on three dozen television channels around the country. The property has ample parking, and there was room to add a five-story building with more than 200,000 sq. ft. of classrooms and television production offices (Pristin 2004; Bacon 2005).

Lakewood Church took the property through a long-term lease with the city, to which it paid $11.8 million in rent in advance for the first thirty years. The church faced competition for the property from Crescent Real Estate Equities Company, which owns a 5-million-sq.-ft. office complex surrounding the arena. Crescent wanted to tear down the arena and put up a new office building. However, executives at Crescent now believe that the church will attract new restaurant and retail tenants to the complex. The city is pleased with the arrangement because, according to a city spokesman, the rent paid by the church was equal to the appraised value of the arena (Pristin 2004).

Gold Club to God Club

The Gold Club, in Atlanta, Georgia, was a notorious night club in the 1990s, but in 2004 the building was turned into a church. Pastor Dan M. Garrett pointed out the analogy between remodeling the building and the work of the church in redeeming souls: "It's all about transformation. . . . What we did to this building, cleaning it up and fixing it up, that is what God does for us" (Hart 2004).

The Gold Club was a prominent strip club, with celebrities and star athletes among its patrons. In 2001, federal prosecutors charged the owners with racketeering in a sweeping indictment that included charges of prostitution, credit card fraud, money laundering, and links to organized crime. The planned trials promised lurid testimony from NFL and NBA players concerning sex with strippers. Before trial, however, most defendants were able to plea bargain. The owner was imprisoned and fined, and relinquished the building to the government (CNN 2001; Hart 2004).

While the prosecution prepared its case, Dan Garrett, a pastor who had recently returned to his hometown of Atlanta, was looking for a church of his own. His wife suggested they rent the Gold Club, which brought the spotlight of media attention on the fledgling church. Two hundred volunteers helped with the renovation, and many more came to see the changes. Most of the new congregation expressed delight at the church's location. A kindergarten teacher and member of the congregation said, "I think it's hilarious. . . . It's a real testimony of what God's grace can do."

The church planned from the beginning to use the space only temporarily, and after a few months moved to a permanent home in a renovated AMC theater. Clearly, a major purpose of the temporary use of the Club building was to gain publicity for the new church. As Pastor Garrett noted, "Just a few months prior, twenty of us had sat around tables in the fellowship hall of North Druid Hills wondering how we could get the word out that we were starting a new church, and then on Kick-Off Sunday Christian Church Buckhead was the feature story on every TV and radio station in town!" (Garrett 2005). Church historian Jeanne Halgren Kilde pointed out that there was a tradition among Protestant Evangelicals of seeking publicity for their revivals, so that they sometimes used theaters, considered as sinful venues at the time, with the justification that they would "convert" the space (Hart 2004).

First Baptist Church at the Mall, Lakeland, Florida.
Photograph: Larry Ledebur

"I'm One of Those Crazy Baptists That Bought the Mall"

These words are on the t-shirts worn by members of the congregation whose church is officially named The First Baptist Church at the Mall. Located in Lakeland, Florida, about an hour from both Tampa and Orlando, the church moved from the building it had occupied for ninety-five years in downtown Lakeland to the mall on the outskirts of town in 1999.

Worship services have been held in the former Montgomery Ward store, with the plan to move into a larger space, a renovated former Sam's Club with seating for 2,400. Two movie theaters, seating five hundred people, are used for seminars and family movies. Other former retail shops, such as Radio Shack, are now the locations

First Baptist Church at the Mall, Lakeland, Florida.
Photograph: Larry Ledebur

for Sunday school classes and church offices. The mall also houses a 7,000-sq.-ft. library, an on-site restaurant, a clothing and food bank for the poor, and a dock leading to the lake (Whitaker 2004).

The church has grown much larger since it moved to the mall. About 2,700 people attend each weekend, out of a membership of 5,600. The congregation bought the 475,000-sq.-ft. mall for $5.6 million and spent $2.3 million on renovation (Slaybaugh 2004). The parking lot has space for 1,800 cars. Pastor Jay Dennis, quoted in *Christianity Today*, remarked, "What once was a retail center where people bought things is now a spiritual center where the most important thing in life is offered free" (Wilson 1999).

"From an Office Building to the House of the Lord"

In these words, Christ Church Kirkland pastor Norm Willis expressed his congregation's joy at the conversion of an office building in Kirkland, Washington, to a church home. The church began in 1972 as a home ministry, and continued for two decades without a building of its own. With exploding growth of its congregation, the church purchased a 48,000-sq.-ft., steel-framed office building in 1992 to hold church offices and Sunday meetings (Christ Church Kirkland 2009).

The church bought the entire building with an eye to the future, even though they initially needed only the sanctuary space on the top floor. The building is on a hillside, so there is an entry from parking areas directly to the top and bottom floors. The church rented out the lower two-thirds of the space for nine years until, with the establishment of a church school, the elders decided that the church needed the entire building.

The classrooms required very little adaptation from their former uses as offices, and are clustered around a two-level atrium used for communal spiritual and learning activities of the school. The worship space is in a renovated area on the top floor, with a new steel cross incorporated into the roof, which helps the building's structure and also provides an appropriate spiritual symbol. Also on the top floor is a café, intended to encourage community interaction, under a newly created skylight.

The exterior of the building is primarily a steel box. To make the entrance area more congruent with the church's "classical" approach to religion, the architects built "a freestanding tilt-concrete 'loggia' and entry plaza columns. These elements establish a new, visually strong presence, and do not require modifying the building's existing metal skin" (Frye 2003).

The architect of the project identified the advantages of the adaptive reuse of office buildings for churches, especially those that include a church school. "[O]bvious benefits include fewer neighborhood impacts as compared to locating in a residential area, empty buildings are occupied and put to good use, and the peak traffic associated with weekend church services comes on non-peak days" (Frye 2003).

"The Wrecking Ball of Heaven Is Swinging"

Church properties are not immune from the credit crisis that dominated the real estate market during recent years. The rise of the megachurches in the 1990s corresponded with the rapid increase in real estate prices, and lenders were willing to provide large loans to new churches on the assumptions that the congregations, and therefore donations, would grow, and that the property would appreciate at a rapid rate. With the downturn, some churches, including megachurches, are behind in their mortgage payments or facing foreclosure (Sataline 2008; Story 2008).

One example of such a megachurch is Without Walls International Church, located in Tampa Bay, Florida, which soon may be literally without walls. The seventeen-year-old church, located in a prime location, put its property on the market in March 2008, with an asking price of $30 million. The property includes a 4,500-seat sanctuary, a 94,000-sq.-ft. office building, a television studio, and a health club (Bearden and Helgeson 2008). With a softening of the real estate market, the church has not found a buyer, and in November 2008, the holder of the mortgage, Evangelical Christian Credit Union, foreclosed on the church. The credit union was demanding immediate repayment of a $1 million loan, the $12 million mortgage on the Tampa Bay property, and the $12.5 million mortgage on the church's branch in Lakeland, Florida.

In the case of Without Walls International, recent events within the church exacerbated the financial problems brought about by the national credit crisis. In 2007 the popular copastors, Randy and Paula White, announced their divorce, for which

Randy White said he assumed full responsibility, though no details were made public. There was the threat of a U.S. Senate investigation into the finances of this church and several others, which seemed to suggest a disproportionately lavish lifestyle for the leadership.

These events were particularly damaging for churches like Without Walls, which depend on the personal charismatic leadership of the pastors for their popularity. For many of the flock, these revelations indicated that the church was not built on a sound religious foundation, and they lost confidence. Over half of the 22,000 membership of Without Walls has left in the last couple of years. Among those who remain, many fear for their own financial security in the sagging economy. As a result, donations have fallen drastically, and the church can no longer meet its financial obligations (Day 2008). J. Lee Grady, editor of *Charisma,* an evangelical magazine, expressed the view that God was punishing churches like Without Walls: "The wrecking ball of heaven is swinging. It has come to demolish any work that has not been built on the integrity of God's Word" (Grady 2008).

Conclusion: Thinking Outside the "Box"

The renowned urban planner Jane Jacobs argued that "Old ideas can sometimes use new buildings; new ideas must use old buildings" (Jacobs 1961). We are challenged to think creatively and innovatively about new ideas for old buildings whether they were secular or sacred in their former use.

In *Big Box Reuse,* Julia Christiansen documents creative uses of secular buildings, including schools and churches. Big-box stores present unique opportunities. As Garreau (2008) says, "Big boxes are not only one-story, one-room places originally cre-

ated for retail sales. They are of breathtaking size—some of them as much as 280,000 square feet or six football fields. They are marked by dazzlingly tall ceilings—18 feet or more—that beg to have additional levels, balconies and cantilevers added to them. And they offer world-class heating, ventilation and air-conditioning." They are both older buildings awaiting "new ideas" and new buildings awaiting old ideas.

References and Works Consulted

Associated Press, 2005. "Nation's Largest Church Opens in Stadium," July 17. www.msnbc.msn .com/id/85625629/.

Bacon, Sheila. 2005. "Features: What We Build: From Hoops to Hope." *Constructor,* September/October. http://constructoragc.construc tion.com/features/build/archives/2005–09 Lakewood.asp.

Bearden, Michelle, and Helgeson Baird. 2008. "Tampa's Without Walls Church for Sale." *Tampa Tribune,* March 4. www.2tbo.com /content/2008/mar/04/042011/tampas -without-walls-church-sale/.

Christ Church Kirkland. 2009. "Our History." www.cckirkland.org/about/history.html.

Christensen, Julia. 2008. *Big Box Reuse.* Cambridge, Mass.: MIT Press.

CNN. 2001. "Sex, Sports and the Mob: The Gold Club Trial," June 15. http://archives.cnn.com /2001/LAW/06/15/gold.club.trial/index.html.

Day, Sherri. 2008. "Without Walls May Lose Property. *St. Petersburg Times,* November 5. www.tampabay.com/newsw/religion/article 892007.ece.

Frye, Thomas, Jr. 2003. "Church Praises the Benefits of Adaptive-Reuse." *Seattle Daily Journal of Commerce,* Special Section "A & E Perspectives," November 20. www.djc.com/news/ad /11151115.html.

Garreau, Joel. 2008. "Big Box & Beyond: Today's Temples of Consumption Don't Have to Be Tomorrow's Ruins. What's in Store?" *Washington Post,* November 16.

Garrett, Dan. 2009. "A Brief History of Christian Church Buckhead." www.christianchurchbuck head.com.

Grady, J. Lee. 2008. "Preparing for a Charismatic Meltdown," November 19. Fire in My Bones blog. http://fireinmybones.com/index.php?col=111908.

Hart, Ariel. 2004. "Religion Journal: Where Strippers Held Sway, Now the Gospel Does." *New York Times,* March 6. www.NYTimes.com.

Jacobs, Jane. 1961. *The Death and Life of Great American Cities.* New York: Random House.

Pristin, Terry. 2004. [Jeff Yip contributed reporting for this article.] "Commercial Real Estate: A Sports Arena Gets Religion." *New York Times,* March 10. www.NYTimes.com.

Sataline, Suzanne. 2008. "In Hard Times, Houses of God Turn to Chapter 11 in Book of Bankruptcy." *Wall Street Journal,* December 23. http://online.wsj.com.

Slaybaugh, Rae Ann. 2004. "Innovative Church Awards 2004." *Church Solutions Magazine,* August 1. www.churchsolutionsmag.com/articles/48/cover1.html.

Story, Louise. 2008. "Foreclosures Don't Spare the House of God." *New York Times,* December 27. www.nytimes.com/2008/12/27/business/27church.html.

Whitaker, Aja. 2002. "Church Finds Sanctuary in Buying Former Wal-Mart." *Tampa Bay Business Journal,* June 14. http://phoenix.bizjournals.com/tampabay/stories/2002/06/17;focus5.html.

Wilson, Mike. 1999. "Mall Gains Second Life as Church." *Christianity Today,* June 14. www.christianitytoday.com/ct/1999/june14/9t714c.html.

11

CONCLUSION

Robert A. Simons and

Youngme Seo

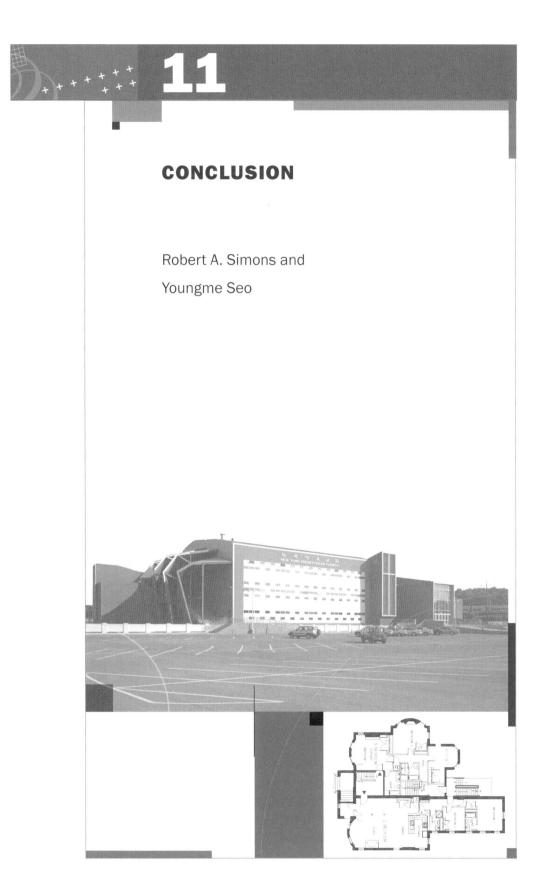

Purpose and Scope

Purpose and Scope This book has strived to inform developers, planners, architects, public officials, not-for-profit companies, and owners and managers of religious buildings about finding new uses for religious buildings in the United States. There are likely between five thousand and ten thousand underutilized, abandoned, or otherwise empty churches and other religious buildings in the United States. Every year over a thousand become vacant or available for redevelopment. The market absorbs some of the prominent, historic, attractive, and well-located structures, but others may languish for years.

In tough economic times (which typically lower project costs) and in general, rehabbing these desirable structures may present a profitable opportunity for developers. Rehabbing also permits sellers to recoup some value from these assets. Neighbors and other stakeholders may be better off, but some neighbors may be anxious about, and not fully supportive of, a new use for a former religious building.

This chapter systematically analyzes seven case studies of the rehabilitation of religious buildings and three of school buildings in the United States, and then provides a summary of the lessons learned and policy recommendations. The cases, which have a variety of end uses and financing mechanisms, were selected from a representative sample that was geographically diverse within the Midwest and Northeastern United States. The case studies include information about each case project, redevelopment plans, financial data and output, and strategies and lessons. The redevelopment outcomes were classified into five categories based on their uses (for-sale and rental residential projects, commercial, office, or cultural). Some projects mixed several of these uses.

Below, we analyze the case study data from three different angles: project background information, financial data and outcomes, and strategic outcomes and lessons. After these analyses, we discuss lessons learned from the case studies and make recommendations for those involved in adaptive reuse of religious buildings. The lessons learned are presented along the project development time line, starting with preavailability, through site acquisition, planning, construction, and ending with occupation and management.

Case Study Profiles

1. Conversion of the Red Door Church in Cleveland Heights, Ohio, and its 1.5-acre mini-campus to twenty units of condominiums, including fifteen new units

2. Adaptive reuse of the Dutch Reformed Church into the 18,000-sq. ft. Jamaica Performing Arts Center in Queens, New York

3. Adaptive reuse of the Deutsche Evangelical Reform Church into the Urban Krag Rock Climbing Gym in Dayton, Ohio

4. Adaptive reuse of Saints Peter and Paul Catholic Church in South Boston, Massachusetts, into forty-six upmarket condominiums

5. Conversion of the Asbury Methodist Church in Buffalo, New York, to the semimarket, commercial Babeville Performing Arts Center

6. Disposal of twenty church properties in the Archdiocese of St. Louis, Missouri, including the demolition of the St. Aloysius Church for twenty-three for-sale house lots

7. Conversion of a former Catholic church, school, and an old sanctuary on a 2.2-acre site in Fayetteville, Arkansas, to

for-sale condominiums and rental apartments

8. Conversion of West Tech High School in Cleveland, Ohio, on a 20-acre site to a mix of 189 low-income and market-rate housing, with sports fields sold as for-sale housing

9. Conversion of two adjoining historic public schools on 5 acres into the Clinton Cultural Campus, a mix of seventy low- and market-rate housing units, in Hot Springs, Arkansas, including a wider description of the developer's business model over numerous historic elementary schools in Little Rock, Arkansas

10. Adaptive reuse of a high school campus with four buildings in Albuquerque, New Mexico, to mixed use of apartments, condominiums, retail, and office space

Analysis of the Case Studies
Project Background Information

The first table, shown in Exhibit 11-1, summarizes the background information on the seven church projects and three repurposed schools. Project background includes information about original uses, size of site and building, location, construction year, sellers, buyers, and information related to site preparation, such as demolition and brownfield issues. In addition, the table illustrates the geographic location of each project and its final reuse. Average and median values are calculated for both religious buildings and overall (including the seven churches and three school projects), but only church averages are reported here.

The geographic location of the case studies varied, covering eleven cities in six U.S. states, including Arkansas (Fayetteville, Hot Springs, and Little Rock), Massachusetts (Boston), Missouri (St. Louis), New York (Buffalo and Queens), New Mexico (Albu-

querque), and Ohio (Cleveland, Cleveland Heights, and Dayton). More than half of the cases are in the central city.

The seven religious buildings, including four Catholic and three Protestant churches, were redeveloped for various uses: four residential projects (two composed primarily of for-sale condominiums, one condo/apartment mix, and one conversion to building lots), two performance halls/theaters (one nominally for profit, one purely nonprofit), and a recreational climbing center. We also include three school case studies, converted to a mix of low-income and market-rate housing. All of the projects utilized historic preservation tax credits, as well as other public subsidies. Some also are struggling financially.

The buildings were constructed between 1844 and 1968. More than half of these buildings are now over one hundred years old, and are located in downtown or inner-city neighborhoods where population had gradually declined so that the buildings were no longer used for their original religious or educational purposes. However, some projects, such as the St. Joseph Church, Fayetteville, Arkansas, are located in a smaller community that was gradually gentrified and redeveloped. The repurposed church cases we evaluated tended to be on a main street or in commercial areas.

The church sites are relatively small, ranging from 0.23 acres to 5 acres, with an average size of 2 acres. The rehabbed building size ranges from 8,000 sq. ft. to 52,000 sq. ft., with an average of 32,000 sq. ft. The ratio of the building size to site size ranged from a low of 0.28 to high of 1.46, with an average of 62 percent (i.e., a floor-area ratio of 0.62).

Four of the projects required at least some demolition of freestanding structures. One building was torn down completely,

Exhibit 11-1 Background Information

Case	Location	Real Estate End Use(s)	End Use Building sq. ft.	Prior Use(s)	Project Land Size (acres)	Original Proje Building Size (sq. ft.)
Red Door Church	Cleveland Heights, Ohio	21 residential condominiums, 5 rehab, 16 new	45,000	First Anglican church	1.5	14,000
Jamaica Performing Arts Center	Jamaica, Queens, NY	High end not for profit theater and meeting place	18,000	Dutch Reformed church	1.5	8,000
Urban Krag	Dayton, Ohio	Rock climbing gym in a former church	8,000	Former Protestant church	0.23	5,000
Saints Peter and Paul	Boston, Massachusetts	44 residential condominiums, 38 in church and 8 in rectory	52,000	Catholic church and rectory	0.82	17,800
Babeville Performing Arts Center	Buffalo, NY	1,200-seat performance hall	32,000	Church	5	25,000
St. Louis Diocese/St. Aloysius	St Louis, Missouri	Diocese divestiture and 25 single housing lots for sale	no building	Catholic churches	3	46,000
Fayetteville Church Complex	Fayetteville, Arkansas	8 units of apartment, 17 units of condo, 8 units of condo	37,000	Catholic church campus church, school, rectory, school, and former historic church	2.18	37,000 sq. ft. old sanctuary, 21,989 sq. ft. school building 7,830 sq. ft. S Joseph Church
West Tech High School	Cleveland, Ohio	189 residential apartments, 46 new for-sale houses	368,000	Public high school	20	368,000
Clinton Cultural Campus	Little Rock, Ark.	70 units of apartment	90,000	Inner city junior and senior high schools, inner city elementary schools	5	90,000
Albuquerque Central High School Campus	Albuquerque, New Mexico	70 units of apartment, 164 units of condo, and 15,700 sq. ft. of retail and office space	179,000	Public high school	7.26	183,500
Low			8,000		0.23	5,000
High			52,000		5	46,000
Median Religious Only			34,500		1.5	15,900
Average Religious Only			32,000		2.0	19,300
Median All Cases			45,000		2.6	25,000
Average All cases			92,111		4.6	84,144

Final Building sq. ft./land Area (floor area ratio)	Year of Original Construction	Demolition?	Brownfields or Unusual Site Preparation or Construction?	Seller	Buyer/ Developer Acquisition	Community Development Corporation Role?	Other Item of Interest
0.69	1932	school wing torn down	none	single user Protestant congregation	private developer via direct sale	none	
0.28	1859	no	had to backfill basement, add 4 feet of height	single user Protestant congregation to city	city as developer with not for profit user	not for profit group is tenant	
0.79	1862	5,000 square foot sanctuary floor area	none	private owner developer	private business owner	neighborhood embraced project	city landmarks commission and zoning commission saw big picture benefit of project
1.46	1844	garage building	none	hierarchical-Catholic church	private developer via RFP	no	
0.15	1876	no	basement backfill	city acquired property from church for demo or redevelopment	private for profit company	none	project was motivated by philanthropy
NA	1904	all parish buildings church, school, gym, convent, and rectory	none	hierarchical-Catholic church	private developer via RFP	the community wanted the building preserved	
0.39	1936, 1968	no	none	hierarchical-Catholic church	private developer	none	Catholic church had outgrown site and was able to use proceeds for new church and school
0.42	1912	no	none	school district to city	private developer via RFP	helped facilitate, alumni group was proponent	
0.41	1920, 1914	no	none	school district	private developer with non-profit sponsors	ARC-co developer	
58.00	1914	yes	none	city acquired property through condemnation law suit	private developer via RFP	none	campus sat empty for 25 years before redevelopment
0.28	1844						
1.46	1968						
0.54	1869						
0.62	1880						
0.42	1890						
6.95	1888						

and two projects were partially demolished. Three projects retained all the buildings in their entirety.

The majority of buyers for the vacant and abandoned church properties are local private developers. Out of the seven religious building cases, six were bought by developers or by developers in partnership with a nonprofit organization. Only one case, the Jamaica Performing Arts Center, was developed by a public entity.

Financial Data and Outcomes

This financial section addresses project cost, public subsidies, and financial outcomes. Exhibit 11-2 shows the data on various cost aspects of these projects, the role that public subsidies played in their financing, and the sources of funds and rate of return that developers earned.

Total project costs, which include construction expenses, acquisition price, and demolition costs, ranged from $500,000 in Dayton to $20.9 million in Queens, New York, with an average overall project cost of $8.2 million. The acquisition cost for many of these properties was relatively cheaper than market rate, and sometimes the property was donated. Excluding projects for which the property was donated, acquisition prices ranged from $50,000 for an 8,000-sq.-ft. building on 0.23 acres, to $2.4 million for a church in South Boston with views of downtown. The average price was $854,000 per project, with a median of $650,000. The final developed cost per gross building square foot averaged $174, but the range between low and high was very large. The projects were generally redeveloped between 2002 and 2008.

The acquisition cost calculated by building square foot for the five church projects that had repurposed buildings and attempted to create marketable space ranged from $5.50 per square foot in Dayton, Ohio, to $46.20 per square foot in Boston, with an average of $21.20 per square foot and a median of $15.56 per square foot.

Transforming the project cost into a ratio, the highest property acquisition cost in relation to total project cost was about 55 percent for the church site to housing lots deal in St. Louis. The highest property acquisition cost as a proportion of total project cost was 23 percent for a well-located church-to-condos site, and was zero once. The median cost of the site in proportion to total project cost is 14 percent, with an average of 19 percent.

Public subsidies played a significant role in the financing of four of the seven church projects profiled in the case studies. (Neither the site demolished for building lots nor the two projects converted to residential condos were eligible for public funding.) Major public subsidies included historic tax credits, and New Market Tax Credits. Other subsidies used were small business administration (SBA) loans and property tax abatements. The average proportion of public subsidies was a substantial 30 percent. The highest public subsidy was in the case of the Jamaica Performing Arts Center, completed with 100 percent public subsidy, and the lowest was the Fayetteville, Arkansas, case, which required a mere 22 percent in public money. With respect to multiple subsidies, the Babeville case in Buffalo, New York, benefited from the efforts of historic preservation tax credits and New Market Tax Credits of 27 percent of the total project cost.[1] In the cases that used historic preservation tax credits, this represented a key financial boost to injecting equity into the project.

The last point addressed in Exhibit 11-2 is developer profit compared to total cost. In the five church cases where profit data are available, one shows negative cash flows. The others already are profitable, or expect to be. The average rate of return (including developer-projected return of projects still underway in late 2009) is over 10 percent. Two of the schools projects were struggling, with the Clinton Campus running just below break even. The West Tech High School project was initially unsuccessful, and substantial funds were lost by the first two of the equity players that ran, before the project was turned around by shedding most of the debt through foreclosure and its low-income tax credit requirements.

Strategic Outcomes and Lessons

This section summarizes project features, including the property acquisition process, construction management, marketing, and financial success, as well as lessons learned from individual projects. This information is provided in Exhibit 11-3.

Most of the developers acquired the properties by a request for proposal (RFP) or in a direct transaction. RFP is a common tool for transaction of the property owned by a public entity or for a church property sold in a hierarchical organization such as the Catholic Church, in which leaders above the parish level administer church properties.[2]

In general, large-scale projects that cannot be easily phased and that have excessive unusable interior space are not recommended. Projects in which redevelopment work can be easily phased because the property consists of a campus with separate structures appear more manageable. This phasing allows for risk reduction and market testing.

Since the historic buildings were constructed fifty to 160 years ago, careful construction management was needed. The developers in these case studies used experienced architects, designers, and planners to deal with physically deteriorated buildings that required substantial repurposing to become market-ready. Some common features of their construction management were the maintenance of renovated exterior features and reconstruction of the interiors to modernize them while maximizing architectural beauty, such as stained-glass windows and ceiling detail. Since there is a risk of cost overruns, an inexperienced rehab developer may face a choice between acting as his or her own general contractor and having a fee builder or using a construction manager approach.

The local media, the Internet, and the multiple listing service (MLS) were frequently used as marketing tools. In any case, hitting several price points and product types is desirable and can increase lease up or sales activity.

The nonprofit project, the Jamaica Performing Arts Center, was occupied by captive nonprofit tenants, and the Performance Arts Center in Buffalo was occupied by the owner with some space leased to another tenant. The Urban Krag was also an owner-occupied single business.

In general, the neighborhoods around the vacant buildings were positive toward, and sometimes strongly supportive of, redevelopment. Most neighbors welcomed preserving the historic landmarks in their community. The local governments also strongly supported redevelopment projects because the projects preserved historical buildings and because they had potential to increase the property tax, and (where applicable) the income tax base. In some cases, grassroots organizations played a pivotal role in getting and retaining the local government's support. In contrast, the redevelopment of St. Joseph Church in Fayetteville, Arkansas, met opposition from

Exhibit 11-2 Financial Data and Outcomes

Case	Property Acquisition Cost	Property Acquisition Cost/final Building sq. ft.	Property Acquisition Cost as a % of Total Project Cost	Demolition Cost	Demolition Cost/final Building sq. ft.	Total Project Cost
Red Door Church	$700,000	$15.56	9%	$32,000	0.71	$8,110,488
Jamaica Performing Arts Center	City owned	NA	NA	-	0	$20,850,000
Urban Krag	$50,000	$6.25	10%	-	0	$500,000
Saints Peter and Paul	$2,400,000	$46.15	23%	$5,000	0.001	$10,610,000
Babeville Performing Arts Center	$175,000	$5.47	2%	-	0	$9,758,882
St. Louis Diocese/St. Aloysius	$600,000	NA	55%	$341,250	NA	$1,100,000
Fayetteville Church complex	$1,200,000	$32.43	18%	0	0	$6,600,000
West Tech High School	$600,000	$1.63	2%	0	0	$34,000,000
Clinton Cultural Campus	$520,000	$5.78	7%	0	0	$7,997,504
Albuquerque Central High School Campus	$-	$-	0%	0	0	$41,000,000
Low	$50,000	$5.47	2%			$500,000
High	$2,400,000	$46.15	55%			$20,850,000
Median Religious Only	$650,000	$15.56	14%	0	0	$8,110,488
Average Religious Only	$854,167	$21.17	19%	$54,036	0.14	$8,218,481
Median All Cases	$600,000	$6.01	9%	0	0	$8,934,685
Average All cases	$693,889	$14.16	14%	$37,825	0.09	$14,052,687

Cost per Final Gross Building Square Foot	Average Cost per Dwelling unit/user unit	Tax Credit Programs?	Other Public Subsidy	Public Subsidy in % of Total Project Cost	Profit as % of Total Project Cost	Financing Loan to Value Ratio	Sources of Private Equity
$180	$386,214	none	none	0.0%	12%	80%	$1 million developer cash in deal
$1,158	NA	none	none	100.0%	none	0%	None; City funds
$63	NA	none	SBA loan	0.0%	Owner occupied building	70%	Private equity (family)
$204	$230,652	none	none	none	5% + 2 units	80%	Developer cash and a line of credit
$305	NA	HPTC, NMTC	property taxes used to pay down portion of rehab cost	27.0%	Too early— likely slight negative	24%	HPTC, NMTC
NA	NA	none	10 year tax abatement on new construction	none	>10 %	20%	
$118	$200,000	HPTC	none	21.6%	Projected 33%	21%	Cash and HPTC (apartment portion)
$92	$179,894	HPTC, LIHTC	land bank, forgivable second mortgage, residential property tax abatement for for-sale units	74.0%	Large negative	64% at origin	LIHTC, HPTC, Letter of Credit, Developer cash
$89	$114,250	HPTC, LIHTC	tax adjustment	62.4%	Slight negative	32.3%+	Owner equity, FHLB grant, LIHTC, HPTC
$226	$117	HPTC	gap financing	40.0%	Property has a positive cash flow profit; cannot be calculated until sale of condos	80%	Historic tax credits
				148.6%			
$63	$200,000			0.0%	likely slightly negative	0%	
	$386,214			100.0%		80%	
$180	$230,652			22%	profitable	24%	
$174	$272,289			30%	profitable	42%	
$149	$189,947			34%	profitable	47%	
$160	$185,188			41%	profitable	47%	

Exhibit 11-3 Strategic Features and Lessons

Case	Site Acquisition	Construction Management	Marketing	Dealing with Neighbors and Public Process	Location Location Location
Red Door Church	Direct transaction	Maximized space and attractive design	A lot of out of town buyers, single women	Easy. No tax abatement	Proximity to employment and a stable established neighborhood
Jamaica Performing Arts Center	City owned	OK; delay due to flood. Tricky basement excavation went fine.	Captive, non-profit tenant	Retained existing use, CDC support strong	Main street, urban
Urban Krag	Direct transaction	Hired architect and engineers to prepare plans, general contractor to do construction. Low budget single user.	Business was market "free" through local media.	City used priority boards to facilitate projects	Historic district
St. Peter and Paul	RFP	Retained original building features	Units sold themselves	No residential abutters. Community approval positive	Irish neighborhood
Babeville Performing Arts Center	Direct transaction	Hired professionals to coordinate rehab of building	Owner occupant and space leased to a tenant	Community supported reuse of the church	Downtown
St. Louis Diocese/ St. Aloysius	RFP	Demolition and salvage contract good	17/25 lots sold off	Supported by political and church leaders	Located in the infill development neighborhood
Fayetteville Church complex	Direct transaction	Partnership was experienced in construction, management and sales.	MLS and local media	Feedback from neighbors and public meetings	Historic district of university town
West Tech High School	RFP	Disastrous management. Fee builder not CM at %.	Low income filled fast. Downtown not comp. for this area; 4 miles away.	Strong city support	In the central city
Clinton Cultural Campus	Direct transaction to the non-profit	Trouble; ran out of funds to complete work.	LIH easy to lease; market harder	Preserved	Near central business district
Albuquerque Central High School Campus	RFP	Project done in phases over 8 years.	Internet and multiple listing service	Community wanted the building saved	Downtown of the city

Financing and Cash Flow	Lender Acceptance	Deal Structure and Partnerships	Others Interesting Factors	Big Lessons from This Case
Successful financially	Balky construction lenders	Private sell off	High-end condo. Part rehab part new on small campus	Location good, acquisition cost cheap, and marketing time good; kept red door theme; oversized lot; carriage houses did very well; nice use of stained glass
Rent to city $1 a year	NA	City lease to tenant	Public performance hall	What you can do in NYC; expensive and culture very high priority; neighborhood group carrying the ball for the long haul; strong city support; basement ceiling height increased
Small business operating at same location since 1996		Owner owned and maintained	Building saved from demolition	City's landmark commission did not make owner replace slate roof, which would have been a deal killer. Local neighborhood organization embraced project as "savior" of building that was in a state beyond repair. City hall cooperation.
Sold out quickly	No issues	Private sell-off		Hit market window, no NIMBY problems, no residential abutters, built a large new building inside an historic shell. Very nice use of religious architectural details in old ceiling.
Multiple sources of financing	Challenge to obtain financing	Developer owned and maintained	Iconic structure saved	Mostly single tenant with related companies. Geothermal energy system. Downtown landmark saved from demolition with a lot of community and tax credit money. Basement ceiling height lifted.
House lots sold over time	No issues	Developer sells lots, not builder-developer	Building saved from demolition	Archdiocese had good transparent disposal plan, carried it out, and delegated responsibility to real estate marketing professionals. Sometimes best use is to tear it down. Listen to residents and parishioners, and church leadership.
Condo units sold quickly	No problems financing	Partnership holds property and sells off condos	Entire church campus reused	Quick absorption of underpriced, small condo units (750 sq. ft.) in former religious school. City's progressive zoning code was helpful.
Unsuccessful financially	Lenders too eager	Apts: letter of credit took over ownership and management. For sale: private partnership w/ house builder	Building preserved	School building too big, original developer inexperienced, no real market study, unreasonable optimism, difficult floor plans, construction contract structure, new units in gymnasium. Financial disaster, foreclosed upon, only 3rd and 4th owners making money.
Ongoing	Low LTV	Fee builder and NFP owner	Historic building being used	Some units almost unrentable; mediocre design. Tax credit equity can get pulled back when markets tighten. Non-profit organization learning finance; on the job training. Financially not above water.
Gap financing by city and mortgage; quick absorption and cash flow	Lender reaction positive	True private/public partnership. Several partners within the deal	Apartment, condo, offices, mixed-use	This project done in phases to capitalize on an evolving real estate market. Master plan approved by city allowed for flexibility to respond to market opportunities. Very low acquisition price. City subsidies for parking and gap financing, diverse product types. New units in gymnasium. Rent out slow; selling units to ride out the market.

neighbors who did not fully understand it. The developer overcame this opposition by soliciting feedback from the community and showing willingness to revise the plan. The Boston project, on the other hand, met almost no opposition because there were no abutting residential neighbors.

With respect to financial outcomes, some cases were successful while others were not. At least three case studies out of seven can be considered successful, while two cases in progress continue to look promising but have not yet achieved expected absorption, due to the Great Recession. Two church projects and two repurposed schools, however, needed to be "fed and watered," requiring ongoing cash injections to suffer from negative cash flow or (in one case) mortgage default. The different financial results are due to various reasons, such as location, marketing, public subsidy, and capability of the developers to appropriately hit the market window. Residential condominium end uses are timing- and market-driven and generally receive no subsidies, but do require local support. For slow-to-sell properties, a developer should consider leasing units for a period until the market recovers to assist cash flow.

Conclusions and Insights from the Case Studies

The redevelopment projects for religious buildings have similarities and differences. They were similar in that they saved historic buildings from demolition and helped to revitalize communities in downtown and inner cities. Another similarity is that, with the exception of residential condos, most cases we studied received substantial public subsidies such as historic or new market tax credit equity. The differences resulted from final reuses of the project due to the differences of structure, the size, and the location of churches.

A project's success can be established in many ways, not all of which are financial. Rehabs by nonprofits, for example, are not meant to generate high rates of return. When using cash flow as a measure, we found that projects tended to have a positive cash flow when the developers had accurately estimated market demand through thorough market studies and preparation, so that the buildings were redeveloped with the highest and best uses that allowed them to hit market windows and the right price points. Financially unsuccessful projects suffered negative cash flow because they were spearheaded by inexperienced or incapable developers and/or encountered poor market conditions. Sometimes inexperienced developers anticipated markets that were never there to begin with.

To summarize the case studies, there are several successful redevelopment cases in which historically valuable religious buildings were saved from demolition and redeveloped through adaptive reuse. Not all redevelopment was financially successful, but all of the redevelopment projects for the historic buildings should be praised for historic preservation, sustainability, community revitalization, and economic development.

Lessons Learned

The lessons learned from the cases studies are presented along a time continuum from the preavailability of a building to the completion of the project.

Determining When a Property Is Ripe for Redevelopment

Abandoned and closed religious buildings usually become surplus as a result of declining population, enrollment, attendance, coupled with migration of congregation members to the suburbs, coupled with financial stress on the owning entity. Neglect, deterioration, and physical damage can turn the properties into eyesores. Deteriorated properties can have considerable negative impact on communities because they either lower nearby housing values or simply generate a bad impression. The building's state then reflects badly on the ownership entity, whether that is a hierarchical religious institution such as the Catholic Church, a government body like a city government, or simply the individual stand-alone congregation that owns the building.

Former religious structures located in growing, prosperous, or revitalizing areas may well present opportunities for market-driven adaptive reuse. When no adaptive reuse is commercially viable, these buildings may still serve many other purposes, including housing another religious congregation, providing a location for a nonprofit organization with a social service mission, or being turned to public use as schools or centers of local government.

Identification of Best End Uses for Redevelopment

Final end uses of abandoned, closed, or obsolete religious buildings are partly predetermined by various site attributes that can be grouped into five categories: seller characteristics, macroeconomic conditions, demographic trends, microlocation characteristics, and building characteristics. The five most common end uses of the buildings that we surveyed were conversion to condominiums, apartments, retail outlets, cultural centers, or offices. Our experience suggests that the developer should strongly consider the interconnected attributes of a site in determining its final use[3]:

- *Attributes for condo housing:* Seller characteristics: nonhierarchical religious organization, financially independent congregation. Demographic trends: higher

educational level. Macroeconomic conditions: lower interest rate. Microlocation conditions: close to park, lower rental vacancy rate in immediate area. Building characteristics: smaller building, corner location, at a distance from the highway and main road. Look also for extra land or extra structures in good shape, such as a rectory. In many successful condo conversions, extra land or a spacious lot became a new housing development complementing the reuse of the former church.

- *Attributes for cultural:* The characteristics most predictive of cultural reuse were microlocational, including a lower rental rate and limited other market uses. With some exceptions, successful cultural reuses were generally newer structures. A corner location and access to a main road are also desirable characteristics for these reuses.

- *Attributes for office:* Demographic characteristics include a higher percentage of white residents in the census tract. Microlocational characteristics include an inner-city location, low vacancy rate, and easy access to a highway. Smaller buildings are preferable, lower interest rates are positively associated with office repurposing, and distinctive or dramatic space is a plus.

- *Attributes for retail:* Seller characteristics: a nonhierarchical, financially self-contained religious group. Demographic trends: higher education level, younger population, more whites in the census tract. Macroeconomic conditions: lower interest rate. Microlocational characteristics: close to lake and highway, lower rental vacancy rate, higher rental rate, more owner-occupied housing. Building characteristics: newer, smaller, one-story church at a corner location. Distinctive architecture is an advantage.

Acquisition of the Properties

The two common ways of selling surplus religious properties are through public request for proposal and direct transaction. The properties are usually but not always sold to bidders who are willing to pay the highest price. Auctions and batch acquisitions of multiple properties are unusual in our experience, and usually occur when leaders of a centrally organized denomination decide to make multiple properties available concurrently.

If developers are seeking to acquire a property associated with a hierarchical religious organization, they should consider developing a proposal that meets the organization's mission. For example, they may prefer a project design that includes affordable-housing units to a more lucrative offer that does not provide a similar social good. If the property owners (seller) belong to a stand-alone religious institution, one in which an individual church's ties to its denominational leadership are not financial, the sellers may not be in a financial position to prioritize intangible benefits (social goods). These sellers often count on the sale to fund a move to a new place. Get details on their new facility, if there is one. Finally, certain religious organizations, including but not limited to the Catholic Church and Orthodox Jewish congregations, are also often concerned with what the eventual end use is, and how this reflects on their image in the community. Thus, they may preclude sale at any price if certain potentially undesirable uses (bathhouse, tannery, bar, brothel) are proposed. Each group's list of excluded use is likely to be different.

Sale of the Property

The selling entity should set a realistic price based on an independent professional's appraisal of how much it can get for the property, not on how much it needs or hopes to get. Organizations that are concerned about protecting their image or achieving a nonfinancial objective should require bidders to offer detailed plans for the property's end use. All sellers should keep the following points in mind:

- When a property is old and in poor condition, the asking price needs to be realistic.
- The seller cannot plausibly put many conditions on the sale without diminishing demand, especially in a soft market.
- Lobbying for a project may be important.
- The owner and local government planners need to have a dialogue about a building's future to establish common goals and a strategic plan.
- Potential rezoning issues can affect both demand and price for the property.
- Many development deals of this type are somewhat precarious financially, especially in the long-run operations phase (after sale has been completed). Lowering debt is key to project success, and one of the best ways to accomplish this goal is to acquire the property at a low price. Institutional sellers anxious to sell for top dollar should remember not to focus too narrowly on the short run. Accepting a lower sale price may be better than dealing with the long-term consequences of maintaining a facility that is either closed or struggling to survive.
- Instead of focusing solely on net proceeds from sale of surplus assets, sellers should consider the social benefits of redevelopment of their buildings. These benefits include providing affordable housing, gaining goodwill by preserving a community icon, fostering environmental sustainability through infill and reuse of building materials, and generating the positive externalities that these

potentially cathartic projects can have on the neighborhood. Thus, one legacy to the neighborhood can be one of leading by example, and continued support of the neighborhood, even after the facility has left.

Planning Process

Sellers and potential buyers and their government and historic preservation partners should scope out potential problems and opportunities for developing the property before and during the city planning-approval process.

- Choose projects with no residential abutters.
- Sometimes a building just needs to sit vacant until neighbors realize that reuse is a viable option. This is particularly true when the reuse is in the middle of a residential area. Eventually, board-up vacancy tends to lead to more compliancy on the part of adjacent stakeholders to redevelopment plans.
- Historic preservation advocates should understand the cost of reuse and should recognize that each pot of money comes with its own set of strings. It is costly to save buildings and easy to burn through a lot of money.
- Some reuses, such as adult entertainment, bars, and low-income housing, may evoke a negative response from the neighborhood. NIMBYs may object to poor people living in a rehabbed structure.
- If needed, engage in NIMBY management by hiring a professional planning firm to run public meetings.
- City hall may lack the staff or expertise needed to properly support a complex project, which may require careful financial planning and navigation of antiquated ordinances. On the other hand, a catalytic project that jump-starts the re-

vitalization of a neighborhood and has substantial positive externalities deserves public subsidy.

Architectural Issues

Not all buildings are suited for repurposing. Some are simply too large and cannot be developed in phases. The case study portion of this book offers prototypes for rehabilitating buildings of several different sizes. It is important to buy the property as cheaply as possible, while avoiding buildings with deal-killing structural problems. Also:

- Look for distinctive marketing features, especially ones visible from the street.
- Look at the upper ceiling features as penthouse walls and ceiling detail. Avoid leaking roofs, as water damage may cause structural problems and potentially toxic mold.
- Approach the sale of a church as an opportunity to build a new multistory building inside a historic shell.
- Shallow basements can be excavated with careful engineering, offering more space for use.
- If there is a school building on the church campus you are developing, evaluate it for reuse as well.
- Avoid structures with a lot of dead hallway space. This would make the net-to-gross space ratio too low and indicate high operating costs.
- Also, avoid extremely large structures that cannot be broken down into phases or viable parts and marketed in phases.

Market Analysis

Church rehabs can be tricky projects, and even developers with good instincts should supplement their gut feel with a professional market study. At a minimum, we recommend conducting a highest and best use study and some type of market niche analysis. A few developers in our cases encountered pricing mishaps partly because they failed to conduct realistic market studies, and accordingly missed market windows or had leftover inventory when the market went soft. A well-constructed market study can guide marketing strategies and pricing, thereby aiding absorption and maximizing project benefits.

- Broaden the scope and options on the highest and best use matrix if you see an advantage in an innovative reuse. For example, sometimes a simple public meeting hall is a better end use for an old church than any housing use.
- The developer needs to know the pulse of the market. A thorough analysis of demographic data, such as population growth/decline rate, age range, gender, and income/educational level is very important, and worth the effort to obtain.
- It is important to be market-specific rather than following the same formula for all markets. Secondary data often become a problem if not presented in a form that exactly meets the marketer's needs. In an increasingly risky market, relying on more detailed statistical models could be rewarding. See, for example, the models set forth in Chapter 3.

Financing Tools and Strategies

The developer has four options regarding markets and funding: (1) seek a cultural not-for-profit use and act as a fee developer rather than trying to make a profit from ownership; (2) forgo tax credits or other substantial subsidies so that you can build nimbly to the market, usually by constructing residential condos; (3) build apartments with historic preservation tax credits (HPTC) or low-income housing tax credits; (4) use HPTC and New Market Tax Credits to redevelop for commercial use (retail office, or owner-occupied) by either a firm or its tenants.

Look for creative sources of equity:
- Contribute property or make the property owner a partner in the deal.
- Rezone property to accommodate a more valuable use.
- Look to government sources for bond and tax increment financing. Play up the sustainable aspects of the project (infill, neighborhood revitalization, etc.) for local public subsidy, and potentially for gap financing from philanthropic organizations.
- Syndicate tax credits to generate equity for a project.
  - Historic tax credits are available for many recycled building projects.
  - Low-income housing tax credits provide opportunities to catalyze redevelopment efforts in transitional or distressed neighborhoods by reusing an historic building while providing expanded housing opportunities for residents.
  - Be careful to monitor compliance with tax credit program rules and regulations.
- The ownership entity can be used to gain certain tax advantages, to increase equity sources while maintaining control of a project, and to spread risks and liabilities.
- The Developer's Toolbox (in Chapter 6) provides a convenient reference for those thinking about structuring a project's financing and includes citations to further sources of information.
- Be careful to maintain adequate income to cover debt service and expenses.
- Utility costs in some of these old structures can be detrimental to the success of a project.
- Anticipate surprises during construction.

Despite the best-laid plans, these rehabs can have large contingency budgets, which are still insufficient to cover cost overruns. We have found that big buildings invite trouble; too many sins hide inside. Due diligence is the rule.

- A thin construction budget at the beginning may force cuts later on. The cost estimation has to be very good.
- Be careful that plans are in order that meet the requirements of tax credit supervisory agencies.
- Look for best practices. For example, can windows be rebuilt instead of manufactured new?
- Too many floor plans require lots of documentation. The ideal building has rooms that are all basically the same: a cookie-cutter style can be good.
- Storm and sanitary lines can be a nuisance: they get old and deteriorate. They can also be broken and covered over during retrofitting, creating big problems down the road.
- Structure arrangements with contractors. You can choose to use either general contractors or fee builders. A general contractor is the better choice for an inexperienced developer because (subject to a properly executed contract) the construction firm absorbs any surprises.

Financing Issues

Because lenders tend to be unfamiliar with rehabilitated projects, they may not readily find comparables. This may lead to a lower loan-to-value ratio. The developer should bring comparable sales (comps) to the lender.

Historic preservation tax credits: There are several kinds. The federal historic preservation tax credit program offers a 20 percent credit on qualifying rehabilitation expenses for work performed in accordance with the standards established by the Secretary of the Interior. HPTC replaces equity in this type of deal. It is key to get a good architectural consultant who has a personal and working relationship with the approving agency because rules are strict and the structure's appearance from the street trumps market and energy cost considerations. Accordingly, energy costs may be higher in properties redeveloped with HPTCs. Residential deals must always be rentals for five years (e.g., no residential condominiums), so using these credits may limit building functionality and restricts the developer's flexibility.

Low-income housing tax credits (LIHTC): The key financing mechanism that makes marginally viable residential rental projects work is LIHTC. This source both replaces equity in the deal and provides huge tax benefits. Applicants compete for funds at the state level. The lower the income group targeted by the project, the better the chance of winning funds. However, these projects also carry the risk of lower rents and higher vacancies negatively affecting market-rate rentals. In mixed-income neighborhoods, a proposed project with a low-income housing component may cause NIMBY issues with neighbors who do not want the stigma of low-income housing in their backyard. Staying in compliance with LIHTC operations is tricky. Do not underestimate how difficult it is to maintain long-term positive cash flow for these mixed low-income projects—they are called not-for-profit deals for a reason. We have found that former religious buildings are typically not a good fit for this program, but school structures (either on religious campuses or stand-alone) are. Furthermore, providing low-income housing is an excellent social goal that is compatible with the missions of most religious selling entities.

Other financial inducements: The above tax credit programs can be used in combination with each other, and HPTC also may be potentially used with New Market Tax Credits. Local property tax abatement, if available, could be used with any of the above.

Profitability

Meeting cash flow goals is important. Our analyses suggest that condos have the potential for the highest profit, while low-income housing–mixed apartments are lucky to break even. Another important issue is to attempt to replicate a successful business model. Since there is a substantial learning curve for this type of redevelopment, a clever developer could consider the first project as a learning experience, then repeat the procedure for similar projects in their market area. This should lead to lower development costs, fewer management mistakes, and greater profitability.

More details:

Cultural

Cultural projects are huge subsidy deals, with profit likely only for fee builders and soft-cost consultants.

- We identified several instances in which buildings were adaptively reused as museums and cultural facilities for public performances.
- In some instances a small owner bought an old church, rehabbed the building inexpensively, and rented space for artists to live and work within the complex.
- Well-heeled colleges and universities have purchased former churches for many purposes. The open floor plan can work well as a concert hall, art gallery, or occasionally as administrative offices.
- Private museums have purchased an old iconic church to house art collections.

Retail

In most situations, we found retail to be a marginal reuse for religious buildings. The typical retrofit was just okay, not ideal, with low rent. Examples include a climbing wall and boutique crafts stores.

- These reuse projects can work when the church is within an existing retail district, such as in a New England town with a closed church within a downtown business district.
- Restaurants are a common retail reuse because the open hall can be converted to a dining area while the rear of the sanctuary becomes the kitchen. Microbrewery/bars are also possible adaptive reuse outcomes.

Office

There were very few pure general occupancy office rehab projects in our experience. The most likely outcome is when the building is reused by a firm for its own purposes. Once the space is controlled this way, this may be a great value to the firm because the unique space can showcase the architectural firm's creativity.[4] This is a frequently overlooked potential reuse for church facilities, particularly those near the city center.

- Local landmark commissions could encourage office reuse by providing grants for studies by local architectural firms. Communities could identify potential projects where there has been a glut of churches on the market.
- Medical reuse of old churches or school auditoriums in former church buildings is not unusual. The open space of an old sanctuary (e.g., the seated worship area) can become a physical therapy area. Auditoriums in general have been known to become medical offices or back office space.

Apartments

Our experience with LIHTC projects (rare among religious buildings, a better physical fit for former school structures) is only just okay. The outcomes seemed satisfactory for the property or for a fee developer or builder, but are tough on owners. These deals are financially skinny and tend to have higher-than-expected vacancy. If the deals are done purely as a HPTC play, then after five years, the developer can flip them to condos.

- Although apartments are one way of saving a community icon, rents cannot be stretched beyond the local marketplace or units will not absorb.
- Projects need to have a mix of incomes; they cannot be exclusively low income.
- Adaptive reuse of a church for apartments is uncommon.

Condo

Residential condominium uses tend to have the best financial outcomes. Take care to hit the market window in a market with solid market fundamentals.

- For top dollar, condo location is important. Having nice views and proximity to cultural and academic centers is a formula for a successful development.
- Pricing and market mix are important. Two- to three-bedroom townhomes and carriage houses make for an interacting mix. Smaller, lower-priced units have been well received.
- Some smaller churches make nice single residences.

Luck and market cycles

Do things in small chunks. Do not get caught with too much extra inventory. For example, watch the Standard and Poor's Case-Shiller Index (it contains a month-by-month index of housing price trends in the twenty largest U.S. markets) or other local indicators for emerging bubbles.

- Incremental phasing seems to work in a risky marketplace. Too many units cannot be absorbed quickly, and price points have to be on target. Small units of 700–1,000 sq. ft. proved to be lucrative in three of our case study locations. Price points above marketplace have a hard sell, and the developer can end up with unsold units. If markets soften, renting units for later sale can generate some cash flow.

Nonmarket outcomes

Former houses of worship most often have public interests and nonmarket community stakeholders who are unlikely to view market dynamics as the sole or acceptable measure of highest and best use. Clashes between market-driven interests and nonmarket stakeholders occur particularly when the structure has historical or architectural significance, contains religious art embedded within it, represents a significant community landmark, or has alternative public uses.

Policy Recommendations

Policy Recommendations for Developers

Do developers need policies? No. They need strategies. In a down market, rehabs are cheaper. This means less equity in. They can also be greener, in that they use more embodied energy. Lenders are uncomfortable with new concepts, so get sales comps for them. This book provides some. Develop cautiously and do your homework. Replicate the project if market conditions permit. In addition, remember, sometimes the best deal you do is the one you walk away from. Do not let your love for the structure blind your financial judgment.

Policy Recommendations for Planners

- Hierarchically organized religious entities arrive at their disposal decision en masse (i.e., in batches—no pun intended). They should make this process a rational and systematic one because they have influence in the community and because their facilities are capable of generating positive externalities. The negative impact that a closed church can have on nearby property values may justify subsidies to developers.
- Communities need to have funds to fill the financing gap.
- Neighbors do not like change but have to be educated about adaptive reuse options. Often opportunities are missed because the community has its head in the sand.
- Communities that allow planned unit development or flexible zoning to accommodate different uses are ahead of the curve in getting reuse projects approved.
- Consider the green or sustainable angles to these infill projects, and strive to reward them accordingly.

Policy Recommendations for Current Owners of Potentially Disposable Properties

A financially hierarchical religious organization should prepare a plan for future uses of the closed buildings before closing any of them. The plan should take into account a projection of parishioner enrollment in the near future. Then the decision can be made to dispose of a building temporarily (by leasing or mothballing) or permanently (selling it).

The considerations and the problems associated with the new adaptive reuse include any changes negatively or positively associated with the new redevelopment project, including effects on public safety, public health, and the environment. Additionally, the redevelopment plans should meet the goal of community development and the objective of community development.

The redevelopment plan is valuable for the community and the local government in terms of preserving these historical buildings, revitalization of the community, and increase in tax bases, or potential property tax liability if the property changes away from a not-for-profit use. The local government should actively cooperate with the project developers to make the project successful. The local government also should play a role as an intercessor in harmonizing the community and the developer.

Part of the controversy surrounding market-driven adaptive reuses could be avoided or minimized if the seller of the property—the former congregation or church hierarchy—has clear, consistent, and articulated policies on which types of market enterprises are acceptable activities in the formerly religious structure. These vision and implementation policies should include the reasonable interests of nonmarket stakeholders. Both the seller and potential purchaser have strong vested interests in minimizing the controversy and conflict that often surround proposed market uses.

And now, dear reader, you are done. You know what we know. After you have perused the case studies that follow this chapter, go find, sell, and/or facilitate the rehab of some old religious buildings. Good luck in turning those old prophets into new profits, and leave no building behind!

Notes

1. The three school projects also used extensive tax credits, including both historic preservation and low-income housing tax credits.

2. Hierarchical organizations have centralized decision-making with respect to property ownership and budgets, as well as religious matters. Religious buildings in these denominations are effectively subsidiaries of the parent organization in every way. In contrast, some organizations may follow the same religious philosophy, and also have a layered administrative or religious hierarchy (for example, some Protestant sects or Orthodox Judaism), but their real properties are financially self-contained. Finally, there are many stand-alone congregations, whose properties are also financially self-contained. Only the first category meets the hierarchical definition for purposes of this book.

3. For reference purposes, comparisons are given relative to apartment outcomes, which typically were less common in repurposed religious buildings, and more common in former school buildings.

4. Because many companies own real estate in a separate legal entity for liability and tax purposes, this implies that the occupying firm pays a subsidiary real estate firm a market rental.

THE RED DOOR CHURCH
Cleveland Heights, Ohio

Robert A. Simons, Gary DeWine,
and S. Subha Vyakaranam

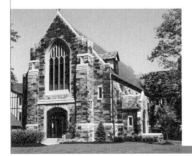

The Red Door Church was originally built as a modest-sized First English Lutheran church. It is located on a minor arterial street, on a 1.5-acre lot in Cleveland Heights, an inner-ring suburb of Cleveland, Ohio. The congregation that built the church had been displaced from Chester Avenue in Cleveland due to a street-widening project, so they moved up the hill to Cleveland Heights. In the 1930s an 8,000-sq.-ft. school wing was built, and a day care was added in 1952.

Introduction

As is common in Rust Belt metropolitan areas, Cleveland's population declined and spread away from the core city in the latter decades of the twentieth century. In 1950 the church membership numbered three hundred faithful, but by 2002, fewer than fifty remained, not a sustainable level. "We had to ask ourselves, 'is it better stewardship to close the building or continue to struggle along?'" said Rev. Robert Hanson, the church's last pastor (O'Malley 2004). The congregation voted to dissolve the fellowship that had begun 123 years earlier. On September 1, 2002, the faithful of First Lutheran gathered for the last time. Thereafter, the church was offered on the market as a religious facility.

When no church-use buyers emerged, a developer group, led by Josh Simon, operating as Derbyshire Partners LLC, acquired the property for about $700,000. Another partner, Andrew Brickman, took over at later stages of the project. The proceeds from the sale were distributed to soup kitchens, homeless shelters, and social service agencies, and the property was redeveloped into residential condos with the marketing name Brownstones at Derbyshire. The school wing was removed, and the church itself was converted to five condo-

miniums. The balance of the lot was developed into an additional fifteen residential condos. All homes were custom finished. The developers built the shell up to the plastering, and then allowed buyers to custom-design their interior finishes. This allowed for substantial interior changes.

The project was built in four phases, and sold out within a year and half. The prices ranged from $174,000 to $550,000, or from $156 to over $200 per building square foot. This price was almost twice the ambient market level. Two units that were resold sustained market increases of 5 percent per year. The $8.3 million project netted the developer a return in excess of 12 percent, a handsome profit.

Site History

The building redeveloped as the Brownstones at Derbyshire was originally built between 1932 and 1936 as the First English Lutheran Church. The original stone Tudor church contained about 12,000 sq. ft., including worship space, a basement activities room, and a small suite of offices. The sanctuary is about 35 feet high at its highest interior point and has several beautiful stained-glass windows.

The facility is located in a pleasant, 1900s vintage "City Beautiful" inner-ring suburban neighborhood on the corner of Derbyshire Road and Euclid Heights Boulevard, in the western part of Cleveland Heights, Ohio. The site is about 6 miles from downtown Cleveland and about 1 mile from the Cleveland Clinic–University Hospital–University Circle cultural area, a powerful and growing economic driver with over forty thousand jobs. The original neighborhood was designed to appeal to the discriminating taste of the social, business, and professional leaders of the Cleveland community. First platted in 1892, the neighborhood was designed on the principles of Frederick Law Olmsted. It is a mixture of curving and straight streets with graceful boulevards linking to downtown Cleveland. Cleveland Heights was so named because it sits on a plateau east of Cleveland. It was once known as Turkey Ridge because of the large number of turkeys roosting there.

The church itself is handsome, constructed from hewn gray granite and sandstone. The 1.5-acre lot is particularly large, with ample parking and frontage on two streets. (See Exhibit 12-1.) Finally, in 2002, it was placed on the market and offered as a religious facility. The building was continuously under nonhierarchical ownership. Aside from some asbestos floor tile in the basement area, the building was in good shape when the congregation decided to put the property on the market.

Market Conditions

Residential market conditions in Cleveland Heights were adequate at the time the project was built. Aside from a struggling school district, city income and racial dynamics were stable. However, the population was dropping perilously close to the fifty-thousand threshold, where communities must compete for federal community development block grant dollars, thus putting their city planning department at risk. City planners resisted encouragement of denser multifamily housing until 2000, when the Cleveland Heights population was clocked at 49,750. This sobering milestone impelled a new willingness to accommodate denser projects such as condominiums, especially ones with substantial property values that were marketed to yuppies and empty nesters.

From a market standpoint, the project was attractive because the property is located on an east-west commuting route, two lanes each way, plus turn lanes with a divided median into downtown Cleveland with moderate but not excessive traffic. The property has immediate access to the University Circle cultural area, with its museums, nonprofit organizations, Case Western Reserve University, University Hospitals, and the Cleveland Clinic. The site is also located in proximity to the funky Coventry district, which is an eclectic mixture of retail and nonchain restaurants. Exhibit 12-1 shows the general area with local features.

The 8.7-sq.-mi. city of Cleveland Heights contains 49,958 people (2000 estimate), or about 3.6 percent of Cuyahoga County's population. There was a 5.7 percent loss of population from this city since 2000. About 27 percent of the population was in the eighteen to thirty-four age group, and 15 percent are sixty-five years and over.

There are 20,913 households in Cleveland Heights, nearly 11 percent of which live below the poverty level. This is about 3 percent lower than the poverty rate of Cuyahoga County and about the same as that of the entire state. There are several universities near Cleveland Heights. Many professors from Cleveland State University, Case Western Reserve University, and John Carroll University reside there. Cleveland Heights has an excellent public library system, but the city's public schools are struggling. The violent crime rate was 0.3 per one thousand people, which is quite low when compared to the rest of Cuyahoga County.

Demographics of Housing Market

This inner-ring suburb experienced market appreciation rates of about 3 percent per annum between the 1990 and 2000 censuses, slightly above average for the Cleveland metropolitan area. Housing stock is largely brick and colonial-style frame homes, dating from the 1920s and selling for about $100 per square foot. The project hit the market window perfectly; the units went on sale just before the market slowed in late 2006 due to the subprime loan fiasco. Marketing time increased, and housing prices for single-family homes dropped about 10 percent.

In 2000, the city of Cleveland Heights had a 96 percent housing occupancy rate, higher than the county rate of 93 percent. The homeownership rate in Cleveland Heights was 62 percent, lower than the 63 percent figure for the county and 68 percent for the

Exhibit 12-1 Red Door Church Site Location and Site Plan

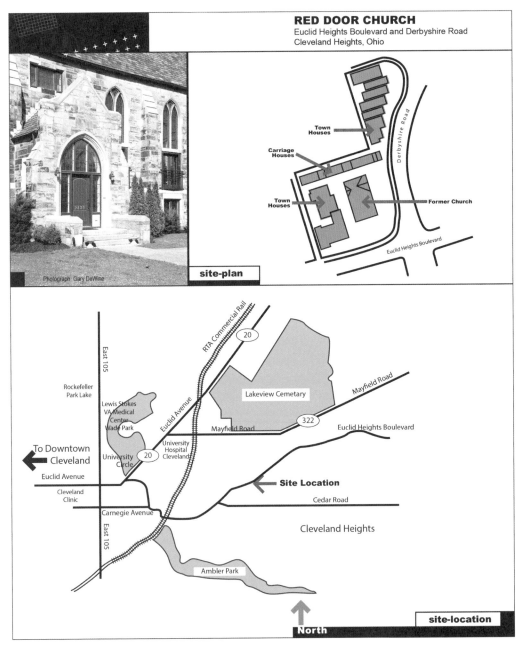

Exhibit 12-2 Census Data 2000 and 2007

		Ohio	Cuyahoga County	Cleveland Heights	Census Tract 1411
Population					
	2000	11,353,140	1,393,978	49,984	4,091
	2007	11,466,917	1,295,958		
	% Change	1.00%	-7.03%		
Age (2000)					
	Less than 18	25.41%	24.92%	23.89%	9.09%
	22 - 39	24.93%	24.71%	28.53%	60.11%
	40 -59	22.78%	22.32%	24.42%	12.47%
	60 and over	17.27%	19.60%	15.43%	13.49%
Median Household Income					
	2000	$40,956	$39,168	$46,731	$32,373
	2007	$46,597	$44,358		
	% Change	13.77%	13.25%		
Race (2000)					
	White alone	84.92%	67.41%	52.73%	81.89%
	Black or African American alone	11.35%	27.27%	41.45%	8.51%
	American Indian and Alaska Native alone	0.24%	0.17%	0.18%	0.22%
	Asian alone	1.16%	1.85%	2.72%	6.28%
	Hawaiian and Pacific Islander alone	0.02%	0.02%	0.00%	0.00%
	Some other race alone	0.79%	1.52%	0.73%	0.46%
	Two or more races	1.53%	1.75%	2.20%	2.64%
Education (2000)					
	Bachelor or higher	21.10%	25.15%	50.00%	71.59%
	High School above age 25	36.09%	30.04%	15.58%	5.87%
Unemployment					
	2000	3.22%	3.86%	2.58%	2.86%
Housing (2000)					
	Households	4,446,621	571,606	20,932	2,389
	Housing Units	4,783,051	616,903	21,826	2,484
	Owner Occupied Units (%)	69.11%	63.17%	62.00%	21.83%
	Renter Units (%)	30.89%	36.83%	38.00%	78.17%
	Median Rent Apartment	$515	$541	$640	$657
	Median House Value (Owner Occupied)	$100,500	$110,100	$110,100	$140,100

Source: 2000 and 2007 U.S. Census
Note: 2007 tract data is not available

state of Ohio. The city's median gross rent for the year 2000 was $640, much higher than the $541 median for the county. The average sale price of single-family houses in Cleveland Heights in 2000 was $140,575, more than that of $124,827 in the county, and the average sale price of two-family houses was about $130,000, almost double the county average of $69,000. The sales price of condominiums in Cleveland Heights averaged $66,026, about 10 percent higher than the county average (Citydata.com 2008).

The city of Cleveland Heights has several programs that support home ownership. It has a housing preservation office that distributes loans and grants funded by the U.S. Department of Housing and Urban Development. Another important resource for homeowners is the Home Repair Resource Center (HRRC), a nonprofit organization established to maintain and strengthen the housing stock in Cleveland Heights. These aggressive housing maintenance programs make Cleveland Heights somewhat unusual, and are a vestige of its history as a national example of an integration-maintenance community following passage of the Fair Housing Act in 1968. The census tract where the Brownstone project is located has a higher income, larger percentage of white householders, higher homeownership, and a substantially higher average sales price than the city as a whole.

Redevelopment Process

The controlling entity prior to redevelopment was the original congregation, the First Lutheran Church, which was known locally as the Red Door Church for its distinctive red door. The congregation initially put the church on the market as a religious facility. A Jewish synagogue group looked at the facility but did not buy it, in part because the north-south orientation of the

church's sanctuary space was incompatible with the east-west needs of traditional Jewish worship. Most Jewish congregations have the ark and sacred scrolls on the east wall, facing Jerusalem.

When no religious institutional buyers emerged, lead developer Josh Simon, as Derbyshire Partners LLC, acquired the property for $700,000. The developer team combines Florida and local Cleveland talent Andrew Brickman, who helped direct later stages of the project. Simon had earned his BA in business and had spent time with his family's real estate company. He had previously done about eight other real estate development deals in the area, including converting two office buildings to residential lofts in downtown Cleveland. He was looking for his next residential project when he heard about the availability of the Red Door Church from a relative who played golf with the real estate agent representing the property. Simon liked the church building and thought it would be "fun and interesting" to convert it into condos (J. Simon, personal communication, November 2007). The size of the property also allowed for the development of new townhomes in addition to rehabbing the church.

Rezoning was not required because the area was already zoned multifamily and the proposed project density of about fifteen units per acre was well under the allowable number of about eighty-five units. The city of Cleveland Heights was helpful in expediting the approvals, although some friction with inspectors inevitably took place. Neighbors generally supported the project, with the exception of one adjacent single-family detached property owner, who voiced concerns about lack of privacy. The issue was that the rear of the carriage house units was set back in close proximity to the abutting neighbor's backyard. The solution was to install frosted glass on the carriage houses' back windows, which maintained the abutting neighbor's privacy.

The developers requested a tax abatement from the city of Cleveland Heights as an incentive to save the church building. Their rationale was that demolishing the building as part of the development plan made more economic sense than saving it because the site zoning would allow higher-density construction in the church's place. At one point a demolition permit was actually pulled, allowing the developer the right to demolish the church. Eventually the city rejected the developer's request, deciding that the abatement was not necessary to make new housing construction viable in an affluent neighborhood. In the end, the church was subdivided into five condominiums without the property tax abatement. Even without this incentive, the church units are so desirable that attached parking did not have to be provided. Keeping the church also made the adjacent townhomes more desirable and valuable.

The project benefited from the city of Cleveland Heights's support. Richard Wong, of the city's planning department, was a strong supporter and facilitator of the adaptive reuse. Richard was a "solutions guy." The city's building commissioner, Tony Carbone, allowed the building inspector in the field to approve changes to the floor plan and resolve code issues rather than requiring the developer to resubmit plans or commence a new review process. This flexibility saved time and money because it allowed for the efficient use of tradesmen.

Forum Architects' Gary Ogrocki was project director, and Scott Dimit was the design architect for the project, which was featured in Northeast Ohio's *Properties Magazine.* "Units in the church building, designed by Scott Dimit, who was design architect for

Forum Architects, LLC at the time, are three levels, sub-grade, first floor, and second floor ranging from 2,500–3,200 square-feet. Some units retain the original 35-foot ceilings with Gothic arches and windows. Many units preserve architectural details, which have been incorporated into the interior design. Original leaded-glass, pointed-arch windows along the sides of the building have been replaced with new, high efficiency windows. Original doors have been re-used and eight original light fixtures have been retained" (Schuemann 2004).

With respect to actual construction within the church itself, the entire interior was gutted and rebuilt with all new carpentry and interior walls, electrical, plumbing, security, and HVAC. Units were wired for new technology based on individual buyers' requirements. The church's stone facade, roof, and red door have all been retained, and new curved balconies have been added. As Simon told *Properties Magazine,* "Brand new homes were built within the framework of the old church" (Schuemann 2004).

Development Plan

The development plan remained largely intact, with twenty units proposed originally and twenty built. There are three housing products: five prime units in the rehabbed church itself, ten town house units, and five smaller carriage houses with tuck-under parking. All units have a trademark red door. The church building inspired the design of the new construction units, which matches the steeply pitched main roof of the sanctuary. The exposed foundation bases were selected to match the pattern and color of stone on the church. (See Exhibit 12-3.)

The five rehabbed church units were largely a gut job, with stained-glass features and exterior doors retained. The architects did a fine job of maximizing the space and converting the church into three-story lofts, with three bedrooms and two-and-a-half baths and an average of 2,800 sq. ft. on a 900-sq.-ft. footprint. The all-new construction featured granite countertops, top-of-the-line bathrooms, and a master suite on the second floor. The developer commented that the company construction superintendent was particularly important to the interior construction of the five church units; his expertise allowed work to move along smoothly to completion. Parking for

Exhibit 12-3 Red Door Church Photographs and Plans

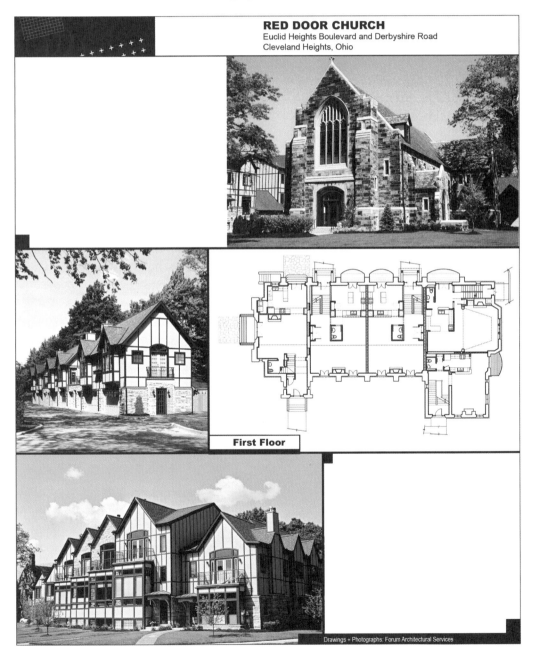

RED DOOR CHURCH
Euclid Heights Boulevard and Derbyshire Road
Cleveland Heights, Ohio

First Floor

Drawings + Photographs: Forum Architectural Services

the units is located under the adjacent carriage house units. Initial marking prices were $450,000, or $192 per square foot.

The ten townhouses, with wood-frame construction and stone fronts, were new construction on the out lot and site of the former educational wing. The architects designed two-story-plus loft units, with three bedrooms and two-and-a-half baths averaging 2,600 sq. ft. on an 800-sq.-ft. footprint. The all-new construction also featured granite countertops, top-of-the-line bathrooms, and gourmet kitchens. Parking is behind the units, mostly without interior access. Initial marketing prices were $420,000, or $168 per square foot.

The five carriage house units are much smaller, second-story walk-up loft units. The architects oriented these units toward an entry-level buyer, with one bedroom and two baths and an average 1,100 sq. ft. on a single floor with a patio. The same top-of-the-line features were available. Initial marking prices started at $175,000, but the units were in heavy demand, and later units sold for up to $300,000, or over $200 per square foot. Parking for the carriage house and church units is underneath the units themselves. Developer Simon said that demand for the carriage house units was unexpectedly brisk and he wished he had more to sell. Refer to Exhibit 12-1, which shows the site development layout for the Brownstones at Derbyshire.

Resale activity is highly satisfactory. The two properties that resold both averaged a 5 percent annual appreciation rate. This is highly acceptable for an expensive product in a down market.

Project Financing

The novelty of adaptive reuse in the Cleveland market made financing difficult to secure. Lenders were not familiar with multi-family development in the neighborhood and consequently could not see the potential financial success of the project. They wanted to see presales before making a commitment. Financing was eventually secured through the efforts of a local loan officer of Provident Bank. The loan officer grew up in the neighborhood, and her local firsthand knowledge provided a sympathetic ear.

Exhibit 12-4 provides a summary of the financial aspects of this project. In order to protect the proprietary nature of the project, certain industry assumptions have been used in the financial analysis. In addition to the site acquisition cost of $700,000 and site preparation cost of about $410,000, there was a small amount of demolition and asbestos removal. Soft costs such as legal, design, engineering, and marketing totaled $630,000. Project hard costs, before finish work, were $5.2 million, and the work was completed in four phases. The finish work was deferred until units were sold, and buyers had a large role in determining how the $900,000 in-unit interior finish allowance was spent. Construction financing cost about $200,000, which was relatively low, about 3 percent of project cost, because of the phased development. No units were finished speculatively. Profit was taken from the project at the end, with no up-front developer fee. Overall project cost was $8.1 million, or $180 per square foot, exclusive of sales commissions.

Marketing and Absorption

All twenty units sold in eighteen months. The original marketing plan was to sell the units to employees of two large hospitals within a mile of the property, Cleveland Clinic and University Hospitals, and the institutional community of the University Circle cultural district. However, the actual purchasers tended to be suburbanites who

Exhibit 12-4 Red Door Church Development Costs

1.5 acre former church site

Cleveland Heights, Ohio

Development date 2005-6	Factors	Dollar Amount	% of Project Costs
Lot size (land square feet)	65,340		
Floor/area coverage	69%		
Gross building area	45,000		
Net usable space (100%)	45,000		
# current owners	20		
# parking spaces	40		
Development Cost Information			
Land/site acquisition (including option), includes buildings	$10.71	$700,000	9%
Site preparation			
Remediation: removal of asbestos	$0.25	$10,000	0%
Other site preparation inc. parking	$3.00	$402,000	5%
Demolition school building 8,000 sq. ft.	$4.00	$32,000	0%
Construction costs			
Gut church building 3,000 sq. ft.	$10.00	$30,000	0%
New construction 45,000 sq. ft.	$114.44	$5,150,000	63%
Buyer finish allowance	$20.00	$900,000	11%
Total building hard costs	**$135.11**	**$6,080,000**	**75%**
Soft costs			
Architect, planners, legal, surveying, power		$630,000	8%
Market analysis (internal)		$5,000	0%
Subtotal before construction loan		$7,859,000	97%
Construction loan/carry one year term	8%, int. only	$251,488	3%
Subtotal		$8,110,488	100%
Developer's fee		$0	0%
TOTAL DEVELOPMENT COST		$8,110,488	100%
TOTAL DEVELOPMENT COST/sq. ft. building		$180	
Sales			

	Units	Average sales Price/unit	Total sales Revenues
Units for sale in church building	5	$490,000	$2,450,000
Units for sale row houses	10	$460,000	$4,600,000
Units for sale. Carriage houses with tuck under parking	5	$275,000	$1,375,000
Total gross sales			$8,425,000
Less commissions @1.5% (sweet deal with realtor)			$126,375
Net sales proceeds			$8,298,625

THE FUNDING GAP		$188,137	
GAP (surplus) AS % OF DEAL		2%	
Profit analysis			
Project equity (20%)	$1,622,098		
Return surplus plus developer fee		**$188,137**	
Developer's return on equity		**12%**	

Note: some industry standard assumptions have been made by the authors in preparing this pro-forma

wanted to be closer to the city and out-of-towners who moved to Cleveland. Interestingly, all of the customer traffic came from a development sign placed on the corner of Derbyshire and Cleveland Heights Boulevard. A marketing arrangement for web and print advertising was made with Progressive Urban Real Estate, which was paid a reduced commission rate of 1.5 percent for each unit sold. The arrangement with the real estate company was that all inquiries, either by phone or email, were referred to Derbyshire, and the developer handled sales in-house. This arrangement worked for both parties. In terms of actual buyers, out-of-towners made up half of the purchasers, with almost all the premium units in the church going to out-of-towners. Only three of the twenty units were sold to married couples.

Total sales proceeds after sales commissions were $8.3 million. Assuming an industry-standard 20 percent developer cash in the deal, this works out to a return on equity of $188,000, or 12 percent.

Lessons Learned

- *Location:* The property is well located proximate to a dynamic employment node in a stable neighborhood.
- *Low acquisition cost and a generously sized lot:* The site was bought cheaply, and the lot was large enough to allow for a substantial number of new units to offset the fixed cost of site acquisition.
- *Cooperative local government:* No rezoning was required because the site was already zoned multifamily, and the neighbors largely did not object to the develop-

ment. The city cooperated, but offered no financial inducements.

- *Good architectural design:* The units all contain the architectural feature of the former church's red front door. The church construction built entirely new units inside the church while retaining the attractive outside shell. The developer and his architect preserved much of the aesthetics of the church building. Each unit within the church retains a piece of the small church's interior grandeur.
- *Hit the market window:* Market timing was excellent, and phased development and deferring finish costs until buyers were found kept financing costs low. A special arrangement with a knowledgeable local boutique realtor also kept marketing costs in check. This was a highly successful project.

Conclusion

This was a highly successful project evidencing thoughtful architectural design and a 12 percent (or better) return on equity for the developer. The product of development of condos within the church and new construction was well received by purchasers.

References and Works Consulted

City-Data.com. www.city-data.com.

O'Malley, M. 2004. "Church Goes through a Conversion to a New Townhouse Development." *Plain Dealer,* June 3, B1.

Schuemann, N. 2004. "Sanctuary in Cleveland Heights: Adaptive Re-use Project Transforms Empty Church into Luxurious Living Spaces." *Properties Magazine, Inc.,* December, 33–38.

U.S. Department of Commerce. Bureau of the Census, 2000 and 2007.

13

Adaptive Reuse of the

DUTCH REFORMED CHURCH

into the Jamaica Performing

Arts Center

Queens, New York

Robert A. Simons

This case describes the renovation of the empty First Dutch Reformed Church at 153–04 Jamaica Avenue in Queens, New York, into an additional facility of the Jamaica Center for Arts and Learning (JCAL) in the form of a new four-hundred-seat theater, the Jamaica Performing Arts Center (JPAC). (See Exhibit 13-1.) It has taken ten years to bring the Performing Arts Center project from idea conception to occupancy. The $20.85 million project, first occupied in 2009, is sponsored by the city of New York Department of Cultural Affairs, which put together internal funding from a number of city sources, aided by substantial leadership from the Queens Borough president's office, the New York City mayor, and the city council. The Greater Jamaica Development Corporation championed the project in the community and successfully won its acceptance. JCAL has a strong record of service in the community, and this is a second facility they have in their service area to expand artistry and programming. The building is rented from the city of New York for $1 per year.

Introduction

"Originally built in 1859, the First Reformed Church at 153rd and Jamaica Avenue in Queens, New York, is a Romanesque Revival structure featuring two asymmetrical towers. There was a major addition in about 1902, which was later torn down in the 1960s" (Padalka 2006). The building sits on about 1.5 acres. Before renovation the building had a shallow basement, one large sanctuary of about 8,000 sq. ft., and some smaller rooms.

Site History

In the early 1970s, about the same time the congregation using the building moved into another church nearby, the city of New York designated a 10-acre site around the original church as an urban renewal area so that it could build an office complex for the Social Security Administration (SSA). The Greater Jamaica Development Corporation (GJDC), the local not-for-profit economic development entity, supported the city's plan, according to Carlisle Towery, executive director for GJDC. In the original proposal, the Social Security Administration was going to employ an elevated pedestrian bridge between buildings and preserve the church as an auditorium, partly because then–Senator Patrick Moynihan liked public art. The city therefore bought the church building and grounds from the Dutch Reformed Church at fair market value. Eventually, however, the SSA built its project without the church, opting instead for an internal auditorium.

After the Social Security building plans proceeded without the church property, the city retained ownership. It nominally maintained the church and tried to find a user, leasing the property out to another church group from about 1980 until 1990. After the group left, the facility sat vacant for many years (C. Towery, personal communication, July 2008). According to Alex Padalka, "Without regular maintenance, the structure's slate roof, stained-glass windows, brownstone, sandstone, and terra cotta began falling apart" (Padalka 2006). The property was overlooked and underutilized, and waiting for a champion.

Market Conditions

The Jamaica Performing Arts Center is located in Queens County, New York. Queens is the largest in area and the second most populous of the five boroughs[1] of New York City. According to the 2000 U.S. Census, Queens County had a total population of 2,229,379. The City-Data Web site estimated about a 2 percent increase in population (2,270,338) in the county from the year 2000 to 2007 (see Exhibit 13-2). Queens County has the largest Asian American population outside the Western United States, ranking fifth among U.S. counties (City-Data 2008).

The site itself has excellent access. It is located along a busy commercial street about a half-hour subway ride from Manhattan, and it is very close to the E line NYC subway and the Long Island Railroad.

Exhibit 13-1 Jamaica Performing Arts Center Location and Site Plans

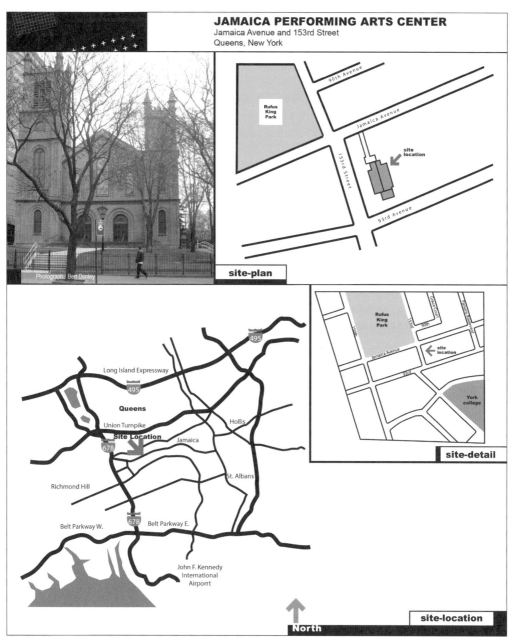

Exhibit 13–2 Census Data 2000 and 2007

	New York	Kings	Brooklyn Borough	Census Tract 1142.01
Population				
2000	18,976,457	2,465,326	2,465,326	1,382
2007	19,297,729	2,528,050		
% Change	1.69%	2.54%		
Age (2000)				
Less than 18	24.63%	26.72%	26.72%	32.27%
22 - 39	26.62%	27.95%	27.95%	24.10%
40-59	26.48%	24.30%	24.30%	22.94%
60 and over	16.88%	15.34%	15.34%	11.58%
Median Household Income				
2000	$43,393	$32,135	$32,135	$37,422
2007	$53,514	$41,406		
% Change	23.32%	28.85%		
Race (2000)				
White alone	67.93%	41.21%	41.21%	12.81%
Black or African American alone	15.74%	36.22%	36.22%	53.47%
American Indian and Alaska Native alone	0.42%	0.35%	0.35%	0.00%
Asian alone	5.50%	7.54%	7.54%	2.03%
Hawaiian and Pacific Islander alone	0.04%	0.06%	0.06%	0.00%
Some other race alone	7.13%	10.21%	10.21%	22.36%
Two or more races	3.24%	4.42%	4.42%	9.33%
Education (2000)				
Bachelor or higher	27.37%	21.85%	21.85%	13.64%
High school above age 25	27.75%	26.72%	26.72%	23.49%
Unemployment				
2000	4.32%	5.94%	5.94%	10.43%
2007				
Housing (2000)				
Households	7,060,595	881,006	881,006	413
Housing Units	7,679,307	930,866	930,866	435
Owner Occupied Units (%)	52.99%	27.06%	27.06%	58.07%
Renter Units (%)	47.01%	72.94%	72.94%	41.93%
Median Rent Apartment	$672	$672	$672	$678
Median House Value (Owner Occupied)	$147,600	$229,200	$229,200	$190,200

Source: 2000 and 2007 U.S. Census
Note: 2007 tract data is not available

Redevelopment Process

The redevelopment process that produced the Jamaica Performing Arts Center began in 1998, when "to prevent the church from deteriorating completely, three local cultural groups—the Jamaica Center for Arts and Learning, the Cultural Collaborative of Jamaica, and the Black Spectrum Theater worked together to save the structure" (Padalka 2006). These players coordinated with the NYC Department of Cultural Affairs (DCA) and the development corporation to spearhead the transformation of the church property into a performing arts center. Prior to that time, the work of "babysitting" the property had fallen largely to the Greater Jamaica Development Corporation (GJDC). A number of improvements were made to the property in order to market it to potential users, such as clearing debris and small outbuildings away from the church, leaving only the original structure. The church was also too close to 153rd St., which abutted the side of the building. Arrangements were made for the street to be realigned away from the church. The development corporation spent twelve years maintaining the building at an annual cost of $12,000 to $15,000, before eventually turning it over to JCAL in 2007.

The building's champion was Queens Borough President Claire Shulman, who found the initial public money to restore it. According to the Department of Cultural Affairs' Victor Metoyer, this meant that, in New York City internal politics, the Queens Borough president owned the project. She was in the driver's seat, and was the lead in ensuring the project would get completed. Shulman's successor, Borough President Helen Marshall, later allocated additional public money to sustain the project's momentum.

The church's redevelopment project was funded through the NYC Department of Cultural Affairs and construction coordinated through the NYC Department of Design and Construction (DDC). At this book's press time, DCA has about four hundred projects of all types underway, according to Kate deRosset, project director of DCA. Several are major adaptive reuse projects with cultural end uses. Funds are used for projects that strengthen an organization's capacity to provide high-quality cultural services to the public, thereby generating substantial social but not necessarily financial return. This includes projects with positive externalities, such as encouraging economic activity, enhancing quality of life, and sustaining New York City's reputation as a world-class cultural center. The Department of Cultural Affairs provides programming and operating support for more than nine hundred cultural organizations, including city museums, the botanic garden, theaters, centers of arts education, and city zoos. Thirty-three of these nine hundred organizations are on city-owned property and receive substantial general operating funds through the department. Jamaica Performing Arts is one such institution. The two organizations already had an operating agreement from other existing operations in Queens. The new facility is expected to attract artists and audiences engaged in a broad array of cultural activities from Queens and beyond. The actual programming is left up to the local art association with no quota or expectations on artistic output other than adhering to certain agreed-upon management and governance practices (K. deRosset, personal communication, June 2008).

Jamaica Performing Arts, according to Deputy Director Anita Segarra, was involved in the project design from the beginning. In the late 1990s, the project started with an $8 million budget, which grew to about $21 million in 2008. The four-hundred-seat theater was intended to fill a strategic niche between an existing ninety-nine-seat Queens facility and the one-thousand-seat theater at York College, a few blocks away. The theater plus a conference/business center were core to the project, although the business center's importance shrank over time. The performing arts group plans to use the facility several times a week for various arts and cultural performances. Plans include renting out the building to other local nonprofits and individuals. Overall, it is expected that the building will be used four to five nights a week with income going to the center (A. Segarra, personal communication, July 2008).

Development Plan

The process of finding an architect to oversee the design process was not a smooth one. The project called for a renovated building of 18,000 sq. ft., with an 8,000-sq.-ft. footprint. The original architectural design firm, which led the project for several years, lost the confidence of the stakeholders and was replaced with Wank Adams Slavin Associates (WASA) of New York in 2003. The firm is over one hundred years old and has had extensive experience with performing arts centers and rehabbing old buildings. Preservation architect for the project, Douglas Emilio, indicated a similar notable project is the adaptive reuse of the 135th Street Gatehouse as the Harlem Stage, a performing arts center located on Manhattan's west side in New York City. The firm's New York City office has performed hundreds of preservation and rehab projects the last five years (D. Emilio, personal communication, June 2008).

Administratively, the architect's contractual client on this project was the NYC Department of Design and Construction (DDC), the city agency that executes hiring and administers construction. The NYC Department of Cultural Affairs (DCA) is DDC's internal city client and is providing funding for the project, which was contractually administered by DDC.

The architectural team worked with Peter George Associates of Haddonfield, New Jersey, to produce "a design that included theater-quality acoustics" (Padalka 2006). This design placed a 325-seat main floor in the beautiful and acoustically desirable ground floor theater space. A seventy-five-seat balcony and an overhanging third-floor conference room provide additional audience space. The project has a multistory "smart" tower with the building's electronics and a "wow" lobby to welcome visitors.

After four project design presentations at Queens Borough Hall, the community stakeholders were on board. Another important purpose of these presentations was to demonstrate community support for the project in order to facilitate obtaining additional funds from the Queens Borough president (M. Calin, personal communication, June 2008). This effort was successful, and construction began in 2004.

Problems Underground

There were some major design and construction issues with the project's underground foundation, which had to be expanded to accommodate support space. Lowering the basement floor was the source of considerable difficulty and delay. The lower level design called for approximately 8,000 sq. ft. for a coat-check office, small lounge for refreshments, pantry, restrooms, dressing rooms, practice space, a prop entrance, and an offstage waiting room. The design fit all of those elements into a cellar that was originally only 5½ ft. deep, requiring significant work to raise the ceiling by digging a deeper base. A full 10-ft. depth was needed for the rest of the foundation. The project team dropped the foundation by more than 4 ft. to create the building's new 10-ft.-deep cellar.

To accomplish this task, the crew dug holes under the perimeter wall in a checkerboard pattern, filling in the first squares with concrete, and then repeating the process for the remaining squares to complete the new, deeper wall. The crew also excavated the main floor area of the rest of the basement to the lower depth. It was determined, however, that the existing building footings were insufficient and additional underpinning for more than half the building was needed. This presented technical challenges, and the effort to shore up and expand the foundation lasted six months, cost about $500,000, and wrapped up in the spring of 2006.

Some danger was involved. According to lead architect Mircea Calin, the ground-level wood-joint floor was holding up the walls of the building, which create a 2-ft.-thick brick shell. The architect's design required the removal of the first floor to complete the work in the basement. However, removing the first floor created a risk that the whole structure could collapse. Therefore, it was necessary to pour a new 50' × 100' concrete first floor on top of the existing wood floor before excavating. At the same time, new concrete posts were poured down to the new basement finish floor, and then a second concrete basement floor was created. When the concrete slab and columns reached the required structural strength, the existing wood floor and columns were removed. The sidewalls were very carefully backfilled in 2- to 4-ft. sections to support the underpinning, so the integrity of the building would be maintained (M. Calin, personal communication, June 2008).

The entire four-story interior structure was new. The first floor of the project includes the entry hall, box office, office, stage with storage underneath, and 325 seats. The theater has a flat floor with seats on moving platforms that extend and retract. The entry hall is breathtakingly beautiful, with stunning stained-glass windows and modern artwork. (See Exhibit 13-3.) The architects saved a few of the pews inside the main seating area for historical accents, but otherwise the seating in the theater is all new. The architects also salvaged a few balcony-support cast-iron columns and front fascia for aesthetic purposes, and replicated the crown-molding look from the original ceiling.

Above ground, all the critical electronic component systems were incorporated into a 34-ft.-high, one-story shell, not including the attic and steeple. Thus, utilities were incorporated into a mechanical tower built inside the building. The second-floor mezzanine contains balcony seats, the control room, and an office. It is situated over part of the lower seating area of the theater. The architects removed the historic balcony face and reconfigured it further out on the second floor.

The third floor has an office, bathroom, and a conference room. The author found that this area felt like an owners' suite at a major league ballpark—a donor "wow" zone overlooking the theater from just the perfect spot. This fine venue is available for internal and external meetings.

The fourth floor contains the mechanical systems. It also has two hard-sucking, sensitively designed, copper-clad roof dormer cutouts for HVAC supply and air return. There is also a 50' × 100' tension-grid catwalk, where all the lighting and sound equipment is located.

Building-code compliance was a challenge because there was only one exit to

Exhibit 13-3 Jamaica Performing Arts Center Photographs

JAMAICA PERFORMING ARTS CENTER
Jamaica Avenue and 153rd Street
Queens, New York

Photographs: WASA/Studio A

the street. To alleviate concerns about fire safety, the team built an internal safe area in the first-floor foyer with separate HVAC and enough room for folks to stay as they file out in case of a fire. This safe zone alleviates the need for a claustrophobic internal staircase and instead creates a nice, open feeling in the building by exposing two monumental open stairways.

Reconstruction of the building exterior had to accommodate the church's landmark designation from city, state, and federal preservation bodies. Because the slate roof had suffered extensive damage, the team replaced it entirely and added new supports. All of the exterior brick needed replacement, said Leonard Franco, WASA's partner-in-charge of the project (Padalka 2006).

To accommodate the HVAC systems, the architect decided to perforate the roof with small, semihidden dormers constructed of traditional materials. The Landmark Commission approved this alteration. They also allowed a modestly sized HVAC unit to be installed outside, but sheltered by vegetation.

Meeting landmarks requirements was a core part of the redesign. Certain elements that would have been cost-prohibitive required extra negotiating, said Louie Rueda, deputy commissioner of the Design and Construction Agency. "All of the exterior will be reconstructed to comply with landmark requirements," he added. "The landmarks commission is pretty flexible. They worked with us" (Padalka 2006).

One of the inventive changes from those negotiations was to replace the stained-glass windows lining the auditorium with acoustically insulated glazed-glass panels, complemented by electronically controlled shades to filter out light. The team also salvaged enough stained glass to supplement the three damaged windows facing Jamaica Avenue, those in the main lobby, the back window of the third floor conference center, and two smaller windows on the sides (Padalka 2006). Of the thirteen stained-glass windows in the building at the time of redevelopment—most of them in bad shape—the team relocated the best three pieces in front, including one in each mechanical stair tower. The design team decided to not install stained glass in the theater itself because the predominant objective was acoustic—keeping art sounds in and any airport noise out. Hence, the rest of the former stained-glass windows went back to the church's original congregation,

located a few blocks away (D. Emilio, personal communication, June 2008).

One late problem that arose in the summer of 2007 delayed the opening of the building until September 2008. The basement flooded twice during construction because a backflow device was not installed properly. This problem is not uncommon in older cities that have combined storm water and sewage systems. In August 2008, the on-site construction manager, PMS, installed 23,000 gal. of water-retention storage tanks to avoid future flooding.

Project Financing

This is a straight public subsidy deal. It was funded with all New York City funds. The deal is structured so that the city of New York owns the building and Jamaica Performing Arts is a tenant under an operating agreement with the city.

As of September 2008, the funds for the project, all of which came from New York City, totaled $20.85 million. The bulk came from the Queens Borough president's office ($10.7 million), with NY city council and the NYC mayor's office kicking in $4.6 million and $5.1 million, respectively. The funds were rounded out with a State of New York grant for $450,000. From the deal perspective, the project is all equity and no debt. However, NYC capital dollars are bond financed. Although the building is on the historic register, no historic credits, New Market Tax Credits, or tax abatement were used because the city is a public nonprofit entity and cannot take advantage of these potential tax benefits (V. Metoyer, personal communication, June 2008).

Construction costs totaled $1,158 per square foot, the bulk of which were hard costs. The cost breakdown is as follows: soft costs, including consultant design fees and related DDC fees, totaled $2.49 million, 12 percent, or $138 per square foot. Hard costs, including construction, construction manager fees, and equipment, totaled $18.36 million, 88 percent, or $1,020 per square foot. The cost of site acquisition was minimal when the city obtained the property back in 1973. Some costs, like maintenance of the vacant historic church incurred over twelve years by the development corporation, are excluded.

From a real estate development perspective, this is a pure subsidy deal. The city of New York owns the property and receives rent of $1 per year on a ten-year operating agreement with a ten-year renewal option. Operating subsidies for utilities and other operating expenses are provided by the city. The goal is to nurture and sustain the performing arts community in Queens and hope the project will do well by attracting large audiences. As a matter of policy, the city set no formal, quantified threshold for the city's return on its investment from the programming at this facility. The expected returns are primarily social.

Lessons Learned

- *Implementation takes time:* At the end of the ten-plus-year development process, the center is a top-of-the line, stunning community asset for the performing arts. Projects in a complex political environment like New York City require patience, perseverance, and teamwork plus a lot of money.

- *Finding lost space in the basement*: Rehab construction challenges can be overcome with careful planning and precise implementation. Retrofitting a basement is tricky under a 150-year-old building, but is possible with the right engineering expertise.

Conclusion

Despite the stunning existing church structure, the project cost $21 million for an 18,000 sq.-ft. project, more than $1,000 per square foot. While this cost may seem high even for a large city with high real estate values, people in the hinterlands will undoubtedly be amazed at the massive amounts of resources expended for a single project. Only in New York City!

Note

1. A *borough* is a form of government that administers each of the fundamental constituent parts of New York City.

References and Works Consulted

City-Data.com. www.city-data.com.
Padalka, A. 2006. "Historic Church Undergoes a Conversion into a New Arts Center." *New York Construction.* http://newyork.construction.com/features/archive/2006/02_feature 1b.asp.

Adaptive Reuse of the

DEUTSCHE EVANGELICAL

REFORM CHURCH into the

Urban Krag Rock Climbing Gym
Dayton, Ohio

Gary DeWine

The Urban Krag is a rock-climbing gym in the former Deutsche Evangelical Reform Church, located at 123 Clay Street, Dayton, Ohio. The Deutsche Evangelical Reform Church filtered through several successive church uses over the years. Its last use was as the Spiritualist Temple of the Burning Bush with a real snake-charming minister. The building then sat empty and deteriorating for almost twenty years, until developer Karl Williamson bought the property. A common commercial reuse of a church is as a restaurant. Williamson put the building to a less conventional use by redeveloping it as a rock-climbing facility. This case considers both the construction and legal challenges, primarily zoning, which he overcame to put the building into productive use.

Introduction

Karl Williamson became acquainted with rock climbing while on a trip to Glacier National Park. He enjoys the mental challenges of the sport along with the lessons of self-reliance and problem solving that interior rock-climbing venues provide. The first indoor rock-climbing gym appeared in Seattle in 1987. Now there are more than five hundred in the United States (*Urban Climber Magazine* 2008). In 1994, Williamson began an eight-month search for a building of sufficient size in which to construct an 8,000 sq.-ft. vertical climbing wall of textured and sculpted vertical terrain. Typically, gyms are located in industrial buildings that have sufficient height for the required wall: the wall eventually constructed for Urban Krag required a five-story building. A warehouse would have been suitable, but Williamson wanted to locate his business in a more distinctive building that people would remember (Morris 1996). He discovered the former Deutsche Evangelical Reform Church build-

A church converted to condominiums immediately north of the Urban Krag in the Oregon Historical District. Photograph: Gary DeWine

ing while walking through the Oregon Historic District and decided it was the right fit. (See Exhibit 14-1.) The church may have been as little as one month away from demolition when Williamson began negotiations to purchase the building.

Though unusual, the Urban Krag is not the only reuse of a church as a rock-climbing gym. The Bristol Climbing Centre, formerly the fifteenth-century St. Weburghs Church in Bristol, England, is another example. Originally standing in the center of Bristol, the church had been disassembled and reconstructed on a suburban site. A shrinking congregation eventually led the diocese to lease out the building. The lease agreement with the operators of the rock-climbing gym requires that the original church elements not be changed so that the building might one day revert back to a church (Cockram 2006).

Site History

The 5,000 sq.-ft. Deutsche Evangelical Reform Church is located in the center of the Oregon Historic District of Dayton. The Oregon neighborhood developed between 1830 and 1910. It hosts well-preserved architectural styles ranging from Federal Italianate to Greek Revival and Queen Anne. The neighborhood was nearly demolished under the Federal Urban Renewal policies of the 1960s. Fortunately, it survived the wrecking ball that destroyed the neighborhood just east of it. Now Oregon's Historic District attests to the neighborhood's prosperity in the early nineteenth century. Modern visitors enjoy a unique shopping and dining experience amidst almost twelve city blocks of restored commercial and residential buildings from the late Victorian period.

The Oregon Historic District contains

Exhibit 14-1 Urban Krag Site Location and Site Plan

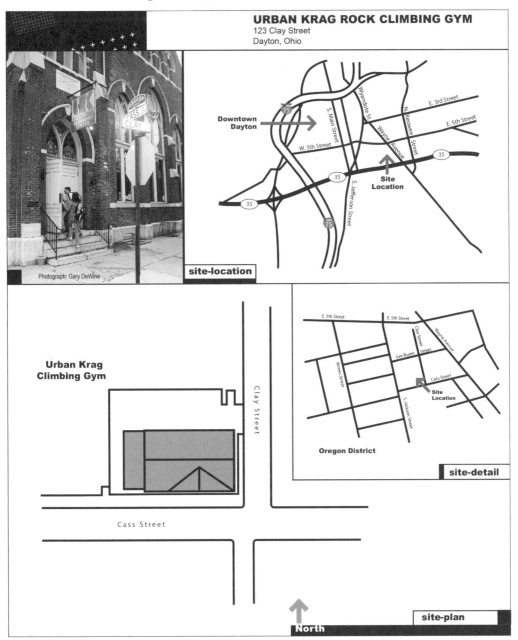

many churches, each of which ministered to a different ethnic religious group. Serving the German community was the Deutsche Evangelical Reform Church, built in 1862. For well over a century, the church witnessed countless baptisms, marriages, and funerals. Its membership declined as people moved from the Dayton neighborhood to the suburbs. The neighborhood landmark church was vacated in the 1970s.

The church was purchased by local developer Tim Patterson in the 1980s. In the mid-1990s Patterson successfully converted two other churches in the neighborhood into condominiums. He prepared plans to convert the Deutsche Evangelical Church building into seven condominiums units. The church was put up for sale. Potential developers shied away from Patterson's plan to redevelop the church, however, because they believed that the structure had deteriorated beyond salvation. Gaping holes in the building's slate roof allowed the elements easy entry, destroying the interior of the building. The church was placed on the city of Dayton's list of buildings to be demolished. Infill development of the very small 0.23-acre lot seemed to be the logical next step (Williamson, personal communication, July 2008).

Market Area Demographics

The population of the city of Dayton has been declining since the 1960s. This is in part due to the slowdown of manufacturing in the region and the growth of Dayton's affluent suburbs. As of the 2000 census, the median income for a household in the city was $27,523, and the median income for a family was $34,978. Males had a median income of $30,816 versus $24,937 for females. The per capita income for the city was $34,724. About 18.2 percent of families and 23.0 percent of the population were below the poverty line, including 32.0 percent of those under age

eighteen and 15.3 percent of those age sixty-five or over (Dayton, Ohio 2014).

Redevelopment Process

Because use of the church as a rock-climbing gym would place a business in the heart of a residential area, Dayton's zoning ordinance presented a major obstacle. Fortunately, the president of the Oregon Historic District Society, Barry Buckman, understood that Williamson's proposed use was the only hope for saving such a deteriorated structure. Both Mr. Buckman, a practicing architect with Rogero Buckman Architects of Dayton, and his neighborhood group had been working to preserve the old church. Buckman's initial reaction to the proposal was "the concept seemed a bit jarring. But then I thought, 'Fantastic!'" Buckman supported the project so enthusiastically that he signed on as the project's architect. Getting the Oregon District Society to buy into the idea, though, was another thing, since zoning ruled out locating a business in the middle of the historic residential neighborhood (Rogero-Buckman Architects Web site 2005).

The city of Dayton uses priority boards, which are groups of elected citizen volunteers, to resolve neighborhood issues and assist in advocating for business projects such as the Urban Krag. Karl Williamson found support with the Southeast Priority Board and from the neighborhood residents who saw the value and importance of a small but significant project. The project received great support from the neighbors in the Oregon Historic District. At public hearings, seven or eight would attend to voice support for the project (Morris 1996).

Having the neighborhood buy into the idea of a commercial use for the church was just a first step in the approval process. More than twelve meetings were required over a twelve-month period before the project could

Exhibit 14-2 Census Data 2000 and 2007

	Ohio	Montgomery County	Dayton City	Census Tract 21
Population				
2000	11,353,140	559,062	166,193	3,969
2007	11,466,917	538,104	146,360	
% Change	1.00%	-3.75%	-11.93%	
Age (2000)				
Less than 18	25.41%	24.63%	25.02%	16.18%
22 – 39	24.93%	25.04%	26.10%	35.53%
40 -59	26.82%	26.59%	23.76%	22.55%
60 and over	17.27%	17.83%	15.54%	20.99%
Median Household Income				
2000	$40,956	$40,156	$27,423	$22,927
2007	$46,597	$43,939	$28,927	
% Change	13.77%	9.42%	5.48%	
Race (2000)				
White alone	84.92%	76.53%	53.35%	80.65%
Black or African American alone	11.35%	19.89%	43.24%	11.26%
American Indian and Alaska Native alone	0.24%	0.24%	0.32%	0.35%
Asian alone	1.16%	1.29%	0.62%	0.35%
Hawaiian and Pacific Islander alone	0.02%	0.05%	0.02%	0.00%
Some other race alone	0.79%	0.39%	0.52%	1.97%
Two or more races	1.53%	1.62%	1.94%	5.42%
Education (2000)				
Bachelor or higher	21.10%	22.83%	14.37%	24.75%
High School above age 25	36.09%	30.42%	31.88%	25.81%
Unemployment				
2000	3.22%	3.38%	5.50%	5.64%
Housing (2000)				
Households	4,446,621	229,177	67,476	2,098
Housing Units	4,783,051	248,443	77,337	2,389
Owner Occupied Units (%)	69.11%	64.68%	52.67%	28.93%
Renter Units (%)	30.89%	35.32%	47.33%	71.07%
Median Rent Apartment	$515	$525	$448	$428
Median House Value (Owner Occupied)	$100,500	$94,800	$66,700	$88,400

Source: 2000 and 2007 U.S. Census
Note: 2007 tract data is not available

proceed to the construction phase. When discussing the process over a decade later, Williamson still expressed exasperation at the number of meetings it took simply to get the project approved, though he delegated meeting attendance to Buckman, the project's architect. John Gower, director of planning for the city of Dayton, was also very supportive of the project. Gower understood the merits of the project and provided sufficient input from the governmental and planning side so the planning commission approved a conditional use of the building (Williamson, personal communication, July 2008).

Because of the building's age and its location within the Oregon Historic District, the Landmarks Commission was also required by law to approve, deny, or approve the project with modifications (Landmark Commission Application Process 2013). Fortunately, this group acknowledged that Williamson was the only "white knight" willing to make an investment in the property, and they facilitated the Krag Rock project by reaching compromises that accommodated the limitations of Mr. Williamson's pocketbook. For example, Williamson's plans called for replacing the building's deteriorated slate roof with asphalt shingles, a $50,000 project. The Landmark Commission wanted the building's exterior appearance to be maintained by repair or replacement of the original roof. The $150,000 cost of a new slate roof, however, was a potential deal killer. The commission decided to accept asphalt replacement shingles that appeared original to the untrained eye, and permitted Williamson to block in the windows facing the parking lot. These decisions saved the building from destruction.

Development Plan for the Property

The redevelopment of the church, from Karl Williamson's first contact with Tim Patterson to the Urban Krag Rock Climbing Gym's opening day, was accomplished over a two-year period. In addition to zoning hurdles, the building posed major structural design challenges. The building was in deplorable condition when Williamson purchased it for $50,000. The roof had simply disappeared in many areas. The double-hung stained-glass windows had been removed, and the gaping holes in the roof allowed the weather and pigeons free entry. Williamson stated, "[The building] was pretty much a giant check. It was expensive to save the building" (St. Clair 2002).

Williamson's vision for the property required almost 75 percent of the 5,000 sq.-ft. sanctuary floor area to be removed. The design called for the climbing wall to be constructed from the basement floor up to the top of the gable. Caution had to be exercised in removing the floor, which provided support for the exterior walls around the perimeter of the building. Removal of the floor would weaken the exterior walls and possibly lead to the collapse of the church. Structural engineering professionals, in addition to architect Barry Buckman, were required. They solved the problem by adding structural steel I-beams in the basement walls. Additionally, installation of a 20-ft. concrete footer was necessary to address the faulty condition of the 1860s limestone foundation. The basement, along with providing an open area for the climbing walls, now contains lockers, showers, a weight room, and classroom space for personal instruction.

The interior space (shown in Exhibit 14-3) is both visually stimulating and interesting. Large clusters of stained-glass Gothic-style windows allow avenues of natural and colored light to fill the space. The red brick of the exterior walls, from which much of the plaster has fallen away, contrasts nicely with the exposed 150-year-old beams of the roof trusses. This interior space, which predates the Civil War, is much more interesting than a windowless industrial building of cold steel beams.

Heating the space efficiently required a creative approach. Heated air would collect and become trapped in the vaulted ceiling. Barry Buckman explained, "The ceiling has two chimneys. We used them to pull air from the top of the space to the furnaces. The furnaces are positioned at the base of the chimneys. The air is heated and pumped out at floor level. Of course the warm air rises to the vaulted ceiling where it is again

Exhibit 14-3 Urban Krag Photographs

URBAN KRAG ROCK CLIMBING GYM
123 Clay Street
Dayton, Ohio

Photographs: Gary DeWine

Photograph: Karl Williamson

sucked back down the chimneys. So you have continual movement of the heated air from the ceiling to the basement so the heat does not stay at the top of the ceiling but is reused to heat the space" (Urban Krag Climbing Center 2007).

Entry to the rock gym is through the former church's original street-level doors, leading to the front desk, seating area, and a pro shop. A log cabin church stood on the site in 1837 but burned to the ground. The only thing to survive was a 300-lb. brass bell, which now is used as the counter bell that customers can ring if no one is at the desk (Archdeacon 2007). To the right of the front desk is a railed observation area providing an open view of the climbing walls from the basement to the rafters.

In the back and on one side are 8,000 sq. ft. of climbing area, with a total of eleven climbing walls and 109 ever-changing routes. The climbing walls, which are the biggest in Ohio, are built to Climbing Wall Industry Group (CWIG) standards. The climbing walls are freestanding and not dependent on the old walls of the church. They were constructed independently, with each supporting up to 4,000 lb.

Behind the five-story lead wall with its 30-ft. overhang, there is a slightly smaller wall in addition to a shorter bouldering wall (Morris 1996). The variety of terrain at Urban Krag is a feature that sets it apart from other climbing gyms. The steep bouldering area is full of high-difficulty problems: a deep, horizontal cave for bouldering that also turns into a lead wall; a pillar; a massive overhang; two stations for teaching rappelling; several high-quality, full-length cracks of varying degrees of difficulty, some of which meet up mid-route with other cracks; and a bolt ladder composed of metal fittings driven into the climbing face. Though the current trend in climbing seems to be flowing away from traditional and aid climbing, Urban Krag keeps a wide perspective on the sport, offering classes in top-roping, leading, rappelling, and even aiding. This variety is part of Williamson's conscious effort to avoid being "tunnel-visioned," or catering to only one type of climber (Urban Climber Magazine 2008).

The clientele at Urban Krag mirror the setup of the gym in its diversity. As with any climbing gym, most of the customers are beginners: people stopping in for the first time, birthday parties, Scout troops, and, of course, church groups. But then there are the regulars whose climbing interests range from bouldering and sport climbing to ice climbing and even caving. "Some climb for social reasons," observed Rick Kappel, a local schoolteacher who has climbed for fifteen years. "I climb for mental sanity and fitness" (Urban Climber Magazine 2008).

Financing

The project was funded with a $350,000 SBA loan from Unity National Bank supplemented by $150,000 in family financial backing. When this case study was conducted in July 2008, the family loan had been paid off, the SBA loan was refinanced at a lower interest rate, and Williamson expected the building to be owned free and clear by 2011. Exhibit 14-4 briefly describes where the $500,000 was spent, in addition to a significant amount of sweat equity.

Williamson had $300 in his checking account when Urban Krag opened for business. When asked about marketing and promotion, he indicated that newspapers and television were the no-cost means of getting the word out about the rock-climbing gym in the former Deutsche Evangelical Reform Church. The novelty of a gym in a former church was a hot news item.

Exhibit 14-4 Use of Funds for Urban Krag

Building Purchase	50,000
Design Fees	13,000
Climbing Wall System	200,000
Building Improvements	
Roof	50,000
Heating and Cooling	21,000
Windows and Doors Reset	20,000
Showers and Locker Room	45,000
New Plumbing	26,000
New Electrical	23,000
Structural—Steel and Foundation	48,000
Total	$500,000

Lessons Learned

- *Low opportunity cost:* This is an excellent example of an opportunity found in a church building facing the wrecking ball. For many months Karl Williamson did not take a paycheck, but his commitment has paid off. With only a nominal amount of investment he is meeting his monthly expenses on the building he will own outright.
- *Flexibility in historic preservation requirements is key:* The Landmarks Commission rightly recognized that requiring a totally restored slate roof would be a deal killer on the cost side. They allowed the developer to install a cheaper replica, and the deal got done.
- *Even small deals need qualified design professionals:* Even on a small budget, Williamson rightly recognized that he needed the help of architectural and engineering design professionals to bring his climbing gym vision to reality. The architect's involvement both professionally and as president of the Oregon Historic District Society was crucial in pushing the project along. The design services were money well spent.

- *Engage residents and city hall:* The neighborhood grasped that Karl Williamson's vision for the property was not an off-the-wall use. Skeptics could have written off the idea of a rock-climbing gym, but instead the neighborhood and the city government embraced the idea, facilitating the project through city hall bureaucracy.

Conclusion

"Some say the wildest thing that ever happened inside that 148-year-old church at the corner of Cass and Clay Streets in Dayton's Oregon Historic District was when bizarre preacher Wavil B. Lewis moved his Spiritualist Temple of the Burning Bush in there. Still, in my book, he's second fiddle to Karl Williamson. He's a true rock star" (Archdeacon 2007).

References and Works Consulted

Archdeacon, T. 2007. "Dayton's Urban Krag a Climber's Paradise." *Dayton Daily News,* November 25, B2.

Cockram, Michael. 2006. "Postcard from Bristol." *Architecture Week,* September 20, C1.1, http://www.architectureweek.com/2006/0920/culture_1–1.html.

Dayton, Ohio. 2014. http://en.wikipedia.org/wiki/Dayton,_Ohio.

Landmark Commission Application Process. 2013. City of Dayton. www.cityofdayton.org/departments/pcd/planning/Pages/Landmarkprocess.aspx.

Morris, J. 1996. "Cliffhanger." *Dayton Daily News,* October 12, C1.

Rogero-Buckman Architects Web site. 2005. Projects: Urban Krag. www.rbaoh.com/Krag.html.

St. Clair, S. 2002. "Boulder Dash Climbing Wall Facilities Race for the Next Level." *Recreation Management,* February 3. recmanagement.com/features.php?fid=200203fe03&ch=2.

Urban Climber Magazine. 2008. "Plastic Paradise: Urban Krag—Dayton, Ohio." www.urbanclimbermag.com/themag/plasticparadise/urban_krag_dayton_ohio.

Urban Krag Climbing Center. 2007. www.urbankrag.com.

Adaptive Reuse of

SAINTS PETER AND PAUL

CATHOLIC CHURCH

into Residential Condos

South Boston, Massachusetts

Robert A. Simons

uilt in 1844, the former Saints Peter and Paul Church, with its adjoining rectory at 45–55 West Broadway in Boston, Massachusetts, was a Roman Catholic church in the predominantly Irish section of South Boston. In 2001, the Catholic Archdiocese of Boston divested itself of the 35,700-sq.-ft. building property, including 28,000 sq. ft. of built space, selling it as is to West Broadway LLC, headed by developer James McFarland.

The McFarland firm selectively gutted the 60-ft.-high building and redeveloped the former church into six stories of high-end residential condos. The smaller rectory, which was developed first, was kept mostly intact. (See Exhibit 15-1.) The entire project included forty-four units, with eight units in the adjacent rectory and thirty-six in the former church building itself. The market was growing and firm at the time of redevelopment from 2002 to early 2004, with prices ranging between $230,000 and $790,000 ($285 per square foot to $415 per square foot) for units that averaged 1,100 sq. ft. Twenty-five percent of the units were set aside as affordable, which was helpful in winning the right to develop the property.

Two separate outside real estate brokerage firms handled the sales transactions. The project absorption averaged about three units per month. The project's rate of return was about 5 percent on overall development revenues of $11.7 million before considering the value of the units retained by the developer.

Notable features of this case include maximizing space in a large church and dealing with only limited issues with neighbors by constructing a new multistory building inside an existing statuesque and dignified structure while retaining as much architectural detail as possible, hitting the market window, and winning a profit by using a vertically integrated management structure.

Site History

Saints Peter and Paul Catholic Church, built before the Civil War, was a mainstay in the religious life of Irish Catholic South Boston for decades. The facility included a church, rectory, and small garage on 0.82 acres near I-93 and I-95, on a main commercial street just south of downtown Boston, a stone's throw from the Broadway Red Line T subway station. At the time of redevelopment, the building was surrounded by nonresidential uses, including retail and service uses. The project has been catalytic, however, and two adjacent multifamily residential projects with more than a hundred units were built nearby.

The gray granite, 17,800-sq.-ft. main church building contained a full basement and worship space on the 60-ft.-high first floor, in addition to organ and choir space. Distinctive church features included stained-glass windows, a bell tower steeple, 3-ft.-thick, gray granite walls, and vintage handcrafted stonework over the Broadway entryway. The rectory was 12,000 sq. ft. on five residential floors. The red brick rectory had nice woodwork inside and was in very good condition. There was also a small service garage on the property.

The building was a Catholic church from 1844 to 1995. The rectory was always occupied with church personnel during this time. After the church building was closed, it sat empty for five years, from 1995 to 2000. The archdiocese then sold the building in an open-bid format, before the binge of church closures and sales that occurred in Boston a few years later (Grillo 2000).

Market Area Demographics

According to the 2000 U.S. Census, the Boston metropolitan statistical area (MSA) had a total population of 5,819,101, making it the eleventh largest MSA in the nation. Saints

Peter and Paul Church is located in predominantly white and historically Irish South Boston, in a census tract where 43 percent of the population is in the twenty-two to thirty-nine-year-old age group, and 17 percent of the residents are sixty years or over. The census tract is located in Suffolk County, which is the third largest county in the state of Massachusetts with a population of 690,000, according to the 2000 census.

In the year 2000, there were 963 households in the census tract, 43 percent of which were one-person households. That figure is higher than for Suffolk County

Exhibit 15-1 Saints Peter and Paul Location and Site Plan

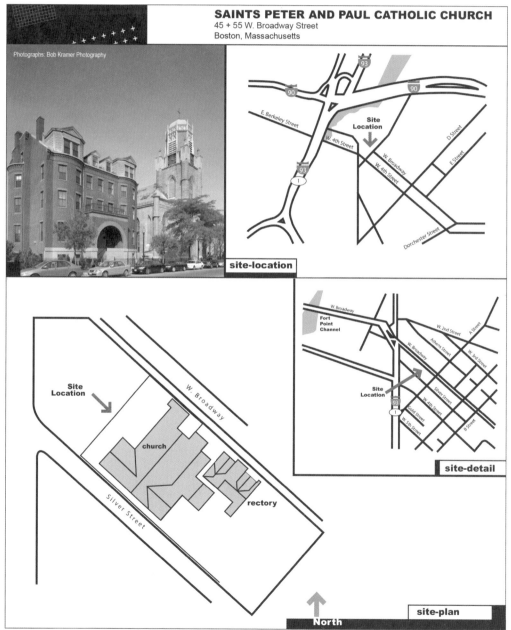

Exhibit 15-2 Census Data 2000 and 2007

	Massachusetts	Suffolk County	Boston City	Census Tract 612
Population				
2000	6,349,097	689,807	589,141	1,983
2007	6,449,755	713,049	613,117	
% Change	1.59%	3.37%	4.07%	
Age (2000)				
Less than 18	23.56%	20.09%	19.67%	11.25%
22–39	26.83%	35.31%	36.36%	43.02%
40–59	26.96%	22.03%	21.52%	22.89%
60 and over	17.26%	14.26%	13.55%	17.40%
Median Household Income				
2000	$50,502	$39,355	$39,629	$37,188
2007	$62,365	$50,181	$50,476	
% Change	23.49%	27.51%	27.37%	
Race (2000)				
White alone	84.50%	57.70%	54.44%	94.70%
Black or African American alone	5.31%	21.89%	24.94%	0.50%
American Indian and Alaska Native alone	0.24%	0.44%	0.44%	0.00%
Asian alone	3.75%	6.98%	7.53%	2.72%
Hawaiian and Pacific Islander alone	0.03%	0.03%	0.04%	0.00%
Some other race alone	3.73%	8.28%	7.93%	0.00%
Two or more races	2.43%	4.69%	4.69%	2.07%
Education (2000)				
Bachelor or higher	33.19%	32.45%	35.56%	27.30%
High school above age 25	27.27%	25.74%	23.99%	24.97%
Unemployment				
2000	3.01%	4.43%	4.59%	3.50%
Housing (2000)				
Households	2,444,588	278,776	239,603	963
Housing Units	2,621,989	292,520	251,935	1,086
Owner Occupied Units (%)	61.72%	33.92%	32.23%	33.78%
Renter Units (%)	38.28%	66.08%	67.77%	66.22%
Median Rent Apartment	$684	$791	$803	$750
Median House Value (Owner Occupied)	$182,800	$201,300	$210,100	$153,300

Source: 2000 and 2007 U.S. Census
2007 tract data is not available

(36 percent) and the Boston MSA (27 percent). The residents' median age is 31.7 years. There are approximately 295 schools, both public and private, in or near Suffolk County, and nearly 164 public libraries (City-Data.com 2008).

The multifamily housing market in the county (including condos and apartments) is dominated by structures with twenty or more units. They total about 60,574. Three- and four-unit structures (73,731) are also common. The median selling price of a condo in December 2007 was $270,000, which remained unchanged from December 2006. The median selling price in May 2008 for single-family homes fell 9.2 percent to $322,500, compared with $355,000 in May 2007 (Boston.com 2008).

In general, this project's market timing was good. All property markets were stunned by the events of 9/11, about the time that the deal was coming together. The condo market started to heat back up in late 2002, was fine through the project's marketing window in 2004, and started softening up again in 2005 and 2006.

Redevelopment Process

The controlling entity for disposal of the church-rectory complex was the Catholic Diocese of Boston. They put up the buildings for sale through a packaged competitive bid in 2000. James McFarland was the successful bidder. McFarland, along with his sons Bernard and John, became the developer, owner, and builder of the project (Grillo 2000).

James, an Irish immigrant, arrived in Boston as a young adult. He opened a property development firm in the late 1960s and started buying and rehabbing houses, doing general contracting for the Boston Housing Authority and the Boston Redevelopment Authority (BRA), and doing general structural repairs to housing. McFarland also had his own redevelopment business. The McFarland family firm had done about fifty separate housing-related development and redevelopment projects before taking on Saints Peter and Paul, including one nonresidential church rehab project. (J. McFarland, personal communication, June 27, 2008). Saints Peter and Paul was their first venture into converting a church into housing. It was a vertically integrated project, so the McFarlands wore several hats: developer, owner, and builder.

Acquiring the Property

McFarland happened to be between jobs with time on his hands in early 2001, when the request for proposal to acquire the church as is came out. This meant he was able to develop a thoughtful and comprehensive proposal, which is a very time-consuming process. About twenty firms submitted bids to the archdiocese to purchase buildings. McFarland won the bid competitively and straight up, partly because of his experience, but also because he was willing to set aside 25 percent of the units as affordable housing. His bid price ($2.4 million), plan to have housing as the end use, promise not to demolish buildings, and already lined-up financing package were also keys to winning the bid.

McFarland incurred a business risk once he won the bid because he owned the building outright and could not resort to the usual property option approach. The hardest and riskiest part of the deal, he said, was buying the buildings without already having planning approval or building permits.

McFarland's construction lender was Andover Bank, with which he had a successful ten-year relationship. His approach to property development, which had led to his success, was to minimize risk in cost overruns.

His flawless credit history made it easier for him to secure financing. McFarland also had market comparables and agreed to some pre-sale conditions when he met with the lender.

McFarland selected an architectural firm, R. Wendell Phillips and Associates, Architects, which had substantial restoration experience. The architect prepared several compelling renderings, which were helpful later in public meetings about the proposed project.

The plan was to redevelop the buildings into for-sale housing. The first floor and basement were generally combined into twelve two-story duplex units, averaging about 1,200 sq. ft. each. Floors two and three had nine and eight units, respectively. These flats averaged 700 sq. ft. The affordable units were distributed among both the flats and duplexes. Floor four, the penthouse level, had seven units, all duplexes. Their average size was 1,800 sq. ft. The biggest one was 2,000 sq. ft. Many had excellent church roof features, such as structural arches and painted ceilings. They also had little pocket balconies with views of the city.

Development Process

The project was vastly simplified because it used no city money, no tax credits, and required only an advisory role from the historic property commission. The public agency spearheading the redevelopment effort was the Boston Redevelopment Authority. The BRA process included public vetting, design review and plan approval, and then a trip to the zoning board. The project required rezoning because the area was zoned for industrial uses and had to be rezoned to residential multifamily. James McFarland said that "the hardest and riskiest part of this deal was buying the buildings without having planning approval or building permits" (J. McFarland, personal communication, June 27, 2008).

The BRA process required public input. The architect prepared renderings and floor plans, and they went with the developers and BRA to three neighborhood public meetings over three months. Over the course of these meetings, there were no substantial changes to their original proposal. Because Saints Peter and Paul was among the very first churches the Boston archdiocese sold, the project was somewhat of a novelty. Also, the fact that the archdiocese had boarded up the church's windows after extracting most of the stained glass gave the project the benefit of appearing to "unblight" the neighborhood.

Community reaction to the project was generally positive because there were no residential property abutters, and thus the project was an INBY, i.e., "in nobody's back yard." The sparsely attended meetings attracted only a dozen folks and few local residents, and no organized opposition emerged.[1]

The public process was reasonably quick and smooth: it took eight months overall, and there was only one delay-causing glitch. After the public meetings, BRA rezoning and design review went fine. Because the buildings were not in a historic district, not on the historic register, and not asking for historic preservation tax credits, the Boston Historical Commission was involved only as a nonbinding advisory body. The commission's input was still required as part of the BRA review, but "best efforts" to historically preserve the building (rather than strict adherence to particular standards required by Historic Preservation Tax Credits, for example) were sufficient. For example, cutting utility dormers and pocket deck balconies and adding an ADA-compliant handicap access ramp were minor issues. The BRA approved the project, and the Historical Commission went along.

The next and the last step before pulling permits was the Boston Zoning Board. The case was heard, but the Boston Zoning Appeals initially tabled it. One city councillor objected and wanted more consideration of the parking ratio. The project had only one on-site surface space per unit. Another hearing was scheduled for a month later. McFarland's attorney did some lobbying, mostly by pointing out the opportunity cost of having the building remain empty, desolate, boarded up, and abandoned. The next zoning board vote came back with unanimous approval of preliminary plans. About six more months were required for detailed plan approval from the BRA. The developer pulled permits just after Christmas of 2001 and started construction on January 2, 2002 (J. McFarland, personal communication, June 27, 2008).

Project Financing

The developer acquired the project with $1 million of his own funds, plus a private line of credit secured by other projects. The balance of the development funds came from a construction loan from Andover Bank. No historic credits were used, despite the fact that the building could have been made eligible. (See Exhibit 15-4.)

Michael Ecker was a senior loan officer at Andover Bank at the time the deal was struck in 2001. The construction lender had known James McFarland since about 1990, and they had a highly satisfactory professional relationship. The McFarland team had done a lot of housing rehab projects in Boston's South End, and the builder had the required skill sets and a reputation as a low-cost builder. The banker remarked, "If I had to rank McFarland on a scale of one to ten, he would be a twelve." When McFarland was putting together the bid package, the lender toured both buildings. The rectory seemed

an easy play, but the plan for the church's cavernous, empty space was overwhelming. Cutting through the 3-ft.-thick granite walls for windows also seemed daunting. A vision was needed.

In terms of business risk, the lender was confident that McFarland would keep the rehabilitation cost low and that the units, priced accordingly, would compete well in the market. The lender also saw considerable upside in the premium penthouse units, which made the lender more comfortable with the project. The market risk was not so clear. Boston's Big Dig was going on. However, the project's proximity to the city, highways, and Subway "T" station was persuasive. McFarland also had done his homework with some appraiser comps, showing market demand at about $300+ per square foot. The bank wanted no input into project design, and stayed by the numbers.

In terms of project phasing, the lender and builder both agreed that the easier rectory project should go first. The bank would not advance funds to start the church building itself until 75 percent of the rectory inventory (six units) was under purchase and sale agreements, accompanied by a 5 percent deposit. McFarland was free to start redeveloping the church with his own money, if he chose. With respect to loan payback, the bank's release fee was based on about 85 percent of sales price, payable on each sale (M. Ecker, personal communication, July 1, 2008). The interest rate varied between 9 percent and 6 percent, averaging 7 percent. Total financing costs were $800,000, or 7.5 percent of project costs.

Construction

As set forth in the winning proposal to the archdiocese, the McFarlands' guiding concept was to keep the outside of the two buildings intact. This was accomplished except for taking out the little service garage, and adding several small utility dormers and some cut-in balconies for the penthouse units. Some windows also had to be added for light.

Construction on the rectory building began first and was straightforward, since that building was kept largely intact. McFarland demolished and relocated several nonload-bearing interior walls to create legal and market-ready entrances to the units, and to meet building codes. The rectory originally had been set up as a single residence, so it had to be reconfigured to accommodate the eight proposed units.

Redeveloping the church was next. Before selling the property, the archdiocese had decommissioned the buildings as religious structures. It also removed the largest stained-glass windows, but left about ten smaller and more ordinary stained-glass windows, mostly located in little arches, which were retained as part of the renovation. The church pews and organ were disposed of and sold at a discount.

The main construction challenge was cutting six 25-ft.-high windows into the south-facing back of the church to add light; this was a challenge because the church's exterior walls are composed of 3-ft.-thick granite. The developers tried three contractors before one could figure out how to do the job right (B. McFarland, personal communication, June 27, 2008).

The church was 60 ft. high inside, and there was an existing basement and first-floor level. The project required adding four new stories to the interior of the building, all built inside the existing church structure. This was accomplished efficiently, with functionality as the focus. Gutting the structure was done incrementally: Gut, build up, then repeat. As Bernard McFarland said, "we were gutting the church

building from day one until we were done." The church basement was a generous height of 10 ft. high to start, and so it needed no expansion. McFarland added footings for new load-bearing walls, installed plumbing stacks, and set drain lines in the new basement floor (B. McFarland, personal communication, June 27, 2008).

The front door entryway was done with little connection to the structure's past grandeur. A bell and clock tower were preserved but not restored. It will always be 12:15 at the top of 45 West Broadway.

The main challenge and value-added opportunity occurred at the top of the building. The McFarland team was able to save columns, upper archways, some stained glass, and crown moldings in the premium upstairs units. These units also have cutout balconies with incredible views of the city skyline.

The project was completed in early 2004, after a construction period of twenty-seven months. Construction costs totaled $7.1 million, not counting marketing sales expense or acquisition cost.

Marketing and Absorption

The developer initially determined that the project could not support apartments because market rents were too low. Therefore, he chose the residential condo route. As part of the bid process, an appraiser provided outside sales comps, showing support for prices at about $300–$350 per square foot.

Two real estate brokerage firms handled marketing of the project. Gibson Domain, now Gibson Sotheby's, marketed the bulk of the market-rate units. Theresa O'Neill sold the eleven affordable units. Both arrangements were exclusive representation with a 5 percent commission, so there was no developer overhead required. All sales occurred as presale during the construction. Marketing and sales commission costs were

5 percent of the $11.7 million project revenues, or about $585,000.

Unit absorption was brisk. All units sold within eighteen months, with most sold in the last nine months. Sales amounts were between $225,000 and $725,000, with values between $285 per square foot and $415 per square foot. The buyer profile was 10 percent young families with small children; 45 percent young, upwardly mobile couples; and 45 percent young, upwardly mobile singles. The majority of buyers came from outside the

Exhibit 15-3 Saints Peter and Paul Photographs and Plans

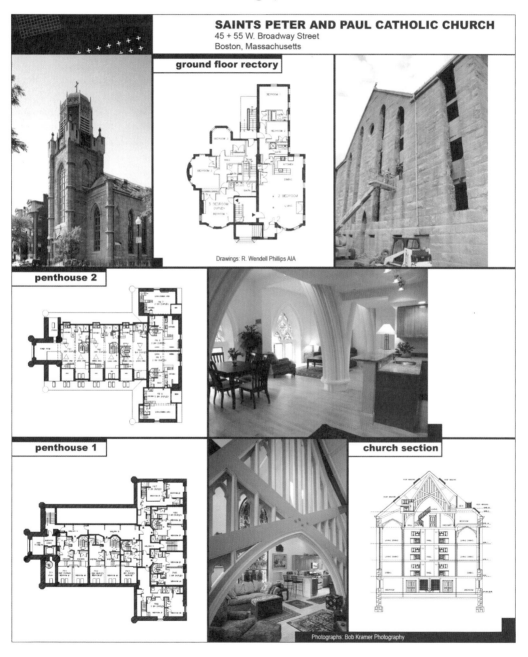

View of Boston from a penthouse condominium. Photograph: Robert Simons

Boston metro area. Religious affiliation was not a factor at all in the buyers' purchase decision. Rather, they were attracted by the location and stone building.

Project condo fees now average $350 per month, exclusive of property taxes. This includes landscaping, cleaning public areas, all heating and cooling, public electric, parking lot maintenance, and replacement reserves.

With respect to uses of funds, total property development costs were $10.6 million, excluding sales expense of $585,000. Property acquisition costs were $2.4 million (23 percent of project cost), or about $83 per square foot for the existing 29,000 building sq. ft., but only $46 per square foot for the final building square footage of 52,000 sq. ft. Site prep, including a bit of asbestos remediation, demolition, parking, and landscaping was $115,000, or 1 percent of project cost. Gutting the building cost $300,000, or 3 percent of project cost. Construction hard costs, excluding acquisition cost, totaled $6.7 million (63 percent of proj-

ect costs), or $129 per building square foot. Soft costs, including legal, planning, property appraisal, and architectural fees, were $1.1 million, or 10 percent of project cost. All-in development costs, excluding marketing, were $204 per building square foot. Including marketing, gross per square foot costs were $215 per building square foot.

The project cleared $515,000 in net profit, a project rate of return of 5 percent. The developer also got builder profit on hard costs, and kept two units for investment purposes. Overall, this deal was excellent for all involved. Refer to Exhibit 15-4 for detailed financial information.

Lessons Learned

The following lessons can be learned from this successful project.

- *A catalytic project with a good public outcome:* Neighborhood approval was not problematic. No residential abutters (INBY) meant easy public approval. In the medium run, the church and rectory

Exhibit 15-4 Saints Peter and Paul Church Project Development Costs

0.82 acre former church and rectory site
Boston, Massachusetts

Development date: 2002-04	Factors	Dollar Amount	% of Project Costs
Lot size (land square feet)	35,700		
Floor/area coverage	146%		
Gross building area	52,000		
Net usable space (100%)	49,000		
# current owners	44		
# parking spaces	44		
Development cost information	**Per building sq. ft.**		
Land/site acquisition (including option), includes buildings	$46.15	$2,400,000	22.64%
Acquisition cost per original building sq. ft.	$82.76		
Site preparation			
Remediation: removal of asbestos		$10,000	0.09%
Other site preparation inc. parking		$100,000	0.94%
Demolition garage building		$5,000	0.05%
Construction costs			
Gutting and building prep		$300,000	2.83%
New construction 52,000 sq. ft.	$128.56	$6,685,000	63.07%
Total building hard & acquisition cost	**$182.70**	**$9,500,000**	**89.62%**
Soft costs			
Architect, planners, legal, surveying		$305,000	2.88%
Market analysis/appraisals		$5,000	0.05%
Subtotal before construction loan	**$188.65**	**$9,810,000**	**92.5%**
Construction loan/carry 27 months term, variable rate	7%, int. only	$800,000	7.5%
TOTAL DEVELOPMENT COST	**$204.04**	**$10,610,000**	**100.0%**

REVENUES	Units	Average sales price/unit	Total sales revenues
Affordable units in church @700 sq. ft. each	11	$ 104,218	$1,146,400
Market units in church @1000 sq. ft. each	18	$ 230,444	$ 4,148,000
Premium units in church @1700 sq. ft.	5	$ 582,000	$ 2,910,000
Market units in rectory @1400 sq. ft.	8	$ 365,300	$ 2,922,400
Retained penthouse units @1900 sq. ft.	2	$ 286,600	$ 573,200
Total gross sales	**44**		**$11,700,000**
Sales expenses fee @5%			$ 585,000
Net sales proceeds			**$11,115,000**
PROFIT	5%	$515,000	

Gross project profit, before builder profit, etc., excluding value from 2 retained units

rehab was a positive catalytic project. The site went from no residential abutters to a considerable number of residential abutters. This is a good public outcome.

- *Avoid formal historic designation:* No historic designation meant less red tape, quicker public approvals, fewer hassles with regulators, and a quicker entry into the market. The project was timed right, and hit the market window. Of course, the opportunity cost was that historic tax credits were not available as a source of equity to the project.
- *Design challenges can be overcome:* Cutting in windows through 3-ft.-deep solid stone for light was a challenge, but could be overcome.
- *Know your market:* Despite the big-ticket acquisition cost of $2.4 million (about 23 percent of project cost) and the need to buy with cash to seller, with no option, and without prior formal planning approval, the market could support the acquisition cost. Because McFarland bought a two-story building but was able to develop six stories by constructing a building within the church shell, he essentially bought about 22,000 sq. ft. of internal development air rights.
- *Advantage of being the owner, developer, and builder:* Financially the project was a success, even without historic preservation subsidies. The business strategy exemplified vertical integration as the de-

veloper, builder, and owner were the same entity taking all the profit.

The McFarland team had a combination of luck and skill on their home turf. After the success of the Saints Peter and Paul redevelopment project, they next planned to bring the six-story Allele residential condo project to market on an abutting parcel south of 45 West Broadway.

Note

1. There are opposing views. For example, elsewhere in this book there is some evidence that former parish or other stakeholders had issues with the development, although this did not appear to impact the public approval process. A successful and well-adapted deal such as this one can't please all of the people all of the time. The economist's jargon is "Pareto Optimal" (at least one person is better off and nobody is worse off), and almost no deals are.

References and Works Consulted

Boston.com. 2008. www.boston.com.
City-Data.com. 2008. www.city-data.com.
Grillo, T. 2000. "Condos Set for South Boston Church Developer Plans 50 Mixed-Income Units of Housing." *Boston Globe,* November 4, E1.
U.S. Department of Commerce. 2000. Bureau of the Census.
Vigue, D. 2003. "Converted Houses of Worship Become Homes of Distinction, as Churches Go up for Sale and Developers Shout 'Bingo!'" *Boston Globe,* May 11, E1.

Adaptive Reuse of

ASBURY METHODIST CHURCH

into Babeville Performing Arts
Center, Contemporary Art Gallery,
and Corporate Offices
Buffalo, New York

Gary DeWine

Almost every major city in America contains church buildings near the central business district that are either decaying from lack of maintenance, underutilized, or shuttered. Diminished congregations with limited finances are unable to maintain large buildings that may be more than a hundred years old. The building deteriorates due to deferred maintenance, a deterioration that accelerates rapidly when the roof needs repair. The Delaware Avenue Asbury Methodist Church was one such building. It could easily have become a parking lot due to neglect but was saved by the intervention of the Buffalo community.

Introduction

The Delaware Avenue Asbury Methodist Church, located at 341 Delaware Avenue, has been a Buffalo landmark since its erection in the 1870s. (See Exhibit 16-1.) The iconic church building is an imposing structure constructed of red medina sandstone with two monumental church spires, one rising to 125 ft. while the other reaches 185 ft. The Methodist church closed in the early 1980s. After accommodating two succeeding Protestant congregations, one an owner and the second a tenant, the building was left empty in 1995. The north tower and building facade deteriorated to the point that falling sandstone forced the city of Buffalo to close the streets and sidewalks below.

In 1996 the city of Buffalo began planning for the demolition of the church at an estimated cost of $1 million. While the city was attempting to acquire the title to the property from the last church owner, two saviors of the building materialized in the form of Ani DiFranco, owner of the record company Righteous Babe Records, and Scot Fisher, president of the company.[1] DiFranco and Fisher began a grassroots effort to save the church. Community activists, historic

preservationists, and public outcry subsequently kept the church from demolition. Eventually, Righteous Babe Records used its financial resources to acquire and rehabilitate the property, which is on both the National and State Historic Registers.

The building, first named by Ms. DiFranco as "The Church," is now referred to as "Babeville." Almost $10 million was spent refurbishing the building, of which $7.2 million was hard costs. Under Ms. DiFranco's ownership the Asbury Church has become a one-thousand-seat performance hall, a contemporary art gallery with a cinema, and corporate offices. The expectation is that Babeville will become an artistic catalyst for downtown development in Buffalo (Sommer 2006).

The Babeville project is more of a study in public policy, landmark preservation, and maintenance of a community's urban fabric than it is an example of a real estate project in which success is determined by net operating income. This case study therefore gives special attention to the process used to gain control of the property, the financing of the $10 million renovation, and the actual redevelopment of the building.

Site History

Buffalo-based architect John H. Selkirk (1808–78) designed the church late in his career. Selkirk's commissions included private residences, businesses, and churches in the then-economically thriving young city. The church was constructed in downtown Buffalo on the corner of Delaware and West Tupper. Completion of the two buildings, which are now the Babeville project, was carried out in two phases in 1871 and 1876. The first building, which is 10,000 sq. ft., was a chapel and parish house consisting of two floors and a basement. The second floor of this building is notable for its vaulted assembly hall with stained-glass windows beginning at floor level and extending to the top of the gable. The second building, which is attached to the chapel and parish house, is the 6,000-sq.-ft. main sanctuary, designed in the Gothic Revival style. Decorative stone buttresses, an element often seen in European churches, line the outside walls of the sanctuary building on each side. Two architecturally interesting steeples constructed of stone with dormers and louvers flank the front facade. The taller steeple soars almost nineteen stories and is one of Buffalo's tallest buildings.

Exhibit 16-1 Babeville Performing Arts Center Location and Site Plan

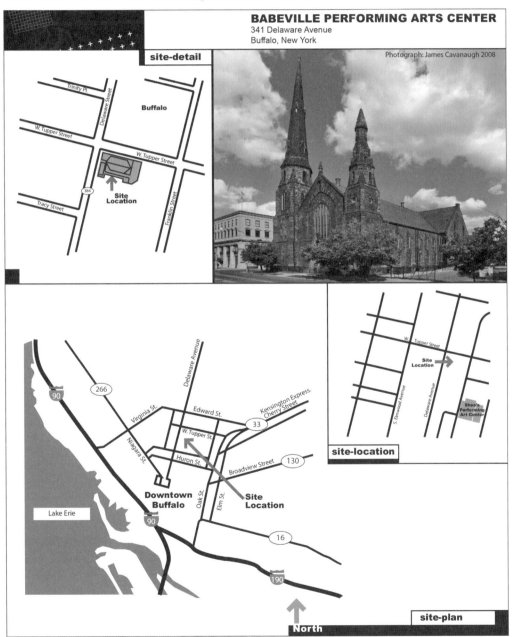

As Eve M. Kahn of Traditional Building explains, the church interior is constructed of "cast-iron columns with leafy gilt capitals, plaster chandeliers ribbed like rose windows [and] rosewood-inlaid oak and mahogany pews." The exterior and interior are a Gothic masterpiece, with windowpanes of painted art glass decorated with "flowers, palmettes, scrollwork and grapes, rather than biblical tableaus" (Kahn 2006).

The Methodist congregation vacated the Asbury Church in the early 1980s. Kingdom Evangelical Missionary Church of Texas purchased it in 1992. The church was sublet to another Protestant denomination, which stripped the sanctuary of pews and other furnishings and sold them to local antique dealers. According to Scot Fisher, the city of Buffalo saw this as vandalism that devalued the asset, and the city encouraged the mortgage holder, Key Bank, to take Kingdom Evangelical to court (S. Fisher, personal communication, August, 2008). That court action led to the building's eventual sale to the city of Buffalo in 1999 for $175,000. The deal included an adjoining parking lot, which the city wanted to use to raise revenue for the redevelopment: "We plan to use income from the lot to stabilize and maintain the church," said David State, deputy corporation counsel (Fairbanks 1999). However, the city had no viable offers for redevelopment and no developer was willing to assume the risk. The church, Fisher says, "was inches away from being a parking lot, and a year from catastrophic [building structure] failure" (S. Fisher, personal communication, August 2008).

Demographics

At the onset of the Great Depression, Buffalo had 573,000 inhabitants, making it the thirteenth-largest city in America. In the seventy-five years that followed, this once-mighty metropolis lost 55 percent of its population, a decline most dramatic in its blighted inner city but also apparent in its broader metropolitan area, one of the twenty most quickly deteriorating such regions in the nation. Twenty-seven percent of Buffalo's residents are poor, more than twice the national average (see Exhibit 16-2). The median family income is just $33,000, less than 60 percent of the nationwide figure of $55,000 (Glaeser 2007).

In general, when cities shrink, poverty isn't far behind, for two reasons—one obvious, the other subtler. The obvious reason: urban populations fall because of relocation of industry and drop in labor demand; as jobs vanish, people living in a city become poorer. The subtler reason: declining areas also become magnets for poor people, attracted by cheap housing. This is exactly what happened to Buffalo, whose median home value is just $61,000, far below the state average of $260,000 (Glaeser 2007).

Redevelopment Process

Scot Fisher and Ani DiFranco recognized that hope was fading for the church building. Setting aside $1 million in cash for the rehabilitation of the church, they sought advice from Robert Kresse, a local attorney and trustee of the influential Margaret L. Wendt Foundation. Mr. Kresse, a preservationist who had helped to save Buffalo's St. Mary of Sorrows Church through its conversion to the King Urban Life Center, advised Fisher and DiFranco that the $1 million would not get the project very far. He also concluded, however, that the church facade's status as a community landmark obliged the church's owner, the city of Buffalo, to maintain it. Coincidentally, Righteous Babe Records was at the time considering relocating its offices to New Orleans because it was being displaced from rented

Exhibit 16-2 Buffalo Demographic Data

	New York	Erie County	Buffalo City	Census Tract 72.01
Population				
2000	18,976,457	950,265	292,648	1,650
2007	19,297,729	913,338	264,292	
% Change	1.69%	-3.89%	-9.69%	
Age (2000)				
Less than 18	24.63%	24.23%	26.34%	3.76%
22-39	26.62%	23.70%	26.25%	46.48%
40-59	31.20%	30.10%	29.16%	42.48%
60 and over	16.88%	19.98%	16.98%	4.55%
Median Household Income				
2000	$43,393	$38,567	$24,536	$15,192
2007	$53,514	$45,076	$29,706	
% Change	23.32%	16.88%	21.07%	
Race (2000)				
White alone	67.93%	82.29%	54.72%	42.42%
Black or African American alone	15.74%	12.94%	37.22%	55.27%
American Indian and Alaska Native alone	0.42%	0.63%	0.78%	1.94%
Asian alone	5.50%	1.36%	1.30%	0.36%
Hawaiian and Pacific Islander alone	0.04%	0.03%	0.05%	0.00%
Some other race alone	7.13%	1.38%	3.50%	0.00%
Two or more races	3.24%	1.38%	2.43%	0.00%
Education (2000)				
Bachelor or higher	27.37%	24.54%	18.29%	6.36%
High school above age 25	27.75%	29.87%	29.11%	31.12%
Unemployment				
2000	4.32%	4.53%	7.29%	0.00%
Housing (2000)				
Households	7,060,595	380,890	122,672	208
Housing Units	7,679,307	415,868	145,574	265
Owner Occupied Units (%)	52.99%	65.32%	43.46%	0.00%
Renter Units(%)	47.01%	34.68%	56.54%	100.00%
Median Rent Apartment	$672	$516	$472	$333
Median House Value (Owner Occupied)	$147,600	$88,200	$58,800	NA

Source: 2000 and 2007 U.S. Census
Note: 2007 tract data is not available

space. Seeing a solution to both its own and the church's problems, Righteous Babe approached Buffalo City Hall in 2000 about partnering with the city to restore the property. A handshake deal was made, and the Common Council of the city of Buffalo passed legislation that Righteous Babe Records was "the designated official developer" of the Asbury Church. Righteous Babe Records performed a complete due-diligence assessment of the building. This would allow everyone to know what they were getting into. This was done on Righteous Babe Records' dime with no city or foundation monies!

In October 2001 Righteous Babe presented the city with a $4.7 million plan to renovate and rehabilitate the church. They proposed that the city assume responsibility for the $2.2 million exterior renovations, while Righteous Babe Records committed $1.3 million to turning a portion of the church building into corporate offices. The plan called for an additional $1.2 million, to be financed through an "undefined public-private partnership," to convert the large sanctuary to a performing arts venue. Righteous Babe Records would then assume responsibility for the venue's ongoing maintenance and operating costs.

Though the city was receptive to seeing a plan for the property's redevelopment, Righteous Babe found itself frustrated by the city's inability to make a financial commitment in the wake of the economic decline that followed 9/11 (Meyer 2001). Scot Fisher, a straightforward businessman, found himself questioning the city's financial sophistication. In an interview, Fisher stated, "Mayor Tony Masiello was very hot on the project to put the church to reuse. The city had taken a lot of criticism for its lack of action. I soon came to the conclusion the city lacked the brainpower to put a deal

together" (S. Fisher, personal communication, August 2008).

Fisher's next step was to hire his own financial consultants and legal counsel to package the deal for eventual presentation to the city. He recalls the initial lender met with Righteous Babe Records for nine months asking after each meeting to be provided with "additional information." Eventually, when Righteous Babe Records thought it had met all the initial lender's conditions of personal guarantees and deposits of funds, the lender told it that the church property had no value as collateral and the loan could not be made. The initial lender was replaced by HSBC.

Meanwhile, the church's condition was worsening. Water was pouring into the church from both the roof and two spires. Particularly problematic was the north tower. Against the advice of legal counsel, Righteous Babe Records decided to spend money on a building it did not yet own. It took steps to make the building weather-tight and spent $60,000 for emergency repairs to the church's roof and spires. Had these actions not been taken, $350,000 of damage may have been added to the rehabilitation cost. The company also retained design professionals who began planning an ambitious program to preserve and reuse the church. After much discussion, Righteous Babe and the city worked out the financing deal in the spring of 2003.

Simultaneously with hiring its own team to put together a financing package, Righteous Babe assembled two architectural teams to design the interior and restore the exterior. Architectural Resources of Buffalo was retained to design the corporate offices of Righteous Babe Records and the space to be rented by a tenant, Hallwalls Galleries. Flynn Battaglia Architects of Buffalo was retained to coordinate the complex reconstruction of the church building, design the adaptive reuse of the sanctuary, and serve as historic adviser in securing historic tax credits. Lehigh Construction Group, which had experience with other notable historic preservation projects in the Buffalo area, was hired as part of the design-build team to restore the church.

Original construction drawings did not exist, but a laser-based drafting system called Quanta Point allowed building drawings to be produced to an accuracy of one-sixteenth of an inch at a cost of $16,000. Righteous Babe also retained a soil-testing firm, masons, and engineers to perform various analyses. These analyses produced important information, including the discovery that the main sanctuary's facade had a bulge of 3–4 in. that likely occurred within three to four years of the building's completion in 1876. Inspection revealed that not enough mortar was used to bond the sandstone face with the subsurface of stone rubble, which allowed water to seep between the two surfaces. The consensus was that the bulge occurred because the architect, Selkirk, was at the end of his career and could not physically inspect the quality of workmanship. This defect required tuckpointing and the addition of metal pins to stabilize the exterior facade.

Development Plan

Righteous Babe Records had from the beginning planned to occupy the building. The design plan as it evolved called for the original sanctuary or parish house, located behind the main sanctuary, to become the corporate offices of Righteous Babe Records and a tenant. The approximately 5,000-sq.-ft. second floor provided sufficient room to house staff in an open-space setting, construct a row of executive offices, and have storage space. The cathedral ceiling and

stained-glass windows make it an interesting space in which to work. In January 2006, Buffalo's Hallwalls Contemporary Arts Center became the building's first resident since the last congregation departed. "When I heard that Righteous Babe Records would be buying the church and that they would have room for a tenant, I jumped on the opportunity right away," says Executive Director Edmund Cardoni (Frontuto 2006). Hallwalls took space on the first floor of the rear parish house chapel, which has become a gallery and offices. Space in the basement was made into a sixty-seat state-of-the-art screening room. An elevator, installed as part of the renovation, links the basement, first, and second floors.

The 6,000-sq.-ft. main sanctuary was preserved as a one-thousand-seat concert hall. The interior of the sanctuary was restored to its original grandeur, absent the church pews. Since the previous occupant had sold the church pews, Righteous Babe Records was not obligated to replace them as a condition of using historic preservation tax credits. This allows the space to be configured for varying types of events. Concerts, weddings, fund-raisers, public high school functions, and corporate meetings and dinners now take place in the former sanctuary. (See Exhibit 16-3.)

Eve Kahn describes the renovated interior of the sanctuary: "[Ani] DiFranco had the walls painted in the boldest colors found in Selkirk's palette: yellows, oranges, greens. To supplement the creamy overhead light from 1870s chandeliers, surviving gaslights have been electrified and recessed ceiling cans and under-balcony fixtures were added" (Kahn 2006). The balcony area now has pews purchased from an Episcopal church that was undergoing renovation several doors away. The acoustics of the building required tweaking by sound professionals. The building was not designed for amplified sound, and consequently contemporary sound systems created a chamber of echoes. This was corrected through the addition of fabric sound panels and curtains along with the design of a directional sound system.

The initial work on the building, which Righteous Babe began even before it actually owned the property, was exterior stabilization, reconstruction, and restoration. This work, which began in 2003, included the installation of a new slate roof on the

Exhibit 16-3 Babeville Performing Arts Center Photographs and Plans

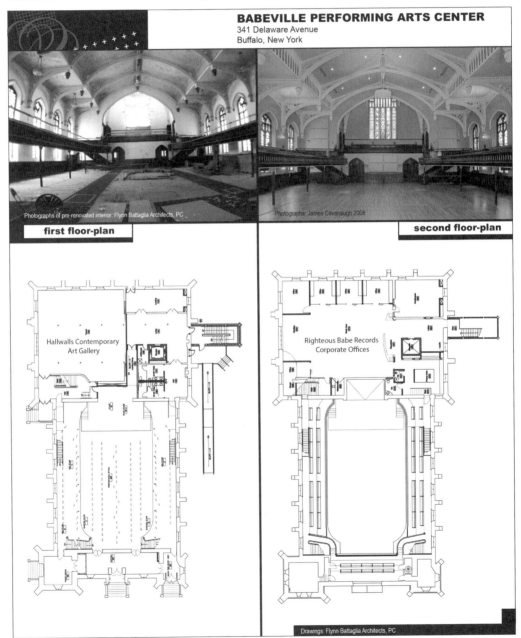

main sanctuary and pointing of the 185-ft. north tower. Trained steeplejacks were hired to do this challenging repair. The other, shorter tower was partially disassembled and rebuilt.

The only addition to the building was a stair tower constructed on the south side of the building to provide access into the rear of the building containing Hallwalls and Righteous Babe Record's corporate offices. There was originally no entrance on this side of the church, which abuts a parking lot. Now an ADA-compliant ramp leads to the three-story-tall stair tower. The ramp is designed to be an architectural attribute, not a code afterthought. It is faced in sandstone with railings in scale with the building and serves as a main entrance into the building, the art gallery, and corporate offices. The stair tower is constructed of structural steel I-beams, an echo of Buffalo's industrial heritage. It is glazed in transparent glass on all three sides. Its shape, when viewed from the side, is the same as the pointed Gothic-style windows of the main sanctuary. It is a well-thought-out, sensitive design solution.

Lost Space in the Basement

The basement under the main sanctuary was originally a system of Edgar Allen Poe–like catacombs. The decision was made to lower the 6-ft.-high basement space an additional 2 ft. This proved to be an easier challenge than one might suppose. The soil under the church is composed of sand, making removal easy. An opening was made in the basement wall, which allowed a small landscaper's skidster or bobcat to remove the hundreds of tons of sand. Timbers salvaged from a nearby building demolition were used as columns to strengthen the floor above. A new foundation around the perimeter, along with the addition of

a new floor, had positive results. The space now accommodates patron restrooms, four dressing rooms (including one with a shower), and an intimate lounge area with a bar for small performances. A complete kitchen for catered events is also contained in this space. The area could become a permanent club in the future as the entertainment scene evolves along Delaware Avenue.

Heating and Cooling

Scot Fisher explained that heating and cooling the vast space within the building was a challenge. The cost of utilities to heat the large volume of open space was an item that needed to be creatively addressed. The building was never designed for air conditioning. Moreover, the owner did not want to clutter the outside grounds of the building with massive condenser units.

At Babeville, an air-handling system capable of both heating and cooling was installed without putting it on the roof, which was gabled and so had no room for the units. The solution was to put—a better word is *hide*—the equipment in the north tower, where the bell tower louvers and openings are a source of fresh air. Righteous Babe Records, wanting the building to be as green as possible, had thirty geothermal wells dug to a depth of 300 ft. on the south side of the church property. A ground-source heat pump ejects heat from the building in summer and adds heat in the winter. Since the temperature of the earth is a constant 54°F at that depth, heating requirements are greatly minimized. Babeville was the first commercial space in Buffalo to have such a system. The result is that the monthly gas bill is a modest $3,000 when it could easily have been much more given that the building, which now includes the utilized basement area, totals more than 25,000 sq. ft.

City Approvals

The building did not require any rezoning. Had the building immediately transitioned from church to concert hall, both assembly uses, without sitting empty, much of the code-compliance requirements and remodeling expense may not have been necessary. In any event, the building is now code compliant. The church building is located within a historical district, and the Buffalo preservation board twice reviewed the project, first to approve the exterior restoration and second to green-light the design of the two-story stair tower.

The neighborhood and community were very supportive of the project. Whenever a public meeting took place, people in favor of the project would be present to lend support. They would also write letters and make calls to members of the Buffalo Common Council encouraging support.

Project Financing

The financials for the Babeville project are set forth in Exhibit 16-4. The sources of funds for the $9.8 million project were as follows: about $2.8 million came directly from Righteous Babe Records in the form of equity ($1,264,401 in partnership equity, plus a direct infusion from Ms. DiFranco) and loans ($1.2 million), while historic preservation tax credit and New Market Tax Credits generated about $4.2 million, or 41 percent of total sources of funds.

The arrangement that Righteous Babe Records made with the city, which faced a $1 million bill to demolish the church, was for the city to pay for exterior renovation and structural repairs while Righteous Babe paid for interior improvements. Financing had been a major stumbling block for the project to move forward; the city supported the project but had trouble coming up with its share. The stalemate on how to shake the money out for the city's share was broken late one night by Jessie Schnell, who was Flynn Battaglia Architects' project manager during the planning phase. Ms. Schnell's idea was that the future real estate taxes to be paid by Babeville, projected at $200,000 annually, could be directed to amortize the $1.2 million loan from the Buffalo Economic Renaissance Corporation (BERC), which was responsible for putting the city's portion of the package together. At the end of the day, the city of Buffalo, through BERC, provided a total of $2.7 million, $1.5 million of which was an equity infusion from the city to Righteous Babe Records, who would begin paying real property taxes. The deal had no private bank debt at all.

The city of Buffalo utilized the state of New York's "Payment in Lieu of Taxes" (PILOT) program, which allows the real property taxes to be directed to the city to repay the $1.2 million BERC loan. This is much like tax-increment financing where real property taxes are directed to pay for some project-related public improvements.[2]

Total cost of the project was $9.8 million, 73 percent of which was spent on actual construction, and the contingency was a very modest 2 percent. A total of $2.5 million was soft costs, of which the design fees, legal fees, and tax credit placement fees were each about 7 percent of total costs. The balance of soft costs was small, with no developer profit or development fee and minimal finance charges. The tax credit fees were paid to Buffalo's Local Initiative Support Corporation as a fee for serving as the conduit for the New Market Tax Credits. Scot Fisher indicated the fees made the New Market Tax Credits barely worthwhile pursuing. "It [New Market Tax Credits] was barely a net positive" (S. Fisher, personal communication, August 2008). Also, for each year of the tax credits Righteous Babe

Exhibit 16-4 Righteous Babe Records Sources and Uses of Funds

Sources of Funds	
General Partnership	$1,264,401
Righteous Babe Records	354,960
Buffalo Economic Renaissance Corp.	1,500,000
New Market Tax Credits	2,539,521
Historic Tax Credits	1,700,000
Subtotal Equity	$7,358,882
Loan from Righteous Babe Records	$1,200,000
Buffalo Economic Renaissance Corp.	1,200,000
Subtotal Debt	$2,400,000
Total	**$9,758,882**

Uses of Funds	
Hard Costs	
Site Acquisition	$175,000
Construction Costs	
Construction Costs - Phase 1	$3,237,210
Construction Costs - Phase 2	3,654,532

Stabilization/Repairs	67,260
Construction Contingency	176,502
Subtotal	$7,135,504
Soft Costs	
Design Fees	$738,000
Construction Management	107,861
Legal Fees	602,325
Accounting	116,068
Construction Loan Interest and Insurance	48,146
Operational Costs	31,204
Erie County Industrial Development Fee	83,990
Tax Credit Fee	681,784
Title Fees and Expenses	39,000
Subtotal	$2,448,378
Total Expenses	**$9,758,882**

Records is to provide a "premium audit report," which costs $25,000.

Lessons Learned

- *Landlord flexibility with rent-paying tenants:* When Hallwalls Contemporary Arts Center emerged as an occupant, required earlier plans had to be modified to accommodate a rent-paying tenant who would bring additional synergy to the project. This necessitated finding lost space in the basement for dressing rooms in the main sanctuary building. Landlords need to be flexible when opportunities arise.
- *Assemble a team of super professionals:* The due-diligence process of assembling building professionals, finance experts, and legal counsel let Righteous Babe Records know what it was getting into. Consequently they had no big surprises, just minor ones.
- *Engage community support:* Righteous Babe Records also engaged the community and local newspapers, which had a sympathetic ear for what the company was trying to do.
- *Recognize the limitations of city hall:* Scot Fisher soon came to the realization that the well-intentioned Buffalo City Hall did not have the capacity to put the financing together. He then engaged his own team to assemble the financing package, which was presented to the city.
- *Green building opportunities:* The use of green building technology, in this instance the geothermal heating system, will pay off handsomely in the near term.

Conclusion

The Babeville Performing Arts Center was never intended to provide income, but it was meant to eventually be financially self-sustaining. This goal has not yet been attained; the project is not expected to break even financially in the near future, even with almost no debt. The center continues to operate with a funding gap each year and struggles to meet expenses, requiring funds from Righteous Babe Records annually. In the words of Scot Fisher, "This project was based on honest to goodness philanthropy. Ani [DiFranco] could have invested in the stock market but chose to give something back to the Buffalo community. Our plan was to save the architecture and save the building. We accomplished our goal" (S. Fisher, personal communication, August 2008). Delaware Avenue is a main artery in and out of downtown Buffalo. This was an empty and desolate neighborhood fifteen years ago. Now, as a result of Babeville and other investment, it is starting to boom. Being a community champion has its own rewards.

Notes

1. The Buffalo-based independent record label star Ani DiFranco owns the record company, Righteous Babe Records. The company, according to *Inc. Magazine,* grosses $5 million in sales annually. The majority of income is derived from CD sales and concerts.
2. Righteous Babe is also eligible for state of New York Empire Zone benefits. Under this program the city of Buffalo, Erie County, and Righteous Babe Records agree on the disposition of the property taxes to be generated by the Babeville building over the next fourteen years. "PILOT payments are preferable to property taxes because they go directly to the municipality and are easier to redirect toward purposes like this [renovation of Righteous Babe Records] with city and county approval," John Riccione (CFO of Buffalo Economic Renaissance Corporation) said. "What's more" he added, "property taxes can fluctuate with assessment values. A PILOT is more stable. Bankers like to have a PILOT in place because it ensures a stable income stream for ten years" (EDC Advance/NY 2006).

References and Works Consulted

EDC Advance/NY. 2006. Monthly newsletter of the New York State Economic Development Council, 17, no. 1 (February).

Fairbanks, P. 1999. "City to Purchase Landmark Church." *Buffalo News,* March 17. http://www2 .buffnews.com/newslibrary/.

Frontuto, A. 2006. www.Buffaloathome.com.

Glaeser, E. 2007. "Can Buffalo Ever Come Back?" *New York Sun,* October 19. http://www.nysun .com/opinion/can-buffalo-ever-come-back/ 64879/.

Kahn, E. 2006. "Righteous Reuse." *Traditional Building,* December. http://www.traditional -building.com/Previous-Issues-06/December Project06babe.html.

Meyer, B. 2001. "Firm Wants to Turn Church into Concert Hall." *Buffalo News,* October 25. http://www2.buffnews.com/newslibrary/.

Sommer, M. 2006. "The House That Ani Built." *Buffalo News,* January 8. http://www2.buff news.com/newslibrary/.

ARCHDIOCESE OF ST. LOUIS
Sale of Twenty Church Properties and St. Aloysius Gonzaga Property Reuse into Magnolia Square Residential Development
St. Louis, Missouri

Gary DeWine

This case considers the real property management decisions of the Catholic Archdiocese of St. Louis, Missouri. The archdiocese serves nearly 522,000 Catholics in eleven counties. In 2005, the archdiocese closed and sold twenty churches. Proceeds from the transactions exceeded almost $20 million. The money, less any outstanding debt, followed church members to their new parishes.

This case study also describes the decision-making process leading to the closing of the twenty churches and briefly details the sale of the properties. In addition, it presents a case showing how one of the properties, the Church of St. Aloysius Gonzaga, was demolished for a 2.9-acre single-family residential development.

The Archdiocesan Management Structure and Planning Process

The Roman Catholic Church establishes either an archdiocese or a diocese to oversee the location and boundaries of individual parishes. A diocese that is important because of its size or historical significance is referred to as an archdiocese. Each diocese is headed by a bishop (or archbishop) who is the administrator over the geographic area encompassing his diocese. The diocese or archdiocese owns all the real estate assets of the individual parishes within its boundaries. Thus, the Catholic Church has a centralized hierarchical administrative structure, unlike most Protestant denominations and branches of the Jewish faith, which operate as individual, stand-alone facilities with decision-making authority at the local level.

The Archdiocese of St. Louis is further subdivided into ten deaneries, each of which is headed by a *vicar forane,* or a dean. The deanery is responsible for coordinating pastoral activities, ensuring that churches and furnishings are maintained and the parish books are properly managed, and seeing that the norms of the archdiocese are followed. The smallest geographical subdivision within the Roman Catholic Church is the parish. The parish has fixed boundaries and a priest who exercises pastoral care over the community through the authority of the bishop. Parishes have a parish council made up of members who advise the parish priest.

There is no canon law (universal law of the Catholic Church) on the process of how to decide which parish churches will be closed if the need arises. The decision ultimately rests with the bishop. For example:

- When the closing of churches became necessary in Cleveland, the bishop grouped parishes within the same geographical area into a cluster, allowing each cluster as a group to recommend for his consideration which parishes should remain open, close, or merge (Briggs 2007).

- The New York City Archdiocese announced the closing of twenty-one parishes in 2007. This brought to an end a process that dragged on for more than five years. This caused much uncertainty and frustration in many parishes (Luo 2007).

- In Massachusetts, a state senator asked for "transparency" and "sunlight" calling on government officials to investigate, supervise, and second-guess religious authorities' difficult parish-closing decisions (Garnett 2006).

In the Archdiocese of St. Louis, the pastors and laity of the South City and the Northeast County deaneries expressed a strong desire to assist the archdiocese in long-range pastoral planning. In June 2003, both of the deaneries began a planning process that sought "means of sustaining viability in the face of population transition, a substantially diminished number of Catholics in these regions, the continued aging of current parishioners, declining Catholic school enrollment, historically disappointing efforts at evangelization, consequent budgets shortfalls, and other broader social and cultural challenges" (Strategic Pastoral Plan—Northeast County Deanery 2004).

The deanery-based initiative for planning was designed with the assistance of Meitler Consultants, Inc., of Hales Corners, Wisconsin. This company has prepared thirty-seven comprehensive diocesan strategic plans and seventy regional plans for Catholic schools and parishes throughout the United States (Meitler Consultants 2007). Objective data were used and analyzed in the decision-making process. The deanery-based initiative worked independently, with no preconceived plan from a higher level of leadership, such as the archdiocese. A task force representing the various regions of each deanery was formed, and along with the consultants, visited each parish and school to interview the pastor and school principal. These site visits allowed the task force to understand each church's ministries and the challenges faced by each parish and school.

Parish and Population Trends 2003

The general population of the Northeast County Deanery decreased by only 1 percent between 1990 and 2000. In contrast, it is projected that the Catholic population in the deanery will decrease 28 percent during the next decade, resulting in fifteen thousand fewer Catholics. The Catholic population is aging or relocating, and the local replacement population is not constituted of young Catholic families. In twelve of the twenty-five parishes, more than half of the parishioners are over fifty-five years of age. In contrast, 74–84 percent of the non-Catholic population within the parish boundaries is younger than fifty-four years of age. The decline in Catholic population has been

experienced without exception throughout the deanery. In an increasing number of instances, parish membership does not mirror the racial or ethnic makeup of the local neighborhood community in which the parish is located (Strategic Pastoral Plan—Northeast County Deanery 2004).

In 1970, the parishes of the South City Deanery had a registered Catholic population of 96,800. By 2003 that population was estimated to be down to 50,500. In 2003 there were ten parishes with fewer than 350 households, and the number of sparsely populated parishes increased to twelve by 2008. Six parishes had more than a thousand households in 2003, but this number was down to five parishes by 2008.

The Catholic population of the South City Deanery, like that of the Northeast County Deanery, is aging. In fact, the Catholic population is generally older than the total population. As the older Catholic population moves or dies, the population taking its place may be either not Catholic, or Catholic but less active in the church (Strategic Pastoral Plan—South City Deanery 2004).

Thus, the Catholic population within the two deaneries was decreasing, and this trend was expected to continue. The population of several of the parishes was aging and was not being replaced by younger members. Shifting racial demographics were also contributing to parish membership decline.

The Characteristics of a Viable Parish

The Pastoral Planning Process identified the following set of characteristics as indicators of a vibrant and viable parish and school for the future (Strategic Pastoral Plan—Northeast County Deanery 2004; Strategic Pastoral Plan—South City Deanery 2004):

- A quality Eucharistic (mass) celebration
- Effective evangelization, religious formation, and stewardship

- Catholic schools supported by parishes meeting enrollment expectations
- Maintenance of facilities
- Sufficient offertory income
- A base of eleven hundred to twelve hundred households

As determined through the Pastoral Planning Process, the ideal membership to sustain a parish and its activities is eleven hundred to twelve hundred households. In contrast, in 2003 the average size of a parish was 750 households in the Northeast County Deanery and 620 households in the South City Deanery. Seating capacity at a church in either of the deaneries ranged from three hundred to nine hundred. In the Northeast County Deanery, 32 percent of available seating capacity was used each Sunday. In South City, 29 percent was used. Reconfiguring the territorial parishes in the Northeast County Deanery would result in parishes averaging eighteen hundred households, versus just 750 households per parish before the reconfiguration. In South City, reconfiguration would see an average parish size of 1,123 households, versus 620 households before closing parishes (Strategic Pastoral Plan—Northeast County Deanery 2004; Strategic Pastoral Plan—South City Deanery 2004).

The Pastoral Planning Process identified the presence of an elementary school as a component of a stable parish: a parish without a school, it concluded, has a limited future. Key indicators of a stable school are a balanced budget, a stable income stream from the parish, and sufficient cash reserves to cover expenses for three months beyond regular income (Strategic Pastoral Plan—Northeast County Deanery 2004; and Strategic Pastoral Plan—South City Deanery 2004). Several parishes in both deaneries had closed their elementary schools, and enrollment in the several operating schools was decreasing.

The Pastoral Planning Process also considered a parish's financial abilities to have a balanced budget and to provide a high-quality ministry. It reviewed offertory and donation income to determine if a parish would keep pace with increases in operating expenses in the future and found that many parishes had eliminated lay parish staff positions to maintain parish budgets, consequently affecting the quality of their ministries.

Priests—a Future Decline in Numbers

In 2004, the North County Deanery contained twenty-five parishes served by twenty-seven priests. It was projected that in six years only seventeen priests would be able to serve. In the South City Deanery, which contained thirty-five parishes, it was projected that only twenty to twenty-five priests would be available in the future. A lack of seminarians studying to become priests, along with priests retiring at the age of seventy-five, would make it impossible for the archdiocese to staff each parish.

The conclusions of the Archdiocese Pastoral Planning Process resulted in the decision to close and sell a total of twenty out of sixty parish church properties. The plans were forwarded to Most Rev. Raymond Burke, the archbishop of St. Louis, in December 2004. The Northeast County Deanery contained thirteen church properties to be sold while the South City Deanery contained seven.

The Building and Property Disposal Process

In February 2005, Archbishop Burke officially authorized the closing of parishes in the Northeast County and South City deaneries. Thomas Richter, P.E., director of the Archdiocese Office of Building and Real Estate, was responsible for orchestrating the sales process. His office supports the archdiocese by providing expertise, information, and services related to facilities management and real estate. These services include direction and oversight of construction, maintenance of plans and blueprints, coordination with legal counsel on sale and lease agreements, facility inspection, and consultation with other offices on property management issues. To ensure that the process would go smoothly, Richter's office began planning for the sale of church properties six to eight months before the archdiocese made a final decision about which properties would in fact be closed.

The archdiocese's real property disposal plan called for the hiring of real estate companies with prepared marketing plans in place. The plan was to be implemented as soon as the decision about which parishes were to close was made. Because empty buildings can quickly become a blighting influence on a neighborhood, the archdiocese did not want a time lag between church closure and sale. It hoped for the closed buildings to be put back into productive use as soon as possible. Richter's plan was to get ahead of the curve. The archdiocese's goal was to obtain the listing price but also to remain flexible with the price when presented with a proposal that would leave a positive legacy. The archdiocese preferred to sell the church for another religious use or to a school, and it would not consider uses that were distasteful or objectionable to the church (Prost 2005).

North County Deanery

The properties in each of the deaneries were substantially different. The North County parishes were established in the 1950s and 1960s. According to Richter, the archdiocese was building four to five new churches per year immediately after World War II (T. Richter, personal communication, January

2008). The parcels on which the churches were built ranged between 3 and 10 acres. The areas north of I-40, which make up the North County Deanery, saw rapid demographic change along racial lines in the 1980s with the newer residents, predominantly African Americans, not being Catholic. While the parish churches remained a physical and spiritual presence in the neighborhoods, their membership and financial resources declined.

The building design of North County Deanery buildings made them attractive for reuse as either schools or churches. Richter stated, "Quite often the churches were in the building that was eventually intended to be transformed into a gym, after a new permanent church was built. That was part of their appeal since these churches were easily adapted by schools and the smaller Christian Church groups" (Watkins 2007).

Trammell Crow, which has a national real estate practice devoted to unique properties, was hired to represent the archdiocese in the sale of the North County Deanery properties. An important reason for the archdiocese's selection of Trammell Crow was that it had a group dedicated to selling one-of-a-kind properties such as churches or schools. The archdiocese believed that Trammell Crow's experience in selling such properties would help develop a marketing plan to effectively attract viable potential buyers, and would not leave the false impression that it wanted to attract out-of-town buyers. Reasonable values were established for the properties to facilitate a sale. The archdiocese had formal appraisals done for Northeast County Deanery properties. Since there were no recent church or school sales to draw upon, they needed an expert's help. These appraisals were very thorough and, when compared to the eventual sale price, also very accurate. In general, the asking price was 10 percent above the appraised value, while the replacement value of the church campuses was estimated to be five times the asking price.

For-sale signs were placed on the properties to be sold while the church continued to operate. This upset pastors, and Mr. Richter said later that he might forgo the use of for-sale signs in the future. Trammell Crow's marketing plan, which included targeting other denominations, resulted in a number of quick sales that allowed the archdiocese to transfer the property promptly after formal closing of the church (T. Richter, personal communication, January 2008). Exhibit 17-1 shows the sales.

In the Northeast County Deanery, the Alexian Brothers, a Catholic order providing health care services, purchased one property for use as an adult day care center. Two local public school districts and one Chris-tian elementary school purchased former church properties, and one church was sold for commercial use. All the other properties were acquired for use as churches by other Christian denominations (Prost 2005).

South City Deanery

The South City Deanery properties were built in the early 1900s or earlier and tend to be large, old churches. Although some churches had distinctive architecture, the Strategic Planning Recommendations for the churches designated for disposal took only condition and size into account, not historic or aesthetic value. The planning recommendations of the South City Deanery observed, however, that "private philanthropy might find preserving some of these historic buildings an attractive endeavor" (Strategic Pastoral Plan—South City Deanery 2004). This statement hinted that a sold

Exhibit 17-1 Northeast County Deanery Church Sales Summary

Acres[1]	Church Name	Appraised Value[2]	Asking Price[3]	Sale Price	Square Footage	Price per Square Foot	Outcome	Sale Date
7.69	Transfiguration	1,890,000	2,173,500	$1,950,000	33,704	$57.84	Local School District	02/29/05
9.74	Our Lady of Good Counsel	2,150,000	2,365,000	2,136,159	74,843	28.54	Local School District	07/05/05
6.59	Our Lady of Mercy	990,000	1,138,500	990,000	17,716	55.88	Local School District	07/28/05
7.54	St. Pius X	1,000,000	1,100,000	1,025,000	24,771	41.38	Church	08/02/05
2.7	St. Catherine	1,150,000	1,265,000	1,265,000	46,563	27.17	Church	08/22/05
7.26	Our Lady of Fatima	1,600,000	1,840,000	1,600,000	46,374	34.50	Chevrolet Dealer	08/31/05
6.64	St. Christopher	1,360,000	1,564,000	1,400,000	25,754	54.36	Church	09/16/05
9.84	St. Bartholomew	850,000	935,000	935,000	32,066	29.16	School	10/07/05
6.16	St. Sebastian	1,700,000	1,870,000	1,689,340	46,606	36.25	Local School District	11/29/05
7.33	St. William	1,450,000	1,450,000	1,265,000	31,386	40.30	Church	04/03/06
4.78	North American Martyrs	2,000,000	2,300,000	1,350,000	38,662	34.92	Church	06/20/07
5.84	Corpus Christi	2,500,000	2,500,000	1,000,000	112,246	8.91	Adult Day Care Center	02/09/07
8.16	St. Aloysius	825,000	905,500	600,000	30,490	19.68	Church	07/13/07

Notes:
1. Size range 2.7 to 9.8 acres
2. Appraised value average $1,487,308
3. Asking price average $1,646,654

The former Our Lady of Good Counsel purchased by Riverview Garden School District from the Archdiocese of St. Louis. Photograph: Paul Calabrese

church might become a use other than a church or school.

The South City Deanery is located within the city of St. Louis, south of I-64. This area of the city saw substantial population decline in recent years, accompanied by a glut of vacant church buildings from many denominations. The archdiocese therefore recognized it would need to be receptive to end uses other than churches and schools. This required real estate agents who understood the local market and could market the properties for an appropriate end use. The archdiocese selected two real estate companies to market South City Deanery churches: Hilliker Corporation, a prominent St. Louis commercial, retail, and industrial real estate company, and Linda M. Wash Real Estate, a boutique real estate company. Both companies had contacts with the major players in the South St. Louis marketplace to facilitate such sales.

Hilliker had already represented St. Louis Public Schools in the sale of several school properties. Because of its experience, the archdiocese decided to trust the agency's instincts in setting an asking price without formal appraisals. Hilliker's instincts proved to be pretty good. They based their estimate of value on a cost per square foot

for the different buildings. These numbers were then adjusted up or down based on the neighborhood and overall quality of the building (T. Richter, personal communication, January 2008).

The archdiocese used a request-for-proposal procedure when considering the sale of the properties in the South City Deanery. In this process the Hilliker and Wash companies took would-be buyers on tours of the church campuses and set bid deadlines for the properties to encourage buyers to make their best offer for consideration by the archdiocese. The real estate agent then submitted a completed purchase agreement and a bid package, including the planned use of the property, track record of the buyer, and source of buyer financing. The process, with set deadlines, was successful: it generated purchase or lease agreements that ultimately became purchases for all seven of the properties.

A typical property contained, in addition to a church building, a rectory, school buildings and a convent for teaching nuns, a gym, and athletic fields. Parcel size of sold properties ranged from 0.75 to 2.1 acres. A requirement of the church property disposal process was that purchasers could not cherry-pick the components of individual parish properties. All the buildings and land on a property were to be part of the purchase agreement; a developer could not purchase only the church. However, the archdiocese made several exceptions to this policy. One exception was the Holy Innocents Church in the South City Deanery. Unlike the other parish complexes, with related and sometimes attached buildings, the layout of Holy Innocents allowed the archdiocese to offer the buildings individually. The entire property was listed at $1.6 million, but buildings also were listed separately at prices ranging from $550,000 for the forty-eight-year-old church to $300,000 for the rectory (Prost 2005). The archdiocese also assisted when two purchasers had an interest in separate portions of a property. It worked with the city to facilitate lot splits, allowing the sales to take place. Exhibit 17-2 shows the sales figures within the South City Deanery.

The South City Deanery's request-for-proposal process resulted in the sale of one building to another Christian denomination. Three buildings were sold to schools; Tom Richter later said that he would have made more of an effort to sell properties as charter schools had he been aware of the demand. The remaining properties went to secular uses. These uses included offices for an advertising agency and a lease/purchase agreement by the Compton Heights Band for a band practice facility. Ultimately Rothschild Development purchased St. Boniface, in the Carondelet area of St. Louis, for adaptive reuse as a performing arts theater. As is discussed in more detail below, St. Aloysius Gonzaga was sold to a developer and razed for construction of single-family housing.

Purchase Contract and Deed Restrictions
The purchase contract for sale of the church properties was generally the same as in a typical commercial transaction. It did, how-

EXHIBIT 17-2 South City Deanery Sales Summary

Acres	Church Name	Asking Price	Sale Price	Square Footage	Price per Square Foot	Outcome	Sale Date
1.5	Holy Family Church and Rectory	$1,600,000	$525,000	44,090	$19.85	Purchase, Advertising Agency Offices	03/10/06
	Holy Family School and Parish Hall		350,000			Regional Catholic School, Sale/Lease Purchase	12/20/07
1.9	Holy Innocents	1,650,000	1,750,000	56,624	30.90	Church	12/08/05
1.2	Immaculate Conception	1,375,000	475,000	25,074	18.94	Band Practice and Performance Facility	04/03/08
2.1	St. Aloysius Gonzaga	1,475,000	600,000	46,652	12.86	Demolished for Housing Development	10/28/05
2.1	St. Boniface	1,775,000	1,150,000	47,559	24.18	Adaptive Reuse— Theater Sale	10/31/05
1.2	St. Hedwig	900,000	572,000	22,258	25.70	Church—Lease/ Purchase	12/05/06
0.75	St. Thomas of Aquinas Church	475,000	250,000	6,186	40.41	Church	04/14/06
	St. Thomas of Aquinas Rectory		85,000	3,843	22.12	Sold to Individual	06/09/08

Holy Family Church located in St. Louis purchased by CFX Advertising to be used as corporate offices. The stained glass windows were removed by the Archdiocese of St. Louis. Photograph: Paul Calabrese

ever, contain language requiring removal of religious artifacts and fixtures by the archdiocese. Should the end user not be a church, stained-glass windows could be removed at the expense of the archdiocese and replaced with plain-glass windows.

A straightforward list of deed covenant restrictions was part of the purchase agreement. These covenants run with the land and are binding on future purchasers until the church structure has been demolished. A summary of the deed restrictions and covenants is:

- No use of the church name or any derivative of it
- No Roman Catholic worship services unless authorized by the Roman Catholic Church
- No human abortion, sterilization, or euthanasia services, including advocacy or counseling

- No display, sale, rental, or viewing of pornography
- No services providing massages or tattoos
- No use as a tavern, bar, nightclub, dance hall, hall or restaurant in which alcoholic beverages are served, although incidental alcohol sale is allowed
- No live performances directed to an adult audience
- No use as a bingo hall

Seven South St. Louis Deanery churches were closed on July 1, 2005. All were either sold or leased by July 1, 2006. A lot split took place with one property allowing the school portion to be purchased by Marian Middle School, a not-for-profit Catholic girls' academy, while the church portion became the offices for an advertising agency. Also disposed of was a school property, St. Anthony of Padua, which became a charter school. St. Anthony's Church was retained by the archdiocese as a neighborhood parish serving a diverse ethnic community of Hispanics, African Americans, and Vietnamese.

The church consolidation and merger process took place over a period of seventeen months. The archdiocese sold or leased virtually all of the former parishes in the two deaneries. This efficient process resulted in no reports of vandalism or deterioration of assets (Watkins 2007).

St. Aloysius Gonzaga Property Reuse into the Magnolia Square Residential Development—Site History

As it is with a person, the decline of the Church of St. Aloysius was gradual. The physical structure began to droop. The church had been constructed over a honeycomb of clay mines, and over the years the building settled unevenly. The bell tower weighed down the south side, and cracks split the walls. The parishioners began to age. Young families were moving out. A few years ago, the school

closed, and the exodus of young families accelerated (McClellan 2005).

St. Aloysius Gonzaga Parish was established in 1892 in the Fairmont area of St.
Louis at 5608 North Magnolia Avenue, near
the Hill area of south St. Louis. (See Exhibit
17-3.) The first church was a simple frame-
construction building; not until 1925 was a
permanent church erected. The initial membership was predominantly of German origin. A mission was established in 1903 for
the Italians residing in the neighborhood,
which raised funds to later establish St. Ambrose Parish. The parish of St. Ambrose

Exhibit 17-3 Magnolia Square Residential Development Site Location

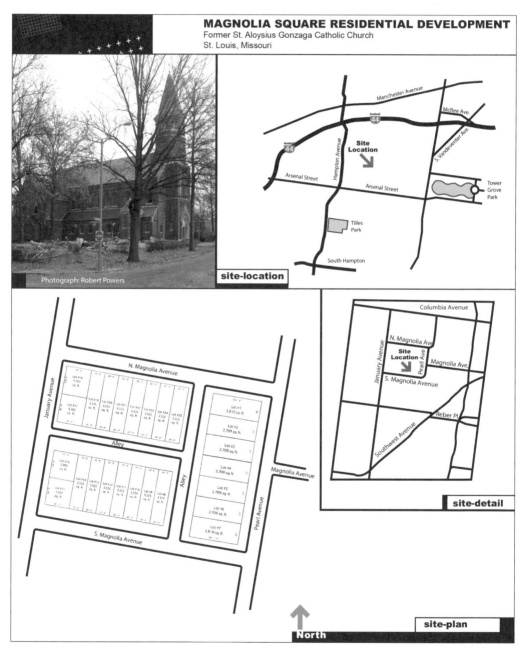

would eventually play a pivotal role in the fate of St. Aloysius Gonzaga.

The campus of St. Aloysius Gonzaga contained a rectory constructed in 1904, a convent built in 1911, and a school building dating from 1914 (the school building was replaced in 1962). Original plans from the 1890s called for an elaborate Gothic church to be erected. Though the foundation of this building was completed, construction of the church then had to be delayed until 1925 so that church debts could be paid off. The church eventually built on the site was in the Romanesque style, and the foundation of the original church was later used as a gym building with a bowling alley.

Saint Aloysius Gonzaga was one of twenty St. Louis parish properties closed in 2005 and later sold. A changing demographic, aging population, and budget shortfalls caused the closure. Membership of St. Aloysius peaked at eight hundred families in the 1950s, then declined. The school was closed in 2002 because of decreasing enrollment and increasing operational costs. By 2004 one-third of the 350 households registered with the church were over the age of sixty-five, far below the archdiocese's goal of eleven hundred to twelve hundred households per parish. Mass attendance used only 19 percent of the church's seating capacity. The authors of the Pastoral Planning Process noted, "The parish's physical plant requires significant repairs and upgrades in order to conduct the ministries of a vibrant parish" (Strategic Pastoral Plan—South City Deanery 2004). They concluded it was best to close the church.

Redevelopment Process

The archdiocese received two proposals for the purchase of the Church of St. Aloysius Gonzaga property, which had an asking price of $1,475,000. The first proposal was from Rothschild Development of St. Louis, which submitted a bid to purchase the property for around $1 million. Rothschild is an experienced St. Louis converter of old properties to new use. This proposal would have retained the church, rectory, and convent buildings for residential condominiums. Rothschild planned to ask St. Louis City Hall to provide tax incentives such as tax abatement or tax increment financing. Historic tax credits would be an additional ingredient to make the financing work. This proposal would have satisfied the historic preservationists who unsuccessfully rallied to save the old group of buildings.

The second proposal, which the archdiocese accepted, was Wohlert Company LLC's plan to transform the site into a development of single-family housing to be named Magnolia Square. The project manager and principal, Jim Wohlert, explained in an interview how he successfully developed and executed his plan. He became aware of the possible sale of St. Aloysius in 2003 and began making tentative plans to bid on the property. He participated in the Hilliker Corporation's marketing tours of the various properties to see what was being offered and to assess the competition. He then developed a plan that called for the demolition of the buildings and subdivision of the site into twenty-five lots for single-family housing. Though Wohlert Company's $600,000 offering price for the site was lower than the Rothschild offer, its end use was more acceptable to the archdiocese. "We've built other homes in the area," said Wohlert, "and the Archdiocese wanted the church and all of its outbuildings torn down" (National Trust for Historic Preservation 2006).

However, some historic preservationists were interested in saving the church complex. The church's location at the end of a street and the layout of the other buildings on the grounds created strong visual links with the surrounding residential buildings. These aesthetic qualities set a high standard for urban design and neighborhood planning. A *Preservation* online article notes that a report written for the Landmarks Association of St. Louis describes the property as "one of the best examples of urban planning by a parish in the entire city." Steve Patterson, a St. Louis real estate agent, and Michael R. Allen wrote extensively about the attempt to save St. Aloysius Gonzaga on their respective Web sites. Patterson claims he heard from many residents who never realized they had any say in the demolition. "There are a lot people wanting to save the building," he says. "The demolition of the church will mean the loss of a very unique urban setting—a rarity in the area." John Norquist, former mayor of Milwaukee and CEO of the Congress of New Urbanism, had previously used the church building as an example of how to terminate a vista. When informed that St. Aloysius was to be razed, he was shocked and miffed. "Tell them I used it in my presentation" (Patterson 2009).

Though the project faced opposition, Wohlert had several allies. Early in the planning phase the Wohlert Company presented its vision for Magnolia Square to Joe Vollmer, the alderman who represents the area in which the church was located. Vollmer was aware that members of the parish did not want the church buildings used as living quarters, a restaurant, or a recreation hall, and also that his constituents feared that the buildings could stand empty and become eyesores (Sutin 2006). He became convinced that Wohlert had the only viable plan for the property, and Wohlert recalls that this early communication with Vollmer eliminated problems later in the process. Another supporter of Wohlert's project was Father (now Monsignor) Vin-

View of the former St. Aloysius Gonzaga mentioned by John Norquist as an example of an urban design technique to terminate a vista. Photograph: Ron Powers

cent Bommarito, pastor of St. Ambrose Church, which had merged with St. Aloysius Gonzaga. Like Alderman Vollmer, Father Bommarito wanted to support St. Aloysius's former parishioners, who did not want to see the church turned into condos. Father Bommarito had also reached the strategic conclusion that the demolition of St. Aloysius would help to maintain St. Ambrose parish's good health because the proposed housing complex would offer his parishioners a local alternative to moving to newer suburban developments (V. Bommarito, personal communication, January 2009).

Preservationists held out hope that the city of St. Louis Preservation Board would be the forum to save the building. In December 2005, the board heard a preliminary application for a demolition permit. Several individuals, who had neither financial nor legal interest in the property, spoke in favor of preservation. Speaking in support of the demolition were the developer Jim Wohlert, Alderman Vollmer, and Father Bommarito.

Two votes were taken at the meeting. The board first voted four to two against granting a demolition permit. A second action to expressly deny a demolition permit passed in a five-to-one vote.

In St. Louis, however, preservation review allows the local alderman to ultimately control the process, and Alderman Vollmer had already decided to support Wohlert's plan for the construction of Magnolia Square. The preservation review process, in this instance, was put aside for political expediency. As the gatekeeper of the Hill neighborhood, Alderman Vollmer introduced a bill in city council to designate the church property as blighted and to simultaneously approve the Wohlert Company plan for residential development. "Aldermanic courtesy," which informally means the other aldermen will defer to the judgment of the representative of the area, gave the necessary support for the buildings to be demolished and the residential development to move forward. It was no longer necessary to appear before the St. Louis Preservation Review Board.

Market Conditions

According to the 2000 U.S. Census, St. Louis City had a total population of 348,189. The city population increased to 350,759 by 2007 (City-Data.com 2008).

The housing market in the city is composed of 53 percent renters, which is much higher than the state average of 30 percent. At the time this case study was completed there were 176,354 houses, of which 147,076 were occupied: 68,917 by owners, and 78,159 by renters (City-Data.com 2008). The housing boom that lifted housing prices from 2003 to 2005 did not seem to have much effect on the St. Louis housing market. The median home prices reached $138,800 in the fourth quarter of 2005, much below the

$213,000 national level, according to Property & Portfolio Research, Inc. (Sadovi n.d.).

Development Plan

To understand the development plan for the St. Aloysius Gonzaga site, it is important to have an understanding of the fifty-square-block area in south St. Louis known as The Hill. The neighborhood is one of the city's purest ethnic neighborhoods, occupied largely by second- and third-generation Italians. The residents call their neighborhood "la Montagna," "the mountain." As its name implies, The Hill remained remote from the rest of St. Louis, helping to solidify its strong ethnic identity. An anchor of the staunchly Catholic neighborhood is St. Ambrose Church, which serves as a focal point of community life. Its associated school has educated several generations of The Hill's children.

St. Louis, like many Midwestern cities, has recognized a need to retain residents by providing suburban-style housing. The Hill neighborhood has benefited from success with infill residential development. Its original buildings are a heterogeneous mixture of styles of modest working-class detached single-family homes, the majority of which evidence good maintenance despite some being more than a hundred years old. Throughout the neighborhood are individual lots on which new single-family residences have been erected.

There are fewer opportunities for residential projects with substantial numbers of units, though some do exist. One example of a large-scale project is Parc Ridge Estates, which is located ¼ mile from St. Ambrose on the former Truman Restorative Center, previously a city-owned nursing home. The developer of the property saw a market for newlyweds, singles, families, and retirees who wanted to stay in the

Exhibit 17-4 Census Data 2000 and 2007

		State Missouri	County St. Louis City	Census Tract 1131
Population				
	2000	5,595,211	348,189	3,428
	2007	5,878,415	350,759	
	% Change	5.06%	0.74%	
Age (2000)				
	Less than 18	25.49%	25.70%	13.48%
	22-39	25.02%	28.02%	34.63%
	40-59	26.24%	23.37%	25.26%
	60 and over	17.57%	16.99%	23.45%
Median Household Income				
	2000	$37,934	$27,156	$33,623
	2007	$45,114	$34,191	
	% Change	18.93%	25.91%	
Race (2000)				
	White alone	84.84%	43.77%	81.45%
	Black or African American alone	11.12%	51.01%	11.99%
	American Indian and Alaska Native alone	0.47%	0.30%	0.00%
	Asian alone	1.08%	2.03%	4.29%
	Hawaiian and Pacific Islander alone	0.05%	0.03%	0.00%
	Some other race alone	0.81%	0.78%	0.44%
	Two or more races	1.63%	2.07%	1.84%
Education (2000)				
	Bachelor or higher	21.58%	19.08%	21.40%
	High school above age 25	32.73%	27.50%	22.76%
Unemployment				
	2000	3.44%	6.81%	3.87%
Housing (2000)				
	Households	2,197,214	147,286	1,671
	Housing Units	2,442,017	176,354	1,784
	Owner Occupied Units(%)	70.28%	46.86%	46.91%
	Renter Units(%)	29.72%	53.14%	53.09%
	Median Rent Apartment	$484	$442	$529
	Median House Value (Owner Occupied)	$86,900	$63,500	$65,300

Source: 2000 and 2007 U.S. Census
Note: 2007 tract data is not available; do not need County Data

neighborhood or relocate from the suburbs. Construction on this competing residential development of thirty-six homes and twenty-two villas began in April 2006—about the same time as Magnolia Square—with prices starting at $297,000. This project had a six-month jump on Magnolia Square and has sold out, with the exception of five attached townhomes.

Wohlert designed the Magnolia Square project to complement the existing housing around it. The most prominent style of home in the neighborhood is the small "shotgun house," so named because if a bullet had been fired through the front door, it would have passed straight through the living room, bedroom, kitchen, and out the backdoor. These were built for blue-collar workers in the early twentieth century. Alleyways are a part of the neighborhood. Wohlert, in designing the subdivision plans, included narrow lots with small front yards set back 10 ft. from the street. Nineteen of the twenty-five lots would be retro shotgun style. The others would be in a more conventional two-story colonial style. The alleyways behind the houses allow for housing density similar to that existing in the neighborhood, providing an urban context. However, the homes have been criticized for their suburban design and selection of materials, which were brick veneer on the fronts of the houses and vinyl siding covering the sides.

Wohlert's company had previously built four homes in the neighborhood with a starting price point of $250,000. Individual owners could add upgrades that could raise the price to a top at $325,000. In contrast, older homes in the neighborhood tend to be small with an average sale price of $180,000. The twenty-five lots on the St. Aloysius site range in size from 2,700 sq. ft. to 3,810 sq. ft. In submissions to the city in November 2005, base finished house prices

ranged from $196,000 to $289,000. Pricing in 2007 had moved up to between $254,900 and $369,900. Building square footage varied between 1,200 and 2,500 sq. ft. The developer requested to be allowed a 10-ft. front yard setback, a side yard of 3 ft., and a variance to the 4,000-ft. lot requirement to align with the surrounding neighborhood. Wohlert Company's intention was to sell lots at a starting price of $75,000.

Wohlert formed Dimartino Homes LLC in 2004 to be the builder. By 2006 he anticipated a soft market: his contacts on the material supply side (trade association and component manufacturers for the home building industry) indicated the market was contracting. Wohlert therefore made a strategic decision in 2006 to sell twelve lots to Prather Homes of Kirkwood, Missouri, and five lots to Heyde Homes of St. Louis, to reduce the debt being carried by the company. Wohlert, through Dimartino Homes, retained seven lots for new home construction.

By December 2008, over half of the lots had been sold to home purchasers, with fourteen houses constructed. As of December 2012 only one undeveloped lot, which is owned by Wohlert, remains. The other two developers built on four lots in 2009 and one each in 2011. A house built by Prather Homes is being marketed as a just-completed builder's closeout with an asking price of $400,000. The St. Louis Assessor's records and other real estate sources indicate the other newly constructed homes sold between $249,000 and $470,000.

To summarize, the project was able to absorb three to four lots a year, over the seven-year build out. The diocese made about $600,000 on sale of lots to Wohlert, who then wholesaled eighteen of the twenty-five lots to other builders, retaining seven for himself to build on. The total value of lots sold (excluding the houses constructed on

Exhibit 17-5 St. Aloysius/Magnolia
Square Time Line

7/1/2005	St. Aloysius closes
10/28/2005	St. Aloysius purchased by Wohlert
12/7/2005	Planned unit development plans submitted to St. Louis Planning Commissions
12/19/2005	Developer appears before St. Louis Preservation Review Board requesting a demolition permit
1/23/2006	St. Louis Board of Alderman Committee hearing for redevelopment of St. Aloysius into Magnolia Square
4/14/2006	Demolition of St. Aloysius
5/17/2006	First lot sold and house constructed
9/28/2008	A strategic decision is made by Wohlert to sell seventeen lots to other developers
10/1/2008	Two of twenty-five lots remain unsold
9/21/2010	Wohlert sells one of his two remaining lots
12/13/2012	Only one lot remains of the original twenty-five lots and is owned by Wohlert

them) was $1.3 million, or about 19 percent of the total project. The value of the constructed homes is about $7 million.

The city's development agency, as a condition of receiving approval for tax abatement, required brick on the street side of each of the new houses along with the installation of street trees in the tree lawn and retention of several mature pin oaks. It also required Wohlert to use city-certified minority contractors for portions of construction in order to gain ten years of tax abatement. Exhibit 17-5 details the redevelopment process. It shows a time line of the redevelopment process, which is followed by Exhibit 17-6, which shows several of the constructed single-family homes.

Market Absorption

Wohlert's sale of a majority of the inventory of lots to Prather Homes shows that the original developer's energies would best

be directed to acquisition, remodeling, and sale of individual properties in the neighborhood. Relinquishing control through the sale of the lots was a prudent decision in a contracting market. Good business sense told him it was time to reduce debt and sell the lots. Moreover, he had a policy of not building homes on speculation. Consequently, he was not carrying much unsold inventory.

In December 2008, eight lots remained unsold, four of the fourteen completed houses were for sale, and the builders were sitting on some undeveloped lots until the market picked up again. By December 2012, as is discussed above, market recovery and the desirability of the product had resulted in nearly complete absorption of the units, shown in Exhibit 17-7. The land-development side of the project had a double-digit rate of return.

Reuse of Salvaged Artifacts

Wohlert Construction realized a substantial savings on the demolition of St. Aloysius when it allowed Bellon Wrecking and Salvage to resell material from demolition. The Bellon family took the salvaged material and installed them in the Church Key Tavern. The pews became booths, the choir loft was turned into a bar, and the padded kneelers became the bar's footrests (Hixson

Salvaged materials from St. Aloysius were used to decorate the interior of the Church Key Tavern located in St. Louis. Advertising states "Heavenly Spirits—Sinful Merriment" will be found within.
Photograph: Paul Calabrese

and Lay 2007). Former parishioners were upset to learn of the use of the church furnishings, though Monsignor Bommarito explained in an interview that there was nothing wrong with the secular reuse of the salvage (J. Wohlert, personal communication, January 2009).

Lessons Learned

With respect to the archdiocese property-disposition program, the following suggestions for sale of church properties can be made:

- *Conduct mass property disposal in a planned, orderly process:* The archdiocese

Exhibit 17-6 Magnolia Square Residential Development Photographs

MAGNOLIA SQUARE RESIDENTIAL DEVELOPMENT
Former St. Aloysius Gonzaga Catholic Church
St. Louis, Missouri

Photographs: Paul Calabrese

Exhibit 17-7 St. Aloysius/Magnolia Square Absorption

Magnolia Square Development Absorption—June 2008 and December 2012
Transfer Date Archdiocese to Wohlert 11/01/2005

Address	Construction Status 2012	Lot Size	Frontage	Depth	Date of Purchase	Buyer/Owner June 2008	December 2012 Status
2633 Pearl	Built	3,810 sq ft	45'	85"	12/14/2006	Individual Owner	
2637 Pearl	Built	2,709 sq ft	32'	85"	6/21/2007	Individual Owner	
2641 Pearl	Built	2,709 sq ft	32'	85"	8/23/2007	Individual Owner	
2643 Pearl	Built	2,709 sq ft	32'	85"	9/28/2006	**Prather Homes**	Sold 6/06/11
2647 Pearl	Built	2,709 sq ft	32'	85"	4/12/2007	Individual Owner	
2651 Pearl	Vacant Lot	2,709 sq ft	32'	85"	11/1/2005	**Wohlert**	Unsold Lot
2655 Pearl	Built	3,810 sq ft	45'	85"	11/1/2005	**Wohlert**	Sold 9/21/10
5617 S. Magnolia	Built	3,525 sq ft	30"	117'	9/28/2006	**Prather Homes**	Sold 9/22/08
5619 S. Magnolia	Built	3,525 sq ft	30"	117'	9/28/2006	**Prather Homes**	Sold 3/30/09
5623 S. Magnolia	Built	3,525 sq ft	30"	117'	9/28/2006	**Prather Homes**	Sold 3/18/09
5625 S. Magnolia	Built	3,525 sq ft	30"	117'	9/28/2006	**Prather Homes**	Sold 4/8/09
5629 S. Magnolia	Built	3,525 sq ft	30"	117'	5/17/2006	Individual Owner	
5631 S. Magnolia	Built	3,525 sq ft	30"	117'	7/18/2007	Individual Owner	
5635 S. Magnolia	Built	3,525 sq ft	30"	117'	8/7/2007	Individual Owner	
2656 January	Built	3,200 sq ft	59"	54"	9/28/2006	**Prather Homes**	Sold10/24/08
2644 January	Built	3,200 sq ft	59"	54"	9/28/2006	**Prather Homes**	Unsold Home
2636 January	Built	3,200 sq ft	59"	54"	6/5/2008	Individual Owner	
2632 January	Built	3,200 sq ft	59"	54"	8/31/2006	**Prather Homes**	Sold 7/1/11
5636 N. Magnolia	Built	3,525 sq ft	30"	117'	6/6/2007	Individual Owner	
5632 N. Magnolia	Built	3,525 sq ft	30"	117'	12/21/2007	Individual Owner	
5628 N. Magnolia	Built	3,525 sq ft	30"	117'	8/23/2006	**Broadwing LLC**	Sold 5/26/09
5626 N. Magnolia	Built	3,525 sq ft	30"	117'	5/20/2008	**Heyde Homes**	Sold 10/6/08
5622 N. Magnolia	Built	3,525 sq ft	30"	117'	5/26/2008	Individual Owner	
5620 N. Magnolia	Built	3,525 sq ft	30"	117'	3/19/2008	Individual Owner	
5616 N. Magnolia	Built	3,525 sq ft	30"	117'	10/10/2007	Individual Owner	

Bold = Developer

followed an orderly process and used several professional real estate sales companies to market and sell the properties. Although pastors and parishioners found it upsetting to hang for-sale signs on parishes to be closed, it was nevertheless an effective marketing strategy. Sending direct mailings to targeted audiences was also effective. Property tours and a short deadline for submission of buyer offers resulted in quick decision-making on the part of purchasers.

- *Avoid subdividing parcels offered for sale:* The archdiocese intentionally marketed entire individual parishes for purchase. Consequently, desirable portions could not be acquired separately. However, the archdiocese did show flexibility when two purchasers had an interest in separate portions of the same property.

Exhibit 17-8 Development Cost Information

Magnolia Square
St. Louis, Missouri
Site area: 2.1 acres (91,500 square feet)
Lot Size Range: 2,709 square feet to 3,525 square feet

DEVELOPMENT COST INFORMATION	
Land Acquisition Cost	$600,000
Site Preparation Cost	
Demolition	341,250
Asbestos Remediation	57,148
Tree Removal	4,600
Construction Costs	
Utilities—Sanitary and Storm	79,170
Alleyway	36,855
Grading	3,185
Soft Costs	
Plan Prep. Arch. and Engineer	16,380
Surveying	4,557
Demo Fees and Planned Unit Development Fees	26,537
Metro Sewer District Fees	23,660
Total Development Costs	**$1,193,342**
Cash Flow at Completion	
Number of Sales	23 (excludes 2 lots retained)
Average Sales Price	$58,000
Total Proceeds from Sales	1,334,000
Gross Profit	**$140,658**
Financing and Investment	
Value of Sales	$1,334,000
Gross Profit	140,658
Equity	1,193,342

Note: a substantial part of the demolition cost was recovered by selling the right to salvage the contents of the buildings

- *Be flexible on sales price in considering non-financial benefits:* Sometimes the archdiocese did not take the highest bid, but rather accepted a lesser purchase price when a proposed project met other, non-financial objectives, such as retaining parishioners in the neighborhood or facilitating a religious reuse of a property by a kindred religious group. An example is the sale of church property to the Alexian Brothers for an adult day care center.
- *Communicate with the parishioners:* The parishioners of St. Aloysius were not aware of what might happen to nonsacred church furnishings, and were upset that salvaged pews were reused in a bar. This perhaps could have been avoided by better communication.

With respect to the St. Aloysius Gonzaga demolition and housing lots project, the following lessons are evident:

- *Listen to the neighbors:* The neighborhood clearly communicated a cool reception to the idea of condominiums as a reuse of the church. However, Father Bommarito clearly indicated that adaptive reuse was never a consideration. It is usually troublesome to advance a project when the neighborhood is opposed.
- *Line up interests of church leaders and politicians:* Using the local political process facilitated deference to local wishes (primarily the local parish church and councilman) to not have the buildings reused as condos. Passing a city ordinance that declared the church as blighted made it possible to circumvent the preservation review process and any historical preservationists.

Conclusion

The project was mostly successful, but absorption lagged due to a decline in the housing market. The developer diversified risk by selling lots to other builders, earned an acceptable return, and was able to retain two lots for future use or sale.

References and Works Consulted

Briggs D. 2007. "Parishes Assigned to 'Clusters' Cleveland Diocese Move Could Be First Step to Some Consolidation, Closings." *Plain Dealer,* February 8, A1.

City-Data.com. 2008. www.city-data.com.

Garnett, R. 2006. "Downsizing and the Catholic Church." *USA Today,* July 16. http://usatoday 30.usatoday.com/news/opinion//editorials /2006–07–16-religion-edit_x.htm.

Hixson, S., and J. Lay. 2007. "The 'Key to Your Salvation Lies in The Grove." *Sauce Magazine,* February 2. www.saucemagazine.com/a/172.

Luo, M. 2007. "Archdiocese to Shut 21 N.Y. Parishes." *New York Times,* January 19. http:// www.nytimes.com/2007/01/19/nyregion/ 19cnd-church.html?n=Top%2FReference%2F Times%20Topics%2FPeople%2FL%2FLuo%20 Michael.

McClellan, B. 2005. "Church, Steeple Are Woven into Fabric of Life for Man, His Family." *St. Louis Post Dispatch,* September 14, B1.

Meitler Consultants, Inc. 2007. www.meitler.com.

National Trust for Historic Preservation. 2006. www.nationaltrust.org/magazine/archives/ arc_news_2006/020/06.htm.

Patterson, S. 2009. "CNU's Norquist Uses St. Aloysius in Presentation on Urbanism." Weblog post. *Urban Review STL,* January 25. http://www.urbanreviewstl.com/?p=603.

Prost, C. 2005. "Want to Live in a Church? The Largest Sale of Parish Buildings in Its History." *St. Louis Post Dispatch,* June 10, C1.

Sadovi, M. n.d. Special to the *Wall Street Journal Online.*

Strategic Pastoral Plan—Northeast County Deanery. 2004. Best Set of Recommendations, December 12.

Strategic Pastoral Plan—South City Deanery. 2004. Best Set of Recommendations, December 9.

Sutin, K. 2006. "New Residential Developments Rise in Neighborhood near the Hill." *St. Louis Post Dispatch,* March 24.

Watkins, B. 2007. "Old Parish Properties Have Owners, Uses." *St. Louis Review,* January 21. www.stlouisreview.com/aricle.php?id=12413.

ST. JOSEPH CHURCH

CONVERSION CASE STUDY

Fayetteville, Arkansas

Gary DeWine

The St. Joseph Church campus is a 2.2-acre property located within the Washington-Willow Historic District, along a major two-lane street leading to Fayetteville's central business district. It is a neighborhood of Victorian-era houses and streets shaded with large trees. The area has slowly gentrified from student housing to single-family homes, which are predominantly owner-occupied. The church site contains three buildings, which are the subject of this case study. (See Exhibit 18-1.) Two of the buildings have been transitioned to condominiums; the third has been redeveloped as apartments with a condo conversion planned in the future.

Introduction

The first building is the 7,778-sq.-ft. old sanctuary, which became Willow Avenue Condominiums. It was built in 1936 to replace the site's original church. It subsequently served as a meeting hall, a residence for four Franciscan Brothers, and church offices. The building was recently placed on the National Register of Historic Places.

The second building on-site is the 21,989-sq.-ft. former school building, constructed in 1968. A relic of 1960s institutional school architecture, the building was truly an ugly duckling. It became Lafayette Loft Condominiums.

The third building is St. Joseph Church, a 7,830-sq.-ft. building at the corner of Lafayette and Walnut. The building was designed in the international style by a protégé of noted architect Warren Seagraves, who is held in high regard in the Fayetteville community. The sanctuary contained seating for 430. The building was built in the 1960s, and underwent a major remodeling in 1993 to accommodate the installation of a large pipe organ. Other improvements made at that time included a new choir loft, reloca-

tion of a confessional, and new entrances. After its redevelopment, the church was renamed Seagraves Condominiums.

The campus also contained a single-family home and a duplex residence on separately deeded lots. These properties were sold to the developer as part of the church and school real estate transaction, and are not addressed in this case study.

Three offers of over $1 million were made for the property before it was sold. Eventually, Alexander, Merry-Ship & Alt, a major developer in Fayetteville specializing in adaptive reuse, negotiated an offer of $1.2 million, which took into account the cost of roof repairs and asbestos abatement. The property was to be developed through North College Development Co., LLC, for the purpose of transforming the three major buildings on the church campus into separate condominium projects (Rob Merry-Ship, personal communication, January 2008).

The three buildings were converted to condominiums over a period of twenty-four months. Willow Avenue Condominiums, the former old sanctuary, became eight rental units renting for between $750 and $900 a month. The developer plans to sell the units in the future. Lafayette Condominiums, the former school building, contains seventeen units that sold for prices ranging from $84,000 to $257,000, or from $155 to $210 per building square foot. Since completion, three units have resold. The three units originally sold for an average of $134,540 in the spring of 2005, and within a year resold for an average of $174,000, almost a 30 percent price appreciation.

Seagraves Condominiums, constructed within the interior of St. Joseph Church, contains eight units. Sales prices have ranged from $284,000 to $473,000, or from $196 to $237 per building square foot. When this case study was conducted in 2008, two units remain in inventory with a list price of $300,000 each. The project is projected to provide the developers a 30 percent return when the last two units are sold (S. Alt, personal communication, January 2008).

Site History

Maurice Coffey purchased the plot of land that became the Lafayette Street Project for $100 in 1872. Coffey, a Catholic, donated the land to the Catholic Church, which held it until 2002. The St. Joseph Church campus

Exhibit 18-1 Lafayette Street Project Location and Site Plan

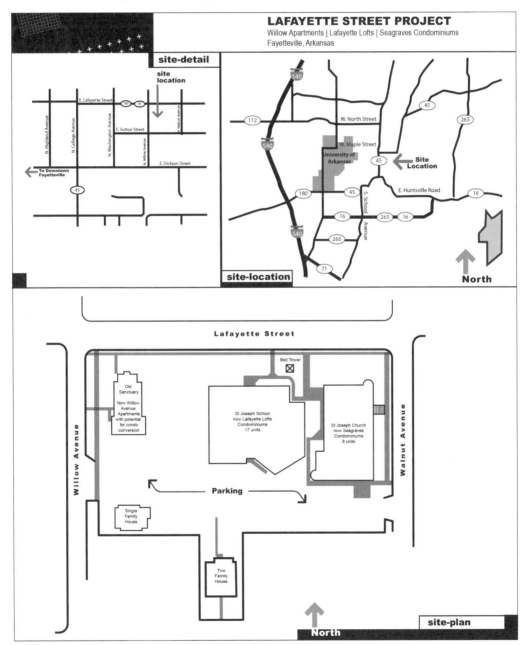

served the Catholic community of Fayetteville, Arkansas, for 130 years. Over time, the church acquired abutting residences, which supported church activities.

The aesthetic layout of the church campus provides those approaching from downtown Fayetteville a sense of place within the historic Washington-Willow neighborhood. The stand-alone bell tower further adds to the visual experience. The bookends of old and new buildings preserve religious motifs, such as carved relief on doors, stained-glass windows, and religious symbols.

In the 1990s, the parish served by St. Joseph Church concluded that it had outgrown the site. The available parking space for church services of fifteen hundred parishioners was inadequate, and the school facility was too small to accommodate five-hundred-plus students. According to church spokesman Paul Warren, the church considered expanding by acquiring houses abutting the property, but decided that it did not want to level a block of the historic district for parking space (City of Fayetteville Planning Commission 2003). In 1995, at the recommendation of the Pastoral Council, the church accepted a long-range plan calling for purchase of land for construction of a new church and fellowship hall. The Pastoral Council later recognized, however, that it would be financially impossible for St. Joseph's to support the expense of maintaining two separate properties. In February 1999, Pastor John Antony presented a new plan calling for the construction of a new school, parish offices, and a combined worship center and parish hall with seating for a thousand. The cost of the new facility was estimated to be $3 million. Canon law required that a facility of that cost have Vatican approval, which the parish received on May 8, 2001 (St. Joseph Catholic Church and School 2013). A church committee then decided to relocate the church and place the Lafayette Street property for sale. The church interviewed four real estate companies with which to list the property. Given the uniqueness of the property, each recommended placing the church on the market as "for sale by owner."

Reed and Associates Real Estate Appraisers of Springdale, Arkansas, concluded that the church and school buildings on the 2.81-acre property could be razed for single-family homes, reused by another church, or adapted for residential-office use. The appraisers set a value of $1,370,000 to $1,520,000 for the property. The lower end of the range assumed that the buildings would be razed for single-family homes, which was the only reuse that the site's zoning permitted. The upper end of the price range assumed that the property could be rezoned as institutional, allowing for reuse of the structures (Reed & Associates, Inc. 2001). The report indicated it would take two years to market the property. Simultaneously with the appraisal, Morris and Associates Environmental Consultants prepared a report and survey detailing the condition and presence of asbestos in the building.

The church initially marketed the property informally "by owner" hoping to secure a buyer. When the property remained unsold in October 2002, the church listed it with the local real estate firm of Lindsey and Associates with an asking price of $1.5 million and reached out to Richard P. Alexander of Alexander, Merry-Ship & Alt to seek his advice on what could be done with the church property. Alexander's firm, the AMA Real Estate Group, ultimately bought and developed the property. Refer to Exhibit 18-2 for a time line of the project.

AMA Real Estate group was formed in 2002 by a partnership of Richard Alexander, Rob Merry-Ship, and Sheree Alt. The

Exhibit 18-2 Time Line

1997	2000	December 2002	May 2003	August 2003	Spring 2005
St. Joseph purchases property for relocation	St. Joseph informally puts original property on the market "for sale"	Developer and St. Joseph begin negotiations	Fayetteville Planning Commission votes 5-4-0 to recommend planned rezoning and development of church	Fayetteville City Council approves planned zoning district	Construction completed over preceding 24 months

partners each bring an area of expertise and specialization to the real estate development process. With over fifty combined years of experience in real estate sales, development, and property management, the three have contributed substantially to Fayetteville's downtown revitalization.

Alexander, Merry-Ship & Alt specialize in the adaptive reuse of functionally obsolete buildings. Examples of their work are found throughout Fayetteville, and include a range of new uses, including a hotel, office spaces, retail stores, restaurants, and residences. A few notable examples are the Rollston Building and the UARK Bowl. The Rollston Building, one of their first projects, was an early mixed-use development that involved converting a one-story warehouse into two restaurants and six luxury apartments. The UARK Bowl, originally built in 1949 as a bowling alley with a ballroom on the second floor, was converted into a mixed-use building in 2000, and included a mix of event space, meeting rooms, retail space, and high-end condominiums (Alexander, Merry-Ship & Alt 2007).

Market Conditions

Fayetteville, with a population of 58,047, is located in the northwest corner of Arkansas. It is home to the University of Arkansas, with almost 23,000 students. It has been recognized as one of America's most livable communities and a *Money Magazine* "Best Place to Live." A notable feature of downtown is the Walton Arts Center, which is Arkansas's largest performing arts center and hosts many events throughout the year (*CNN Money Magazine* 2007; Partners for Livable Communities 2007).

Washington County ranks 128th out of 3,141 counties in the United States in terms of residential property appreciation. The U.S. Census Bureau estimated that the county had a total of 79,921 homes in 2006, representing a 23.3 percent increase from the 15,109 homes counted in the 2000 census. The 2000 census found that the county's median owner-occupied home value was $90,100, which was greater than the state of Arkansas's median value of $72,800. The values of owner-occupied dwellings in 2006 had increased by $58,900, or 65.4 percent in the county. The county had 35,748 owner-occupied houses and condos and 24,403 renter-occupied apartments (City-Data.com 2008).

Planning Process

In December 2002, Alexander, Merry-Ship & Alt negotiated a purchase agreement of $1.2 million for the St. Joseph Church property. The purchase agreement allowed for a ninety-day investigation period, and required the buyer to have the property approved for rezoning or change of land use along with obtaining proof of financing.

Exhibit 18-3 Census Data 2000 and 2007

		Arkansas	Washington County	Fayetteville Township	Census Tract 101.04
Population					
	2000	2,673,400	157,715	57,783	4,915
	2007	2,834,797	194,292		
	% Change	6.04%	23.19%		
Age (2000)					
	Less than 18	25.44%	25.05%	19.73%	22.44%
	22-39	24.63%	29.63%	34.23%	28.34%
	40-59	25.72%	23.03%	19.46%	28.95%
	60 and over	18.39%	13.22%	11.10%	15.12%
Median Household Income					
	2000	$32,182	$34,691	$31,345	$47,636
	2007	$38,134	$42,689		
	% Change	18.49%	23.05%		
Race (2000)					
White alone		79.94%	87.98%	86.84%	92.80%
Black or African American alone		15.63%	2.13%	4.84%	2.71%
American Indian and Alaska Native alone		0.69%	1.28%	0.98%	0.31%
Asian alone		0.71%	1.65%	3.01%	2.77%
Hawaiian and Pacific Islander alone		0.06%	0.48%	0.05%	0.00%
Some other race alone		1.54%	4.45%	2.24%	0.31%
Two or more races					
Education (2000)					
Bachelor or higher		16.66%	24.54%	41.18%	60.22%
High school above age 25		34.10%	30.50%	20.61%	14.22%
Unemployment					
	2000	3.67%	5.37%	9.92%	2.26%
	2007				
Housing (2000)					
Households		1,042,807	60,183	23,691	2,183
Housing Units		1,173,043	64,330	25,326	2,310
Owner Occupied Units (%)		69.38%	59.43%	42.12%	62.70%
Renter Units(%)		30.62%	40.57%	57.88%	37.30%
Median Rent Apartment		$453	$490	$480	$614
Median House Value (Owner Occupied)		$67,400	$88,300	$97,700	$129,500

Source: 2000 and 2007 U.S. Census
Note: 2007 tract data is not available

The project found support among the city leaders. Fayetteville's mayor and city council have vowed to maintain the city as the only real downtown in northwest Arkansas, and to encourage projects that minimize sprawl by creating residential infill opportunities in the historic part of downtown. The St. Joseph project's preservation of the character of the Washington-Willow neighborhood near downtown suited their vision.

The first application that the developers submitted to the city of Fayetteville called for the creation of a planned residential zoning district. According to Planning Commission correspondence, the proposal was for an infill project designed to use the existing structures and infrastructure by converting the site's school, church, and administrative offices into multifamily dwellings. The developers' plans called for the old St. Joseph school building to become twenty one- and two-bedroom residential condominium units. The church would become nine one-and two-bedroom condominium units. The two houses already on the site were included in the sale. One, a duplex, would be remodeled, and the other, a single-family home, would remain unchanged. The 1936 vintage old sanctuary would be made available as a center for community meetings or performances. Because the developer intended to seek National Register status for the old sanctuary in order to take advantage of historic tax credits, the facade of the building would be preserved in a manner consistent with U.S. Department of Interior guidelines. The developers planned to retain the building as investment property with possible sale of the units in the future. Finally, the proposal considered some site use for a commercial purpose, such as a coffee shop (R. Merry-Ship, personal communication, January 2008).

Opposition to the project materialized. Letters and zoning commission minutes indicate that many residents did not fully understand what was being proposed. Some opponents were under the mistaken impression that the site would be converted entirely to apartments, and others were not aware that the condominiums planned for the site would adaptively reuse the existing buildings. The neighborhood homeowners' association said flatly that it would not support a developer tearing down the buildings to make way for new construction condominiums or apartments. Neither the city nor the homeowners' association wanted to see the site turned into "party central" student apartments catering to University of Arkansas undergraduates or new-construction "McMansions." Residents said that apartments would not fit in the predominantly single-family housing area and feared that the development would destroy the neighborhood's historic character. The usual arguments against rezoning were also made, such as concern that the development would create extra traffic, parking problems, and would decrease property values.

Paul Warren, the church's spokesman to the public and representative at Planning and Zoning Commission hearings, was instrumental in answering critics' negative comments about the project. His familiarity with the issues allowed him to provide an articulate voice explaining how the project would benefit the neighborhood. Mr. Warren pointed out that the site, which had been obviously vacant for a year, was attracting trash dumpers along with a vagrant who took up temporary residence in the church. Mr. Warren also explained the challenges the church had confronted in attracting a buyer. Other churches had been approached but declined because of the

Exhibit 18-4 Lafayette Street Project—The "Deal" at a Glance: St. Joseph Church Campus Conversion

Project	End Use	Building's Square Footage	% of Total Square Footage	Number of Units	% of Total Number of Units	Tenure
Single-Family House	House	1,750	3.60%	1	3%	Sold Off
Two-Family House	Two-Family House	1,300	2.70%	2	6%	Sold Off
Sanctuary Church	Condos	15,000	31%	8	22%	Owner
School	Condos	22,000	46%	17	47%	Owner
Old Sanctuary	Rental Apartments	8,000	17%	8	22%	Rent
Totals		48,050		36		

city's per-pew parking requirements. Mr. Warren said that "we solicited the Montessori School, the University of Arkansas, the Arts Culture in Fayetteville, which we thought would be a wonderful opportunity for a museum or an art studio or some other kind of use . . . unfortunately, there is no money out there at this point in this economy for those types of ventures" (City of Fayetteville Planning Commission 2003).

While Mr. Warren defended the church's decision to sell the property to the AMA Real Estate Group, the developers worked with Kathy Thompson, president of the Washington-Willow Neighborhood Association, to solicit residents' feedback on the project. In deference to residents' vehement opposition to a four-hundred-seat auditorium in the neighborhood, Mr. Alexander abandoned plans to use the old sanctuary building as a venue for concerts and receptions. The developers decided that the entire project would be residential, and eventually the project overcame community resistance. "This is one of those situations where everyone gets all upset about some-

thing, and after it is all said and done, people say, 'This is okay, it's nice,'" said Ms. Thompson (Walter 2003b).

The Planning and Zoning Commission recommended approval of the revised project by a five-to-four vote, and the Fayetteville city council approved the creation of a Planned Zoning District around the site in August 2003. In order to gain Planning and Zoning Commission approval, the developer was required to satisfy a Park Land Development Ordinance requiring 0.66 acres be set aside for recreational use. The developer satisfied the ordinance by setting aside 0.18 acres and paying $11,262 to the city as park fees in lieu of creating a 0.66-acre park. The new park was constructed between the school and the 1936 vintage sanctuary building (Walter 2003a).

Development Plan

The city of Fayetteville has a history of legislatively assisting and administratively encouraging infill residential development in the downtown area. The goal is to minimize sprawl. The Lafayette Street project ben-

Acres	% of Total Acres	Absorption	Absorption as % of Total	Tax Credits	Price Points	% of Total Value	Unit Size
0.16	7%	OK	100%	Surplus Sold—NA	$75,000	1%	
0.19	9%	OK	100%	Surplus Sold—NA	$155,000	2%	
0.56	25%	2 unsold	75%	No	$284,000 to $473,000	43%	1,400 to 2,000
0.9	41%	Nice Pre-sold	100%	No	$84,000 to $257,000	36%	500 to 1,250
0.39	18%	High Occupancy	90%	Historic Tax Credits	$750 to $900/ month	18%	600 to 1,000
2.2							

efited from the city's progressive Planned Zoning District ordinance. The ordinance's purpose is to permit and encourage redevelopment by allowing simultaneous approval of a development plan and rezoning. Mayor Dan Coody said the city ruled in favor of a Planned Zoning District for the St. Joseph campus because it wanted to make sure that the site attracted the right kind of development. "The last thing we need in Fayetteville are large, vacant, derelict buildings in our downtown area," Coody stated (Walter 2003b).

The developers had a vision for the entire city block encompassing the sanctuary, schoolhouse, and rectory. Their long history of living in Fayetteville and development experience provided insight into building a product that would be well received. They considered several development plans with more or less density, and decided upon a configuration of thirty-three condos in three buildings. The developers chose the Little Rock architectural firm of Fennell, Purifoy, and Hammock to craft the design solutions required by the three architecturally differ-

ent buildings. (See Exhibit 18-4 for details.)

The developers agreed that the redevelopment would respect the religious heritage of the property. All religious images on the exterior were to remain. Special interior design considerations were made for the two-story-tall stained-glass image of St. Joseph by providing an interior balcony so the icon was not cut in half. A skylight that lit the former altar was used to provide light in the kitchen of one unit. Finally the church bell tower, a separate structure on the property, was retained to maintain a sense of place in the historic fabric of the neighborhood. In the words of developers, the plan was to do the "right thing" with the church (R. Merry-Ship, personal communication, January 2008).

The developers provided products at three different price points, which attracted an eclectic mix of incomes and age groups. The former church, built in the 1960s in the international style, became Seagraves Condominiums, featuring eight units between 1,400 and 2,000 sq. ft. priced between $250,000 and $500,000. The design challenges for this building included reconfiguring the vast interior space into separate condos and adding a second floor within the sanctuary, which doubled the building's interior from 7,500 to 15,000 sq. ft. Seagraves Condominium is the most luxurious of the three buildings. All units have hardwood floors in the living room and kitchen, granite countertops, a fireplace, and 10-ft. ceilings. Balconies and windows were added, but the majority of the exterior remained unchanged (S. Alt, personal communication, January 2008).

The school building became Lafayette Loft Condominiums, with seventeen units ranging in size from 500 to 1,250 sq. ft. The developers used anodized bronze windows, EFIS (a textured stucco-like product applied over concrete block), and small balconies to create a stark but visually intriguing building. The somewhat ugly old school building became an attractive addition to the site separating the two architecturally different church buildings. Units in this building were designed to be affordable with an urban feel. An example is the exposed aluminum HVAC ductwork suspended from the 15-ft., black-painted ceilings. Hardwood flooring runs throughout the units, with the exception of the bathroom. Lafayette Loft Condominiums sold out before completion. Selling prices ranged from $84,000 to $260,000, with an average selling price of $170 per square foot. One member of the AMA Group commented that the units were likely priced below the market and could have commanded a higher price (R. Merry-Ship, personal communication, January 2008).

The oldest of the three buildings is the old sanctuary, now the Willow Avenue Condominiums. Unit sizes range from 600 sq. ft. to almost 1,000 sq. ft. The building interior was remodeled in the spirit of classicism with traditional elements and design considerations fitting with the building's

original design. Because the rehabilitation of this building benefited from federal historic preservation tax credits, the original owner was required to hold it for five years before selling the building or individual condominium units. The building has remained 90 percent occupied since completion. Rents range from $750 to $900 depending on the size of the unit. A final credit to the developers is that one of their competitors' daughters purchased a unit as her residence. Exhibit 18-5 shows St. Joseph Church, the former school, and the old sanctuary in their adaptive reuse.

Project Financing
The project was financed with a $4.5 million line of credit from the First Tennessee Bank of Memphis. The loan matured four years after closing, with a one-year interest-only construction period followed by a three-year carry period. The credit amount stepped down by $1.5 million at the end of years two, three, and four. The rate charged on the financing was the thirty-day LIBOR, plus two hundred basis points. Historic tax credits contributed to the financing of apartments in the original 1936 St. Joseph's Church.

Exhibit 18-6 shows the development costs for the twenty-five condo units in two phases. The total development costs were $4.3 million. Site acquisition was fairly high, at almost $1 million (24 percent of project cost). Site preparation and gutting the building were about 5 percent of total cost each. Building hard costs for construction were the lion's share of costs, at $2.4 million (55 percent). Project soft costs were a modest 8 percent, including architects, planners, and lawyers. Financing costs were 5 percent of total costs, as was the developer fee of $200,000, likewise at 5 percent. Revenues after sales commissions are projected to be $5.5 million, but this includes sale of

Exhibit 18-5 Lafayette Street Project Photographs and Plans

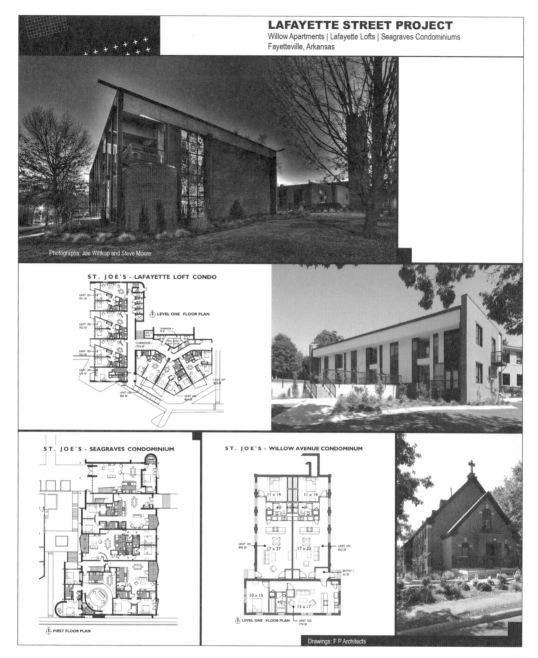

LAFAYETTE STREET PROJECT
Willow Apartments | Lafayette Lofts | Seagraves Condominiums
Fayetteville, Arkansas

Photographs: Joe Wittkop and Steve Moore

S T. J O E ' S - LAFAYETTE LOFT CONDO

S T. J O E ' S - SEAGRAVES CONDOMINIUM

S T. J O E ' S - WILLOW AVENUE CONDOMINUM

Drawings: F P Architects

two separately deeded existing houses, and two premium condo units remaining unsold as of early 2008. If all units are sold without excessive additional interest expense, profit will be a handsome 30 percent.

Exhibit 18-7 shows the development costs for the eight apartment units. The total development costs were $1.1 million. Site acquisition was fairly high, at $200,000 (19 percent of project cost). Site preparation was about 1 percent of total cost. Building hard costs for construction made up the

Exhibit 18-6 Lafayette Street Condos: Project Development Costs (25 units)

St. Joseph Church Campus Conversion   Fayetteville, AR

	FACTORS	DOLLAR AMOUNT	PERCENT OF PROJECT COST
Lot size (land square feet)	77,872		
Floor area ratio	0.48		
Gross building area	37,000		
Net usable space (100%)	95%		
# current owners	25		
# parking spaces	53		
DEVELOPMENT COST INFORMATION			
Land/site acquisition (including option), includes buildings	0	$996,000	23.37%
Site Preparation			
Remediation: removal of asbestos and roof repairs	0	$150,000	3.52%
Parkland development fees	0	$11,261	0.26%
Parking lot resurfacing	4	$32,000	0.75%
Construction Costs			
Gut building	$5.42	$200,444	4.70%
Construction costs	$54.86	$2,030,000	47.64%
Buyer finish allowance	$3.25	$120,267	2.82%
Total building hard costs	$63.53	$2,350,711	55.16%
Soft Costs			
Architect, planners, legal, surveying, power,	$0.00	$320,711	7.53%
Market analysis (internal)		$0	0.00%
Subtotal before construction loan	$0.00	$3,860,682	90.59%
Construction loan/carry one year term	8%, int. only	$200,444	4.70%
Subtotal	$0.00	$4,061,126	95.30%
Developer's fee	$0.00	$200,444	4.70%
TOTAL DEVELOPMENT COST		$4,261,571	100.00%
TOTAL DEVELOPMENT COST/SF building	$115.18		

Sales

	units	average sales price/ unit	total sales revenues
			$ -
Single family house	1	$75,000	$75,000
Duplex house	1	$155,000	$155,000
Church*	8	$365,000	$2,920,000
School	17	$144,000	$2,448,000
Total gross sales			$5,598,000
Commissions to the agents			$58,000
Net sales proceeds			$5,540,000
THE FUNDING (GAP) or SURPLUS		$1,278,429	
(GAP) SURPLUS AS % OF DEAL		30.00%	

Profit analysis

Project equity (20%)	$852,314	
Return -surplus plus developer fee		$1,478,874
Developers return on equity		173.51%

* Assume two unsold units @ $300,000 to be sold in 2008

Exhibit 18-7 "Old Sanctuary" Apartments/Condominiums

(8 apartments)	FACTORS	DOLLAR AMOUNT	PERCENT OF PROJECT COST
lot size	16,988		
floor area ratio	0.47		
gross building area	8,000		
net leasable space (90%)	8,000		
# current owners	1		
# parking spaces	14		
DEVELOPMENT COST INFORMATION			
land/site acquisition (including option)	$25.50	$204,000	18.88%
site preparation			
Remediation: removal of asbestos	$0.25	$2,124	0.20%
other site preparation incl parking	$4.00	$6,000	0.56%
		$-	0.00%
construction costs			
rehab and functional upgrades	$30.00	$240,000	
new finish	$55.00	$440,000	
total building hard costs	$85.00	$680,000	62.92%
soft costs			
legal		$50,000	4.63%
architect planners, etc.		$47,600	4.40%
market analysis		$-	0.00%
leasing fees		$-	0.00%
subtotal before construction loan		$989,724	91.58%
construction loan/carry one year term	10%, int. only	$39,589	3.66%
Subtotal		$1,029,312	95.24%
developer's fee	5%	$51,466	4.76%
TOTAL DEVELOPMENT COST		**$1,080,778**	100.00%
TOTAL DEVELOPMENT COST/SF building		$135.10	
ANNUAL OPERATING CASH FLOW			
Number of tenants	8		
market rent gross/month, weighted average	$0.92	$88,320	
market vacancy	5%	($4,416)	
other costs @20% of gross	$17,664	($17,664)	
government subsidies		$-	
Net operating income		$66,240	
Financing and Investment			
Value (NOI/Cap rate)*	10.00%	**$662,400**	
Debt Service (% 20 year amortization, 7 year b	0.109546	$58,051	
Before Tax Cash Flow		8,189	

bulk of costs, at $0.68 million (63 percent). Project soft costs were a modest 9 percent, including architects, planners, and lawyers. Financing costs were 4 percent of total costs, and the developer fee of $51,000 was 5 percent. Total development costs were $135 per building square foot.

Gross rent collections are about $90,000, and net operating income after expenses is projected to be $66,000 annually, yielding a total project value of $0.66 million. Projected debt service is about $58,000, yielding a pretax cash flow of $8,200. When the historic tax credits are factored in, the after-tax value to the developer is estimated to be $51,400 for the first five years, a return on equity of a little over 10 percent.

Marketing

The developers used their intuition rather than a formal real estate market analysis to determine what type of product would be accepted. Familiarity with Fayetteville and the success of other projects led them to conclude that the condominiums could be marketed to multiple target groups.

The target market groups included:

- purchasers from outside the market area but within the northeast Arkansas area, such as Bentonville, Rogers, and Springdale;
- University of Arkansas alumni looking for a second home;
- professionals employed by the University of Arkansas;
- investors who would rent out a leased condo as a fully furnished "executive boarding house" apartment;
- empty nesters wanting to downsize;
- Walmart vendors with a semipermanent residence in the area;
- Tyson Chicken employees; and
- Walton Arts Center patrons.

Lessons Learned

- *Active marketing by the seller:* Paul Warren's proactive actions on behalf of St. Joseph Catholic Church in meeting with potential developers and neighborhood residents and in speaking publicly about the project helped orchestrate the transaction.
- *Careful management of community approval process:* The developers effectively used links to a neighborhood homeowners' association to inquire about residents' concerns and to prepare responses to neighbors' objections about congestion and parking. The developers demonstrated that thirty-three additional dwellings, many occupied only part-time, would certainly cause less traffic than hundreds of church parishioners on Sunday and a kindergarten-through-seventh-grade elementary school.
- *Know your market:* The developers knew part of their market (small, well-designed units) and provided a product that purchasers enthusiastically accepted. These moderately priced units moved quickly.
- *Lack of a formal market niche analysis:* Without a market study, however, the developers misjudged demand for the less expensive units within the school. Three units resold within a year for over 30 percent more than the original selling price while two of the eight luxury units within St. Joseph Church remained unsold when this case study was conducted. Accordingly, the developers probably should have relied less on intuition and performed a thorough market niche analysis to determine actual market demand.

Conclusion

The success of this project can be attributed to several participants. The city of Fayetteville's public policy of simultaneously approving a development plan and rezoning encouraged the developer to pursue the project. The active involvement of the seller resulted in securing a purchase for the property. Finally, an experienced developer had a vision for the property being repurposed along with making a handsome profit. This project made sense in the market.

References and Works Consulted

Alexander, Merry-Ship & Alt. 2007. "Past Projects: The UARK Bowl Events Center." www .amaregi.com/projects.

City-Data.com. 2008. www.city-data.com.

City of Fayetteville Planning Commission. 2003. Meeting Minutes, May 1.

CNN Money Magazine. 2007. "Money Best Places to Live." http://money.cnn.com/magazines /moneymag/bplive/2007/snapshots/PL0523 290.html.

Partners for Livable Communities. 2007. "America's Most Livable Communities." Information Please Database. http://www.infoplease.com /ipa/A0931290.html.

Reed & Associates Inc. 2001. Real Estate Appraisers-Consultants, Appraisal of the St. Joseph Catholic Church Property, December 6.

St. Joseph Catholic Church and School. 2013. www.sjfay.com/church/welcome/history/.

Walter, M. 2003a. "Fayetteville St. Joseph Sold." *Arkansas Democrat Gazette,* August 23, Section: Business Matters.

———. 2003b. "Fayetteville Officials, Builders Skirmish over Restrictive Requirements for New Houses and Renovations." *Arkansas Democrat Gazette,* October 12, Section: Business Matters.

WEST TECH HIGH SCHOOL

Cleveland, Ohio

Robert A. Simons and

Gary DeWine

This complex and difficult project highlights major issues concerning how to best gauge developer capacity, balance community needs with community wants, extend a niche market not in proximity to the original location, and deal with large projects that are not easily divisible and may take five years or more to complete. The deal can be successful, but not always for the first or even second set of developers.

Introduction

West Tech High School is located near the intersection of West 93rd Street and Lorain Avenue, on the near west side of Cleveland in the Cudell neighborhood. It is about 5 miles from downtown and about 4 miles from the newly gentrified Warehouse District neighborhood. The area developed in the early twentieth century as a working-class community with industries located around the major rail lines that run through the area. Interstate highway I-90 is about ¼ mile away. Existing housing stock in the area is primarily one- and two-family houses of wood-frame construction built in the early 1900s and is generally in stable to substandard condition. About half of the neighborhood residents are of low to moderate income.

West Tech High School was constructed in 1912. It closed as a public high school in the fall of 1996, after eighty years of service, due to shifting population trends. It was sold by the Cleveland Municipal School District in 2000 to an out-of-state developer, "Green" (the names of some participants in this project have been changed).

The redevelopment plan for West Tech included the subdivision of the site into two residential projects. First, the 368,000-sq.-ft. school building complex (multiwing high school building and gymnasium) would house 189 market-rate and subsidized apartments. Second, the balance of the 20-acre property would be developed into thirty-four new market-rate single-family homes and twelve townhouses.

However, when one of the original developer team members pulled out, the remaining principal convinced the local government stakeholders that his experience with a similar adaptive reuse project in Dayton, Ohio, qualified him to complete the project alone. The financial guarantors of the West Tech project agreed to allow him to close on the loan with a letter of credit, but without project bonding, according to Dennis Morton, the HUD administrator at the time of the project (November 2007).

Renovation of the project was complex, and the remaining principal developer was soon floundering. Confronted with evidence of widespread shoddy construction, the lender called the letter of credit, effectively stopping the project from moving forward in its current form. When it became evident that the remaining developer could not complete the project, the West Tech project was offered to the firm holding the letter of credit, the Orlean Company, an Ohio firm with development and management experience of over 4,200 apartments along with other real estate interests. Orlean managed the project for about four years, achieving an occupancy rate of about 55 percent.

In 2007 Orlean had defaulted on its HUD-insured mortgage of $14 million.[1] At the time of the default, Orlean had rented only slightly over half of the 189 loft apartments. The rental income was not sufficient to cover debt service and operating costs, creating a cash flow problem. Public officials blamed a soft market for the default. The local elected councilperson who had supported the redevelopment of the historic school stated, "It was nothing the owners did wrong."

Review of public documents and interviews with management indicate the initially projected rents were well beyond market prices. The developers estimated in their HUD multifamily mortgage insurance application that rents would be $693 for a one-bedroom, $1,100 for a two-bedroom, and $1,200–$1,300 for a three-bedroom apartment. These estimates were too optimistic. The subsidized units proved easy to rent. Most of the market-rate units, however, were not absorbed, and rents were lowered substantially in hopes of attracting tenants. When this case study was initially conducted in mid-2008, the project was still struggling to attract tenants willing to pay market-rate rents, and a substantial number of apartments remained unoccupied due to construction-related issues. The cost of the project had ballooned to over $34 million, with only $20.5 million attributable to actual construction costs. At the beginning of 2013, when the project was under the new ownership and management, the actual rents were just below the rent levels projected in 2000.

The second portion of the reuse of West Tech High included a housing project on vacant fields called the West Tech Residential Development and Parkside Homes. The developer was Rysar Properties, a locally well-known Cleveland housing developer, who had extensive experience in new housing construction in Cleveland's central city neighborhoods. This project involved the platting and subdivision of the former athletic fields into a subdivision of forty-six single-family homes and town houses, priced between $170,000 and $200,000. A total of twenty-five units were built and sold, but the remaining twenty-one units remain undeveloped. The subprime-induced soft market put the brakes on sales, to the extent that substantially reduced pricing was ineffective in generating buyer inter-

est. The new construction portion of the West Tech project missed the strong housing market window and became a hard sell.

This case study seeks to explain the risks involved in a bold undertaking by a succession of developers inexperienced in adaptive reuse, in the conversion of West Tech into 189 apartments with over sixty different floor plans.

Site History

West Tech High School opened as a vocational high school in 1912. Additions were made to the building in 1922 and 1949, and a separate gym was built in 1972. West Tech became the largest high school in the state of Ohio, with enrollment exceeding five thousand students. The physical plant of the building is 368,000 sq. ft., with three stories and a basement. It features extremely wide (12-ft.) hallway corridors (suitable for containing periodic surges of rambunctious high school students) that face two interior courtyards. The main school building is of neoclassical design constructed of high-quality brickwork features. Decorative elements on the facade include terra-cotta reliefs depicting wreaths, books, and garlands. The building was placed on the National Register of Historic Places in 2002 to qualify for historic tax credits.

West Tech High was closed by a federal district judge's court order in the fall of 1996, after more than eighty years of public school service. The city of Cleveland's declining school-age population, coupled with a negative public perception of the school district, contributed to the school's demise. Cleveland residents moving to the suburbs at a rapid pace further accelerated declining enrollment in the urban school district, which dropped from over 150,000 in the late 1960s to under fifty thousand students in 2008 (Ott 2008).

The building sat unsecured for the next four years. Unimpeded access to the building allowed vandals to create a playground for destruction of the interior. The stage area of the auditorium was severely damaged by arson. The Building Department condemned the building in order to facilitate the property's reuse by making it available sooner, and the city sold the property in December 2000 through a request-for-proposal process (D. Morton, personal communication, November 2007). The buyer paid $230,975 for the site. (See Exhibit 19-1.)

Exhibit 19-1 West Tech Site Location and Site Plan

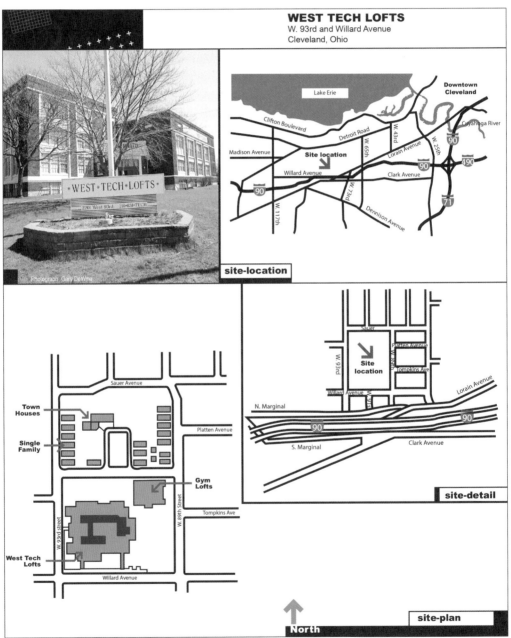

Market Conditions

The city of Cleveland had a total population of 478,403 in the 2000 U.S. Census, making it the thirty-third largest city in the nation and the second largest city in Ohio. The city's estimated population in July 2006 was 444,313, a reduction of 7.1 percent from the previous census figures (see Exhibit 19-2).

There were 190,725 households in the city in 2000, 26.27 percent of whom lived below

Exhibit 19-2 Census Data 2000 and 2007

	Ohio	Cuyahoga	Cleveland City	Census Tract 1011.01
Population				
2000	11,353,140	1,393,978	478,393	2,163
2007	11,466,917	1,295,958	395,310	
% Change	1.00%	-7.03%	-17.37%	
Age (2000)				
Less than 18	25.41%	24.92%	28.46%	19.37%
22 - 39	24.93%	24.71%	27.02%	37.03%
40 -59	26.82%	26.24%	22.83%	26.03%
60 and over	17.27%	19.60%	16.20%	12.07%
Median Household Income				
2000	$40,956	$39,168	$25,928	$21,761
2007	$46,597	$44,358	$28,512	
% Change	13.77%	13.25%	9.97%	
Race (2000)				
White alone	84.92%	67.41%	41.72%	56.54%
Black or African American alone	11.35%	27.27%	50.69%	26.40%
American Indian and Alaska Native alone	0.24%	0.17%	0.29%	0.00%
Asian alone	1.16%	1.85%	1.44%	6.84%
Hawaiian and Pacific Islander alone	0.02%	0.02%	0.04%	0.00%
Some other race alone	0.79%	1.52%	3.60%	5.50%
Two or more races	1.53%	1.75%	2.22%	4.72%
Education (2000)				
Bachelor or higher	21.10%	25.15%	11.43%	17.89%
High school above age 25	36.09%	30.04%	33.19%	32.18%
Unemployment				
2000	3.22%	3.86%	6.44%	3.03%
Housing (2000)				
Households	4,446,621	571,606	190,725	1,115
Housing Units	4,783,051	616,903	215,844	1,169
Owner Occupied Units (%)	69.11%	63.17%	48.52%	21.87%
Renter Units (%)	30.89%	36.83%	51.48%	78.13%
Median Rent Apartment	$515	$541	$465	$434
Median House Value (Owner Occupied)	$100,500	$110,100	$71,100	$57,300

Source: 2000 and 2007 U.S. Census
Note: 2007 tract data is not available

the poverty level. That figure is about double the poverty rate for Cuyahoga County (13.13 percent) and the state (10.6 percent). The violent crime rate recorded in Cleveland was 1.69 per one thousand people, which is high when compared to the rate for Cuyahoga County (City-Data.com 2008).

Demographics of Housing Market

The 2000 census showed that 88.3 percent of the city of Cleveland's 215,856 housing units were occupied, while the county had a 92.6 percent occupancy rate. The home-ownership rate in Ohio was 69.1 percent compared with 63.1 percent in the county, but only 48.5 percent in the city of Cleveland. Cleveland's median gross rent in the year 2000 was $465, lower than the $541 recorded by the county. The average sale price of single-family houses in Cleveland was $62,000, much less than the average price of $124,800 in Cuyahoga County. The two-family structure sale price in Cleveland was $53,334, also below the county average of $69,831. Condominiums sold for about $83,000 in Cleveland, higher than the county's average of $60,293 (U.S. Department of Commerce, Bureau of the Census 2000).

Within a ¼-mile radius of the West Tech site, neighborhood disinvestment is evident. The area is about 73 percent white, and median household income in 2000 was approximately $30,000, higher than the city average but below that of the county. The poverty rate was reported at 30 percent. Very few adults in the neighborhood had a college degree. Housing vacancy, rents, and housing sales prices were about at the city average (U.S. Department of Commerce, Bureau of the Census 2000).

Redevelopment Process

The closure of West Tech was attributed to the lack of students. Community activists disagreed, and asserted that the school district's justification for closing the building was based on the school system's inability to keep kids in public school. The school district has since been reorganized and is under the management of the city of Cleveland. In an interesting twist of irony, the Cleveland School District unveiled plans in 2004 to build a new school on a 15-acre site in the West Tech neighborhood at a cost of $42 million. The new school will relieve overcrowding at three west-side high schools.

The community and construction stakeholders in the redevelopment process of the West Tech School building included the following:

- Cleveland Public Schools (original owner)
- West Tech Alumni Association
- city of Cleveland and Cleveland city council (government partner), represented by the local city councilman
- Cudell Improvement, Inc. (local community development corporation)
- "White" Architects (fee architect)
- "Blue" Construction (fee construction manager)
- "Red" (initial developer, with two entities, "Brown" and "Green")
- the Orlean Company (guarantor of a $2.1 million letter of credit and developer and manager through November 2008)
- U.S. Department of Housing and Urban Development (HUD) (project funder)
- Cleveland Development Partners (nonprofit Cleveland advocacy group)
- NPI/Village Capital Corp. (not-for-profit gap financing lender)
- Rysar Properties (developer of on-site single-family homes)
- state of Ohio (Department of Development loan)
- National City Bank (bought tax credit equity)

- Resource Real Estate Inc. (purchaser of the defaulted $14.5 million mortgage for $2.9 million in late 2007)
- Monarch Investment Group (purchased the property in the spring of 2012)

The building was saved from the wrecking ball through the efforts of community supporters and the West Tech Alumni Association, composed of (presumably nostalgic) former West Tech students, faculty, and staff. The association passed a resolution to "encourage, support, and endorse redevelopment programs that seek to perpetuate and preserve West Technical High School, its building and property as a whole or in significant portions thereof" (H. Davis, personal communication, April 2007). Proposals that surfaced included an employment training and family recreation facility. A local builder proposed razing the building and developing the entire project as single-family housing, but the proposal eventually chosen was to adaptively reuse the school as apartments along with new housing construction.

Public subsidies were definitely available. Since 1990, the city of Cleveland has offered fifteen-year property-tax abatements on new home construction, forgivable second mortgages, land bank lots (from property acquired through property tax foreclosure), and other inducements to facilitate housing development and to attract and retain middle-income residents. This policy made it potentially attractive to acquire a site such as West Tech for demolition and new construction between the late 1990s and the subprime mortgage crisis beginning at the end of 2006.[2]

The plan that was eventually implemented was the result of collaboration by the West Tech Alumni Association, the local Cleveland ward councilman, and local community organizations, including Cudell Improvement Corporation. Cleveland has a long history of strong, neighborhood-based, nonprofit local development corporations providing leadership to encourage and guide development and redevelopment activities. The Cudell Improvement Corporation was the lead organization in soliciting and advancing plans for reuse of West Tech. It was instrumental in the hiring of "White" Architects, a Cleveland-based architectural firm specializing in historic preservation.

The architects prepared both the plans for the conversion of the building to apartments and the application for the building to be placed on the National Register of Historic Places. The latter made the building rehabilitation costs eligible for federal historic tax credits.

The city of Cleveland purchased the building from the Cleveland Metropolitan School District for approximately $110,000. The city then solicited requests for proposals from forty developers. A Technical Advisory Committee and Community Advisory Board were set up by the Ward 18 city councilman to review proposals for the adaptive reuse of West Tech. The committees recommended the "Red" partnership of the "Brown" and "Green" firms. This recommendation was forwarded to the city of Cleveland's director of community development for review. Overall, "Brown" had experience in at least two other historic tax credit projects, one in Ohio (150 units) and the other in California (280 units). However, they abruptly withdrew as the developer of West Tech, leaving only "Green" as the remaining entity.

The city, anxious to move forward with the project, allowed "Green" to proceed alone. As a condition of proceeding, "Green" obtained a $2.1 million letter of credit from the Orlean Company. Orlean was to be paid $50,000 at the successful end of the rehab, and an Orlean subsidiary was also offered the management contract for the property.

Orlean's engagement in the letter of credit would turn out to be a pivotal development for this project.

The West Tech building contained many of the structural and construction peculiarities of a building of its vintage. Because benign neglect had set in even before its closure due to the lack of capital improvement monies available to the Cleveland Metropolitan School District, the building was in poor condition. Operational issues included the need for complete reroofing of the building, as well as abatement of asbestos and lead-based paint. The Cleveland Metropolitan School District, like other inner-city school districts, had a subpar record of preventative maintenance of its operating school buildings—and closed schools are even a lower priority. So when West Tech was closed, it was not adequately secured or maintained (D. Morton, personal communication, November 2007).

Development Plan
Initial Change of Ownership
The initial developer for the property was "Green," a California investment group, which acted as both developer and general contractor. "Green" was the developer when the city of Cleveland shut construction down in the spring of 2002, with about 25 percent of the work complete. The developer/contractor had failed to make payments on construction loans, and was not paying subcontractors. In addition, the work was not meeting the city building code. In fact, according to the city of Cleveland building commissioner, a roofing system was not installed properly. Sadly, openings in the roof of the auditorium had not been made weathertight, causing substantial water damage to the interior. The work was deemed substandard, and the city ordered it removed and replaced (D. Morton,

personal communication, November 2007).

The U.S. Department of Housing and Urban Development's Cleveland office (holder of the mortgage) took the steps necessary to force "Green" off the project. The work completed prior to shutdown included demolition, lead-based paint abatement, and asbestos removal. The company had spent almost $9 million, half of the budget, but completed only 25 percent of the construction. "[Green]," in the words of the HUD administrator, "did not know what he was doing" (D. Morton, personal communication, November 2007).

In November 2002, the Orlean Company and National City Development Corporation (buyer of the low-income housing tax credits) formed a relationship to redevelop the property with "Blue" acting as the new fee construction manager. The Orlean Company had signed a letter of credit in the amount of $2.1 million for the previous developer, and stepped in to assume the developer role with the intention of completing the project when it was recapitalized with additional loans and grants.

The Orlean Company came into the picture as a father-and-son team who managed 4,200 apartment units, a nursing home, and a trailer park in northern Ohio, along with a mortgage business and other interests.[3] Orlean had some previous experience in building rehabilitation, but no direct experience in adaptive reuse or historic preservation. When notified that they "owned the project," Orlean could have walked away, thus limiting their losses to the amount of the letter of credit ($2.1 million). They instead made the expensive decision to step into the developer's shoes.

The city of Cleveland, through the mayor's office and Community Development Department, persuaded Orlean to finish the project with the incentive of recapturing the $2.1 million letter of credit through the sale of the to-be-subdivided athletic fields. The Orlean team, according to the project manager on the West Tech site, believed "that the city would be a safety net" (H. Davis, personal communication, April 2007). This false sense of security led it to take over the project when hindsight suggests that it should have been abandoned. The developers were also swayed by the mayor's pleas for them to continue. The city's initial plan did not permit the school's athletic fields to be developed until 95 percent of the apartment units were rented. By mutual agreement this requirement was changed. In the hopes of generating cash flow for the owners from another market segment, the decision was made to separate the reuse and new construction projects and allow Rysar Homes (also a partner in the main school rehab part of the project) to commence the construction of the new housing.

Construction Headaches

The city had recommended "Blue," a major Cleveland-area building contractor, as construction manager. This well-connected and active firm is now recognized as an expert in the rehabilitation field, and had been successful in projects similar to West Tech. The financial arrangement was such that "Blue" was to receive cost, plus a 3 percent management fee. "Blue" inherited the headaches of the numerous subcontractors hired by "Green." As an example, the drywall contract went from $1 million to $3.8 million. The construction team soon realized that the subcontractors were in over their heads. According to David Orlean, "Blue" changed drywall contractors, but the new firm also had substantial cost overruns, partly because the architectural drawings appeared to be insufficiently detailed to allow sufficiently accurate cost estimates. Because

"Blue" was a fee construction manager—as opposed to a general contractor with a fixed bid amount—cost overruns were passed along to the developer (D. Orlean, personal communication, November 2008).

"White" Architects, who had prepared the application for historic tax credits, was retained to prepare cost estimates for construction and to prepare construction drawings. In the opinion of one of the West Tech project managers, the architect was more interested in style than function. This was evidenced by one apartment suite, known as the "suite from hell," which contains a spiral staircase immediately next to and within the entrance swath of a bedroom door. The stairway "is a head injury waiting to happen." (H. Davis, personal communication, April 2007) Also, some suites present challenges when tenants move in and out, as narrow stairways and spiral staircases cannot be easily negotiated.

A final source of frustration for the owner, as cited by Orlean's project manager, was the conversion of the gym into apartment units. A total of sixteen three-story loft apartments were built within the gym shell. A central corridor provides access to eight units on each side. The original beams and trusses were left exposed along the roof, making a visually interesting space. While high on style, the conversion suffered from some fundamental design issues. Adequate soundproofing was either not specified or not installed between the units. Thus, an alarm clock ringing in one unit would wake the tenant sleeping next door. Consequently, only half of the sixteen units could be rented until the sound issue was corrected. The original construction drawings, prepared by the architect, omitted windows being installed on the outside walls of the gym. When added later, this item significantly increased project costs. The discovery that the original gym floor was contaminated with mercury (surprise!) added a $400,000 remediation cost and delayed work. Changing contractual relationships between owners and main consultants meant roles were not often adequately defined, and the contactors' incentive structure was less than optimum with respect to cost-effective outcomes.

The project developer, architect, contractor, and the city quickly soured on the project. Construction drawings, though not totally accurate, were followed literally by the contractor. This resulted in cost overruns, and daily change orders became necessary to correct errors that could have been avoided with revised drawings. Many design issues remained uncorrected, and several units could not be rented until the problems were corrected under new ownership. The contingency budget for the project was depleted and Orlean, after a personal investment of over $4 million, was unwilling to put more cash in to correct construction-related issues.

The second owner (Orlean) learned too late that the historic preservation architect did not adequately delineate the full scope of work, leading to substantial cost overruns (D. Orlean, personal communication, November 2008). Anticipated cost savings in the purchase of replacement windows were lost when historic preservation requirements forced the developers to use twenty different window styles rather than the two originally planned. Eleven hundred new windows had to be fabricated, costing hundreds of thousands of additional dollars. The National Park Service added (assuming they had been informed earlier) a requirement that all exposed heating ducts had to be painted—well after the ducts had been installed. This item alone cost over $70,000. A final insult was that the newly painted HVAC ductwork suspended from the ceiling had to be disassembled and relocated so that it could not be seen from the street in order to satisfy additional National Park Service historic preservation requirements, though the original location had been approved prior to construction.

Marketing and Absorption

This low-income housing tax credit (LIHTC) project was planned to contain both affordable units, consisting of thirty-eight one- and two-bedroom apartments (20 percent), and 151 market-rate apartments (80 percent), for a total of 189 units.

The plan was for West Tech—located approximately 5 miles from downtown Cleveland—to be marketed to young professionals as an alternative to the relatively successful downtown Warehouse District. As Cleveland's rental market became soft, the Warehouse District struggled to maintain occupancy. Units in the Warehouse District offered concessions and free rent to compete for a very mobile population. According to Dennis Morton, the HUD administrator at the time of the project, Cleveland was in the throes of the worst rental market seen in nearly forty years. When West Tech began to rent up in 2003, absorption was very slow.

Assumptions were made (primarily by way of the comparables included in a consultant's market study) that this property would be an alternative to, and compete with, the historic Warehouse District. The Warehouse District is within walking distance of Cleveland's central business district. The Warehouse District has a distinct fabric of restored buildings, which serve as a home to architectural, advertising, and graphic art firms. In addition, the Warehouse District is home to a myriad of restaurants, galleries, shops, businesses, and nightlife, which creates a sense of place. However, the West Tech area lacks this synergy. The west side of the city of Cleveland (where West Tech is located) does offer some amenities lacking in downtown Cleveland. These include twenty-four-hour pharmacies, all-night and late-night fast food restaurants, large supermarkets, video stores, free all-day parking, and local schools. However, a major detriment to marketing the neighborhood is the poverty of the residents and the high crime rate. At the end of the day, marketing the property has been a steep uphill climb. In retrospect, to think West Tech was an alternative to the trendy historic Warehouse District young, upwardly mobile neighborhood was misguided.

In terms of actual project absorption, the affordable apartments proved easy to rent. The market-rate apartments became problematic for various reasons. The on-premises rental manager indicated that when she came on board, the rents for the market-rate apartments were too high for the location. Rents were reduced from an average of $1,100 to about $950 to accommodate the market. However, all print advertising was required to indicate the complex had low-income units—even though none might be available at that time—implying that the whole project was low-income housing. The connotation may have deterred higher-income tenants, expected to pay market rents.

To the credit of the management team, the building is a safe, secure, and clean facility. Security within West Tech is highly satisfactory (H. Davis, personal communication, April 2007). The neighborhood has documented issues of drug and gang activity, but a keyless entry system has kept neighborhood problems outside. Unfortunately, this is not widely known. A member of the Cleveland Browns football team was attracted to the complex when told about it by another player who was a resident. He was stopped by the Cleveland police while searching for the property due to West Tech's semiobscure location. The police, upon realizing his identity, reportedly "strongly encouraged" him to consider other housing options (H. Davis, personal communication, April 2007).

A final nail in the marketing coffin was that the budget was too low to advertise to the renting public. Having tapped all available corporate and personal funds in an attempt to finish the project, the owners found it difficult to adequately fund an aggressive marketing campaign. Starting in late 2007, the owner made a conscious decision not to throw good money after bad—Orlean saw the writing on the wall. The time line shown in Exhibit 19-3 notes significant events.

Exhibit 19-3 West Tech Time Line

1996	2000	2001	2002	2003	2006	2007	2008	2012
School closed	Sold by city of Cleveland to "Green"	HUD approves mortgage insurance	Spring 2002 rehab work suspended	First tenants move into West Tech	Default on first mortgage by Orlean	Mortgage bought at auction by Philadelphia real estate investor RRE for $2.9 million	Property transfers to purchaser of HUD mortgage RRE for $4.5 million	Colorado-based Monarch Investments purchases property for $6.56 million with 96% occupancy

Project Financing

This is a complex deal that changed substantially over its five-year development period under the original mixed LIHTC-market mix concept. The analysis presented below excludes the for-sale housing on the football fields (discussed later), and reflects only the 368,000-sq.-ft. school building complex. The sources of funds (2001–4) and uses of funds (as built, 2004 only) are discussed below. After that, two snapshots of cash flows for the latest period (2007) and 2003 projections are shown in Exhibit 19-4. This section ends with some cost summaries and estimates of current valuation.

Sources of Funds

The major source of funds for West Tech was a HUD 221(d) 4 Substantial Rehabilitation Mortgage Guarantee. This was a high-profile and important HUD project, and there were hopes that it would lead to the revitalization of the West Tech neighborhood. The HUD funding was originally for $12.5 million and grew to $14.7 million as project costs escalated. Investor equity included an originally budgeted $5.9 million in LIHTC and historic tax credits. National City Bank, which was absorbed by PNC Bank at the end of the Great Recession, was the buyer. These credits increased somewhat as more eligible costs were incurred. The project's second owner (Orlean) contributed additional funds, increasing developer equity. The City of Cleveland Development Fund provided a $3 million low-interest loan from a large-scale economic development and housing project fund. Cleveland Development Partners, a well-capitalized not-for-profit group, provided gap financing of $1.2 million. The letter of credit of the Orlean Company was also in the deal for $2.1 million. The state of Ohio, acting through the Cuyahoga County Department of Development, provided a

$1.5 million loan for asbestos and lead paint remediation.

Funds needed to adequately renovate the West Tech school building project grew from a projected $22.6 million in 2001 to $34 million in 2004, an increase of 50 percent.

Uses of Funds

As the second half of Exhibit 19-4 shows, costs for the nearly completed project (minus soundproofing and other minor build-out items) for the school building complex through September 2004 were $34 million. The largest single item was construction hard costs ($20.2 million, or 59.5 percent). Soft costs for architecture and site acquisition costs were very low (each less than 2 percent of project budget). Environmental issues were about 4 percent of the project budget. Unplanned contingencies and overruns exceeded 10 percent of the project (based on the $34 million figure), and ended up being higher than projected by about $1 million. When unbudgeted cost overruns and operating deficits are added in, required sources of funds ended up being over $36.9 million. Total costs based on the $34 million figure average to $179,600 per dwelling unit, or $92.27 per gross square foot of building area. Net cost per leasable area is in excess of $130 per square foot. These figures do not take into account the lot split that took place for the new single-family and townhome construction, or any costs or revenues related to construction of the forty-six for-sale units.

2003 and 2007 Cash Flows

Obviously the original building cash flows did not meet expectations. Exhibit 19-5 shows the projected 2003 and actual (unaudited) 2007 cash flows. The building size (368,000 sq. ft.), number of low-income units (forty), number of market-rate units

Exhibit 19-4 Sources and Uses of Funds—West Tech High School Project

Sources of Funds

	Oct. 2001	Oct. 2003	Aug. 2004
HUD Insured Mortgage	$12,500,000	$14,690,000	$14,690,000
Ohio Dept. of Development	1,500,000	1,500,000	1,500,000
Investor Equity	5,894,766	8,827,889	8,827,889
City of Cleveland Development Fund	2,000,000	3,300,000	3,300,000
Cleveland Development Partners	700,000	1,200,000	1,200,000
Letter of Credit from Orlean Co.		2,077,000	2,077,000
Architect Fee Give-Back		461,308	461,308
Cleveland Gund Foundation		450,000	450,000
"Green" Develop. Fee Hold-Back		148,619	148,619
City of Cleveland Ward Funding			300,000
National City Community Development Corporation			1,000,000
TOTALS	**$22,594,766**	**$32,654,816**	**$33,954,816**

Uses of Funds			Aug. 2004
Site Acquisition			$600,000
Site Prep			
Environmental Remediation			1,277,764
Demolition/Cleanout			954,459
Roofing / Weatherization			396,419
Security			408,323
Construction Costs			
Land Improvements			477,457
Construction Management			588,465
General Contractor Overhead			58,329
Rehabilitation and Construction			20,214,273
General Requirements			1,713,724
Contingency			2,721,161
Hard Cost Overruns			787,760
Soft Costs			
Architect			550,000
Legal and Organizational			444,119
Interest, Taxes, Insurance			
Misc HUD, Loan Feed, Title and Recording, Bond Principal, Ohio Dept. of Development Partial Payment			1,738,306
Bond Premium and Fees			135,760
Escrow and Working Capital			829,430
Developer's Fee			59,067
SUBTOTAL USE OF FUNDS			**$33,954,816**
Unfunded Cost Overruns			978,034
Deficits for Operating and Debt Service			**2,006,000**
Total Uses of Funds			$36,938,850
Total GAP as of 9/2004			2,984,034

(149), and low-income monthly average rental rates ($475) were the only projections that were reasonably accurate. Expenses, with the exception of utilities, were close to the mark. Market rents in 2007 were $950 per month, well below the projected $1,100 figure. Vacancy was 40 percent, much higher than the 5 percent in the 2003 pro forma. Annual revenues were only about 35 percent of the projected amount ($2.12 million projected versus $780,000 actual). Operating expenses as calculated were only about 2 percent over the projected amount ($790,000); however, this figure excludes property taxes, and the utility figure is for a half-empty building.

In terms of property values that would support a loan, at an assumed cap rate of 8 percent and a net operating income of $1.349 million as projected in 2003 (assuming this is an attainable stable-year figure), the project would be worth $16 million. However,

this value is less than the $22.6 million it was expected to cost to build. Although it was enough to support considerable debt service, it probably could not have supported the amount of debt service actually incurred. The actual value of the project in 2007 based on cash flow is zero because the project has a negative net operating income and cannot support even its operating expenses. At most, even with full lease-up and optimistic assumptions (in a flat market, in a recession) the project would be worth well under $10 million, or less than one-third of its cost![4]

January 2013 Update for West Tech School Building

After the loan default, Resource Real Estate Inc. (RRE) of Philadelphia bought the $14 million HUD mortgage for $2.9 million in late 2007. An outside receiver then managed the property for over a year. In September 2009, RRE foreclosed on the property and

Exhibit 19-5 Cash Flow, West Tech 2003 and 2007

	Projected 2003	Unaudited Actual Data 2007
Revenues		
LIHTC rentals	$228,000	$206,758
Market rentals	1,966,800	536,819 (actual)
Less vacancy @5%	98,340	NA
Other rental revenues	25,000	33,105
TOTAL REVENUES	**$2,121,460**	**$776,682**
Expenses		
Property taxes	$36,800	Not expensed
Util. & oper. expenses	368,000	344,243
Insurance	184,000	125,340
Maintenance and repair	46,000	2,669
Building maint. admin.	120,866	62,803
Management fee	127,288	122,889
Total expenses	**$762,088**	**$778,810**
Net Operating Income	**$1,359,372**	**($2,128)**

Note: utility expenses for 2007 is only for half-occupied building

bought several notes to take clear title of West Tech. It formed RRE HUD MF 2007, LLC as owner of the property. Cuyahoga County Auditor records show that $4.5 million was paid for the property (the $2.9 million HUD insured mortgage, plus purchasing $1.6 million of notes secured by the property).

The RRE foreclosure wiped away all encumbrances and tax credit requirements. RRE operated the property for a three-year period, and changed the tenant base from 20 percent low income and 80 percent market, to 100 percent market rentals. RRE, substantially the third owner of West Tech, then sold the building to Monarch Investment and Management Group of Franktown, Colorado, with 96 percent of the 189 units occupied, in early 2012. The purchase price was $6.56 million, as per Cuyahoga County Auditor records (2013). Monarch manages 10,500 apartment units, mostly in the Midwest. Brian Polley, Monarch's regional manager for northern and southern Michigan, said his company was able to secure the property at a price that allows it to hold the lofts profitably for a long time (Bullard 2012). According to Monarch Executive Manager Chuck Lavezzi, the project is cash-flowing nicely in January 2013, and continues to be a profitable investment. To resolve the project's parking deficiency, Monarch is negotiating to acquire land originally slated for fifteen housing building lots directly adjacent to the former high school building from the Rysar-Orlean group, which confirms negotiations for sale (D. Orlean, personal communication, January 2013).

For-Sale Housing on the West Tech Football Fields

In addition to the West Tech school rehabilitation into apartments, the deal also included development of the 15-acre sports fields into for-sale housing. The builder-developer team selected to undertake this project included Orlean as developer and financier and Rysar Properties as the homebuilder. Rysar had a long-standing reputation in Cleveland for successfully building and rehabbing single-family houses. Under the direction of president and CEO Ken Lurie, Rysar grew from a home-rehabbing outfit, buying and rehabbing five units at a time, to one of the largest housing producers in the metro area. Since 1991, Rysar had renovated and built nearly two thousand homes in every size and style—from lofts to single-family homes—in communities throughout Greater Cleveland. Rysar had done several projects both in weaker markets and larger scale than the forty-six-unit West Tech deal. It seemed like the for-sale portion of this deal would be a way to recover some of the losses the apartment project was experiencing. This was not to be the case.

The Orlean Company, which owned the land in 2005 when the for-sale housing deal was initiated, formed a land partnership with Rysar and transferred the football field land to this new company in a 50–50 split. David Orlean and Ken Lurie are childhood friends who have worked together on several other real estate projects. The team sailed through a zoning hearing with the city of Cleveland, and the football field was rezoned to allow both single- and multifamily housing. Forty-six dwellings were planned for the football field: thirty-four single-family and twelve town houses. The hope was that the synergy would help both parts of the West Tech project.

The partnership valued the land at $130,000. The total out-of-pocket site preparation cost for the forty-six housing lots was $790,000. This included cleaning up the site, planning, engineering, and installing water, sewer, roads, etc. This results in out-of-pocket costs of $17,300 per parcel and a total ready-to-build lot price of $20,000, or about 10 percent of the expected average sale price of $200,000. Streets were laid in, and the single-family part of the building site was ready to go in 2005.

Homes were initially priced in the $170,000–$200,000 range. Each house is eligible for a "free" city-provided second mortgage of $10,000 and property tax abatement for fifteen years. Things went fine at first. Twelve of the single-family homes sold over an eighteen-month period, with the last sale in late 2006. However, at that point the subprime mortgage problem began to emerge, and financing for end users began to dry up. In 2008, nine units were unsold for over eighteen months, and none of the townhomes had sold. Even dropping the asking price by up to 25 percent did not produce a sale. Undoubtedly the market is mostly to blame, as the city, like the nation as a whole, was mired in the subprime contraction of the housing market. Credit became tight, and buyers had trouble qualifying for a loan. Also, the adjacent West Tech project, which was not fully leased in 2008 and in mortgage default, was a detriment in marketing the for-sale housing (K. Lurie, personal communication, June 2008). The for-sale housing missed the market window, and rather than providing a boost to the West Tech building, the projects were dragging each other down.

The future of this project is unclear, according to Ken Lurie. It became a disaster for the partners, and they tried to seek help from other funding sources in a tight credit market. The partnership was unable to pay Cudell, the local development corporation, its fees from housing sales. Rysar had an inventory of 120 homes from other projects in Cleveland when the economy turned sour, and although a few of the projects were saved, the firm was unable to independently survive the housing market shakeout. As of January 2013, twenty-five of the forty-six lots were developed for housing and sold, leaving twenty-one lots. Of these, fifteen are likely to be sold to Monarch for parking, leaving eleven lots to be retained for sale when the housing market recovers (K. Lurie, personal communication, January 2013). (See Exhibit 19-6.)

Lessons Learned

Had West Tech been a smaller project, it might have succeeded soon enough to benefit the first or second developer. The main accomplishment is that a derelict 368,000-sq.-ft. building was spared the wrecking ball. A community eyesore was handsomely rehabilitated at great expense, but it became a white elephant for several years, and funds invested in the project will likely never be recovered (D. Orlean, personal communication, November 2008). The size of this building is by far the largest of any case in this book, and probably made the project less workable because its development was not divisible into market-sized components, not to mention bad luck with respect to market conditions. Once the worst of the housing market downturn had passed, and the project's value was downsized from over $36 million to about $7 million, the project was able to sustain itself after conversion to strictly market-rate housing. Now on its fourth owner, the project appears to be stable and profitable, but at a tremendous loss of public and private money.[5]

- *Too big to phase is not good:* The project size was also associated with a large proportion of hallways, which were dead space and could not be rented out. The net leasable space in this project was very low (well below 70 percent), and the heating costs are potentially exorbitant. Operating expenses were underestimated and in

Exhibit 19-6 West Tech Photographs

WEST TECH LOFTS
W. 93rd and Willard Avenue
Cleveland, Ohio

single family homes

gym lofts

town homes

Photographs: Gary DeWine

some cases never properly projected. No one accounted for the heating of acres of 12-ft.-wide hallways, with their 10-ft.-high double-hung windows. These common areas proved costly to heat in the cold Cleveland winters. Consequently, in late 2008, net operating income appeared to barely meet operating and management expenses, leaving insufficient funds to support mortgage payments.

- *Political will alone cannot create a successful project:* While intentions in the West Tech redevelopment were good, many important signals were missed. A novice developer, "Green," was allowed access to capital in the form of loans, tax credit funds, and grants to undertake a project that would make a seasoned developer shiver. "Brown," which had accomplished smaller adaptive reuse projects, chose to exit and probably made the best decision of any early player in this deal. Cleveland city hall and HUD, each wanting to be a facilitator and bring the RFP selection process to closure, embraced the novice developer without fully taking into account the risks he presented. Civic aspirations of improving the West Tech neighborhood and getting the building rehabilitated probably clouded good judgment. The driving forces behind the West Tech reuse were the high school's alumni association, a local development corporation that derives major portions of funding from the city, and the ward councilman. An impetus for development was that the city had been criticized for directing development monies solely to the downtown Cleveland area (for stadiums, museums, etc.) to the detriment of its neighborhoods. Thus, the West Tech project would quiet critics of city hall. Also, city hall may have been gun-shy of press criticism for stopping the project, so it pushed forward.

- *Sometimes you have to know when to walk away:* A seasoned real estate management company, Orlean, did not grasp the size and difficulty of the task it took on. It should probably never have made the loan guarantee. It was not worth the $50,000 fee and potential management contract. In retrospect, Orlean should have just paid off the $2.1 million guarantee and walked away. But 20/20 hindsight is easy in situations like this.
- *Pay careful attention to the developer, architect, and contractor relationship:* Re-

lationships between the participants soured almost immediately. Architectural drawings required revisions, items were omitted, and change orders could not be administered and approved, creating a bottleneck for the construction manager. Consequently, the construction manager simply built what was on the drawings. Holdover subcontractors from the first developer were retained on the job, some of whom were in over their heads. Many of the units could not be occupied for a variety of reasons. The building did not lend itself to efficient reuse, with sixty different floor plans for 189 units.

- *Proper incentives between developer and builder:* A related lesson comes from the deal structure between the developer and contractor. The available architectural drawings were not accurate enough to generate reliable cost estimates for this unique project, yet they formed the basis for the project's rehab cost budget. Because the school rehab builder acted as a fee construction manager, all architect drawings belonged to the developer, and the builder could pass along any cost overruns, thus increasing overall project cost. A general contractor arrangement would have required the builder to absorb cost overruns, shielding the developer from exposure in this sector.
- *Know your market:* This project is a failure from the perspective of the Orlean Company. Through November 2008, the building achieved only 107 occupied units out of 189. David Orlean noted, "With what we spent on this project, we could have bought everyone a new house." Sad but true. With the over $36 million project cost, 189 homeowners could each have been provided with a newly constructed home valued at over $170,000.

It could be argued that the market study for this project was a perfunctory boilerplate analysis by the project's out-of-town LIHTC consultant, not a genuine critical analysis of the project's true market potential. It was a giant leap to assume that the rents from the Warehouse District 4 miles away would instruct actual rents, even with a solid economic environment. Anticipated income from rent proved elusive for this project. Residents willing to pay high market rents in a low-income neighborhood never materialized. Rents were adjusted down in a vain attempt for the units to be absorbed.

According to David Orlean (interviewed in 2008), the project might have worked if the school had been developed as a straight low-income project with no market rentals. However, local politicians did not support this type of project, so it was never given the market test. Ironically, Orlean had the success formula right: a single type of market user. The current configuration, which is cash flowing successfully at a much lower value, is solely market-rate housing.

Conclusion

By the time the bureaucracy of city hall and the local HUD office realized the developer could not deliver, almost $9 million had been spent. The Orlean Company, which made a loan guarantee of $2.1 million, became the developer. In order to rectify the situation, nearly a dozen stakeholders, representing the "new" owner, lender, government, contractor, and architect, met weekly for over two years to manage the project. One participant described this as the most extraordinary public-private cooperation he had ever seen. The initial budget for the project was $22.6 million in 2001, and by 2004 had grown to $34 million or more, with the property in foreclosure and the mortgage note sold in 2007. Once the project defaulted and the note was purchased at foreclosure, the third owner converted the project to straight market rentals, and this formula is successful. The fourth owner is running the property profitably. Financially they will be the winners, along with the previous owner who bought the HUD note. Another winner is the West Tech neighborhood, which is the beneficiary of a nicely occupied $34 million investment that at last sale was worth about $7 million.

Notes

1. As will be explained later, HUD then sold the mortgage (and therefore conveyed control of the property) for $2.9 million to Resource Real Estate, Inc., a Philadelphia real estate firm, in 2007. It was bought as part of a pool of eleven other multifamily mortgage defaults. This firm held the property for several years, and then sold to Monarch Investments, the current operator.
2. In 2007, the subprime mortgage problem led to increases in mortgage rates, housing mortgage defaults and foreclosures, a contraction of credit leading to a nationally recognized weak market, and lack of qualified and motivated new homeowners. Most projects in Cleveland were delayed or abandoned due to market failure, and through late 2012 housing developers in general faced a bleak market. As of early 2013, the housing market for for-sale properties was still quite soft, although market rentals have improved.
3. Art Orlean, of blessed memory, was co-running the firm at the time the West Tech letter of credit deal was cut. His son David is now in charge. Howard Davis was project manager.
4. In fact, in 2012, the property transferred, fully leased up, for just under $7 million.
5. As a side note, it appears to have had a positive influence on the neighborhood, in that the number of board-ups close to the project is quite small.

References and Works Consulted

Bullard, S. 2012. "Rocky Mountain Firm High on West Tech Lofts." *Crain's Cleveland Business*, March 12, Reporters' Notebook. http://www.crainscleveland.com/article/20120312/SUB1/120309805/0/search.

City-Data.com. 2008. http://www.city-data.com/city/Cleveland-Ohio.html.

Ott, T. 2008. "Cleveland Public School Enrollment Falls to Lowest Level Since 1894." *Plain Dealer*, September 18. http://blog.cleveland.com/metro/2008/09/cleveland_public_school_enroll.html.

U.S. Department of Commerce, Bureau of the Census. 2000.

CENTRAL ARKANSAS CASE

Schools in Little Rock and
Clinton Cultural Campus

Gary DeWine and
Robert A. Simons

This case study has two tracks. The first track follows the story of the two main players involved in a series of historic school redevelopment projects in central Arkansas, including a brief sketch of six school reuse projects in which they shared involvement before they parted ways. The second track is the detailed analysis of the Clinton Cultural Campus, a double school complex in downtown Hot Springs, Arkansas.

Introduction

The adaptive reuse projects of Hot Springs High School and Junior High School Annex are the culmination of a business relationship between a for-profit development company, the Vanadis 3 Companies (formerly known as Vanadis Group or Vanadis), and The Arc Arkansas, an evolving nonprofit agency that advocates for people who have mental and physical disabilities. Vanadis is a boutique developer that has completed the preponderance of school adaptive reuse projects in its market area over a ten-year period. Vanadis recognized early on that these projects are not accomplished independently, but require other players such as the nonprofit group, The Arc Arkansas.

The Arc Arkansas evolved from being a nonprofit sponsor to becoming a developer of historic school buildings. This case briefly explains the history of each organization, and then details both their joint accomplishments in the adaptive reuse of school buildings in central Arkansas and their eventual estrangement as a result of the Hot Springs project.

Vanadis

Paul Esterer founded Vanadis as a commercial real estate development company in 1995. The company, which focuses on the development of downtown historic proper-

ties, also acts as a consultant for nonprofits, developers, and private investors on development opportunities in the state of Arkansas. Vanadis is both an alternative name for Freya, the Norse goddess of love and beauty, and the name of the Esterer family's Canadian islands vacation retreat.

Paul has a background in banking and finance, particularly commercial real estate banking and financial analysis. In 1996 he teamed with Todd Rice to restore an abandoned, pigeon-infested old school building. The duo, who first met on a golf course, shared the belief that artists could be the catalyst for turning around a decaying inner-city neighborhood by being a stable and tolerant population. Their initial venture, a 104-year-old school, became the prototype for downtown loft living in Little Rock and eventually Hot Springs (Silverman 1999).

Vanadis's efforts have resulted in more than $100 million worth of investment and development throughout central Arkansas. Their projects tend toward adaptive reuse of abandoned early-twentieth-century buildings—schools, storefronts, or former hospitals—although new construction projects also form part of the company's portfolio.

The company's success began in 1997 with a $3.7 million conversion of Little Rock's 38,000-sq.-ft., Romanesque-style Kramer School building into twenty-two apartment units. (See Exhibit 20-1.) This project was followed by the Block 2 Lofts in 1999 and 2000, a $21 million development consisting of 250,000 sq. ft. of lofts and commercial space in Little Rock's Rivermarket District. The Block 2 project consists of 145 loft apartments, underground parking, and 33,000 sq. ft. of ground-floor retail space. It was one of many sparks for the Rivermarket District revitalization (Sandlin 2001).

The Vanadis partnership of Rice and Esterer saw early on that low-income housing and historic tax credits, even with their accompanying strings, could be the financial foundation to fund renewal. Cooperative local governments were willing to give old school properties to a development team with funding in place to adaptively reuse the former school buildings.

In Arkansas, Vanadis created the prototypical model of using public incentives to get projects funded. A typical project might include up to fifteen layers of funding, each with potentially contradicting requirements, and multiple mortgage sources. More money could be spent on attorney

Exhibit 20-1 Kramer School Photographs and Plans

fees than architects. Vanadis held discussions with the governor of Arkansas, who saw the value in the projects, to figure out how state government could help make these deals work.

Most people probably do not understand how and where the money for adaptive reuse projects comes from, but they do recognize the loss when an old building is torn down for a parking lot. The community and its decision-makers have to weigh in and support adaptive reuse projects. The rallying of people and resources and marketing the project create a sense of pride, according to Paul Esterer. Early successes set the foundation for future projects, and their model for success would be replicated in other projects.

The Arc Arkansas

The Arc Arkansas, which serves Arkansas's developmentally disabled residents, must raise funds to support programs and activities like all nonprofit organizations do. In the past, their fund-raising consisted of collecting unwanted items and then selling them through thrift stores. This work brought them into contact with North Little Rock Handicapped Services, an organization that provided services to developmentally disabled individuals who earned income in sheltered workshops that took in subcontract piecework from local businesses. In the early 1990s an executive at North Little Rock Handicapped Services, Steve Hitt, recognized that the type of services he was providing needed to change. Hitt met with Cynthia Stone, then the assistant executive director for The Arc Arkansas, to exchange ideas and hear her observations about the programs he operated. She candidly told him she was not impressed with the demeaning and "degrading" services that his organization provided. She suggested

that Steve should listen to what his clients wanted. These discussions led North Little Rock Handicapped services to close their sheltered workshops and two of their three group homes, and in 1996, they merged with The Arc Arkansas (Johnson 2004).

Steve Hitt and Cynthia Stone believe that the future of housing for the developmentally disabled lies in facilities such as the several school buildings adaptively reused under their organization's nonprofit sponsorship. This belief led The Arc Arkansas to assume the role of developer in later projects. The Arc Arkansas believes that the housing developments, which are run as for-profit limited liability companies with The Arc Arkansas as a general partner, will generate modest income in the near term and a substantial increase after the low-income housing tax credit period expires. This income will help fund the Arc's support services for the disabled, including an employment program, a program for parents, and recreation opportunities (Johnson 2004).

The governor of Arkansas appointed Cynthia Stone to the Governor's Task Force on Supported Housing. The task force was created in response to the U.S. Supreme Court's 1999 *Olmstead* decision, which found that the state of Georgia violated the civil rights of two disabled individuals under the Americans with Disabilities Act. The Arc, through Cynthia Stone, used this decision as a launching point to promote the inclusion of Arkansas residents with disabilities in the mainstream of community life, such as improving their housing opportunities. Recognizing that physical barriers in housing construction often preclude inclusion of individuals with disabilities, the state of Arkansas, through the University of Arkansas, funded a $350,000 project for the study of inclusive housing design standards. The University of Arkansas Universal

Design Project now serves as an educational resource for policy makers and contractors in the design of facilities and housing that are, in the spirit of the *Olmstead* decision, accessible to disabled people (C. Stone, personal communication, January 2008).

The Arc Arkansas incorporates universal design principles in each of its projects to create an environment in which the aging and disabled can live with nondisabled peers. Examples of such design features are wheelchair-level door peepholes, lower cabinets,

Exhibit 20-2 Adaptive Reuse of Schools

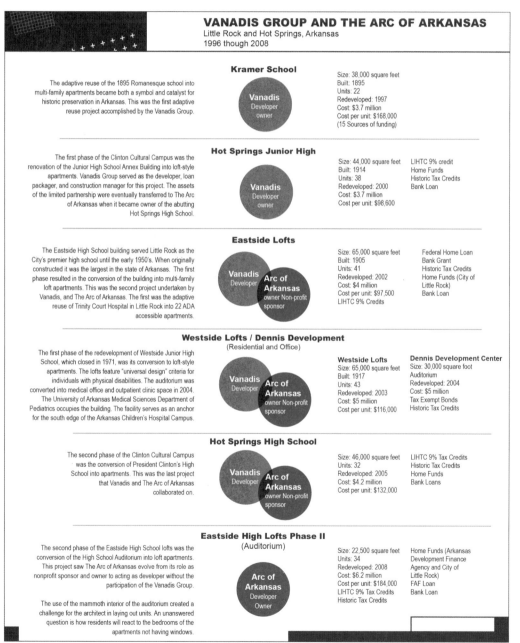

ADA-accessible hallways and walkways, toilet seat and bathtub grab bars, and keyless entry systems. This has created a user-friendly living environment for the disabled (Johnson 2004).

A typical Arc Arkansas project has a resident population of whom 25 percent are eligible for some type of disability income such as Supplemental Security Income of $530 per month along with receiving a Section 8 Housing Voucher. In addition, the projects provide both subsidized and market-rate units. The incorporation of universal design allows for the units to be inexpensively adapted for the changing physical limitations of either the current resident or a new tenant.

In the course of advocating on behalf of the disabled, The Arc Arkansas found itself unintentionally becoming an advocate for historic preservation. In recognition of its work on revitalizing historic buildings and preserving physical reminders of the past, the National Trust for Historic Preservation presented The Arc with its National Preservation Award in 2007.

School Adaptive Reuse Projects of Vanadis and The Arc Arkansas

Exhibit 20-2 shows a chronological history of school adaptive reuse projects undertaken by Vanadis, The Arc Arkansas, or both, since 1996. These projects helped establish Vanadis as the pioneer of school historic preservation through adaptive reuse in Arkansas, while The Arc Arkansas saw its role evolve from sponsor and owner to actual developer. The first project jointly involving Vanadis and The Arc Arkansas was Trinity Court Apartments. The building, which had been vacant since the early 1990s, was a former hospital of 28,000 sq. ft. It was converted to twenty-two ADA-accessible apartments in 1999 (Vanadis 3.com 2008). As project manager and developer, The Arc Arkansas also completed the adaptive reuse of the auditorium at the Eastside High Lofts Phase II in Little Rock to apartments in 2008.

Financing the projects typically involved low-income housing tax credits, historic preservation tax credits, and a mortgage loan. For one project, a tax-exempt bond issue in the amount of $3.9 million was used to convert a high school auditorium to medical offices.

The former public school buildings were acquired at a nominal cost, typically $1. Community and political leadership welcomed the reuse of the buildings, which had all stood vacant for some time. The completed projects contain both subsidized and market-rate units. Vanadis teamed with several other partners and formed the New Argenta Development Group to redevelop Argenta, a historic downtown district in North Little Rock. This urban infill project has seen the Argenta area improve with new mixed-use developments, quality restaurants, and related improvements (Sandlin 2001).

The Arc Arkansas continues to manage its extensive property holdings in Arkansas. At the time this case study was conducted, it was in the process of acquiring the 124-year-old Majestic Hotel in downtown Hot Springs. The Arc plans to rehabilitate the hotel, which sits on 5 acres, into a mixed-use development with residential and commercial uses (S. Hitt, personal communication, January 2008).

Exhibits 20-3 and 20-4 document the accomplishments of Vanadis and The Arc Arkansas in Little Rock.

Clinton Cultural Campus

This is the detailed case study of the Clinton Cultural Campus, an important project that was the result of the collaboration between

Vanadis and The Arc. The Clinton Cultural Campus project in downtown Hot Springs, Arkansas, includes both the Hot Springs Junior High and the Hot Springs High School, where former President Bill Clinton attended high school. The project is located ¼ mile from the central business district of Hot Springs, at 119 and 125 Oak Street. (See Exhibit 20-5.)

Hot Springs is named for its natural hot spring water, which flows from the ground at 147°F. In 1921, a portion of the Hot

Exhibit 20-3 Eastside Lofts Photographs

EAST SIDE LOFTS
Little Rock, Arkansas

Photographs: F P Architects

Springs area became a national park. The city itself is a year-round health and pleasure resort. The downtown is noted for its numerous bathhouses along Bathhouse Row, used for the water's perceived medicinal properties. The city is also home to Oak- lawn Park, a thoroughbred racetrack. Until the late 1960s it was a haven for illegal gambling. The town can be characterized as an older urban area of modest size that declined and is now in the process of rebounding. It is attempting to overcome crime and

Exhibit 20-4 West Side Lofts Photographs, Illustration and Plans

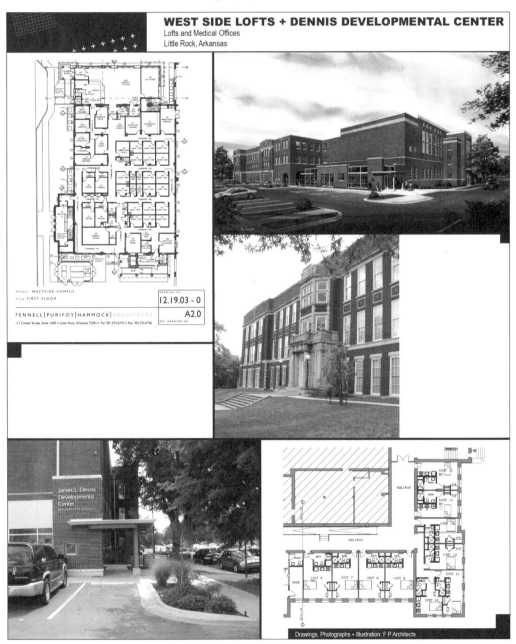

a lack of investment through reinvestment in the aging infrastructure and increased police protection.

The impetus for the adaptive reuse of the Hot Springs Junior High Annex and Hot Springs High School began in 1995 with Todd Rice and Paul Esterer, the managing partners of Vanadis, which had recently redeveloped the Kramer School. Vanadis bought the school for $1 from the city of Little Rock, marking the beginning of a series of adaptive reuse projects that turned

Exhibit 20-5 Clinton Cultural Campus Site Location and Site Plan

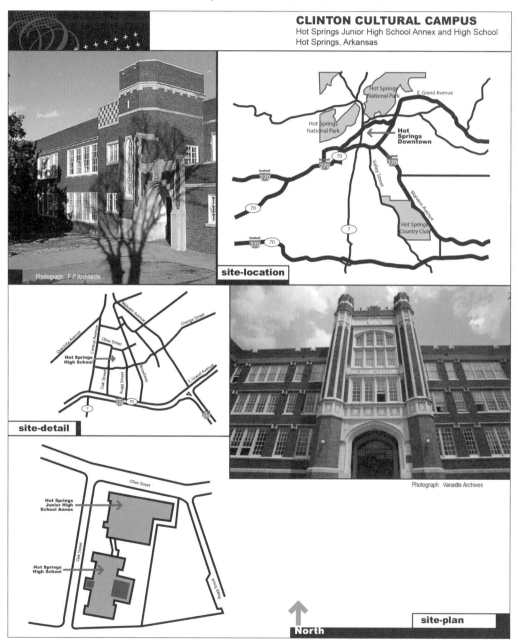

schools into residential space in Arkansas. The developers assembled financing from over fifteen sources to create affordable, loft-style living for artists at the twenty-two-unit $3.7 million Kramer School project. Hot Springs Junior High School was their second school rehab project (P. Esterer, personal communication, January 2008).

Site History

The Hot Springs High School was constructed in 1914, and the junior high was built in 1920. They are located 20 yd. apart in downtown Hot Springs on a campus of several acres. The buildings are constructed of brick and masonry in the Gothic style. Both had been closed and mothballed since 1971. The redevelopment was accomplished in two phases. The first phase, the renovation of the 44,000-sq.-ft., three-story junior high, was completed in October 2000. A total of thirty-eight multifamily loft apartments were constructed at a cost of $3.7 million. Phase II, the redevelopment of the 46,000-sq.-ft., four-story high school building, was completed in 2005 and resulted in the construction of thirty-two units of multifamily apartments at a cost of $4.2 million. A negative attribute of the site is that parking is limited. The site also contains a 20,000-sq.-ft. gym building currently used as a neighborhood recreation center. This building may later be adapted for housing.

Demographic and Market Conditions

As per the 2000 census, there were 25,259 families residing in the county. The population density was 130 people per square mile. There were 44,953 housing units at an average density of sixty-six per square mile. In 2007, there were about 26,908 owner-occupied houses and condos and 10,905 renter-occupied apartments. The median contract rent for apartments in 2007 was $473, a little higher than the state's figure of $421 (www.city-data.com 2008). The estimated median house or condo value in 2007 was $127,000, much higher than the state average ($101,000).

Junior High School Annex Redevelopment Process

The initial driving force behind the adaptive reuse of the junior high school came from local architect David French. He was the president of the Hot Springs Downtown Historical District, a nonprofit organization formed in 2000, which obtained ownership and control of what was to become the Clinton Cultural Campus and Hot Springs High School Loft Apartments. French's group gained control of the entire school site excluding the field house. The group's sole agenda was to see the buildings, which are on the National Register of Historic Places, preserved and reused.

Vanadis's involvement with the Hot Springs project originated from a chance meeting with Hot Springs City Manager Kent Myers. Mr. Myers then arranged for a meeting of Vanadis and the Clinton Cultural Campus Board. At the time, the city owned the former school buildings, which they subsequently sold to the Clinton Cultural Campus nonprofit for $1. The vision was for the buildings to serve as both apartments and workspace for the art community of Hot Springs. A larger plan called for the buildings to provide gallery space, arts-related office space, and a museum focusing on President Clinton's boyhood in Hot Springs. Vanadis was retained as the developer responsible for coordinating and designing the project, obtaining financing, managing construction, and leasing the redeveloped space (Gregory 2000).

Exhibit 20-6 Hot Springs Demographics

	Arkansas	Garland County	Hot Springs	Census Tract 115
Population				
2000	2,673,400	88,068	40,809	2,876
2007	2,834,797	96,371		
% Change	6.04%	9.43%		
Age (2000)				
Less than 18	25.44%	21.48%	20.87%	20.45%
22-39	24.63%	21.05%	21.60%	26.50%
40 -59	25.72%	25.92%	25.20%	24.93%
60 and over	18.39%	27.37%	27.69%	21.63%
Median Household Income				
2000	$32,182	$31,724	$26,790	$20,273
2007	$38,134	$34,947		
% Change	18.49%	10.16%		
Race (2000)				
White alone	79.94%	88.77%	80.77%	52.82%
Black or African American alone	15.63%	7.92%	15.09%	43.71%
American Indian and Alaska Native alone	0.69%	0.64%	0.69%	0.38%
Asian alone	0.71%	0.34%	0.50%	0.59%
Hawaiian and Pacific Islander alone	0.06%	0.01%	0.00%	0.00%
Some other race alone	1.54%	0.65%	0.90%	0.24%
Two or more races	1.42%	1.68%	2.04%	2.26%
Education (2000)				
Bachelor or higher	16.66%	17.97%	16.82%	7.05%
High school above age 25	34.10%	32.76%	31.54%	30.50%
Unemployment				
2000	3.67%	2.74%	3.47%	2.68%
Housing (2000)				
Households	1,042,807	37,796	18,302	1,150
Housing Units	1,173,043	44,953	21,820	1,394
Owner Occupied Units (%)	69.38%	71.16%	58.72%	43.87%
Renter Units(%)	30.62%	28.84%	41.28%	56.13%
Median Rent Apartment	$453	$478	$465	$333
Median House Value (Owner Occupied)	$67,400	$77,200	$70,200	$43,300

Source: 2000 and 2007 U.S. Census
Note: 2007 tract data is not available

Phase I, completed in October 2000, provided six market-rate and thirty-two subsidized units to area artists and their families. Units are contained within each former classroom. Units rent from 70 cents to 85 cents per square foot per month. A description of the apartments states "the key to the development's market ability is its substantial use of open, inviting floor plans that take advantage of large amounts of natural light" (Vanadis 3 2008). The units in the junior high annex attracted many young people who were on their own for the first time.

Initial lease-up of the junior high annex took over eight months, but occupancy could not be sustained.[1] Problems with absorption may have been the result of an increased competition from rental properties in downtown Hot Springs, as the image of downtown living improved during the two years separating the projects (P. Esterer, personal communication, January 2008).

The urban neighborhood provides temptations that attract an unsavory element, such as adult entertainment businesses and liquor stores. The neighborhood contains seedy transient motels from another era, small factories, and warehouses, as well as some well-maintained single-family homes nearby. Furthermore, the disruptive and destructive lifestyle of young tenants resulted in the property carrying a 10–18 percent vacancy rate. Since the junior high school caters to younger tenants, it requires intense maintenance. The maintenance staff's attention is usually taken up by the repair of broken windows and petty vandalism. The project, which started with artists, now has only three to five living in the former school building, making up less than 10 percent of the residents. The units with an open floor plan contain few amenities. "Sparse" has been used as a description. The units, while marketed to the disabled, are not designed for those with physical disabilities. Sinks are not wheelchair accessible, and a resident confined to a wheelchair cannot reach closets. The original design of the building requires the use of a lift to make different levels accessible. It is challenging for building managers to maintain the operation of mechanical lifts when abusive use cannot be controlled, and the barrier-free lift providing accessibility from various levels of three to four steps often is out of operation. The design of a barrier-free environment can be a vexing problem for a designer in an old historic building, particularly when a tight budget limits design alternatives (C. Stone, personal communication, January 2008).

The units facing the auditorium of the high school building next door have a high tenant turnover due to lack of light. Overall, the junior high school annex units do not have the appeal of those in the high school. It is hoped that future employees of a Holiday Inn being constructed on a nearby site will attract mature tenants to the junior high school. The ownership of the Clinton Campus may need to make capital improvements to upgrade the units to attract and retain residents.

Project Financing of the Junior High School

Vanadis's Paul Esterer, who had become especially adept at bringing various sources of funding to projects, secured about $3.7 million of financing, including $700,000 of permanent first mortgage debt. Other funding sources included low-income housing tax credits, historic preservation tax credits, Home Funds, and Community Development Block Grant monies. Regions Bank provided the first mortgage, with Apollo Housing syndicating the tax credits. Verizon bought both the LIHTC and historic tax credits. Tax abatement was not a part of the project, but the project was assisted by a property-tax reduction.

Redevelopment Process

In 2004, when the junior high school annex was 20 percent vacant, control and ownership along with the yet-to-be redeveloped Hot Springs High School was transferred to The Arc Arkansas. Vanadis had just partnered with The Arc Arkansas to renovate the Eastside Lofts in Little Rock into thirty-two loft-style apartments with twenty-one units for low-income households and eleven market-rate units. Vanadis acted as developer and The Arc Arkansas as nonprofit sponsor and owner. A nonprofit sponsor proves beneficial in obtaining a competitively awarded allocation of the limited LIHTC funds from the state of Arkansas because a project with a nonprofit partner scores higher for purposes of the allocation.

The successful experience from the Eastside Lofts project led to The Arc Arkansas and Vanadis teaming up to convert the Hot Springs High School building to apartments. Vanadis again performed the role of developer with the expectation that it would receive a developer's fee for its services. However, The Arc eventually stepped into the role of developer. When this case study was conducted in January 2008, Cynthia Stone, the chief executive officer of The Arc Arkansas, was very enthusiastic to share the frustrations and accomplishments of the nonprofit as it evolved from sponsor to developer of the project.

The facade of the former Hot Springs High School is an imposing edifice, but the campus is on only a minor side street near the Hot Springs central business district. The interior of the building was in surprisingly good condition prior to conversion to apartments. It did not evidence the neglect and vandalism often present at similar

properties that sit empty for years. Floors within the individual classrooms needed only to be sanded and refinished. Walls were added to the interiors for the bathroom and kitchens.

An enclosed corridor connects the junior and senior high school buildings. The units within the high school show careful design on the part of French Haas Architects. The bathrooms and kitchens within the units are situated so that all of the apartment's windows are within the living area. The units contain elements from the original use as a school, with blackboards and lockers remaining as a condition for receiving historic tax credits.

The units within the former basketball gym are particularly impressive as they truly function as artist loft space. The gym was subdivided into four units of two stories each. Each unit has a portion of the jogging track, which runs the perimeter of the building above the gym floor. Portions of this second floor space now serve as an artist work space overlooking the living area. Each unit contains three bedrooms with a combined kitchen and living room. The former auditorium was not utilized as part of the building's conversion to apartments. As is typical for auditoriums of the period, the acoustics are near perfect, and The Arc hopes that it will again be used for public performances (C. Stone, personal communication, January 2008).

A source of frustration between The Arc Arkansas and Vanadis was the inadequate construction budget. As work progressed on the high school renovation, the contingency portion of the budget was depleted due to faulty cost estimates and resulting overruns. Decisions were made to eliminate painting and plastering to keep the project within budget (C. Stone, personal communication, January 2008). Vanadis thought that there were sufficient reserves for this work, but The Arc wanted to be paid $150,000 up front before construction started, although Vanadis warned this might result in a shortfall to cover contingencies (P. Esterer, personal communication, January 2008). The actual shortfall was estimated to be about $400,000. The Arc Arkansas eventually went outside the development partnership to obtain a third loan to replace the funds. The friction from this incident resulted in the developer's fee being deferred or not being paid to Vanadis, and the overall situation led Vanadis and The Arc to part ways.

Project Financing

Project Financing for the High School Project

Financing for the high school was provided by Bank of the Ozarks through a first mortgage for $830,000. Payments are $6,200 per month principal and interest for thirty years at 7 percent, including taxes and insurance. This figure includes partial debt service on the second mortgage of $225,000 from the Arkansas Development Finance Authority. The later loan covered shortfalls to cover painting and plastering.

As of the spring of 2008, The Arc Arkansas had not received the fifth and final payment from the investors and syndicators involved with the tax credits. The payment is being withheld because cash flow requirements of the tax credit agreement are not being met. This problem, which The Arc wanted to handle without the involvement of Vanadis, has been ongoing for almost two years. According to Paul, "You cannot take your eyes off the equity investors. They own you. The paperwork certification requirements require lawyers and cannot be overlooked" (P. Esterer, personal communication, January 2008).

The simplified and aggregated analysis illustrated in Exhibits 20-7 and 20-8 examines the construction and operation of two separate partnerships developed at two points in time, and treats them as one project for the purpose of this teaching case study. Actual figures may differ somewhat from those presented below. Some development partners have likely obtained additional junior debt outside the project structure on these properties, and operating losses are likewise fed from outside project cash flows. The Arc Arkansas appears to be using other income to meet operating and debt service for these properties.

Sources of Funds

The total equity assembled for the Hot Springs Junior High and High School Lofts was just over $5.4 million, or 68 percent of the nearly $8 million total project funding. The largest sources of equity were $3.6 million (45 percent of the equity) of proceeds from the syndication of low-income housing tax credits and $1.4 million (17 percent of the equity) of proceeds from the syndication of historic preservation tax credits. Owner equity and grants were 5 percent of the project's total sources of funds.

The remaining balance of $2.6 million in funding (32 percent) came from debt. First mortgage debt amounted to $1.5 million (19 percent), with the rest of the debt coming from forgivable grants or loans with liberal terms (5 percent of project funds). An unusual lingering construction loan represented 8 percent of project funds.

Uses of Funds

The total project cost $8 million, spread out over both phases during an approximately five-year build-out period. Acquisition totaled $520,000 (7 percent of total project cost). The biggest ticket item was the rehabilitation expense, including contingency

Exhibit 20-7 Sources of Funds

	Hot Springs Junior High Annex School Lofts	Hot Springs High School Lofts	Consolidated Sources	% of Total
Sources of Funds August 2000		**Sources of Funds December 2005**		
Owner Equity	$304,000	$13,180	**$317,180**	**4.0%**
Owner Equity (Federal Home Loan Bank Grant)	$114,000		**$114,000**	**1.4%**
Low-Income Housing Tax Credit Proceeds	$1,844,000	$1,786,220	**$3,630,220**	**45.4%**
Proceeds Historic Tax Credits	$585,000	$765,182	**$1,350,182**	**16.9%**
SUBTOTAL EQUITY	**$2,847,000**	**$2,564,582**	**$5,411,582**	**67.7%**
First Mortgage	$700,000	$830,000	**$1,530,000**	**19.1%**
Second Mortgage/ Arkansas Development Finance Authority (forgivable debt)	$200,000	$225,000	**$425,000**	**5.3%**
Balance of Construction Loan		$630,922	**$630,922**	**7.9%**
SUBTOTAL DEBT	**$900,000**	**$1,055,000**	**$2,585,922**	**32.3%**
TOTAL	**$3,747,000**	**$4,250,504**	**$7,997,504**	**100.0%**

Notes: some of the figures are authors' estimates based on audited data

and contractor profit and amounting to $5.8 million, or 72 percent of total cost. Soft costs, including financing, consultants, and architecture, were almost $1 million, or 12 percent of project cost. Of the soft costs, architecture (5 percent) was the single largest item. The developer fee of $700,000, or 8 percent of cost, rounded out costs. Total cost averaged $114,250 per completed unit, or $89 per gross building square foot.

Operating Cash Flows

Financial statements provided by the owner documenting revenues and expenses show that the two buildings generated about $45,000 of annual net operating income (NOI) when this case study was conducted. Exhibits 20-9 and 20-10 provide a snapshot of the project's income. The relatively high

vacancy in the junior high school is a consistent problem on the revenue side. Project NOI is not sufficient to meet the $136,032 of annual debt service. Thus, the deal cannot support itself on a continuous basis and does not generate positive cash flow before taxes, although additional tax shelters may be available through depreciation and interest deductions (not accounted for here). For example, according to the 2007 financial audit, an affiliate of the high school partnership covered the operating deficit of $112,000 that year (Novogradac & Company LLP, CPA 2007).

Lessons Learned

- *Even the low-income market will recognize design shortcomings:* Some of the units in the junior high building face a wall and

Exhibit 20-8 Uses of Funds

Uses of Funds August 2000		Uses of Funds December 2005	Consolidated Uses of Funds	% of Total
Site Acquisition	$200,000	$320,000	$520,000	6.5%
Environmental Remediation	$25,000		$25,000	0.3%
Hard Costs				
Rehabilitation	$2,313,000	$2,982,132	$5,295,132	66.2%
Contingency/Contractor Profit	$250,000	$194,157	$444,157	5.6%
Personal Property	$50,000		$50,000	0.6%
Subtotal Hard costs	**$2,613,000**	**$3,176,289**	**$5,789,289**	**72.4%**
Soft Costs				
Insurance, taxes, interest, and loan origination	$67,000	$131,453	$198,453	2.5%
Title, recording and inspection	$18,000	$24,735	$42,735	0.5%
Architectural design fee and supervision	$140,000	$222,039	$362,039	4.5%
Legal, organizational, and tax opinion, appraisal, market study, environmental report, tax credit, accounting, survey	$162,000	$115,988	$277,988	3.5%
Operating and rent-up reserves	$110,000		$110,000	1.4%
Subtotal Soft Costs	**$497,000**	**$494,215**	**$991,215**	**12.4%**
Developer's fee/surplus	$412,000	$260,000	$672,000	8.4%
Total Uses	**$3,747,000**	**$4,250,504**	**$7,997,504**	**100.0%**
Average Cost per Unit	**$98,600**	**38 units**	**$132,000**	**32 units**

therefore lack sufficient light. It is unclear if the market will readily absorb bedroom units without windows. Also, the sparse appearance of the units in the junior high presents a challenge for tenants to make the apartment a home.

- *The quality of finish and design in the high school is superior:* All the units rented within thirty days of completion, and the building should have no problem retaining and attracting residents. Spending money on quality design at the beginning is better than retrofitting at some date in the future.

- *Low-income residents can make good neighbors:* Priming the pump for community investment can be through projects that assist lower-income residents. Low-income housing projects are often the first deals of sufficient scale to initiate high-

quality development. This theory was proven in Little Rock with initial projects being ones using low-income housing tax credits as the basis to rehabilitate historic buildings.

- *In skinny deals, it's easier to make money as a developer than as an owner:* Merchant rehabbers can make a profit on this type of project, but that does not ensure positive cash flows for the owners.

- *Maximizing cash flow:* A real concern is that cash flows must improve in the near term if the projects are to be financially successful. Down units, whether from vacancy or needing repairs to be rentable, are drains on income.

- *Budget projections and contingencies:* The business relationship between the fee developer and long-term owner ended on a sour note because of the use of "value engineering" to complete the project. When it became evident that there were not sufficient funds to complete all of the budgeted items, some important items were cut back. Since these rehab deals are tight, budgeting sufficient funds to cover contingencies is important.

- *Understand debt and equity:* A financial plan containing too much debt and inadequate income invites disaster. Caution

needs to be exercised by inexperienced nonprofit entities in understanding the complexities and requirements of the contracts they enter into, especially with respect to the fine print in tax credit syndicator documents. Get an experienced lawyer to help.

- *Knowing when to enter and exit the market:* It's a very good idea to develop a specialty (reuse of old schools) and become

Exhibit 20-9 Stable Year Cash Flows

	Hot Springs Junior High School Annex Lofts	Hot Springs High School	Consolidated Stable Year
	Income 2006	Income 2007	
Revenues			
Net Rental Income	$123,302	$238,446	$361,748
Other Income	$2,163	$-	$2,163
Total Revenue	**$125,465**	**$238,446**	**$363,911**
Expenses			
Administrative	$39,215	$26,087	$65,302
Utilities	$23,997	$19,044	$43,041
Property Taxes and Insurance	$10,510	$23,013	$33,523
Replacement	$62,140	$22,624	$84,764
Legal and Other Prof Fees	$6,106	$11,095	$17,201
Property Management	$9,338	$9,436	$18,774
Bad Debt	$-	$55,734	$55,734
Total Expenses	**$151,306**	**$167,033**	**$318,339**
Net Operating Income	**$(25,841)**	**$71,413**	**$45,572**
Debt Service	$61,632	$74,400	$136,032
Before Tax Cash Flow	**$(87,473)**	**$(2,987)**	**$(90,460)**

Notes: Data available for the stable years for both properties are not the same.
Because of the forgivable loans and debt outside the project but inside the various partnerships, additional debt may be accrued but not paid, and actual debt service may exceed that shown above.

Exhibit 20-10 Rent Rolls

Junior High

# units	Sq. Ft.	Market Rent per Month	Subsidized Rent per Month
32	575	$485	$431
6	1,178	$600	$513

High School

# units	Sq. Ft.	Market Rent per Month	Subsidized Rent per Month
5	782	$485	$413
19	1,100	$650	$513
8	1,460	$750	$588

the biggest market player. However, once you dominate this market, the best redevelopment opportunities may become exhausted, and it becomes time to move on with a new business plan.

Conclusion

In sum, school rehab deals can be adequate in terms of development fees, but skinny in terms of operating profit. Some projects struggle to maintain acceptable levels of return given the substantial risk, especially with complex financing. In this case, the profit can be better earned as a fee developer, rather than an owner.

Time will tell if the Clinton Cultural Campus project is a success. Success can be measured in many ways (one of which is financial, where this property is lacking), but all of these school projects are at least a partial success and should be praised for fostering private-public partnerships, historic preservation, community energizing, and economic development. These buildings can now stand for another hundred years. There will be operating and management issues with these properties, but that can happen in any real estate investment.

Note

1. Absorption at the high school took place in under thirty days. The quick absorption of the high school was attributed to higher quality of design and finishes than in the junior high school (C. Stone, personal interview, January 2008).

References and Works Consulted

The Arc. www.arcark.org.

City-Data.com. www.citydata.com.

Gregory, M. 2000. "Ground Broken on Restoration of High School in Hot Springs." *Arkansas Democrat Gazette,* February 23, B1.

Johnson, S. 2004. "Steven Wayne Hitt. Several Well-Known Schools Have Been Granted a New Life by Arc Arkansas." *Arkansas Democrat Gazette,* June 13, Section: High Profile.

Novogradic & Company LLP, CPA. 2006, *Independent Audit Report for Hot Springs High School Lofts,* February.

———. 2007. *Independent Audited Financials for Hot Springs High School Limited Partnership,* December.

Sandlin, J. 2001. "Downtown North Little Rock Advocated Fear Housing Project Effects Plan for 56 Apartments." *Arkansas Democrat Gazette,* May 19, B1.

Silverman, J. 1999. "Mixed Picture at Little Rock Co-op: Artists Management Spar." *Arkansas Democrat Gazette,* August 29.

Vanadis 3. 2008. Clinton Cultural Campus. http://www.vanadis3.com/clintoncampus.aspx.

THE LOFTS AT ALBUQUERQUE HIGH

The Adaptive Reuse of Four Former School Buildings with Ancillary Development: Residential, Retail, and Office Development

Albuquerque, New Mexico

Gary DeWine

The Lofts at Albuquerque High is a complex adaptive reuse project done in phases to respond to and capture opportunities in an evolving Albuquerque real estate market. The phasing strategy is especially important when large campus sites of separate buildings—either institutional, religious, or schools—are considered for redevelopment. (See Exhibit 21-1 for the original site plan and Exhibit 21-2 for the six distinct phases in the redevelopment process.)

The historic Albuquerque High School, a community landmark, closed in 1976 and was sold to private interests. The campus of buildings, located at 301 Central Avenue and Broadway on the famous Route 66, is a short walking distance from downtown Albuquerque. The buildings fell into neglect under out-of-state ownership, and after two unsuccessful efforts to negotiate a purchase, the city acquired the structures by condemnation in 1996. They remained vacant until April 2001, when Paradigm & Company launched a rehabilitation project named The Lofts at Albuquerque High.

The community wanted to see the buildings restored and adaptively reused. However, the usual obstacles existed: a slumping real estate market in the early 1990s; a declining neighborhood; the negative public perception of abandoned buildings in general; and the poor physical condition of the buildings, which suffered from stripped-out plumbing, broken windows, feral cats and pigeons throughout the grounds, and vagrants and homeless people sheltering in the buildings. The culmination of twenty-five years of neglect in an urban environment was evident.

Despite all these obstacles, the city never considered demolishing the buildings for development of the site. The city's commitment to preserving its historic sites

stemmed from the 1970 demolition of the Spanish Mission–style Alvarado Hotel, a tourist icon owned by the Santa Fe Railroad and Albuquerque's most famous historical landmark. The hotel, which had been within sight of the high school, was architect Mary Jane Colter's first commission by the Fred Harvey Company to design hotels for tourists wanting to experience the American West. Its destruction galvanized the community and henceforth, none of Albuquerque's architectural gems were to see the wrecking ball. This included the historic Albuquerque High School campus.

Developer Rob Dickson first saw the potential value of the high school when visiting his father, who had relocated to Albuquerque, in 1989. Rob is the owner and founder of Paradigm & Company. He is an accountant and attorney by training, but his interests include New Urbanism and opportunities to redevelop traditional neighborhoods. Paradigm & Company came to be selected as the developer for the adaptive reuse of the Historic Albuquerque High School project by the Albuquerque city council through a development agreement negotiated and signed in 1999. Rob's vision was for the property to anchor a revitalized pair of walkable and vibrant urban corridors, or "Main Streets." The developer was able to see beyond all the broken windows and vandalized exterior walls and visualize a jewel of an opportunity (Zissman 2003).

This case is especially interesting because it documents both the frustration and the success of local government in redeveloping a large and blighted property. The city of Albuquerque eventually had to use its police powers to take the property by eminent domain. A condemnation suit was required to sort out ownership that was clouded by a deceased owner and an executed purchase agreement. Having obtained ownership of the property through the courts, the city then used a request-for-proposal (RFP) process to secure a qualified developer. The end result was a mixed-use complex that contains apartment units within two former historic school buildings, new construction condominiums, a former historic high school gym building adapted to loft condos, a parking garage, an office building in a former library building, retail space, and a community of courtyard homes.

Site History

In 1914, the first building of the Albuquerque High School campus was constructed at Broadway and Central, just east of downtown. Referred to as Old Main, the 51,500-sq.-ft. building formerly housed science laboratories, a gym, a library, classrooms, and an 850-seat auditorium. In 1927 the Manual Arts Building (30,000 sq. ft.) was constructed, followed by the Classroom Building (24,000 sq. ft.), a separate Gymnasium Building in 1938 (68,000 sq. ft.), and the Library Building in 1940 (10,000 sq. ft.). The buildings had a combined total of 175,000 sq. ft. All of the buildings are brick, constructed in the collegiate Gothic style, and listed on the National Register of Historic Places.

Market Area Demographics

According to the 2000 U.S. Census, Bernalillo County had a total population of 556,678, making it the most populated county in the state of New Mexico (U.S. Department of Commerce, Bureau of the Census 2000). The City-Data Web site estimated about a 12 percent increase in population (629,292) in the county between 2000 and 2007 (see Exhibit 21-3). The Lofts at Albuquerque High are located in an area that is predominantly white (64 percent) (City-Data.com 2008).

Acquiring the Property

The Albuquerque Public Schools closed the Albuquerque High School buildings in 1976. The district then traded the site for a property near another high school. The first failed attempt to develop the old high school property occurred in the early 1980s by Spruel Development. The project, called Harrington Square, planned for the conversion of the campus to offices and small shops. This plan was followed in 1984 by an ambitious $19.9 million plan to develop the site into restaurants, boutiques, a movie theater, a health club, and offices. The project included $10 million of city-backed redevelopment bonds and historic preservation tax credits. Control of the Albuquerque High School property in the mid-1980s passed into the hands of an out-of-town owner, Charles Hill of Franklin, Massachusetts. During this time the building became the target of vagrants. The double-hung windows were broken, lockers were stolen for scrap, roofs began leaking, and the buildings were left to deteriorate. Due to the broken windows pigeons began to roost throughout the building. Rob Dickson commented, "it cost more for remediation of the pigeon poop than all the asbestos in the buildings" (R. Dickson, personal communication, January 2008). The 7.26-acre site was a blight, which negatively impacted the neighborhood. The neighborhood was in decline, evidenced by a lack of investment in housing maintenance.

The Albuquerque city council created a citizens' task force in 1989 to examine the reuse of the campus. In 1990, the New Mexico legislature appropriated $345,000, earmarked for the reuse or purchase of the buildings from Hill. The building was deteriorating so quickly that the city considered purchasing it without definitive plans for its future use, only a consensus from the community and political leadership that some action was needed.

After a convoluted transaction involving the Federal Deposit Insurance Corporation (FDIC) and a condemnation lawsuit, the city of Albuquerque obtained six of the seven campus buildings from Ricardo Chaves and the Battaglia Family Trust in 1996. As long as the city and developer fulfilled the conditions of the development agreement, the developer would own the buildings and their footprints while the

Exhibit 21-1 The Lofts at Albuquerque High Site Location and Site Plan

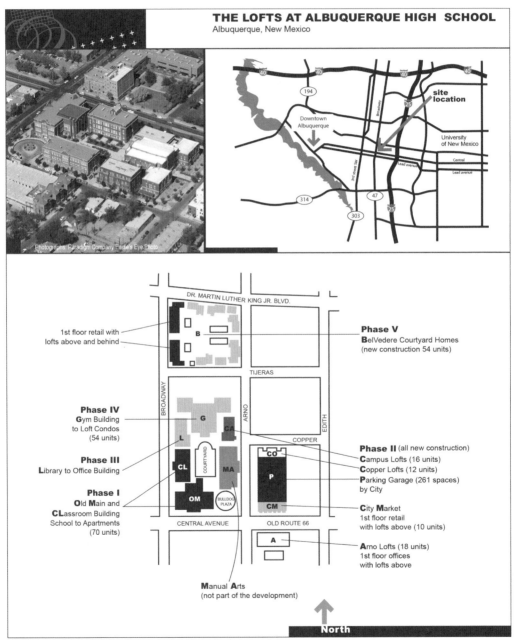

Exhibit 21-2 The Lofts at Albuquerque High Project at a Glance

Phase	Year	Project	Unit Type	Number of Units	Size	Pricing	Project Cost (Millions)	Financing Source (Millions $)
I	2002	Old Main Classroom and Classroom Building Rehab	Rental Apartments	70	500 to 1,300 sq. ft.	$500 to $1,300 month (initial)	$6.3	$1.3 Private equity and tax credits $3.2 Mortgage $1.9 City
I	2002	Streetscape Improvements	Sidewalks, Curbs, Lighting throughout the Development Including Courtyard and Bulldog Plaza				$2.0	$1 US EDA $1 City General
II	Fall 2003	Parking Garage	Public Parking with User Fees, 261 Spaces				$3.4	City Tax Bonds
III	Summer 2004	Campus Lofts Arno Lofts Arno—First Floor City Market City Market Copper Lofts	Condos Condos Retail/ Office Condos Retail Condos	16 18 10 12	Condos 600 to 1,650 Sq. Ft. Retail 5,700 Sq. Ft.	New Construction $88,000 to $264,000	$9.0	Private
IV	Summer 2005	Gym Building Rehab	Condos	54	500 to 1,900 Sq. Ft.	$109,000 to $300,000	$7.5	City Equity & Private Debt
V	2007	Library Rehab	Office		10,000 Sq. Ft.	Leased to a Single User	$1.6	City Equity & Private Debt
VI	Spring 2008	BelVedere Urban Courtyard Living	Condos	54	700 to 2,000 Sq. Ft.	$149,900 to $439,000	$11.7	Private

Total Housing Units: 234   Total Project Cost: $41,000,000

city would own the land and infrastructure elements (Schroeder 2000). The 1996 court order giving the city ownership of the property stipulated a timetable for the redevelopment of the buildings on the property. In 1998, the city began the RFP process that ultimately allowed Rob Dickson and Paradigm to acquire the site.

The future of the school came down to two competing development teams vying for the development of the 7.26-acre site and its buildings: Dickson's and a Phoenix-area developer. The other developer submitted a feel-good project, which had significant support, to create an art and cultural center, a city library, a YMCA facility, non-profit office space, and low-income housing units. This proposal required the city of Al-buquerque to guarantee $30 per square foot triple-net leases over thirty years. The net present value of the city's public subsidy was projected to be $36 million, making it a very expensive project that relied heavily on public subsidy when compared to the Paradigm proposal.

Meanwhile, Dickson retained Todd D. Clarke, CCIM, president of Cantera Consultants, to analyze the local real estate market. Clarke's market study determined that apartments were the highest and best land use (Drummond 2005). Dickson's proposal requested that the city give the buildings to the developers for free, provide $4 million in cash to close the gap between project costs and available private financing, and build a parking structure. The city's cost

Exhibit 21-3 Census Data 2000 and 2007

	New Mexico	Bernalillo County	Albuquerque CCD	Census Tract 15
Population				
2000	1,819,046	556,678	534,564	2,932
2007	1,969,915	629,292	511,893	
% Change	8.29%	13.04%	-4.24%	
Age (2000)				
Less than 18	27.90%	25.26%	25.18%	27.25%
22 - 39	24.45%	26.74%	26.92%	25.82%
40-59	26.20%	26.84%	26.48%	25.14%
60 and over	14.81%	14.44%	14.63%	13.71%
Median Household Income				
2000	$34,133	$38,788	$38,331	$19,329
2007	$41,452	$44,952	$43,677	
% Change	21.44%	15.89%	13.95%	
Race (2000)				
White alone	66.78%	70.72%	70.67%	58.36%
Black or African American alone	1.84%	2.75%	2.82%	5.42%
American Indian and Alaska Native alone	9.47%	4.13%	3.64%	5.32%
Asian alone	1.01%	1.77%	1.83%	0.17%
Hawaiian and Pacific Islander alone	0.07%	0.10%	0.10%	0.00%
Some other race alone	16.98%	15.88%	16.23%	24.11%
Two or more races	3.85%	4.66%	4.71%	6.62%
Education (2000)				
Bachelor or higher	23.45%	30.51%	30.49%	20.83%
High school above age 25	26.59%	24.77%	24.79%	17.03%
Unemployment				
2000	4.41%	3.76%	3.78%	3.73%
Housing (2000)				
Households	678,032	220,939	213,028	1,070
Housing Units	780,579	239,074	230,234	1,267
Owner Occupied Units (%)	69.98%	63.64%	62.65%	40.28%
Renter Units (%)	30.02%	36.36%	37.35%	59.72%
Median Rent Apartment	$503	$560	$560	$422
Median House Value (Owner Occupied)	$94,600	$123,200	$122,700	$85,100

Source: 2000 and 2007 U.S. Census
Note: 2007 tract data is not available

of the public subsidies for Dickson's plan would have a net present value of $11 million, versus $36 million of city-guaranteed rents requested by the other developer. The city commissioned Larry Brooks, MAI, to conduct a third-party analysis to determine the best deal financially for the city. Brooks determined that Rob Dickson's rehabilitation project with its market-rate apartments provided the highest net returns. The city would receive a portion of rental income and sales as reimbursement for the gap financing it was to provide. Accordingly, the city selected Dickson's plan as the winner.

The city had issued almost $7 million in bonds for the redevelopment of the buildings, the landscape elements, and the construction of the garage. The development agreement outlined the specific use of the funds. The gap funds were to be used for design costs, environmental remediation, demolition, roof repairs, and repair to the building facades. The agreement also provided for the repayment of the gap financing from rent, sale, or lease income from the historic buildings. In a 2008 interview, Rob Dickson indicated that these revenues are providing the city with a steady revenue stream as the project moves toward completion (R. Dickson, personal communication, January 2008).

A development agreement with the city took Dickson nine months to negotiate and $125,000 in attorney fees. Development agreements are relatively customized to every project. Paradigm sought to use templates to reduce legal fees and negotiation time, but found little that fit its needs. Dickson personally prepared the actual agreement so that the project could get under way. The agreement outlined the responsibilities of the city and developers, and committed the city to construction of the parking garage and infrastructure improvements.

A last-minute snafu almost caused the deal to evaporate during the property acquisition phase in 1996. Dickson and Paradigm intended to obtain control of the entire site from the city, and the RFP gave the developer the option to pull out from the project if the city did not obtain con-

trol of the whole campus. The city offered the Battaglia Family Trust $750,000 for the seventh building on site, the Manual Arts Building, even though it required such extensive work that it was appraised at negative $400,000. The Battaglia Family Trust wanted $1 million. Rob Dickson chose to proceed with the project without the Manual Arts Building, which was redeveloped independently.

Ricardo Chaves and the Battaglia Family Trust began work on rehabbing the Manual Arts Building into sixteen apartments on the upper two floors with the first floor to become a restaurant or grocery. By late 2008, the building shell and interior framing had been completed, and construction appeared to be slowly moving toward completion sometime in 2009. This remains outside the Paradigm & Company deal.

Redevelopment Process

Once the property had been acquired, Dekker/Perich/Sabatini Architects and Rob Dickson jointly developed a master plan. The original development plan for the Albuquerque High School was conceptual and therefore flexible. The implementation plan was to proceed in strategic phases so that the developer could respond to changes and take advantage of opportunities in the Albuquerque real estate market. Exhibit 21-4 documents the implemented real estate project. The plan called for the adaptive reuse of the five historic buildings on campus as office space or apartments. The central courtyard would be rebuilt incorporating the original elements of a raised fountain and wishing well. A pedestrian gateway and delivery area would be created at the southeast corner of Bulldog Plaza at Central Avenue.

The plan that was formally submitted to the city as part of the RFP process called for vacating some public streets to link the vacant lots to the north and east with the campus. Two four-level parking garages were to be built to serve the residential units created in the old school buildings. The gym and library would become retail or office space. The vacated public streets would become either plazas or access points for ingress or egress. A total of five new buildings were to be built. Their final use was intentionally left unspecified in the master plan. The property was rezoned as mixed use so that the developer could respond to the

Exhibit 21-4 The Lofts at Albuquerque High Photographs and Master Plan

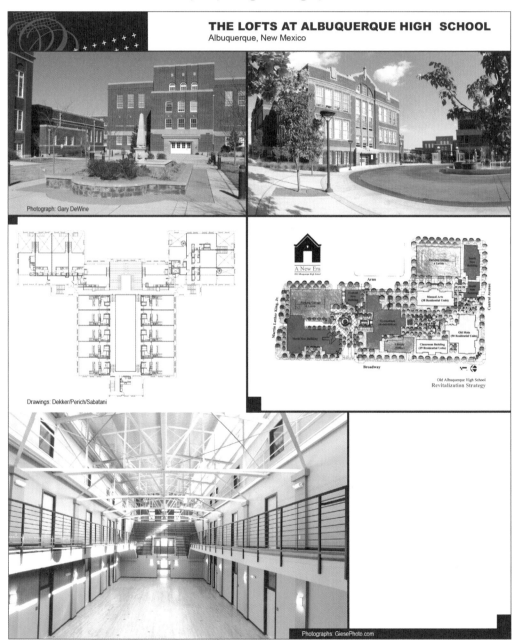

changing real estate market. The rezoning allows the new and old buildings to be used for a mixture of apartments, condominiums, townhomes, retail space, and office space.

Streetscape Improvements

The agreement with the city of Albuquerque required an allocation of $2 million for streetscape and infrastructure improvements around and within the two-city-block main campus, the city block north of the campus, and the half block to the east. The streetscape improvements consist of new curbs, sidewalks, perimeter landscaping of the buildings, and street trees, along with site amenities of lighting fixtures, bike racks, and litter containers. Water and sewer lines also were replaced or relocated. Work began on these improvements soon after work commenced on the Old Main and Classroom buildings.

In addition, the courtyard of the campus was attractively restored and landscaped. Public access is allowed to the courtyard during the day through Bulldog Plaza, a circular vehicular plaza, which serves as temporary parking area for drop-offs and deliveries. Several elements from the past remain within the courtyard, including a bulletin board kiosk, which now houses residents' mailboxes, and an outside seating area with a fountain feature.

The developer designed, managed, and coordinated this work. The project was competitively bid, with the city making reimbursements as work progressed. The improvements were financed with $1 million of municipal general obligation bonds and a $1 million grant from the U.S. Economic Development Administration. The work was started in late 2001 and completed in September 2002 with a large public dedication ceremony.

Phase I: The Old Main Building and the Classroom Building

The first phase of the redevelopment plan called for converting the 51,500-sq.-ft. Old Main Building and the nearby 24,000-sq.-ft. Classroom Building into seventy loft apartments for lease. Conversion began here because the size, shape, and ceiling volumes of the buildings were ideal for residences. Rehabilitation started on these two buildings in April 2001 and was completed with 98 percent occupancy by August 2002. Historic preservation tax credits required the developer to stay as true to the original structures as possible, and so the outside of the buildings is identical to the original construction (*Builder News Magazine* 2007).

The conversion of these buildings was done in two separate contracts: the first to prepare the site, and the second for actual construction. Richardson and Richardson, Inc. acted as general contractor through both contracts. Hap Richardson, president of the company, spent almost a year inspecting the buildings before actual work commenced. There was water damage, but structural repairs were not extensive (Salem 2001). Work done under the first contract included interior demolition, roof work, lead-based paint and asbestos abatement, and cleaning ninety years of accumulated grime from the exterior. Restoration of the windows was also done at this stage. Every window was shipped to Restoration Works of Kankakee, Illinois, to be stripped, rebuilt, and glazed with double-paned glass. The windows were as good as new when returned (Hainsfurther 2002).

The second contract covered the actual construction of the seventy loft apartments. The Old Main Building is T-shaped when viewed from above. The top of the T is the three stories of classrooms running along the front of the building facing Central

Avenue. The bottom of the T is the gym and auditorium; the interiors of the gym and auditorium space were completely removed, creating a space for the one- and two-story loft apartments. Units within this space have floor plans ranging from 500 to 1,300 sq. ft. The front of the Old Main Building and all three floors of the Classroom Building became units of 500–900 sq. ft. All units in this building are lofts with open floor plans, which include a kitchen, a bath, large operable windows, and a platform above the bath that has been creatively used by loft residents for a variety of things—although technically it is not habitable for building code purposes because it is less than 7 ft. tall. The goal for the renovation project was to avoid either removing any classroom walls or adding any interior walls. Fortunately, vandals had not removed the interior doors. The buildings also retained chalkboards and other schoolhouse elements. Clay tile covers the 13- to 16-ft.-wide hallways, representative quality construction from more than eighty years ago. It is likely that the tile floor will last eighty more years.

During the city's design review process, it was suggested that decorative fencing be installed around the entire perimeter of the property. The idea was to make the campus defensible in the then marginal neighborhood. Rob Dickson opted to install fencing only between the buildings because he did not want the building to take on a fortress-like appearance. However, access to the buildings on the property is controlled twenty-four hours a day through a system of keypads and call boxes (R. Dickson, personal communication, January 2008).

Initial rents for the lofts ranged from $500 to $1,100 with an average rent of $750 per month. Tenants pay all utilities, but the fire-suppression sprinkler system also heats and cools through connection with heat pumps, with tenants paying a prorated share. Absorption was quick, reflecting a high demand for reasonably priced units. The lofts have averaged 98 percent occupancy since March 2002. The resident profile is singles and couples of very diverse ages, occupations, and backgrounds.

In late 2008, a condominium regime was filed for the buildings. The seventy loft apartments gradually will be sold as ownership units, as the market allows. At the time this case study was conducted, the owner expected this process to take approximately three years. Unsold lofts will continue to be rented as apartments.

Financing Old Main and Classroom Buildings

The Old Main and the Classroom Building were the first phase of the project. Detailed financials are shown in Exhibit 21-5. The equity portion of the project was funded from the securitization of the historic preservation tax credits, which amounted to almost $1.3 million, and which were purchased for 92 cents on the dollar. Debt financing was a $3.2 million first mortgage via the Fannie Mae Delegated Underwriting and Servicing commercial loan program. The city provided gap financing amounting to $1.9 million. Payment of both interest and principal on the gap financing comes from cash flow, rental operations, and sales of the apartment units at conversion to condos. Total equity and permanent debt are $6.3 million. The hard cost to rehabilitate and construct apartment units totaled $5 million, or 78 percent of the total cost. A total of almost $1.3 million went to soft costs, or 22 percent of the $6.3 million total.

The loft apartments, since initial rent-up, have carried a 95 percent rate of occupancy. This, plus other project income, yields a stable net operating income stream averaging about $350,000 annually. (See Exhibit 21-6.)

In 2006, after debt service, the property had a before-tax cash flow of $233,108. In 2008, after the five-year holding period for historic preservation tax credits had expired, the developer began converting the units to condominiums. This will be done over time with three units always on the market until the supply is exhausted. It is projected that the sales will result in a net profit of almost $8 million to be divided among the partners.

Exhibit 21-5 Sources and Uses of Funds

The Lofts at Albuquerque High
Old Main and Classroom Buildings
Completed 2002

Sources of funds		
Equity		
Historic Tax Credits	$1,261,000	19.9%
Subtotal Equity	$1,261,000	19.9%
Debt		
Permanent Mortgage	$3,200,000	50.4%
GAP Funding (City of Albuquerque) to be repaid from rents and sale	$1,883,000	29.7%
Subtotal Debt	$5,083,000	80.1%
Total Sources	**$6,344,000**	**100.0%**
Uses of Funds		
Site Acquisition	$-	0.0%
Environmental Remediation	$74,309	1.2%
Subtotal	$74,309	1.2%
Hard Costs		
Phase I Construction	$1,247,297	19.7%
Phase II Construction	$3,624,219	57.1%
Additional Hard Costs	$109,639	1.7%
Subtotal	$4,981,155	78.5%
Soft Costs		
Origination, inspection, taxes, city fees, sewer, and water	$102,681	1.6%
Architectural and engineering	$276,574	4.4%
Market study, website, marketing	$140,845	2.2%
Tax credits, legal, owners' association, accounting	$200,988	3.2%
Telecom consultant, mailboxes, and misc. furnishings	$43,233	0.7%
On-site security	$22,816	0.4%
Contingency and additional soft costs	$146,961	2.3%
Developer's fee	$354,438	5.6%
Subtotal	$1,288,536	20.3%
Total Expenses	**$6,344,000**	**100.0%**
Avg. cost per unit 70 units	$90,600	
Avg. cost for rentable sq. ft.	$123	51,487 rentable square feet
Avg. cost for total sq. ft.	$84	75,000 total square footage

Exhibit 21-6 Stable Year Cash Flow 2006

The Lofts at Albuquerque High
Old Main and Classroom Buildings
51,487 rentable square feet
Stable Year Cash Flow   2006

Revenues		
Rental Income	$614,361	95% occupancy
Other Income	$52,595	
Total Revenue	$666,956	
Expenses		
Total Operating Expenses	$293,112	
Net Operating Income	$373,844	
Debt Service	$140,736	
Before Tax Cash Flow	$233,108	
Condo Conversion Projected Income		
Total Units = 70		
Sale of Property as Condos @ $233/SF * 51,487 Marketable SF	$11,996,410	
Less Selling Costs @ 7.25%	$969,744	
Less Refurbishing of Apartments for Condo Conversion	$375,000	
Projected Net Sales Proceeds	$10,751,727	
Less Repayment of First Lien	$2,825,000	
Net Projected Distributable Sales Proceeds	$7,926,727	
To: Tax Credit Investor	$1,585,345	20%
To: City of Albuquerque	$3,170,691	40%
To: BKM, LLC	$1,585,345	20%
To: Paradigm and Company, LLC	$1,717,781	20%

The city of Albuquerque, as a partner, will receive about $3 million for providing the gap financing of $1.9 million for the project in addition to income it received from annual cash flow.

The principals designed the project to have an exit strategy for all the partners at the end of the five-year tax credit "recapture" period, when the apartments could be converted to condos. Since the city could not be the developer and use the tax credits, private ownership was required. The city was relieved of a blighted property, which will provide a sizable income stream and an abundance of goodwill, which can be priceless at any city hall.

Phase II: Parking Garage and Infill Condos

The development agreement called for the city to construct a parking facility on the half-block just east of the campus. The parking facility provides 261 spaces and was completed in the fall of 2003. The garage was financed with $3.4 million in municipal gross tax receipts tax bonds. The facility is public and charges for all usage.

Immediately following completion of the parking garage, work began on construction of fifty-six lofts in four separate loft buildings. During the lease-up of the Old Main and Classroom buildings, Paradigm found that there was significant demand for for-sale lofts. So Phase II was for-sale condos only, with the exception of 5,700 sq. ft. of retail space in the City Market Lofts building.

The first building completed as part of Phase II was the $2 million Arno Lofts on Central Avenue (historic Route 66), completed on the site of the formerly blighted Zia Motor Lodge in the summer of 2004. The Zia was a relic of the 1950s and was acquired by Mr. Dickson from Libra Investments for $365,000. Although this property was not part of the school acquisition, it was redeveloped in conjunction with the rehabilitation of the school property in order to stimulate more private investment in the neighborhood. This was a private deal, unlike the public/private partnership involved in renovating the buildings at the high school (Hainsfurther 2002). The Arno Lofts provide live-work units on the first floor and strictly residential lofts on the second and third floors. The three-story building of 21,000 sq. ft. contains eighteen apartment condominium units from 950 to 1,500 sq. ft. The building has a south-facing gated courtyard and swimming pool.

The three-story city-owned parking garage near the Arno Lofts is bracketed by loft buildings. The south-facing building contains retail on the first floor and ground-level commercial on the west. The east face of the garage fronts a public alley. The three-story $2 million City Market Lofts were constructed on the south side of the parking deck. On the second and third floors, the building has ten condo units ranging in size from 880 to 1,450 sq. ft., and the first floor has 5,700 sq. ft. of retail space. The developers hoped this space would attract a neighborhood market. It is being leased by a salon day spa and a real estate office, with two bays remaining to be leased.

On the north end of the garage are the Copper Lofts, consisting of twelve lofts on three floors. The city insisted that this building's design be a transitional buffer between the school campus and the residential area east of the school. Consequently it was not faced with brick veneer. Instead the building is wood-frame construction covered with stucco, giving it a northern New Mexico look. The building was completed in the summer of 2004 at a cost of $1 million.

The fourth building structure, also completed in 2004, was Campus Lofts. The building is located on the campus proper, on the northeast corner of the courtyard. Accordingly, it is faced with brick of a dark color similar to the brick on the school buildings. The units in this building range in size from 960 to 1,650 sq. ft. Each of the lofts features an open floor plan allowing the occupants latitude in how the unit is laid out and decorated. Fixed areas are the kitchen and bathroom(s).

All of the fifty-six loft condo units were offered for sale with prices ranging from $88,000 to $264,000, depending on square footage, location, and amenities. These sold out and were constructed with no public subsidy.

Phase III: Library Building

Rick Davis of R. Davis Companies planned the redevelopment of the Library Building at Albuquerque High School. Rob Dickson transferred development rights to the building to Rick as compensation for work that Rick's company did during the competitive bid selection process in 1998 and 1999. The redevelopment followed a plan to redevelop the 10,000-sq.-ft. building as a rental office for a single tenant. The building renovation retained all of its major elements, including the original library floor and bookcases that lined the walls. The city-owned parking garage and available on-street parking made the building attractive to a medical records firm, which entered into a five-year lease for the space at market rental rates (R. Dickson, personal communication, January 2008).

Phase IV: Gym Building

The high school gym was originally constructed as a "political present" to New Mexico and its congressional delegation as one of President Roosevelt's Works Progress Administration (WPA) projects. Mr. Dickson described the footprint of the building as akin to a silhouette of Mickey Mouse because of its two small wings connected to the massive central gym space.

The original renovation plan for the Gym Building called for a combination of retail and office uses. However, as demand for owner-occupied housing increased in downtown Albuquerque and the demand for office and retail space declined, Mr. Dickson recognized that his plans needed to respond to the changing marketplace. The success of the modestly priced new construction condominiums of the second phase indicated additional modestly priced units would be quickly absorbed. Accordingly, the units in the Gym Lofts building developed as for-sale loft condominiums priced to attract singles and couples of all ages, incomes, ethnicity, and geographic origin. Mr. Dickson hoped to avoid having leftover units by not selling at a higher price point. He chose not to use historic preservation tax credits, which had previously been used on the Old Main and Classroom buildings, so that he could immediately enter the market with for-sale units to capitalize on the demand for owner-occupied units. Use of historic preservation tax credits would have required Mr. Dickson to hold the property as rental apartments for five years before condo conversion took place, which he was unwilling to do for the Gym Lofts (R. Dickson, personal communication, January 2008).

The project was designed as a "green" project, with the goal that the building be a LEED-certifiable project.[1] Accordingly, construction techniques resulted in a building that is energy efficient while still retaining the architectural character of the original construction.

"I focus on the walk-able, mixed-use, mixed-income neighborhood, well-served by transit, as the fundamental increment of development," says Dickson, who is a member of a group called Congress for the New Urbanism and the National Trust for Historic Preservation. "Any project I do has to fit within the framework of a master plan for such a neighborhood in which that project is located. I'm selling lifestyle in such a neighborhood, not condos" (*Builder News Magazine* 2007).

The interior renovation was designed to preserve much of the building's original elements. The original maple gym floor was refinished, a wall of bleachers remains, and the original ceiling trusses with clerestory windows have been preserved. The exterior renovation required the replacement of the old cast gypsum roof deck system with a steel deck. The original casement windows were replaced with new historically accurate aluminum casements. The original wooden windows were rebuilt, dipped, and reglazed using Low-E insulated glass.

The architect's challenge was filling the large volumes of space in the Gym Building with loft units. The redeveloped interior of the entire Gym Building is approximately 68,000 sq. ft. Ten units were spaced between the support columns on the ground level below the gym, which had served as the cafeteria and kitchen for the school. The cavernous gym was converted into two levels of ten lofts each. The twenty-four remaining units are contained in the wings of the building and below or next to the bleachers. The gym

Exhibit 21-7 The Lofts at Albuquerque High Photographs and Plans

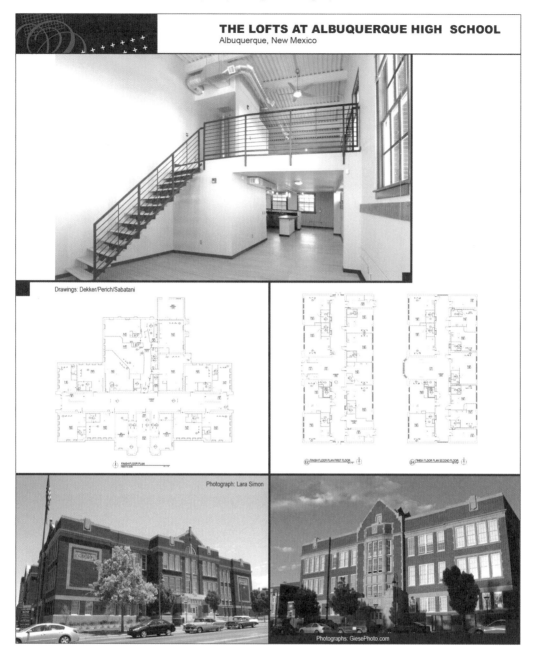

THE LOFTS AT ALBUQUERQUE HIGH SCHOOL
Albuquerque, New Mexico

Drawings: Dekker/Perich/Sabatani

Photograph: Lara Simon

Photographs: GiesePhoto.com

bleachers' central section was kept intact. The clerestory windows in the roof provide natural lighting for the space.

The new structures within the gym had to be structurally independent of the original construction for seismic purposes. The units were framed with a seismic structural system of steel and wood joists. These were covered with drywall and checked for sound transmission.

The interiors of the units range in size from 500 sq. ft. to a spacious 1,900 sq. ft., with larger units having two interior levels and two baths. The interiors provide the owner with bright natural light from the gym windows, portions of brickwork from the gym walls, and a large open space that can be decorated to the taste of the occupant. Exhibit 21-7 shows several images of the campus and one of the lofts.

Phase V: BelVedere Urban Courtyard Living

The final phase of The Lofts at Albuquerque High project was construction of BelVedere Courtyard homes on a 2-acre site, which spans an entire city block north of the school campus. The residents enjoy scenic mountain views from their porches.

The project was designed as a courtyard gated community with every doorway leading inward from the courtyard. The courtyard design was the product of codesigners Terra Designs LLC and Hartman & Majewski Design Group. Seventeen of the fifty-four homes have street entrances in addition to the courtyard entry. Design cues were taken from Spanish and Mediterranean cultures, along with influence from the indigenous Anasazi, an ancient civilization that once resided in multistory, multifamily dwellings in northern New Mexico. According to Abby Roedel, a building with these Native American and Hispanic influences has not been built in Albuquerque in a long time (Roedel 2005). The homes were constructed and completed in the spring of 2008 with 90 percent occupancy by the fall of that year.

The lofts range in size from 800 to 1,000 sq. ft., not including garages and decks. The one-, two-, and three-bedroom courtyard homes, townhomes, and side yard houses range in size from 700 to 2,000 sq. ft., excluding garages or decks. The interiors of the homes feature either the open space of loft living or a traditional design with interior walls and doors. The exterior finish materials are stucco, brick, and siding with either flat or pitched roofs. The project also includes some commercial storefronts along Broadway Boulevard, which is a main street in Albuquerque. The commercial space represents about 7 percent of the project square footage.

BelVedere was designed to capitalize on more traditional households wishing to live in downtown Albuquerque. Three-bedroom units are being offered. Mr. Dickson is curious to see if the units attract families with children.

The project represented an investment of $11.7 million of completely private funding. The development consists of one-, two-, and three-bedroom homes ranging in price from $189,000 to $439,000. The average price per square foot is $183, but including amenities such as garages and decks increases the price to $206 per square foot.

They sold ten BelVedere homes out of the fifty-four before sales activity stalled. "We did not sell either of the three-bedroom townhomes or any of the dozen two-bedroom townhomes, although they all have been leased" (R. Dickson, personal communication, January 2008).

While the rest of the country was in the midst of recovering from the foreclosure crisis, Rob Dickson captured the Urban Revitalization Award from the Home Builders Association of Central New Mexico for the BelVedere Urban Courtyard Living project. BelVedere's fifty-four homes were 90 percent occupied within sixty days of the completion of construction by a combination of owners and renters (Roedel 2005). The project's location in proximity to the high-paying and stable employment generators of local hospitals and the University of New Mexico has been a benefit. Frugal consumers recognize the benefits of saving on fuel costs and living close to work to reduce driving time.

Lessons Learned

- *City intervention with condemnation:* The city of Albuquerque had the political will to use condemnation to acquire the long-vacant historic Albuquerque High School. It is unlikely that the issues of ownership would have been cleared up had the city not intervened. City control of the transaction allowed it to expedite and manage the process, which eventually resulted in the redevelopment of the site.
- *Master planning and market analysis:* The developer used the New Urbanism charrette master planning process and real estate market analysis to determine project viability. This avoided using even more government subsidies as proposed by one of the contending developers.
- *Phased development and flexibility:* Albuquerque's flexible zoning of the property to allow a mix of uses including housing, retail, and offices was sound city planning. The flexibility of the project's master plan allowed the developer to gauge and respond to what the marketplace wanted and allowed market signals that condominiums would be absorbed.
- *Public investment and cooperation:* Allocations of financial resources for rehabilitation of the historic buildings, construction of the parking garage, infrastructure, and beautification assistance were good civic investments. Cities need to have war chests to make such development happen. Over 25 percent of the sources of funds for this deal were public monies.
- *Create a location and know your market:* Real estate is all about location. To jumpstart the project, the developer thought that the "bohemian class" would be the first to take a risk on downtown living.

Thus, the modest apartments had a particular appeal to artists, graduate students, and urbanites, and a new urban address was created.

Conclusion

In December 2005 the Sierra Club recognized East Downtown Redevelopment Project—Historic Albuquerque in a report titled "Building Better: A Guide to America's Best New Development Projects." The criteria for selection were that projects were to preserve existing community assets and involve citizens in the planning. Rob Dickson praised the Sierra Club for supporting walkable, mixed-use, mixed-income neighborhoods well served by transit as well as cars. He further stated that building sprawl is easy, but building great neighborhoods, like those seen in the past, is difficult. That needs to change (Jojola 2005).

The National Association of Realtors says it's all about location, location, location. Rob Dickson saved a location.

A final word. "When this first started, the original Albuquerque High campus was viewed as a project where Bohemians were going to live. Now we are attracting households and residents who wouldn't have looked at this area before," said Rob Dickson (Roedel 2005).

Note

1. LEED, Leadership in Energy and Environmental Design, certification requires that a building, in addition to being energy efficient, contain other elements, such as a location within walking distance to employment, shopping areas, and public transportation; quality architecture and interior design; and "green" features.

References and Works Consulted

Builder News Magazine. 2007. Paradigm & Company, May. http://www.buildernewsmag.com/viewnews.pl?id=632.

City-Data.com. 2008. www.citydata.com.

Drummond, S. 2005. "Born-Again Buildings." CCIM Institute, July/August. www.ccim.com/cive-magazine/articles/born-again-buildings.

Hainsfurther, S. 2002. "Historic Preservation Shows Past, Perfected." *New Mexico Business Weekly*, September 27. http://albuquerque.bizjournals.com/albuquerque/stories/2002/09/30/focus1.html.

Jojola, L. 2005. "East Downtown Work Cheered." *Albuquerque Journal,* December 2, Section: Front Page Metro.

"The Lofts at Albuquerque High." 2008. www.abqhigh.com. U.S. Department of Commerce, Bureau of the Census. 2000. "2000 Census of Population and Housing." www.census.gov.

Roedel, A. 2005. "New Downtown Loft Comes with a Historic Twist." *New Mexico Business Weekly,* October 28. http://www.bizjournals.com/albuquerque/stories/2005/10/31/story8.html.

Salem, Nancy. 2007 *Albuquerque Tribune Online Business.* http://web.abqtrib.com/archives/business/01/07/071601_business_aqhigh.html.

Schroeder, K. 2000. "Old Albuquerque High Plans Are Nearing Final Approval." *New Mexico Business Weekly,* August 7. http:www.nmapartment.com/press/nmbw080720.

Soussan, T. 2000. "Developer Proceeds on Old AHS Project." *Albuquerque Journal,* February 5. http://www.nmapartment.com/press/ajo2052000ahs/.

Wendel, K. R. 2004. "Albuquerque Activity Report—April 2004: Lofty Ambitions." *South-West Contractor,* April. http://southwest.construction.com/features/archive/0404_feature2–5.asp.

Zissman, M. 2003. "The Old Albuquerque High School Campus Is Revived as a Live/Work/Play Community." *Building Design and Construction, Features:* Merit Award, October 1, 35.

ADA: Americans with Disabilities Act. The ADA of 1990 was a broad-ranging civil rights law that prohibits discrimination based on disability status. It affects minimum standards for physical access to handicapped people, described in the ADA Standards for Accessible Design.

amortization: From the French ("to death"); the process of fully eliminating debt over the life of a loan.

appraisal: The practice of determining the value of real property under certain assumptions at a specific point in time.

back-of-the-envelope analysis: An informal calculation of financial feasibility, sometimes performed on a scrap of paper. It uses rounded numbers to quickly develop a ballpark conclusion.

bedroom community: A suburban community that is primarily residential, has little employment, and features above-average public schools, from which most downtown workers commute to their jobs.

berm: In landscaping, a level space, shelf, or raised barrier separating two areas.

big-box: A large (over 100,000 sq. ft.) single-tenant retail building also known as super-center, superstore, or megastore; typically part of a chain.

block club: A club where a group of neighbors who are committed to working together actively address various quality-of-life issues.

board of zoning appeals (BZA): A local board empowered to overturn decisions of a zoning authority.

brownfield: Urban land that is prevented from attaining its highest and best use due to actual or perceived environmental contamination. It may have redevelopment potential if cleaned up.

Brownfield Funds: The U.S. EPA's Brownfield Program gives direct funding for brownfield assessment, site cleanup, loans, and environmental-related training.

call option: A contract that gives the buyer the right (but not obligation) to buy an underlying asset (stock or other) at a specified strike price on or before a specific calendar date. The buyer pays a *premium* to the seller for this right. The reverse is a put option, which some have modeled as being similar to mortgage default.

capitalization rate: Also called cap rate; the percentage of the net operating income produced by a real estate investment divided by its acquisition price (or, alternatively, its current market value).

captive tenant: An existing tenant who has very limited options to move away.

Case-Shiller Index: Standard & Poor's housing price index providing constant-quality house price indices for twenty metro areas in the United States.

cash call: If the entity in which you have invested requires an additional infusion of funds, the management will issue a cash call to members/investors/owners. The cash call is usually proportionate to ownership.

census tract: Census tracts are small statistical subdivisions within a county and typically have between 2,500 and 8,000 people. When first delineated, they were designed to be homogeneous with respect to population characteristics, economic status, and living conditions. The geographic size of tracts may vary based on density.

certificate of occupancy: A document typically issued by a local building department that certifies a building's compliance with applicable building codes and other regulations, proclaiming it to be suitable for occupancy.

certified historic structure: Any building, portion of a building, either listed in the National Register of Historic Places or located within a registered historic district, that has been certified by the U.S. Department of the Interior as historically significant.

chain of title: The history of historical ownership of a property.

churn: A measure of the number of individuals or transactions moving through the market over a specific period of time—sometimes called turnover.

collateral: A borrower's pledge of certain property to a lender as security for a loan.

community development entities (CDE): A vehicle for guiding investment in the New Market Tax Credit program.

Community Reinvestment Act (CRA): A federal law that requires commercial banks and savings associations to help meet the borrowers' needs within all segments of the communities, especially low- and moderate-income neighborhoods. This means lenders must make loans in the same neighborhoods from which they take deposits.

comprehensive plan: Sometimes called a master plan, it is the outcome of the comprehensive planning process. It dictates public policy in terms of transportation, utilities, land use, recreation, zoning capital improvements, and housing.

concentric zone model: Sometimes also known as the Burgess model or solar model, it explains dynamic urban social structures. The model has concentric rings with the central business district (CBD) at the center, surrounded by a transition zone, and by lower-, middle- and upper-class housing, and nonresidential uses.

contingency: Conditional clause in an offer to buy real estate (e.g., inspection) that limits a buyer's or seller's responsibility to close the deal if conditions are not met.

Davis-Bacon: A federal law that requires paying prevailing (union) wages on public works projects. It increases the funds required for rehabilitation.

debt service coverage ratio: The ratio of net operating income available for debt service for interest and principal each year.

discount rate: The investor's interest rate, based on the opportunity cost of capital, used in discounted cash flow analysis to determine the present value of future cash flows, including sale.

Economic Development Authority (EDA): The EDA leads the federal economic development agenda by promoting innovation, competitiveness, and leading America's growth in the worldwide economy. It also provides loans and grants to achieve these goals.

edge city: A satellite community with a concentration of business, shopping, and entertainment outside a traditional downtown. The term was coined in *Edge City: Life on the New Frontier,* by Joel Garreau (1991).

Environmental Protection Agency (EPA): Federal or state-level agency.

Federal Department of Housing and Urban Development (HUD): HUD's mission is to create strong, sustainable, inclusive communities with quality affordable homes. HUD works to strengthen local housing markets to protect consumers and boost the economy, assist creation of affordable rental housing, use housing as a mechanism for improving overall quality of life, and to build inclusive and sustainable communities free from discrimination.

flashing: An architectural term, typically part of a roof, where thin, continuous pieces of sheet metal are installed to prevent the leakage of water into the building from an angle or a joint.

Gantt chart: A visual type of interlinked bar charts, developed by Henry Gantt, showing details on tasks and timing of a project completion schedule.

gentrification: A dynamic urban process in upgrading urban areas when demographic changes bring middle-class residents into a formerly poor neighborhood, exacerbating tensions.

greenfield: Opposite of a brownfield, a piece of virgin land that lacks any constraints imposed by prior urban land uses; hence, there is no need to demolish an existing structure or conduct environmental remediation.

historic preservation tax credits (HPTC): Sometimes called rehabilitation tax credits (RTC), they encourage private sector investment in the rehabilitation of historic buildings. For example, a 20 percent income tax credit is available for the rehabilitation of historic, income-producing buildings that are determined by the U.S. Secretary of the Interior (through the National Park Service) to be a "certified historic structure." Also sometimes available at the state and local level.

HOME: A large federal block grant to states and local governments aimed at creating affordable housing for low-income households.

hurdle rate: The minimum rate of return on a project or an investment required by an investor to put funds in a project.

infill: Structures that fill in a vacant lot within the existing urban fabric.

Ionic columns: A classic architectural feature, the Ionic capital is characterized by the use of volutes, or spiral, scroll-like ornamentation.

keystone: A capstone architectural feature that is a wedge-shaped stone piece at the apex of a masonry arch or vault.

LIHTC "substantial rehab": Part of the LIHTC program, a substantial investment is any amount incurred within a twenty-four-month period that equals or exceeds 25 percent of the adjusted basis of the building.

lintel: A load-bearing building and decorative architectural feature often found over portals, doors, and windows.

load factor: Sometimes called the gross-to-net space ratio. In a real estate lease, the load factor is applied to a tenant's usable space that reflects the tenant's proportionate share of common area space (hallways, restrooms, elevator lobby, mechanical rooms, etc.).

loan-to-value ratio: Used by commercial lenders to express the ratio of a loan underwritten to a value at the time of origination.

loggia: An architectural feature that refers to a gallery or corridor, usually at ground level, on the facade of a building that is open to the air on one side, and supported by side columns or wall openings.

low-income housing tax credits (LIHTC): The LIHTC program is an indirect federal subsidy used to finance the development of affordable rental housing for low-income households, often with a mix of market-rate and subsidized units.

multinomial logit: An advanced statistical technique similar to regression analysis that generalizes logistic regression by allowing the dependent variable to have more than two discrete outcomes.

National Register of Historic Places: The official list of the historic places in the United States deemed worthy of preservation by the National Park Service. The National Register of Historic Places coordinates public and private efforts to identify, evaluate, support, and protect America's historic and archeological sites.

net present value: The sum of the present values (PVs) of the individual annual net cash flows, plus value at time of sale, after considering cost to acquire the property.

NMTC: The New Markets Tax Credit Program was established by the U.S. Congress in 2000 to generate new or increased investment capital into operating businesses and (generally nonresidential) real estate projects located in low-income urban neighborhoods. NMTC grants investors a tax credit against their federal income tax in return for making equity investments in projects through financial institutions called community development entities (CDEs).

Not In My Backyard (NIMBY): Characterizing the opposition by residents to a proposal for some new development nearby because it is close to them, often with the implication that the residents think the developments are needed in society but should be farther away.

other people's money: Leveraging the money of others, usually from a bank or equity investment partners.

Phase I Environmental Assessment: A report prepared for real property that identifies potential or existing environmental contamination liabilities based purely on past use/secondary sources.

Phase II Environmental Assessment: An "intrusive" investigation for environmental contamination that collects original samples of soil, groundwater, or building materials and analyzes them for various contaminants. This investigation is typically undertaken after a Phase I assessment found a high likelihood of environmental contamination.

planned unit development (PUD): Designed grouping of several compatible land uses, like housing, retail, office, and recreation, often with flexible zoning, within one project.

present value: Also known as present discounted value, it is the current value of a stream of variable future payments over time, plus the value of the sale of the property, combined into one figure.

pro forma: A type of real estate analysis used to convey relevant information concerning a development project. It considers ongoing project expenses and income that the project will produce, plus its original development cost.

quality assurance, quality control (QAQC): A set of lightly redundant reviews used to assure the quality of a product and consistency of work product: "two sets of eyes on everything."

radon gas: Comes from the natural (radioactive) breakdown of uranium in soil, rock, and water, sometimes contained in the foundation of a building. If the gas is confined, it can get into the air and make you sick.

rate of return (ROR): The ratio of money gained or lost on an investment relative to the amount of funds invested. The unleveraged net ROR is net operating income divided by project cost.

REIT: Real estate investment trust, a special type of corporation, trust, or association that acts as an investment agent specializing in real estate debt and/or equity under Internal Revenue Code Section 856.

request-for-proposals (RFP) process: A solicitation made, often through a bidding process, by an agency or a seller that has a site it wants redeveloped. Potential buyers submit business proposals to win the right to develop the project.

rezoning: To change the zoning classification and therefore the use-by-right of a property.

shell corporation: A company, typically a limited liability corporation (LLC), that serves as a vehicle for business transactions (such as owning real estate) without itself having any significant assets or operations besides the property.

spot market: A market where financial instruments or commodities are traded for immediate or short-term delivery. Spot markets can be thinly traded with volatile prices.

Stations of the Cross: A series of artistic sculptural representations of Christ carrying the Cross to his crucifixion. Many Catholic churches have one at intervals along the side walls of the nave.

TIF: Tax increment financing is a public-private financing technique used for subsidizing development, infrastructure, and other community-improvement projects through allocation of future property tax payments to retire bonds.

time value of money: The value of money considering a given amount of interest earned, or opportunity cost for an investment, over a set period of time.

transom: The transverse horizontal structural beam, bar, or crosspiece that separates a door from a window above it.

tuck-pointing: A technique of using two contrasting colors of mortar in brickwork, where one color matches the bricks themselves, to give the impression that very fine joints have been made.

Uniform Relocation Act: A federal law that establishes a minimum standard for all federally funded projects that involve acquisition of real property or displacement of people from their homes, farms, or businesses.

urban renewal: A federal urban land redevelopment program that was most active in the 1950s to the 1970s. It featured wholesale movement of lower-income, inner-city populations and commercial areas, replacing them with new commercial and office and public uses.

VAT tile floors: Vinyl asbestos floor tiles.

white flight: Large-scale migration of whites away from racially mixed urban cities to more racially homogeneous suburbs or exurban parts of the same metro area, typically resulting from fear of crime and court-ordered busing for school integration.

zoning variance: The process by which an applicant can request deviation from a zoning ordinance, usually heard by the BZA.

NOTE: Page references in *italics* refer to photos and illustrations.

African Americans, 20, 23–24, 183–84
Albuquerque, New Mexico, 352; demographics of, 353, *356;* support for Albuquerque High project, 355–57
Albuquerque Central High School Campus, *204–7. See also* The Lofts at Albuquerque High (Albuquerque, New Mexico)
Alexander, Merry-Ship & Alt (AMA Real Estate Group), 298, 300–301, 304–5
Alexander, Rob, 300, 304
Allen, Michael R., 172, 288
Alt, Sheree, 300–301
Antony, John, 300
apartments, 142, 215; ADA-accessible, 336–38; in Albuquerque High project, 353, 357, 359–61; churches redeveloped as, *85–88;* in Clinton Cultural Campus, 342, 344, 347–48; condos *vs.,* 39, 260; converted to condos, 73n6, 108–9, 360–61; demographics of residents in, 157, 360; design problems in, 321, 344, 347–48; in Lafayette Street project, 306–10; operating expenses of, 71–72, 132, 360; schools redeveloped as, 138–43, *145–46;* in West Tech High School project, 314–15, 319, 321, 327, *329. See also* housing; rents
appraisals, for valuation of rehab projects, 130–31
The Arc Arkansas, 334, 336–49, *337*
architects: for Babeville Performing Arts Center, 270–71; for Clinton Cultural Campus, 346; in evaluating feasibility of rehab projects, 56–61, 74–75; for Jamaica Performing Arts Center, 238; for Lafayette Street project, 305; for Saints Peter and Paul project, 258; schematic designs by, 61; for Urban Krag, 246–48; for West Tech High School project, 319, 321
architectural features, 203, 285; preserved in Albuquerque High project, 360, 364–65; preserved in Babeville building, 267–68; preserved in Hot Springs schools, 346; preserved in Jamaica Performing Arts Center, 239, 241; preserved in Lafayette Street project, 305; preserved in Red Door Church project, 227, 231; preserved in Saints Peter and Paul project, 254, 258, 260; preserved in Urban Krag, 248–50; repurposing in re-

development, 241; in site attributes, 32, 61, 81–82, 211
Architectural Resources, 270
architectural style: of Babeville building, 266–68; of Christian Scientist churches, 18; in historical value description as variable in statistical analysis, *46;* of Hot Springs Senior and Junior high schools, 342; of Jamaica Performing Arts Center, 234; of megachurches, 19, 22; in Oregon Historic District, 245; of St. Aloysius Gonzaga Church, 287; of St. Joseph Church, 298; of St. Joseph's African American Episcopal Church, 183
Arno Lofts (Albuquerque, New Mexico), 363
ArtCentric (Corvallis, Oregon), 181–84, *182*
arts centers, 83–84, *85–86;* performance spaces proposed in redevelopment projects, 173, 304, 345; St. Joseph's African American Episcopal Church redeveloped as, 183–84. *See also* Babeville Performing Arts Center (Buffalo, New York); Jamaica Performing Arts Center (Queens, New York)
asbestos, 59–60, 64, 75, 300, 320
Asbury Delaware Methodist Church (Buffalo, New York). *See* Babeville Performing Arts Center (Buffalo, New York)
Assemblies of God, 13

Babeville Performing Arts Center (Buffalo, New York), 203, *204–7, 267, 272;* case study of, 266–76; highest and best use analysis of, 84–89, *87–88*
banks, 110, 132–33
Battaglia Family Trust, 354, 357
Bellon Wrecking and Salvage, 292–93
BelVedere Urban Courtyard homes (Albuquerque High project), 366–67
Big Box Reuse (Christiansen), 190–91, 195
big-box stores. *See* retail use/space
Bommarito, Vincent, 287–89, 293, 296
bond financing, 113–15
Boston, Massachusetts, 18, 170, 178–80, 186
Boston Redevelopment Authority (BRA), 258–59
branding, architectural features in, 61
Brickman, Andrew, 222, 226
bridge loans, 112
Brooks, Larry, 356–57
Brownstones at Derbyshire (Cleveland, Ohio). *See* Red Door Church project (Cleveland, Ohio)

mergers of, 13–14, 280, 285; numbers of, *27–29*; numbers of decreasing, 12–13, *15*, 18, 246; numbers of increasing, *14*, 16; reactions to redevelopment projects, 178, 182, 192–94; size of decreasing, 18, 89, 160, 195, 285–86; size of increasing, 13, 194, 300; vacating buildings, 13, 268

consensus building, in planning-approval process, 159–61

conservation easements, sale of, 106

construction costs: for Babeville Performing Arts Center, 274; inadequate budget for Clinton Cultural Campus, 346; for Jamaica Performing Arts Center, 241–42; for Saints Peter and Paul project, 260, 262. *See also* hard costs; soft costs

construction loans, 112, 134–35, 259

construction management, 273; in analysis of case studies, *206;* importance of, 203, 213; problems in, 238–39, 241, 248, 259–60, 264; for Red Door Church project, 228–29; for Saints Peter and Paul project, 259–60; for West Tech High School project, 320–22, 330

contingency budget: depletion of, 65, 67, 213, 322, 345; importance of, 348–49; for new construction *vs.* rehab projects, 65–67, 72; size of, 67, 274, 347–48

Coody, Dan, 305

Copper Lofts (Albuquerque, New Mexico), 363

corporations, ownership by, 125

cost approach, to value of rehab projects, 130–31, 133, 147n1

cost overruns, 213, 257; sources of, 65–67; in West Tech High School project, 321–22, 324, 330

CoStar Group, Inc., 41–42

Cudell Improvement Corporation, 319

cultural heritage, zone of, 21–22

cultural uses, 214; as end-use outcomes for adaptive reuses, 33–34, *35–36*, 37, 39; factors affecting successful redevelopment for, 42, *49*, 209; highest and best use analysis of, 83–84; NYC's redevelopment projects for, 237–38. *See also* arts centers

Davis, Rick, 363

debt, 110–15, 133

debt financing, for Albuquerque High project, 360

debt service, 112, 326, 347

debt service coverage ratio (DSCR), 143

default, 111–12; strategies to avoid, 126, 208; in West Tech High project, 314, 319, 323, 326, 331

Delaware Avenue Asbury Methodist Church (Buffalo, New York). *See* Babeville Performing Arts Center (Buffalo, New York)

demographics, 281; Albuquerque, 353, *356;* of apartment renters, 39, 360; Boston, 254–57; Buffalo, 268, *269;* Catholic, 279; Cleveland, 317–18; of condo buyers, 229–30, 261–62; Dayton, 246–47; Fayetteville, 301, *302;* Hot Springs, 342, *343;* neighborhood, 32, 223–26, 235, *236;* St. Louis, 289, *290*

demolition, 20, 227; in analysis of case studies, 199–200, *204;* Asbury Methodists slated for, 266, 268; of church buildings, 15–16; in cost estimates of rehab *vs.* new construction, 62, 64; Deutsche Evangelical Reformed Church slated for, 244, 246, 248; efforts to avoid, 266, 352; of St. Aloysius, 284, 287–89; West Tech High School slated for, 319

Dennis, Jay, 193

Dennis Developmental Center (Little Rock, Arkansas), *340*

deRossert, Kate, 237

Deutsche Evangelical Reformed Church (Dayton, Ohio). *See* Urban Krag project (Dayton, Ohio)

developer profit, 130, 214, 299, 307, 348, 350; in analysis of case studies, 202–3, *204–5;* in church-to-condos deal, 135, *138;* rates of return on investment and, 143–46; from Red Door Church project, 97, 222, 229; from Saints Peter and Paul project, 254, 262, 264; varying by type of projects, 68–69, 72, 214–15

developers, 56, 146, 215, 330; competing for Albuquerque High project, 355–57; equity of, 103, 104, 111–12; financial tools for, 115, *116–25;* gaining ownership, 354–57; for Jamaica Performing Arts Center, 237, 242; pulling out of West Tech High School project, 314, 320, 323, 330; reducing equity investment of, 103, 111

Developer's Toolbox for financing, 115, *116–25*

development costs, 68, 102, 143, 214, 262, *295*, 306–8, 310; of rehab *vs.* new construction, 62–63

Dickson, Rob, 352–53, 355–57, 363; New Urbanism of, 352, 364, 367

DiFranco, Ani, 266, 268, 271, 274, 276

Dimartino Homes, 291

Dimit, Scott, 227

disabilities, people with, 336–38, 344

documentation, need for ongoing, 58–59

Dutch Reformed Church (Queens, New York). *See* Jamaica Performing Arts Center (Queens, New York)

easements, sale of, 106

East Side Lofts (Little Rock, Arkansas), *339*

Eastside High Lofts Phase II (Little Rock, Arkansas), 338

Eastside Lofts (Little Rock, Arkansas), 346

Ecker, Michael, 259

Eddy, Mary Baker, 18

effective gross income (EGI), 142

Emilio, Douglas, 238

end-use decision process, 79, *79–80*

end-use outcomes, of adaptive reuse of religious buildings and schools: acceptable uses, 33–34, 37, 170–81, 281, 282–84, *282–85;* in analysis of case studies, 203–8; for Catholic churches, *282*, 282–84, *284;* factors influencing, 32, 37, 42, 209–10;

74; goals for redevelopment projects, 184–86, 288, 296; in highest and best use analysis, 82, 83–84; identifying historic value of, 151–52; low-income residents in, 213, 348; opposition of, 158, 159–61, 175, 179, 213, 303; promoting development of, 352, 364, 367; reactions to redevelopment projects, 178–80, 186, 203–8, 211, 222–23, 246, 274, 303; reactions to Saints Peter and Paul project, 179, 186, 258, 262–64; support for redevelopment projects, 176, 226–27, 238, 251, 274. *See also* communities

net operating income (NOI), 132–33, 142–43, 147n2, 347, 360

New Argenta Development Group, 338

new construction: included in redevelopment projects, 227–29, 319, 358, 362–63, 366–67; redevelopment projects compared to, 56, 61–67, 63, 69–72, 70, 104, 161, 191

New Market Tax Credits (NMTCs), 110, 214, 274

New Urbanism, 352, 364, 367

New York City: adaptive reuses for cultural projects in, 237–38; Department of Design and Construction in, 237–38

Norquist, John, 288

North College Development Co., 298

North Little Rock Handicapped Services, 336

not-for-profit organizations, 126, 130, 212; conversion of religious buildings for, 180–85, 203. *See* community organizations

Nottingham, John, 178

Nottingham Spirk building (Cleveland, Ohio), *177–78*

offices, 50, 209, 214; in Albuquerque High project, 353, 357–59, 363–64; in Babeville project, 266, 268–70, 272; churches redeveloped as, 69–71, *70*, 176–78, 181, 185, 284, *285*; as end-use outcomes for adaptive reuses, 33–34, *35–36*, 37, 41; successful redevelopment of, 42, 193–94. *See also* commercial uses

Ogrocki, Gary, 227

O'Neill, Theresa, 260

operating expenses, 71–72, 112, 326, 328–29

Oregon Historic District (Dayton, Ohio), 244–46

Orlean, Art, 331n3

Orlean, David, 321, 327, 330–31

Orlean Company, 314, 319–21, 324, 327, 330

Osteen, Joel, 191–92

Our Lady of Good Counsel (St. Louis), *283*

outcomes, of redevelopment projects, 170, 208, 215, 328–30; nonmonetary benefits of, 33, 43n5, 130, 215. *See also* end-use outcomes, of adaptive reuse of religious buildings and schools

ownership structure, 146; effects on financing, 115, 124–27; tax implications of, 104, 124

Padalka, Alex, 234

Paradigm & Company, 352, 355–57, 362–63

parking, 36, 37, *38*, *40*, 57, 64, 160, 259, 342; for Albuquerque High project, 358, 362–63; church requirements for, 300, 304; in converted commercial spaces, 192–94; for Red Door Church project, 227, 229; in site attributes, 60, 74, 82, 84; in West Tech High School project, 327–28

partnerships, 104, 124–25

Patterson, Steve, 288

Patterson, Tim, 246, 248

"Payment in Lieu of Taxes" (PILOT, NY state program), 274

PCB (polychlorinated biphenyl), 60

Performance Arts Center (Buffalo, New York). *See* Babeville Performing Arts Center (Buffalo, New York)

performance arts centers. *See* arts centers; *specific projects*

permanent loans, 112

phasing, of redevelopment work, 203, 211; in Albuquerque High project, 352, *354–55*, 357–66, 367; benefits of, 215, 259; in Clinton Cultural Campus project, 342, 344; in Red Door Church project, 222, 226, 229

planning-approval process, 154–55, 211; for Lafayette Street project, 304, 310; public involvement in, 159–62; for Saints Peter and Paul project, 258–59; for Urban Krag, 246–48; winning community support in, 157–59

planning process, for rehab projects, 150

plans: for Babeville Performing Arts Center, *272;* for Dennis Developmental Center, *340;* for Lafayette Street project, *307;* for The Lofts at Albuquerque High, *358*, *365;* Magnolia Square Residential Development, *286;* for West Side Lofts, *340*. *See also* site plans

Pledger, Diane, 184

policy recommendations, 215–16

Presbyterian Church (PCUSA), 13

present value (PV), 143

preservationists, trying to save St. Aloysius, 287–89, 296

pro formas, in predevelopment planning, 134, *135, 152*

professionals: specializing in redevelopment projects: Alexander, Merry-Ship & Alt specializing in, 301

professionals, in redevelopment projects: specializing: profitability increased by multiple, 214

professionals, involved in redevelopment projects, 270–71, 275; lack of clarity among, 322; relations among, 330; Urban Krag, 248

profits. *See* developer profit

property ownership, 217n4, 257; in Albuquerque High project, 352–57, 362, 367; by cities, 234, 241, 268, 319, 352–57, 367; as form of equity, 103–5; of Urban Krag, 250–51; of vacant buildings, 209, 342; in West Tech High School project, 326–28, 331 property tax abatements, 214, 227, 292, 319

property taxes, 190, 203, 274, 276n2

property values, 159, 194, 209, 326; effects of adaptive reuse projects on, 104, 132

Protestantism, seven sisters of, 23

public debt, 113–14

public incentive programs, 58

public involvement, 159–62, 184, 206. *See also* community meetings

public opposition, to redevelopment projects, 154; of church-to-condos projects, 158, 180, 186, 288; importance of addressing, 157–62, 161, 203–8, 303–4; off-site effects of, 159; rezoning for, 155–57, 303; Saints Peter and Paul project and, 258, 264n1; to secular uses for sacred buildings, 168, 174–75; sources of, 159, 187, 213

public opposition to redevelopment projects, 154

public subsidies, 150, 152, 211–12; in analysis of case studies, 199, 202–3, 205; for Jamaica Performing Arts Center, 237, 241; for redevelopment of religious buildings, 130, 208; for redevelopment of schools, 319, 355–57; for redevelopment projects, 130. *See also* tax credits

R. Davis Companies, 363

R. Wendell Phillips and Associates, Architects, 258

rates of return, 143–46

real estate entity, *vs.* developer, 146

real estate market, 194, 357, 364. *See also* housing market

rectories, redevelopment of, 6, 138–39, 254, 259–60, 284

Red Door Church project (Cleveland, Ohio), 61–62, *204–7*, 222–31, *228;* expanded highest and best use analysis for, *94–96;* market niche analysis for, *93–97, 98;* redeveloped as the Brownstones at Derbyshire, 89–92, *90–91*

redevelopment plans: for Albuquerque High project, 357–66, 364, 367; for Babeville Performing Arts Center, 271–73; flexibility of, 357, 364, 367; for Lafayette Street project, 303; for Urban Krag, 248–50; for West Tech High School, 314

redevelopment process: for Albuquerque High project, 357–66; for Hot Springs Junior High, 345–46; for Jamaica Performing Arts Center, 237–38; for Magnolia Square Residential Development, *292;* planning approval for, 154–55; predevelopment steps in, 150–54; for Saints Peter and Paul project, 257, 258; for Urban Krag, 246–48; for West Tech High School project, 318–20, *323*

refinancing, motives for, 133

religious buildings, 156, 194; adapted for offices, 69–71, *70,* 176–78; adapted for sacred uses, 16, 20, 22, 268; adapted for secular uses, 16, 20–21, 178–84, 282–83; adapted from secular buildings, 21, 190–95; appropriate reuses of, 169–81, 184–87, 213;

available for redevelopment, *45,* 208; buyers of Catholic properties, *282, 284;* closures of, 12, 170; cultural uses for, 83–84, 214; deterioration of vacant, 14–15, 208–9, 234, 237, 244, 246, 266, 270, 285; highest and best uses for, *85–88,* 168; Lafayette Street project respecting religious heritage of, 305; as landmarks, 17, 22, 25; locations of adaptive reuses of, 33, *34, 45;* market for, 41–42, *52;* number available for redevelopment, 13, 198, 283; outcomes for redevelopment of, 14–16, 215; redevelopment of, 33, *52,* 138–39, 208; redevelopment of schools *vs.,* 68–69; restrictions on redevelopment of, 169, 180, 210, 257, 282–85; schools on campuses of, 68–69, 138; sellers of, 37–38, 56, 226; sold to other congregations, 169, 281–82, 303–4. *See also* church-to-condos projects

rentals. *See* apartments

rents, 99n13, 146, 192, 194, 209; in cultural spaces, 214, 234, 238, 270, 275; income from, 132, 134, 142, *144–45,* 310, 331, *349, 362;* levels of, 37, 39, 58, 71–72, 143, 306, 315, 323, 326, 342, 344, 360; limits on, 109, *118–21,* 140, 142, 215

residential space. *See* apartments; condos; housing

Resource Real Estate, 326–27, 331n1

restaurants/brewpubs, as reuse of religious buildings, 214

retail use/space, *51,* 214; in Albuquerque High project, 353, 358–59, 363, 366; as end-use outcomes for adaptive reuses, 33–34, *35–36,* 37, 41; factors affecting successful reuse as, 42, 209; storefront churches redeveloped from, 190–95. *See also* commercial uses

revenue: in church-to-condos deals, 134, *135;* from school redevelopments, 326, 347, *349,* 360. *See also* finances; rents

Rice, Todd, 334–35, 341–42

Richter, Thomas, 280–82, 284

Righteous Babe Records, 266, 268–70, 274–76

rock-climbing gyms, 244, 250. *See also* Urban Krag project (Dayton, Ohio)

Roedel, Abby, 366

Roman Catholic Church. *See* Catholic Church

Rothschild, Pete, 172–73

Rothschild Development, 287

Rueda, Louie, 241

Rysar Properties, 315, 321, 327

S corporations, 127n17

Saint Louis, Missouri: Catholic Church selling properties in, 278, 280–84, 280–85, 287, 293–96; demographics of, 289, *290*

Saints Peter and Paul Church project (South Boston, Massachusetts), 62, 178–80, *204–7,* 254–64, *255, 261*

schematic design phase, 61

Schnell, Jessie, 274